SECOND EDITION

Teaching Reading and Study Skills in Content Areas

DOROTHY RUBIN
Trenton State College

ALLYN AND BACON
Boston London Toronto Sydney Tokyo Singapore

Dedication

With love to my understanding and supportive husband, Artie,
my lovely daughters, Carol and Sharon,
my precious grandchildren, Jennifer, Andrew, and Melissa,
my charming sons-in-law, John and Seth,
and my dear brothers and sister.

Series Editor: Sean W. Wakely
Series Editorial Assistant: Carol L. Chernaik
Production Coordinator: Marjorie L. Payne
Editorial-Production Service: Benchmark Productions
Cover Administrator: Linda Dickinson
Cover Designer: Suzanne Harbison
Manufacturing Buyer: Louise Richardson

Copyright © 1992 by Allyn and Bacon
A Division of Simon & Schuster, Inc.
160 Gould Street
Needham Heights, Massachusetts 02194

Copyright © 1983 CBS College Publishing

Library of Congress Cataloging-in-Publication Data

Rubin, Dorothy.
   Teaching reading and study skills in content areas / Dorothy
Rubin. — 2nd ed.
    p. cm.
   Includes bibliographical references and index.
   ISBN 0-205-13297-9
   1. Content area reading—United States. 2. Study, Method of.
I. Title.
LB1050.455.R83 1991
428.4'071'2—dc20
                                   91-22986
                                     CIP

Printed in the United States of America
10 9 8 7 6 5 4 3 2 1   96 95 94 93 92 91

Contents

Chapter 8   Integrating Science and Reading/Study Skills Instruction   239

Chapter 12   Diagnostic Techniques for Reading in Content Areas

Preface

Teaching Reading and Study Skills in Content Areas, Second Edition, is a book for content-area preservice and inservice teachers, as well as for any person who needs to learn how knowledge of reading/thinking skills can help enhance the teaching of the content areas. The aim of this book is to help make content-area teachers more effective teachers.

Content-area teachers are well-versed in their specific subject-matter fields; their job is to teach content. No one would dispute this. The problem is that content-area teachers are often frustrated in their efforts to accomplish their goals because some of their students are poor readers and many lack study skills.

A book for the 1990s must address and attempt to offer solutions for major problems noted in the 1980s. "A Nation at Risk" and the many National Assessment of Educational Progress reports, as well as other reports, have heralded the same message: namely, students lack the higher-order thinking skills necessary to read and write well and that students do poorly in science, mathematics, history, and geography. The president of the National Alliance of Business told a U.S. House of Representatives' committee in 1990 that businesses "need assurance that students have achieved a certain level of competency upon graduation, no matter where in the country they went to school." It seems logical that, if students lack reading and study skills techniques, they will have difficulty acquiring subject-matter information, as well as the necessary strategies for processing information.

Teaching Reading and Study Skills in Content Areas, Second Edition, will help content-area teachers recognize that using a directed reading approach to teaching content has as its major aim "getting students to think." The better thinkers students are, the better readers and listeners they can become, and consequently they should achieve much more in their content-area courses.

This book focuses on students as active consumers of information who are involved in their own cognitive processes. It stresses the use of questions that elicit higher-level comprehension responses rather than those that demand merely recall of material. Teachers using a directed reading approach to teaching content will become more sensitive to the various levels of comprehension and will be able to construct questions that demand higher levels of thinking. Because a substantial part of all content-area courses still depends on the successful mastery of textbooks, I give special emphasis to those reading and study skills techniques that students need to become more effective textbook readers.

Teaching Reading and Study Skills in Content Areas, Second Edition, is divided into four parts. In the first part, I set the stage for the rest of the book. I explain the role of the content-area teacher, describe what a directed reading approach to teaching content is, present general guides on using a directed reading approach, stress reading as a thinking process, discuss the developmental tasks of adolescence, and emphasize the special needs of high-risk students. In addition, because we live in a multicultural society, I also give special attention to language and dialect differences and present some possible interferences between English and other languages.

In Part 2, I present chapters on reading and study skills that content teachers should have to help their students read and learn their content material more effectively. I emphasize those comprehension and vocabulary skills that are necessary for reading textbooks and other materials in content courses, and I give special emphasis to study skills techniques. In Part 3, I present chapters on specific subject-matter areas, and for each area I give examples on how reading comprehension and study skills approaches can enhance the teaching of the specific subject-matter area.

In the last part of the book, I am concerned with promoting wide reading in all content areas and in raising content-area teachers' consciousness level to the importance of writing in their content classes. It seems that the goal of all teachers should be to inspire their students with the joy that can be found in books and to help them recognize that writing should be used as a tool to help students learn as well as a means for conveying what they have learned. I stress the interrelatedness of reading and writing and that each acts as a springboard for the other. I also present practical information about informal diagnostic techniques that content-area teachers can use, as well as information about special students who may be mainstreamed into content classes. I place a particular emphasis on handling gifted, borderline, and at-risk students because these are usually found in regular classrooms. In addition, I include a scenario giving a portrait of a secondary school reading specialist so that content-area teachers can gain some insight into both the role of the reading specialist and the ways in which the reading specialist can be of assistance to content-area teachers.

Teaching Reading and Study Skills in Content Areas, Second Edition, is a comprehensive book that contains many hands-on materials for teachers to use with their students, as well as numerous scenarios to illustrate, in an enjoyable manner, the many ideas presented in this book. At the end of every chapter, I present a graphic summary and the key concepts found in the chapter. This stimulates students to think about the material they have read and is consistent with a major goal of this book, namely, that students must be active consumers of information.

Throughout the book the emphasis is on helping content-area teachers recognize that reading is a thinking process and that, if students are to be successful in the content areas, the students must be proficient readers. Effective content teachers are those who can assist students in becoming more knowledgeable individuals and better thinkers.

D.R.

Acknowledgements

I would like to thank my editor, Sean Wakely, for his help, support, and cheerfulness. I would also like to thank Carol Chernaik, editorial assistant, and Amy Pedersen, production editor, for their help and kindness. In addition, I would like to thank my proofreader and copy editor, Carol Smith, for her careful reading of the manuscript and for her helpful suggestions and insights. I would also like to express my appreciation to Dr. Phillip Ollio, Dean of the School of Education, Trenton State College, and Dr. Eileen Burke, Chairperson, for their continued support. Finally, I would like to give special thanks to the following for taking such excellent photographs in a timely manner: Sharon Johnson, Dublin, Ohio; Carol Smith, Monticello School System, Arkansas; JoAnn Lupo, Lawrence High School, Lawrence Township, New Jersey.

Part 1: The Foundation for Teaching Reading and Study Skills in the Content Areas

1

Content-Area Teachers and Reading/Study Skills

OVERVIEW

Introduction: A Scenario

Key Questions

Key Terms in Chapter

Reading Comprehension Skills as a Means to Learning Content Material

The Role of the Reading Teacher in the Middle Grades

Teaching Content in the Middle Grades

The Role of the Content-Area Teacher in Secondary School

What Is a Directed Reading Approach to Teaching Content?

   A Guide for Using a Directed Reading Approach in Reading Content Material

   A Guide for Using a Directed Reading Approach in Teaching a Content-Area Lesson

The Teacher as the Key to Learning

Factors That Affect Teaching Performance and Student Learning

   Important Characteristics of Content-Area Teachers

   Teacher Expectations

   Teacher Planning and Instructional Time

   Interactive Instruction and Content-Area Textbooks

   Motivation and Motivating Techniques

America's Challenge: A Final Word

Graphic Summary of Chapter

Key Concepts in Chapter

Suggestions for Thought Questions and Activities

Selected Bibliography

INTRODUCTION: A SCENARIO

The State Department of Education has just handed down the mandate that no student will receive a high school diploma unless he or she passes a proficiency test in reading, mathematics, and writing. Mr. Johnson, the principal of Central High School, has called together the teachers in his high school to discuss the effects that this mandate will have on them. The principal greets the teachers and tells them that what they have been expecting for some time has taken place; namely, students will no longer be automatically moved along to the next grade, and students will not receive a diploma based on attendance only.

Mr. Johnson then says that the nation is up in arms about the National Assessment of Education (NAEP) reports on the state of education in the United States. (The studies are done on samples of students in grades 4, 8, and 12.) It seems that students have great difficulty with "tasks that ask them to explain or elaborate on what they have read."[1] Students do very little reading in school and for homework, and "their interest in books seems to decrease as they progress in school."[2] Also, "higher-level reasoning activities, such as discussing, analyzing, or writing about what they have read, are reportedly not emphasized routinely for students."[3] Mr. Johnson lowers his voice and says almost in a whisper that what bothered him when reading the various reports was that the average reading proficiency of students increased less dramatically between grades 8 and 12. In addition, "the assessment results indicate that across the grades, most students have a limited grasp of U.S. history."[4] Mr. Johnson states further that both the NAEP and international results show that students' deficits in science increase across the grades.[5] "Moreover," he says, "all the results show that there are large discrepancies according to socioeconomic status. In other words, children who come from lower class homes do less well at all three grade levels assessed. These children are often referred to as high-risk students." Mr. Johnson looks at his teachers and says, "I could go on, but I won't. I think you all get the picture. We need to change some of the things we are doing, and we need to work together to do this. We have to come to grips with facts. We have a number of students, especially high-risk students, who cannot read their textbooks."

[1]Judith A. Langer, Arthur N. Applegate, Ina V.S. Mullis, and Mary A. Foertsch, *Learning to Read in Our Nation's Schools*, The National Assessment of Educational Progress, (Princeton, N.J.: Educational Testing Service, June 1990), p. 7.

[2]Ibid.

[3]Ibid., p. 8.

[4]David C. Hammack et al. *The U.S. History Report Card*, The National Assessment of Educational Progress, (Princeton, N.J.: Educational Testing Service, April 1990), p. 10.

[5]Ina V.S. Mullis and Lynn B. Jenkins, *The Science Report Card: Elements of Risk and Recovery*, The National Assessment of Educational Progress, (Princeton, N.J.: Educational Testing Service, April 1990), p. 7.

The principal continues his talk by telling the teachers that he knows that they are specialists in the teaching of content-area courses rather than in the teaching of reading skills. At this point a number of teachers nod their heads, and some raise their hands. The principal calls on Ms. Brown, a mathematics teacher.

"Mr. Johnson," she says, "I can see how English or social studies teachers may have to teach reading in their classes, but I don't think that it should be my job. I'm prepared to teach math. I like teaching it, and I don't know the first thing about teaching reading."

A number of voices are heard that agree vehemently with Ms. Brown. Mr. Johnson then calls on Mr. Smith, who teaches English.

"Listen, just because I teach English does not mean that I know anything about the teaching of reading. Why don't we just hire more special teachers and have our students who need reading courses take them?"

"That's a good idea, Jim," call out a number of teachers.

Others echo similar comments. After a number of teachers have spoken, Mr. Johnson says that he understands how they feel. "After all," he says, "I was a history teacher before I became a principal. However," he continues, "times have changed dramatically. Money is tight. We can't afford to hire more reading specialists, and we have many students who have reading problems. The public is unhappy that so many students are graduating who can't read. I realize, also, that something more must be done at the lower-grade levels, but if we get students who can't read, we must be prepared to help them. Many of you have spoken to me personally about how frustrated you are many times because students have difficulty reading their textbooks. Actually, a problem in mathematics, political science, English, or science may be a reading problem. We will have to become more proficient in the teaching of reading skills and incorporate these in the teaching of our content areas. I am not asking you to become teachers of reading skills; I am asking you to incorporate reading and study skills techniques in the teaching of your content courses. I believe it should make us better teachers."

Mr. Johnson described the importance of getting teachers to acquire knowledge of reading skills and incorporate this knowledge in their subject-matter courses. However, he explains that this is only part of the problem and that another major difficulty is helping those students who have reading problems acquire positive attitudes toward reading. He continues: "When students learn that they will not graduate unless they pass a competency test in reading, those students with reading problems will be 'up in arms.' We will have to be prepared for this. Also, we will try to utilize the special persons that we have more effectively. During the summer a committee of teachers and other personnel will meet to plan our strategy for making reading part of the content area. Any of you can join the committee. We must have at least one teacher from each content area on the committee. The committee will include our reading specialists as well as the teachers."

Teaching Reading and Study Skills in Content Areas, Second Edition will attempt to make content-area teachers more aware of how knowledge of reading and study skills techniques can enhance their teaching of the content areas. The basic premise of this book is that content-area teachers should be concerned with reading and study skills so that they can help their students learn better and, consequently, be better students. If teachers can help their students to learn better, they will be successful teachers.

KEY QUESTIONS

After you finish reading this chapter, you should be able to answer the following questions:

1. What are the primary goals of the content-area teacher?
2. What are the primary goals of the reading teacher?
3. What is the relation of reading comprehension to learning content material?
4. How does the role of the reading teacher differ from the role of the content-area teacher?
5. What characteristics are common to all successful teachers?
6. What factors affect teaching performance and student learning?
7. How do teacher expectations affect student learning?
8. What is a directed reading approach to teaching content?
9. What are some instructional approaches teachers can use to help students attain key concepts?

KEY TERMS IN CHAPTER

You should pay special attention to the following key terms:

content-area teacher	motivation
directed reading approach to teaching content	reading strategy
	reading teacher
interactive instruction	self-fulfilling prophecy
modeling strategy	strategy
motivating technique	

READING COMPREHENSION SKILLS AS A MEANS TO LEARNING CONTENT MATERIAL

Many content-area teachers, even in the elementary grades, do not consider that they are teaching reading comprehension when they are teaching social studies.[6] Attitudes such as these need to change. Even though the major thrust of content-area teachers is *content*, this goal will not be achieved unless there is reading comprehension. The two are interrelated. The emphasis is on gaining the concepts of the specific content area, but the technique includes reading comprehension skills. In other words, the reading comprehension skills are not activities as ends in themselves; they are a means to an end. For example, finding the main idea of a paragraph or the central idea of a group of paragraphs or an article is not taught in a content-area class for the sake of having students practice finding the main idea. It is done to help students gain certain concepts in content areas. When reading teachers use content-area material, they use it to help students practice finding the main idea or practice any other skill that they are working with. Once teachers understand the difference in orientation between the role of a content-area teacher and a reading teacher, both groups of teachers can work together in better harmony.

The scenarios in the following sections should help teachers gain a better insight into the major differences between the roles of reading teachers and content-area teachers.

THE ROLE OF THE READING TEACHER IN THE MIDDLE GRADES

Scenario: Mr. Green's Fifth Grade During a Reading Period
(A group of six children are seated in a semicircle facing Mr. Green.)
On the board are the following sentences:

Everyone who disliked getting into fights avoided the *pugnacious* man.
He was like a *tornado*—knocking down everything in his path.
His dog was as grouchy as a *scorpion* with a hotfoot.
He was a rough-looking brute—a *battle-scarred King Kong*.
The cat hissed like a *viper*.

Action:

"We've been working with the skill of 'reading between the lines.' What have we called this skill?" "Yes. Good, we've called it *inference*. Can someone tell me what we mean by 'inference'?" "You're right. It refers to information that is not directly stated in the writing but implied—it's something that's suggested. What else did we say about inference?" "Good! We said that to make an inference we must have sufficient information.

"Last night I saw a show entitled 'The Man with the Midas Touch.'

[6]Dolores Durkin, "What Classroom Observations Reveal About Reading Comprehension," *Reading Research Quarterly* 14:4 (1978–1979): 533.

From the title, what would you expect the character to be like?" "Yes, you would infer that he is wealthy, that he has successful business ventures, and that he is quite concerned with money.

"We were obviously influenced by the fairy tale character of King Midas. Well, the fairy tale character did have some relationship to the television character, but there was a twist to it. Look at this caricature I made of 'The Man with the Midas Touch.' What do you think the 'Midas Touch' stood for in the television show?" "Yes, you're right—calamity, disaster, or death. Everyone or everything that the character Mr. Midas came in contact with ended in disaster or death. Obviously, from the title we didn't have enough information to make correct inferences about the character or show.

"Today, we are going to read a story, 'The Pugnacious Pussycat.' After we read the story, we're going to try to draw inferences about the story's characters from the selection, and then we're going to create a new title for the selection.

"Before we begin to read the story, let's go over some words and phrases that are underlined on the chalkboard. Using the context clues, can anyone tell me what *pugnacious* means?" "Very good. It means having an aggressive manner. Does anyone remember the word we met yesterday that would be a synonym for *pugnacious* and *aggressive?*" "Yes, good—*belligerent.* Each of the other sentences has a figure of speech in it. We've worked with this figure of speech. What is it called?" "Yes, it's called a 'simile.' Let's go over each to make sure we understand the comparisons that the author is making."

The teacher and the students go over each one. After they are finished, the teacher asks the students to read the story silently for the purpose of finding out about the main characters in the story. He has the students state the traits of "Harry, the cat." After this is done, he has the students state who the other main character in the story is, and he has the students tell about Bryan. He asks the students whether they think Bryan is bright, and although the author does not directly state that Bryan is bright, the teacher asks what clues are given so that we can draw this inference. He has students find clues in the story and read these aloud. After the students have presented character traits of both Harry, the cat, and Bryan and have found evidence in the story to support their inferences, he has them generate new titles for the story.

After the main points of the lesson have been pulled together, the teacher tells students, "For tomorrow I'd like you to write a short character sketch in which information about a character is implied. You will share your character sketches with one another and then challenge each other to generate good titles for your sketches."

Commentary:

Mr. Green is a good reading teacher. He is interested in helping his students gain skill in "reading between the lines," and his whole lesson is primarily concerned with this skill acquisition. Mr. Green integrates reading with writing, but again the emphasis is on the skill of inference or "reading between the lines."

TEACHING CONTENT IN THE MIDDLE GRADES

Scenario: Mrs. Johnson's Fifth Grade During a Social Studies Lesson
(Mrs. Johnson teaches in a self-contained classroom.)
(A group of ten children are seated in front of the room by the chalkboard. A large map is visible. A bulletin board has an exhibit called "Creative Stories from Other Continents" on display, including a list of the continents and various countries being studied. Next to the list are spelling words related to the countries and continents being considered.)

Action:

The teacher, Mrs. Johnson, says, "We've been working with different continents and countries and we have combined this with our reading lesson and working with the newspaper. Yesterday, we allowed our imaginations to roam, and we wrote some very creative stories. We've talked about some of the countries and their leaders who have been in the news lately. Who remembers some of the countries and leaders we have been talking about?"

After the students give some of the countries and leaders that they have discussed already, Mrs. Johnson tells them that today they will be reading another article about China written by a different author. "Before we begin," Mrs. Johnson says, "let's go over some words that may be unfamiliar to some of you." Mrs. Johnson presents the words in context to the students and goes over each one. She sets purposes for their reading and then asks if they have any questions. Before the students begin reading the selection about China, the teacher reminds them that their purposes are to make inferences about life in China today and to compare this writer's views about China with the views of the writer they had read last time. Because a number of students had difficulty doing this in the last lesson, she would like to again give them some pointers on drawing inferences. Mrs. Johnson proceeds to give students some direct instruction in drawing inferences by using related text material. She does this by using a modeling technique. She verbalizes her thoughts step by step so that her students can gain an insight into how she draws inferences from the material. She then has the students read the selection.

After the students have finished reading the selection, Mrs. Johnson asks the students what inferences can be drawn from the article about life in China today in comparison with life in China two decades ago. A number of students raise their hands to answer. Mrs. Johnson calls on one. After the student has given his answer, Mrs. Johnson asks the rest of the students whether they agree with Jack's answer. Mrs. Johnson asks them to support their position with information that is either directly or indirectly stated in the passage. A discussion ensues in which a number of students take part and try to present and defend their position. When it appears that the students seem to have come to some kind of consensus, the teacher asks them to now compare the views concerning modern China of the writer they are reading today with those views of the writer they had read yesterday. Mrs. Johnson asks the students first to discuss the similarities if there are any and then to discuss the differences if they noted any. She poses this question: "What similarities did you note between the two writers' views?" A number of hands shoot up, and a lively discussion follows. Mrs. Johnson then poses this question: "What differences did you note between the two writers' views?" Again a number of hands shoot up, and another animated discussion follows. Throughout the discussion, Mrs. Johnson asks the students to support their answers with information that is either directly or indirectly stated in the articles.

After the objectives for the lesson have been accomplished, Mrs. Johnson tells the students the following: "Tomorrow, we're going to combine outlining with our study of continents and countries. Then we're going to use the outline as a guide to learn more about the country we choose to study. I would like you to think about which other country you would like to get to know better. At your seats, review some of the things we talked about concerning China, the country we have been reading about. This sheet should help you."

In addition, Mrs. Johnson asks them to think about how the life of a fifth-grader living in China may compare to theirs. She tells them she would like them to jot down some questions they would like to ask such a fifth grader if they could. She further says that perhaps they would be able to do just that because tomorrow she will discuss with them the possibility of having them choose pen pals from the countries they are studying.

Commentary:

Mrs. Johnson is a good teacher also. She is combining social studies with the development of reading skills. In her social studies lesson, she brings in all of the language arts (listening, speaking, reading, and writing); however, her main purpose in this lesson is with helping her students to acquire certain concepts about other nations rather than acquiring specific reading skills. She uses reading and other language arts areas to help her to achieve her goal. During the reading lesson, she used stories about other nations, but her goal there was to help her students to attain the skill of "reading between the lines." Of course, the ultimate purpose for helping students attain the skill of "reading between the lines" or any other skill is to have them use this reading skill or any other to understand what they are reading and to attain information, as well as to maximize their reading enjoyment when reading for pleasure. However, there are times when transfer of learning does not take place so that direct instruction in certain skills using related content material is necessary in the content-area lesson to help students achieve the purposes of the lesson.

THE ROLE OF THE CONTENT-AREA TEACHER IN SECONDARY SCHOOL

Scenario 1: Ms. Brown's History Class (Tenth Grade—Second Period)
Ms. Brown tells her students that they will be starting a new unit and that the theme of the unit is "Minority Groups in American History." She will give them an overview of what they will be studying as well as some of the questions that they will be answering. She explains that it is good to see the whole so that they can see how the parts fit in. After Ms. Brown gives her students a cursory overview, she lists the following questions on the board for them:

1. What are minority groups?
2. What minority groups settled in the English colonies? Why?
3. Why did some minority groups in the colonies receive harsh treatment? What did they do about it?
4. Explain what is meant by, and give examples of, voluntary and involuntary minority groups in Colonial America.

Ms. Brown reads each question aloud and tells her students that these questions will set their purposes for reading. After they have read their assigned reading, they will discuss the answers to the questions. They will also talk about contemporary minority groups and the role that they play in today's history. Now, however, Ms. Brown would like to learn what her students' conception of the term *minority* is. A discussion concerning the term *minority* is undertaken.

Commentary:

Ms. Brown is a content-area teacher, and she's a good one. She likes her subject, she enjoys teaching, and she's well prepared. She majored in history in the teacher preparation program and received her degree 25 years ago. At that time there was talk about making every teacher a teacher of reading, but it was only talk. Her degree and social studies certification did not require her to take any reading courses. Now her main goal is to help her students to learn the concepts of history in an ordered and logical manner. The content matter is supreme, and the emphasis is not on the accumulation of discrete data or facts but on the understanding of generalizations. This type of learning is dependent upon mastery of the structure of the subject matter, that is, learning how things are related.

The role of the content teacher has not basically changed; however, another dimension is being added to it, and this added dimension should enhance rather than take away from the content-area teacher's prime goal. The added dimension is the use of a directed reading approach in the teaching of the content area. (Many good content teachers may have used this approach even though they have not had any reading courses.)

Here is another scenario. The major difference between the teacher in this scenario and the previous one is that Mrs. Smith has received a more recent degree in history and that her social studies certification required a reading course related to the teaching of content material.

Scenario 2: Mrs. Smith's History Class (Tenth Grade—Fourth Period)
Mrs. Smith tells her students that they will be starting a new unit and that the theme of the unit is "Minority Groups in American History." Mrs. Smith continues to tell her students that she has prepared some questions that she feels will help set their purposes for reading and also that she will present an overview of the unit so that they can see better how the various parts that they will be reading relate to the whole. Before she does this, however, she wants to go over with her students some of the terms used in the readings that she feels may cause some difficulty. Mrs. Smith then presents a number of the terms in context and challenges the students to determine the meanings of the terms from the context of the sentence. As Mrs. Smith presents the terms to the students, she also gives them some background information about the terms and tells them that they will be reading more about what she is saying. For example, Mrs. Smith tells her students that the culture of the United States is a blend of many cultures. She asks students in the class to state where they, their parents, grandparents, or great-grandparents were born. She then puts this sentence on the board:

Immigrants from many countries have brought their customs, languages, and beliefs to the United States.

Mrs. Smith asks the students to try to define the term *immigrants*. After Mrs. Smith has the students go over a number of terms and presents her lesson, she tells the class that she would like to spend a little time with them discussing their reading assignment. After they discuss the reading assignment, she tells them that she would also like to give them some study techniques that she herself found helpful when she went to school. Mrs. Smith tells her students first to look over their reading assignment to see if they can determine its organization because organization is important in helping readers comprehend the writer's message. For example, today's reading assignment is one in which the writer states his thesis and then presents a number of examples to support his thesis. Mrs. Smith tells her students that if they read the assignment with a knowledge of this beforehand, this will increase their chances for gaining the key concepts of what they are reading and for retaining the information over an extended period of time.

After discussing the students' reading assignment, she shares with them some study techniques that she found very helpful when she was going to school. For example, Mrs. Smith tells her students that she used to reread a section of a textbook over and over again when she was studying, but this did not seem to help her retain the information. One of her instructors explained to her that learning theorists claim that recall or recitation is an important component in studying and that, therefore, rather than immediately rereading a section over and over again, she should stop at certain parts and try to recall what she had read. Mrs. Smith suggests to her students that since this really helped her, she would like her students to try it. She also tells her students that she always reviewed her previous assignment before beginning her new one. This she did by looking at her reading assignment and trying to recall the main ideas of the paragraphs or the central idea of a section.

Commentary:

Like Ms. Brown, Mrs. Smith is interested in having her students acquire the concepts of history in an ordered and logical fashion, and she emphasizes the acquisition of generalizations. Her prime goal is to teach history, and she is interested in the maximum transfer of learning. However, Mrs. Smith is using her knowledge of reading and study skills to help her students acquire the key concepts of history that she would like them to attain. She is providing her students with the skills that they need to acquire the content material and achieve the purposes of the lesson; in other words, Mrs. Smith is using a directed reading approach to teaching content.

WHAT IS A DIRECTED READING APPROACH TO TEACHING CONTENT?

A directed reading approach to teaching content is one that emphasizes knowledge of the reading process and the components of reading, as well as emphasizing the structure of the particular subject matter, teacher purposes, and student needs. In a directed reaching approach, reading skills and content are integrated; needed reading and study skills are adapted to fit the uniqueness of the subject so that students' learning will be maximized. Such an approach to teaching content includes the direct teaching of any needed reading or study skill using relevant content material so that students can grasp the content concepts being taught. A directed reading approach to teaching content or subject matter takes *nothing* for granted. It requires students to be active consumers of information and to be actively involved in the process of organizing what they are reading. Readers, like consumers, need to know what their purposes are for reading and how best to acquire what they are reading.

The role of the teacher is to help students see how what they are learning relates to the whole; it is one of setting purposes for reading and for providing guidance based on students' needs that will help them to gain the most from the content area they are studying.

In this book, a directed reading approach to teaching content is not limited to the reading assignments only; it also permeates the teaching of the lesson. Chapters 7, 8 and 9 in Part 3 show how many of the skills and information presented in Chapters 3, 4, 5, and 6 can be adapted to specific content areas, and Chapters 12 and 13 present information on how teachers can diagnose students' needs in content-area courses.

Two general guides follow. One uses a directed reading approach for preparing students to *read* content material assignments, and the other is for using a directed reading approach in the *teaching* of a content-area lesson. The two guides have many similar components; the major difference is that the guide for using a directed reading approach in reading content material is presented by teachers to help students gain the most from their reading assignments; whereas the other guide is the one that the teacher would use in presenting his or her lesson to the class or a group of students. Note also that the guide for preparing students to read content material is usually part of the teaching lesson guide; that is, the guide for preparing students to read their assignments is usually presented at the end or some time during the teaching lesson.

A Guide for Using a Directed Reading Approach in Reading Content Material

Guided reading in the content areas, which incorporates a directed reading approach, can enhance the teaching of any content area because it provides interest, direction, and organization to the reading; it is an aid that helps students comprehend what they are reading. Here are the general steps for a directed reading approach to prepare students to read content material. (The guide should be adapted to suit the uniqueness of the specific content area, as well as the students with whom the teacher is working. Moreover, not all steps need to be presented every time an assignment is given. See Chapters 7, 8, and 9 for samples of various guides adapted for particular content areas.)

When teachers are preparing students to read content material, they can do the following:

1. *Use a motivating technique.* For example, a provocative question could interest students in what they will be reading. This will get students' attention and direct their energies toward a particular goal, which is important in any learning situation.

2. *Relate to students' past experiences.* If students see how what they are to study relates to what they have already done, this will increase their chances for gaining the new information because they can fit the new information into an existing meaningful context.

3. *State purposes for reading.* Such purposes will provide direction for students and help them to differentiate between relevant and incidental content. They will help to furnish organization for the material, and they will also provide feedback; that is, students will be able to determine at the end of the assignment whether they have achieved the stated purposes. The purposes can serve also as task reinforcers; that is, students who know that they are mastering a set of objectives will achieve more than those whose only reinforcement is a grade at the end of the term.

4. *Present new terms.* This procedure is needed if students are to be able to understand the key concepts that must be learned.

5. *Give special strategy or strategies for reading the content material.* This would include insights into the organization of the material and provide the tactics that the students should use to gain the most from their reading. The strategies should be directly taught by using relevant content material. However, the amount of information and direction the teacher gives would depend on the students with whom the teacher is working. The lower the students' ability, the more guidance the students will need. (See Chapter 14 for information on special children, and see Chapters 7, 8, and 9 in Part 3 for the adaptation and integration of reading approaches in different content areas.)

A Guide for Using a Directed Reading Approach in Teaching a Content-Area Lesson

1. The teacher prepares for the concepts to be taught.
   a. *Relates to past experiences* of students. This gives continuity to the lesson.
   b. *States the purposes* of the lesson. This will help give direction to the lesson.
   c. *Uses a motivating technique.* This will gain the students' attention.
   d. *Presents the new terms.* This will increase the students' ability to comprehend the concepts to be learned.
   e. *Presents a special strategy, using relevant content material.* This will help students acquire the concepts being taught.

2. The teacher develops the lesson by using different techniques or strategies. For example, the teacher may use a questioning approach. This requires the teacher to know the different levels of comprehension questions so that students will not only give literal-level answers. It requires, also, that students be able to answer questions at various

comprehension levels. The teacher could present a lecture. This would require the students to be adept at notetaking skills, concentration, and the ability to abstract generalizations from what the instructor is presenting. The teacher could use a discovery technique in presenting his or her lesson. This would require the students to be able to do inductive and deductive thinking. The teacher could use a modeling strategy ("thinking aloud"). This would help students gain insights into the thinking necessary to attain information and concepts. Whatever approach the teacher uses, it would require the students to be acquainted with comprehension and learning skills.

3. The teacher prepares the students for their reading assignment. Reading purposes are set; any unfamiliar terms are defined and explained; highlights of what to look for while reading are given, as well as special things to be on the lookout for. Also, any special skills that students need to acquire content concepts while reading are directly taught by using relevant content material. (See guide on p. 12.)

4. Summary of lesson. The teacher helps students to pull together the main points of the lesson. This is done by stating the main or central idea of the lesson and by giving only the important details of the lesson. (See Chapter 3 for a description of various comprehension skills, and see Chapters 7, 8, 9, and 10 for the adaptation and integration of these skills in the content areas.)

Special Note:
A guide for using a directed reading approach in teaching a content area lesson, like a guide for using a directed reading approach in preparing students to read content material, should be adapted to suit the uniqueness of the specific content area. It, too, should take into account the individual differences of the students with whom the teacher is working. Moreover, not all steps need to be presented in every lesson.

THE TEACHER AS THE KEY TO LEARNING

> It is the supreme art of the teacher to awaken joy in creative expression and knowledge.
>
> ALBERT EINSTEIN

Although a school may have the best equipment, the most advanced school plant, a superior curriculum, and students who want to learn, it must have "good teachers" so that the desired kind of learning can take place. With today's emphasis on accountability, the spotlight is even more sharply focused on "The Teacher." When conversation turns to "teacher evaluation," *everyone* seems to be an expert. But despite the surge in educational research, no definitive agreement exists as to how to evaluate teachers. If we were to go back through the ages, we would find such familiar comments as:

> The teachers today just go on repeating in rigmarole fashion, annoy the students with constant questions and repeat the same things over and over again. They do not try to find out what the students' natural inclinations are, so that the students are forced to pretend to like their studies; nor do they try to bring out the best in their talents. As a result, the students hide their favorite readings and hate their teachers, are exasperated at the difficulty of their studies, and do not know what good it does them. Although they go through the regular course of instruction, they are quick to leave when they are through. This is the failure of education today.
>
> CONFUCIUS (c. 551–479 B.C.)

> When he [Abelard's teacher] lit the fire, he filled the house with smoke not with light.
>
> PETER ABELARD (A.D. 1079–1142)

It seems as though time has stood still when we discuss teachers. If we were to ask a number of persons to state the qualities of a "good" teacher, we might produce a statement that reads like this:

> Good teachers need the eyes of an artist to know the varying personalities in their midst. They need a philosopher's insight to be able to deal with each

FIGURE 1-1. This teacher is always available for his students.

individual. They are blessed with a "democratic spirit" and treat each person as someone worthy of dignity and respect, who is capable of self-direction. They have the patience of Job. They help those who need help to help themselves. They are astute diagnosticians. Their analytical ability is well developed. Their ebullience and enthusiasm know no bounds. Their experiences are manifold, their knowledge of the highest; and their judgment is superb.

Our Problem—There are only mortals on earth. Teachers, too, are human beings.

Solution—We must work within our limitations—be optimistic and idealistic, but realize that humans are fallible.

However difficult it is to generate universally agreed-upon statements and evaluative criteria, teachers must realize that they are always under scrutiny, formalized or not. For example, the first day that teachers enter their classrooms, the way they walk, their facial expressions, the way they speak, what they say, how they say it, their voices, their mannerisms, what they are wearing, their ages, their modus operandi, even their genders—all these and more affect their students, regardless of grade level. Will teachers measure up? The answer to this is that they must because the teacher is the key to helping students learn.

FACTORS THAT AFFECT TEACHING PERFORMANCE AND STUDENT LEARNING

Although most people agree that the teacher is the key to improved instruction, there is no unanimity on what factors affect teaching performance and student learning or on the objective criteria for evaluating teacher performance. Who is to do the evaluating? What kinds of instruments should be used? How consistent will the administration of the evaluative instrument be? How will the data be used? All these questions add to the problem.

For many people effective teaching is usually determined by a teacher's ability to produce desirable changes in students' learning behavior. If evaluation were based only on such changes, the task of teacher evaluation would be somewhat simplified. Students could be given pretests at the beginning of the term and posttests at the end of the term. The students' achievement, based on desired outcomes, could then be determined. But there are recognizable difficulties with this method. One is the assumption that students' achievements or nonachievements are directly due to their teachers. This is not so. There are many variables that affect student learning, such as home environment, ability level, motivation, peers, television, illness, and so on. What on the surface may appear to be simple is really not. In one class, children may produce better results on standardized tests than in another, but they may have grown to dislike the subject matter so intensely that they will avoid it in the future. These learned attitudes are not desirable and will remain with the students longer than the subject matter they have learned. How should such teachers be evaluated?

It is beyond the scope of this book to try to answer or resolve the teacher-evaluation controversy. We will concern ourselves with possible descriptions of those characteristics, traits, and competencies that content-area teachers should possess in order to be successful teachers.

Important Characteristics of Content-Area Teachers

The characteristics of good content-area teachers do not vary substantially from those of elementary school teachers in a self-contained classroom except with regard to their orientation toward their subject matter. Although unanimity does not exist among educators as to which characteristics are the most salient in producing good teachers, most educators would agree that characteristics such as knowledge of their content area, verbal ability, a good educational background (including the ability to read with skill oneself), and positive teacher expectations and attitudes would be qualities that good teachers should possess. Also, effective teachers need to be good problem-solvers, who are able to think critically about their teaching behavior and initiate change when needed; in other words, they need to have good metacognitive ability. (See "Metacognition and Reading" in Chapter 2.)

Studies have shown that teachers who have a good educational background and who have good verbal ability are usually better teachers than those who do not.[7] This information makes good sense and should come as no surprise. What is surprising is that there are some teachers who themselves lack necessary reading skills. A four-and-one-half-year study measuring almost 350 teachers' reading skills found "many of the teachers tested demonstrated a wide range of deficiencies or discrepancies in their reading abilities."[8] Although the researchers stated that care should be taken not to generalize from these results, it is clear that teacher deficiencies in reading ability should warrant concern. Another study found that teachers scored low on tests of study skills attainment intended for use with children completing elementary or junior high school.[9] Obviously, if a teacher feels insecure about a subject, the teacher will tend to avoid the teaching of the subject, and when it is taught, concepts and skills may be erroneously taught.

The discussion in the preceding paragraph is or should be of great concern to content-area teachers. Many of these teachers usually take for

---

[7]Charles E. Bidwell and John D. Kasarda, "School District Organization and Student Achievement," *American Sociological Review* 40 (February 1975): 55–70; Eric Hanushek, "The Production of Education, Teacher Quality and Efficiency," paper presented at the Bureau of Educational Personnel Development Conference, "How Do Teachers Make a Difference?" Washington, D.C., February 1970, ERIC No. 037 396.

[8]Lance M. Gentile and Merna McMillan, "Some of Our Students' Teachers Can't Read Either," *Journal of Reading* 21 (November 1977): 146.

[9]Eunice N. Askov, et al., "Study Skill Mastery Among Elementary School Teachers," *The Reading Teacher* 30 (February 1977): 485–488.

granted that their students have attained the reading and study skills that they will need to read content material. This often, unfortunately, is just not so. If students have not been exposed to higher-level comprehension skills, how can they be expected to perform in situations that call for their use of these skills? (See Chapters 3, 4, 5, and 6 for background information on the kinds of skills students need to be effective readers of content-area material.)

From what has been stated, it makes sense that content-area teachers, in addition to the characteristics already mentioned, should be knowledgeable of reading and thinking strategies and know how to incorporate them into their content areas so that they can help students interact with their textbooks to organize meaningful concepts. Sadly, this is often not taking place.

In the opening scenario of this chapter, the principal, Mr. Johnson, expressed concern that students' reading proficiency increased less dramatically between grades 8 and 12. He should be concerned. The reason for the lag in reading performance may be because content reading instruction "has not been universally embraced by secondary preservice and practicing teachers even though they have completed coursework or workshops focusing upon content reading."[10] This is especially devastating because of the suggestions from educators and researchers. For example, many educators feel that the "most logical place for instruction in most reading and thinking strategies is in social studies and science rather than in separate lessons about reading. The reason is that the strategies are useful when the student is grappling with important but unfamiliar content."[11] Unfortunately, surveys show that the contrary takes place; that is, "reading instruction, when it is offered, is the sole responsibility of the reading teacher."[12]

Special Note:
A *strategy* is a systematic plan for achieving a specific objective or result. A *reading strategy* is an action or a series of actions that helps construct meaning.[13]

Teacher Expectations

The more teachers know about their students, the better able they are to plan for them. However, teachers must be cautioned about the self-fulfilling

[10]Roger A. Stewart and David G. O'Brien, "Resistance to Content-Area Reading: A Focus on Preservice Teachers," *Journal of Reading* 32 (February 1989): 396.

[11]Richard C. Anderson, Elfrieda H. Hiebert, Judith A. Scott, and Ian A. G. Wilkinson, *Becoming a Nation of Readers: The Report of the Commission of Reading* (Washington, D.C.: National Institute of Education, 1985), p. 73.

[12]Judith L. Irvin and Neila A. Connors, "Reading Instruction in Middle Level Schools: Results of a U.S. Survey," *Journal of Reading* 32 (January 1989): 306.

[13]Sharon Benge Kletzien, "Strategy Use by Good and Poor Comprehenders Reading Expository Text of Differing Levels," *Reading Research Quarterly* 26 No. 1 (1991): 69.

prophecy—where teachers' assumptions about students come true, at least in part, because of the attitude of the teachers. Studies have shown that teacher expectations about students' abilities to learn will influence students' learning.[14] For example, if a student has a reputation as someone who can't or won't learn or if the student comes from a certain home environment not conducive to learning, the teacher may assume that this student cannot learn beyond a certain level and thus treat him or her accordingly. If such a thing happens, then the teacher's assumptions could become part of the student's own self-concept, further reinforcing the teacher's original expectations.

Teachers who are aware of the effect that teacher expectations have on learning behavior of students can use this to help their students. For example, teachers should assume that *all* their students are capable of learning, they should avoid labeling their students, and they should use positive reinforcement whenever feasible to help students to become motivated.

Teacher Planning and Instructional Time

Teachers using a directed reading approach to teaching content will need to be good planners. Planning helps guide teachers in making choices about instruction; it helps them to clarify their thinking about objectives, students' needs, interests, and so on, as well as to determine what motivating techniques to use. (See section on "Motivation and Motivating Techniques.") In planning, teachers should use student feedback to determine whether to proceed with instruction, to slow down instruction, or to stop and correct or clarify some misconception. Teachers are essential decision makers.

A number of studies have been done on the amount of time students spend on on-task relevant academic pursuits. The problem is that these studies have been done primarily in the area of reading and mathematics at the elementary-grade level. From the studies, it appears that the successful teachers were those who engaged students in academic endeavors and had students spend less time in nonacademic activities.[15] Even though the studies were done at early grade levels, it seems logical and reasonable to assume that the results would be similar at other grade levels as well. The more time one spends on an activity, the more proficient one should become in the activity if the time spent is task-related and students receive knowledge of results or feedback on what they are doing.

It also makes sense that those teachers who are more actively involved

[14]Robert Rosenthal and Lenore Jacobson, *Pygmalion in the Classroom* (New York: Holt, Rinehart and Winston, 1968); Douglas A. Pidgeon, *Expectation and Pupil Performance* (London: National Foundation for Educational Research, in England and Wales, 1970).

[15]Barak V. Rosenshine, "Content, Time, and Direct Instruction," in *Research on Teaching: Concepts, Findings, and Implications*, eds. Penelope L. Peterson and Herbert J. Walberg. (Berkeley, Cal.: McCutchan Publishing Corp., 1979), pp. 28–56.

in all aspects of the teaching-learning situation would be the most effective teachers. Research "supports direct and explicit teacher action associated with planning, motivating, information giving, and mediating student understandings. Conversely, there is no research support for inexplicit teacher actions or for instruction in which teachers assume passive or covert roles."[16]

Interactive Instruction and Content-Area Textbooks

The teacher plays a very important role in how students perceive their textbooks, what they will get from these books, and even whether they will read their books. Teachers who say: "Open your books to page 32, and read silently what it says" or "Read pages 32 to 50 for homework by tomorrow" will get different results from teachers who plan carefully for interactive textbook reading.

In interactive instruction, the teacher plays a crucial role in determining the instructional outcomes. The teacher intervenes at optimal times with optimal strategies to achieve desired learning.

An interactive model of reading and learning recognizes the "teacher's effect on the reader, the text, and the goal of the reading process and the reciprocal influence of the reader, the text, and the goal on the teacher."[17] In interactive instruction, teachers are the key decision makers who must determine how best to use the text based on their students' background of experiences, as well as the text's strengths and weaknesses. The text is used as a tool and as a means for helping students gain content concepts rather than as an end in itself.

Interactive instruction requires knowledgeable, thinking, flexible teachers who are not looking for easy, prescribed packaged programs. Such teachers recognize that "instruction is a complex, fluid endeavor, and that teachers engage in creative orchestration rather than rigid direction following."[18]

Teachers using a directed reading approach to teaching content are engaged in interactive instruction.

Motivation and Motivating Techniques

Often a problem in a content-area course may be because of a student's lack of interest rather than his or her inability to comprehend text material. Motivation, which is internal impetus behind behavior, is an essential ingredi-

---

[16]Laura R. Roehler and Gerald G. Duffy, "Teacher's Instructional Actions," in *Handbook of Reading Research*, Vol. II, Rebecca Barr, Michael L. Kamil, Peter Mosenthal, and P. David Pearson eds. (New York: Longman, 1991), p. 877.

[17]Mariam Jean Dreher and Harry Singer, "The Teacher's Role in Students' Success," *The Reading Teacher* 42 (April 1989): 614.

[18]Roehler and Duffy, p. 877.

ent for success. All of us at one time or another have probably wished we had the drive that someone else seems to have. We may have said: "What spurs him on? He seems to know what he wants, and he goes right after it. He is so determined."

The best motivation is internal; teachers, unfortunately cannot rely on this. As a result, good teachers try to provide motivating techniques for their students. These extrinsic techniques are used to gain students' attention and direct their energies toward a particular goal. The motivating techniques or strategies are limited only by the creative ability of the teacher. Some motivating techniques may be as simple as a provocative question or as elaborate as a teacher dressing up as a historical figure. The type of motivating technique will depend on a number of variables, namely, time constraints, instructional objectives, and teacher creativity.

Some general motivating techniques that have been identified as aids to bringing students and their textbooks together are:[19]

1. Using analogies—the teacher helps students relate their new knowledge to their prior knowledge.

     Example: Biology—Teacher asks students how their skin is like a fortress. (Textbook reading assignment is on the function of the skin.)

2. Relating personal anecdotes—The teacher tells a personal story to give students a hanger onto which they can relate their new information.

     Example: Mathematics—The teacher tells students about her trip abroad and how she never knew how much money she had available to her because the conversion rates seemed to change so often. Also, she saw some people trying to take advantage of foreigners who didn't know how to make the conversions. (Textbook reading assignment is on conversion to the metric system.)

3. Disrupting readers' expectations—This produces a temporary state of surprise and confusion that should heighten students' interest.

     Example: Geography—The teacher tells students a story in which they expect certain things to take place. However, the expectations are incorrect. (Textbook reading assignment explains why.)

4. Challenging students to resolve a paradox. The teacher presents factual information to the students that contradicts their present knowledge and beliefs.

     Example: History—The teacher tells the students that Japan in

---

[19]Adapted from Carla Mathison, "Activating Student Interest in Content Area Reading," *Journal of Reading* 33 (December 1989): 170-176.

FIGURE 1-2. The excitement of learning should last more than fourteen seconds—good teachers make the difference.

World War II sought to dominate Asia and the United States militarily; however, they were totally defeated in this militaristic attempt. A number of decades later, they achieved their goal, but in a different way. (Textbook assignment is on present day Japan and their rise to their present position.)

5. Introducing novel and conflicting information or situations. The teacher brings students' attention to something new, which is in contrast to what they would expect from their experiences.

Example: Mathematics—[20]Teacher asks students to select any three-digit number in which the hundreds digit and unit digit are unequal. They then write their number in reverse order under their original number. Now they subtract the smaller number from the larger number. After this, students take the difference, reverse these digits and add the new number to the original difference. All the students' examples should add up to 1,089. (Students read textbook to find out why.)

Samples: (Numbers chosen)	153	964
	351	964
	153	469
(Differences)	198	495
	891	594
(Sum)	1089	1089

AMERICA'S CHALLENGE: A FINAL WORD

On September 26, 1990, the United States Department of Education released the summary findings of the National Assessment of Educational Progress on American student performance over the past two decades. The report was devastating. Students made little gains and suffered many losses. The data indicated that students' achievement levels are far below the levels that would demonstrate competency in challenging subject matter. It reported that students can read at a surface level; they can get the gist of the material but they cannot read analytically or perform well on challenging reading assignments. Only a small proportion of students write well enough, and most do not communicate effectively. "The achievement

[20]See Alfred S. Posamentier and Jay Stepelman, *Teaching Secondary School Mathematics*, 3rd ed. (Columbus, Ohio: Merrill Publishing Co., 1990), p. 41.

FIGURE 1-3. This teacher never has difficulty getting his students' attention.

of 17-year-olds in reading, mathematics, science, history, and civics represent only modest performance. Large majorities of these students—81 percent to 96 percent—have rudimentary interpretive skills; they can make generalizations, solve one-step problems, and understand basic science. Only 5 percent to 8 percent of our 17-year-olds, however, demonstrate those skills we usually associate with the ability to function in more demanding jobs in the workplace or the capability to do college work. These students can carry out multiple-step problems, synthesize, draw conclusions, and interpret."[21]

A few results of the two-decade summary are being presented here because the time for change is now, and it is the teachers who are one of the major catalysts for this change. The teachers are the ones who work directly with the students. It is they who must help turn the trend by making the teaching-learning environment a dynamic interactive adventure that instills the love of learning and books within the hearts of the students.

(See Chapter 3 for information on the interpretive skills that students need to do well in their content courses and to function effectively in society.)

A Scenario: Al: An At-Risk Student and Teachers' Responsibility

Al is in danger of becoming another life-and-blood dropout statistic. He is one of the young people we talk about who is an at-risk student because he lacks basic literacy skills. Al is in ninth grade, but he cannot read his textbooks. The question is: How did he reach the ninth grade? The answer is simple: social promotion. Al has been promoted based on his chronological age rather than his ability to achieve a certain level of competence at each grade level.

Al has exhibited all the signs of "high risk" throughout his life at school. He comes from a low socioeconomic status home; he has had both behavior and attendance problems, and he looks with disdain on school.

What does Al say about this? On the surface, Al shrugs it off. "Who cares?" he says. "I'm jus' markin' time 'till I get out of here. Most of my friends can't read their books too. Big deal. We'll get by. All we need is the diploma."

Commentary:

The sad thing is that for years many schools have made it easy for the Als of this world to go through the grades and get a diploma without attaining an education.

Who is to blame? Why hasn't some form of intervention taken place sooner? Educators know that the longer children remain nonreaders, the less likely are their chances to get up to their grade levels or their ability levels even with the best remedial help. Also, underachievers in reading tend to have many emotional and social problems, and these are compounded as the students go through the grades. Studies have shown that

---

[21]Ina V.S. Mullis, Eugene H. Owen, and Gary W. Phillips, *America's Challenge: Accelerating Academic Achievement*, The National Assessment of Educational Progress, Princeton, N.J.: Educational Testing Service, September, 1990, p. 3.

severe under-achievement in reading appears to follow the individual all through life.[22]

Fortunately, change is taking place. Al and his friends may be in for quite a shock when they learn that it will be "a big deal" if they do not learn to read. Many school districts across the country have initiated basic skills proficiency tests that students have to pass in order to receive a high school diploma. If Al and his friends can't read, they will not get the diploma for which they have been marking time. If this happens, Al and his friends have two options available to them. The first is to gain needed reading skills; the second is to drop out of school. A number will choose the latter, but there are some—and Al may be one of these—who will choose to remain in school and finally become serious about obtaining an education. If the Als remain in school and become serious about obtaining an education, we, the teachers, have to be prepared to help them.

Content-area teachers (who usually say, "I teach mathematics" or I teach history" or "I teach science" or "I teach English literature," and so on) have to be prepared to cope with students who lack reading ability. Moreover, it will be more difficult for secondary school teachers to send nonreaders into the welcoming arms of open admissions colleges because even open admissions colleges are raising their standards for admission.

Secondary school teachers have an especially difficult task in dealing with the Als of this world because not only do the Als lack basic essential reading skills and thus the means of learning, but they also come trailing years of frustration from the self-fulfilling prophecies of their past school experiences. Further compounding their problems are all the difficulties common to most young adults. The teachers who deal with students like Al need to be persons with special characteristics and abilities. They need to have knowledge of the developmental needs of young adults, of the reading process, and of their own special subject-matter area, as well as the methods and techniques for combining the teaching of their content area with the teaching of reading and study skills. In addition, they need to be flexible and able to adapt their teaching strategies to the situation at hand. It's not an easy mandate.

GRAPHIC SUMMARY OF CHAPTER

Here is a graphic summary of Chapter 1. If you have read the chapter, this illustration should help you remember its main points. Under or beside each heading, you might want to jot down some of the information you recall, as well as some of the key concepts in this chapter. This can act as a

---

[22]Diane Haines, "The Long-Term Consequences of Childhood Underachievement in Reading," Doctoral Dissertation (Ann Arbor, Mich.: University Microfilms International, 1979).

good review. You can then check your key concepts against those that follow the graphic summary.

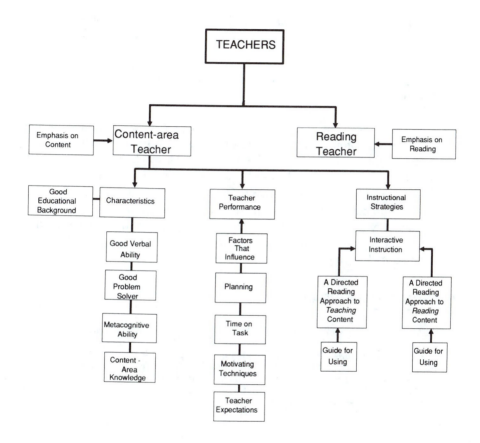

KEY CONCEPTS IN CHAPTER

- The major difference between content-area teachers and reading teachers is that of orientation.
- Reading teachers teach reading for its own sake.
- Content-area teachers use reading skills to help students attain content concepts.
- A directed reading approach to teaching content includes the direct teaching of any reading or study skill using relevant content material so that students can grasp the content concepts being taught.
- The teacher is the key to learning.

- The teacher is a major decision maker.
- A number of factors affect teaching performance.
- Teachers' assumptions about students can in part affect student behavior.
- Teachers play a major role in students' perception of their textbooks.
- Gaining students' interest is essential to their learning.

SUGGESTIONS FOR THOUGHT QUESTIONS AND ACTIVITIES

1. Observe a content-area teacher for a day. Observe a reading teacher for a day. Note the characteristics of both. Compare the two teachers' approaches. Note whether the content-area teacher incorporates directed reading approaches to teach his or her content area.
2. Think of the best content-area teacher you have ever had. Write down the characteristics of this teacher. Think of the worst content-area teacher you have ever had. Write down the characteristics of this teacher. Compare the characteristics of the good teacher with those presented in this chapter.

SELECTED BIBLIOGRAPHY

ALVERMANN, DONNA E. and DAVID W. MOORE. "Secondary School Reading." In *Handbook of Reading Research*, Vol. II. Rebecca Barr, Michael L. Kamil, Peter Mosenthal, and P. David Pearson (eds.) New York: Longman, 1991, pp. 951–983.

Do Teachers Make a Difference? Department of Health, Education and Welfare Report No. OE-58042. Washington, D.C.: U.S. Government Printing Office, 1970.

GROLLER, KATHRYN L., JOSEPH P. KENDER, and DAVID S. HONEYMAN. "Does Instruction on Metacognitive Strategies Help High School Students Use Advance Organizers?" *Journal of Reading* 34 (March 1991): 470–475.

HOUSTON, ROBERT W. (ed.) *Handbook of Research on Teacher Education.* New York: Macmillan, 1990.

MULLIS, INA V.S., EUGENE H. OWEN, and GARY W. PHILLIPS. *America's Challenge: Accelerating Academic Freedom,* The National Assessment of Educational Progress, Princeton, NJ: Educational Testing Service (ETS), 1990.

READENCE, JOHN, R. SCOTT BALDWIN, and ERNEST K. DISHNER. "Establishing Content Reading Programs in Secondary Schools." *Journal of Reading* 23 (March 1980): 522–526.

ROSENTHAL, ROBERT, and LENORE JACOBSON. *Pygmalion in the Classroom.* New York: Holt, Rinehart and Winston, 1968.

SCHALLERT, DIANE LEMONNIER and NANCY LEE ROSER. "The Role of Reading in Content Area Instruction." In *Content Area Reading and Learning.* Diane Lapp, James Flood, and Nancy Farnon (eds.) Englewood Cliffs, N.J.: Prentice Hall, 1989.

STEWART, ROGER A., and DAVID G. O'BRIEN, "Resistance to Content-Area Reading: A Focus on Preservice Teachers." *Journal of Reading* 32 (February 1989): 396–401.

SIEDOW, MARY D., DAVID M. MEMORY, and PAGE S. BRISTOW. *Inservice Education for Content Area Teachers.* Newark, Del.: International Reading Association, 1985.

2

Adolescence: Individual Differences in Reading and Thinking

OVERVIEW

INTRODUCTION: A SCENARIO

Mr. Brown loves teaching. He chose teaching as his profession twenty-five years ago, and he's still excited about it. At the beginning of every year, he greets each student with a smile and tries to make eye contact with each one. Even though he sees his students only for history, he wants them to feel he cares.

Mr. Brown is a good teacher. He is knowledgeable not only of his subject matter, but also of the reading process and uses a directed-reading approach to teaching content. In addition, he has taken courses in child growth and development and continues to attend inservice programs to learn more about the needs and developmental tasks of his students.

Mr. Brown has noticed that over the years, he has had more students in his classes who are nonnative English speakers. He has noticed also that the children today seem to grow faster. Therefore, he was not surprised when he heard an instructor at a recent inservice program state that "children and adolescents today experience the growth spurt earlier, grow faster, attain a greater total adult height earlier than did children and adolescents of sixty and seventy years ago."[1] Variations exist in the time needed to complete growth. Some children go through adolescence rather rapidly and are physically adults in about four or five years after the onset of puberty, whereas others may take seven or more years to reach adulthood. This can have ramifications on students' behavior and consequently affect the teaching-learning situation. Mr. Brown recognizes this and tries to take the individual differences of his students into account when planning instruction because he knows that this will make his teaching more effective.

Good teachers need to take the individual differences of their students into account when planning instruction because the more teachers know about the students with whom they are working, the more effective their instruction will be. Content-area teachers using a directed reading approach to teaching content should know the subject matter that they are responsible for teaching, as well as the reading process; but to be successful content-area teachers, they should also know about the needs and developmental tasks of their students.

Chapter 1 should have helped readers to gain a better understanding of the differences between teachers of reading and content-area teachers. This chapter should help you to gain more insight into the students with whom content-area teachers usually work.

It would be both foolhardy and presumptuous to assume that one short chapter could perform the Herculian task of presenting all the information content-area teachers should have about adolescence and the reading-thinking process. Numerous books have been written on each. However, this chapter can present enough information to raise readers' consciousness levels to the importance of these topics to content-area teachers. It is hoped also that this chapter will stimulate readers to read further in these areas.

---

[1] F. Philip Rice, *The Adolescent: Development, Relationships, and Culture*, 6th ed., (Boston: Allyn and Bacon, 1990), p. 142.

KEY QUESTIONS

After you finish reading this chapter, you should be able to answer the following questions:

1. Why should teachers be concerned with knowledge of the characteristics of adolescents?
2. What kind of thinking are adolescents capable of?
3. What is the relationship of reading to thinking?
4. What is the relationship of intelligence to reading?
5. Why do teachers need to know about the cultural diversity of their students?
6. What are some possible interferences between standard English and Black English that may affect reading?
7. What are some possible interferences between Spanish and standard English?
8. What are some possible interferences between Chinese and standard English?
9. What is the relationship of metacognition to reading and thinking?
10. What are the gender differences in reading?

KEY TERMS IN CHAPTER

You should pay special attention to the following key terms:

adolescence	dialect
bilingual	intelligence
black English	metacognition
cultural diversity	nonstandard English
developmental tasks	standard English

WHAT IS ADOLESCENCE?

Webster's Third New International Dictionary defines *adolescence* as "1: the state or process of growing up: the period of life from puberty to maturity terminating legally at the age of majority."[2] Adolescence has to do with growing up. That's simple enough, but "growing up" is never simple. That's the problem.

[2]*Webster's Third New International Dictionary of the English Language Unabridged* (Chicago: Encyclopaedia Britannica, Inc., 1981), p. 28.

Adolescence is filled with contradictions. It's a time to find oneself, to come into one's own, to find one's identity; it's a time for independence. Many adolescents today are, however, not independent. Emotional independence is difficult without economic independence, and there are not too many adolescents who are economically independent. How can you be dependent and independent at the same time? You can't. This situation obviously can cause problems and does.

Adolescence: A Period of Change

Adolescence is marked by rapid change—change from the slow and steady growth of previous years. This rapid change is quite noticeable not only physiologically, but also psychologically. The turmoil and stress of the teen years is due primarily to this rapid growth period. The upset usually associated with the teen years is due not only to the physiological changes but also to the "lack of changes." Because there is a great amount of variation in the onset of pubescence, which is genetically determined, some boys and girls will mature sooner or later than others. This may be a problem for some individuals. The early-maturing boy will behave differently from the late-maturing boy, and the early-maturing girl will also behave differently from the late-maturing girl.

Developmental Tasks of Adolescence

Adolescence, as we have seen, is that period between childhood and adulthood. Some individuals make the transition smoothly and cope successfully with the specific developmental tasks (problems individuals face at different periods of development) typically associated with adolescence; some encounter great difficulty at this time in their lives. Robert Havighurst defines developmental tasks as those that arise at a specific period in the life of an individual. If an individual is successful in accomplishing these tasks, he or she will be happy and have success with later tasks. If an individual is not successful, he or she will be unhappy, meet with disapproval from society, and have difficulty with later tasks.[3]

Teachers should be familiar with the kinds of developmental tasks that adolescents encounter so that they can gear their instruction to their students' needs. Teachers will be able to make better choices of materials and methods if they know about the students with whom they are working.

Havighurst has identified the following eight tasks that he feels are important ones that must be met and successfully accomplished if a person is to achieve an effective adult role:[4]

---

[3]Robert Havighurst, *Developmental Tasks and Education* (New York: David McKay Co., Inc., 1972), p. 2.
[4]Ibid., pp. 43–82.

1. Achieving new and more mature relations with age-mates of both sexes.
2. Achieving a masculine or feminine social role.
3. Accepting one's physique and using the body effectively.
4. Achieving emotional independence of parents and other adults.
5. Preparing for marriage and family life.
6. Preparing for an economic career.
7. Acquiring a set of values and an ethical system as a guide to behavior—developing an ideology.
8. Desiring and achieving socially responsible behavior.

An adolescent's life in the eighties and nineties seems to have become even more complex and stressful. Adolescents have the same developmental tasks as before; however, the proliferation of drugs and alcohol, the high divorce rate, and the specter of AIDS have changed many adolescents' thinking and behavior. Adolescents need all the help they can get.

Reading is a "tool for the achievement of developmental tasks because it gives knowledge, esthetic enjoyment, and a supply of vicarious experiences that is nearly inexhaustible."[5] It is an excellent means for helping students cope with their emotional and adjustment problems, and as such it can be used to stimulate students to read. If students see that reading books helps them to deal better with certain problems, students may read more. (See Chapter 11.)

CULTURAL DIVERSITY

The United States is a multicultural nation, and this cultural mix is reflected in our classrooms and among adolescents. Contrary to myth, adolescents are not all alike. Like other age groups, they come from different socioeconomic backgrounds, race, and ethnic groups, and these factors greatly shape their lives.

Home Environment

Socioeconomic class, parents' education, and the neighborhood in which one lives are some of the factors that determine an individual's home environment.

Read the following two scenarios of different thirteen-year-olds. The first deals with Al, the young man you met in Chapter 1, "A Scenario: Al: An At-Risk Student and Teacher's Responsibility." The second deals with a

---

[5]Robert Havighurst, *Human Development and Education* (New York: Longmans, Green and Co., 1953), p. 161.

child from a middle-class family. What predictions can you make about each?

Scenario 1: Al S.
Al lives with his mother and six younger brothers and sisters in a small apartment in a large, inner city building. His father left when he was nine years old, so he has some memory of him. Some of his younger brothers and sisters don't have even a faint memory of him. His mother, who doesn't speak English very well, has depended on him for years. At home he became the "man of the house" when he was nine years old. It was at that time that he also became a member of the gang in his neighborhood and has been a member ever since. The gang is the most important thing in Al's life. This year, Al has missed more school than he has attended. He goes only when a truant officer forces him to go. At school Al has been in one pull-out program after another. He has spent more time in pull-out programs than in regular classes.

Scenario 2: David M.
David lives with his parents and sister in a single-family suburban home. His parents are college educated and they are always reading and discussing various topics with David and his sister. They travel a lot together and do many things as a family. They don't all agree, and often they engage in heated debates about different issues; however, they respect one another and recognize that they don't have to agree on everything. On the important issues, they seem to be of one mind.

David's parents are proud of him and his sister. They expect him and his sister to do well, and they both do. David is very interested in birds. During spring break, his parents let him go to another country to study birds. In the summer, his parents went with him to Phoenix, Arizona, so that David could study certain birds.

Commentary:

It seems obvious that Al is on his way to becoming another dropout statistic unless immediate intervention takes place. Has the deck been stacked? Yes, however, even though these scenarios appear to portray stereotypical composites, these children exist. The Als are the at-risk or high-risk children we talk about. Al has all the preconditions one talks about when discussing high-risk students.

According to the National Assessment of Educational Progress, "at all three levels assessed (grades 4, 8, and 12), there were large differences in reading proficiency according to socioeconomic status. Twelfth-grade students from disadvantaged urban schools performed, on average, below the level of eighth-grade students from advantaged urban schools. Similarly,

Black and Hispanic students did less well than White students at all three grade levels assessed."[6]

This is not surprising because studies have consistently reported that children who come from homes where there are many opportunities to read, where there are diverse reading materials such as magazines, encyclopedias, books, and newspapers, and where the people with whom the children live read frequently will be better readers than those without these advantages.[7] Not only is the parents' education a factor in how well children do, but so is the parents' behavior toward their children. Parents who behave in a warm, democratic manner and provide their children with stimulating educationally oriented activities, challenge them to think, encourage independence, and reinforce their children will usually have students who will do better in school than parents who do not do these things.

In addition to child-rearing philosophies, peer orientation also seems to have an influence on students' school behavior. "Adolescents from low socioeconomic status families tend to maintain weaker ties with parents than do youths from middle-class families; they form stronger, more lasting peer relationships."[8]

Dialect and Language Differences

Dialect and language differences are closely related to home environment because the home environment will determine whether the child will speak standard English, a dialect of English, Spanish, Italian, Russian, Chinese, German, or so on. As stated earlier, teachers today have a diverse multicultural mix of students in their classrooms; the more information teachers have about their students' cultural backgrounds, the better able they will be to provide meaningful instruction based on the needs and interests of their students.

According to *Webster's Third New International Dictionary*, the term *standard English* is defined as "the English that with respect to spelling, grammar, pronunciation, and vocabulary is substantially uniform, though not devoid of regional differences, that is well established by usage in the formal and informal speech and writing of the educated, and that is widely recognized as acceptable wherever English is spoken and understood."[9]

The term *dialect* is more difficult to define, however. To some people, a dialect of English is any variation of standard English; to others, it is merely

---

[6]Judith A. Langer, Arthur N. Applebee, Ina V.S. Mullis, and Mary Foertsch, *Learning to Read in Our Schools: Instruction and Achievement in 1988 at Grades 4, 8, and 12*, National Assessment of Educational Progress, (Princeton, N.J.: Educational Testing Service, June, 1990), p. 7.

[7]Ibid., pp. 27–32.

[8]Rice, p. 43.

[9]*Webster's Third New International Dictionary of the English Language Unabridged*, p. 2223.

FIGURE 2-1. Most classrooms have a multicultural mix of students.

a means of expressing oneself; and to still others, it is a variety of language related to social class, educational level, geography, gender, and ethnicity. From these definitions, we can see that standard English could then be considered a dialect and that the definition of dialect is obviously intertwined with that of language. If we were to define dialect in a broad sense, we would be concerned with the language of a geographic area; if we were to define it in a specific sense, we would be looking at the language of a neighborhood, a family, or even an individual (idiolect). Generally, however, when we refer to dialect, we are talking about a structured subsystem of a language, with definite phonological and syntactic structures, that is spoken by a group of people united not only by their speech but also by factors such as geographic location and/or social status.[10]

For some people the term *dialect* seems to have negative connotations associated with it. This is unfortunate because we all speak a dialect. "Dialects inevitably arise within all languages because all languages inevitably change."[11] If the geographical separation between groups of people is very great, and the separation lasts long enough, "the dialects may diverge from

[10]Jean Malmstrom and Constance Weaver, *Transgrammar: English Structure, Style and Dialects* (Glenview, Ill.: Scott, Foresman, 1973), p. 338.

[11]Peter Desberg, Dale E. Elliott, and George Marsh, "American Black English and Spelling," in *Cognitive Processes in Spelling*, Uta Frith ed. (New York: Academic Press, 1980), p. 70.

each other so much that they become two distinct languages."[12] (Persons who speak different languages do not understand one another, whereas persons who speak different dialects do.)

In the United States, standard English is considered the "prestige" dialect and where regional dialects differ very little from each other, perhaps almost exclusively in pronunciation, we would be more likely to speak of an "accent" than a "dialect."[13] In this book, whenever the term *nonstandard English* is used, it refers to a variation of standard English owing to socioeconomic and cultural differences in the United States.

Children speaking in a dialect of English have no difficulty communicating with one another. However, any dialect that differs from standard English structure and usage will usually cause communication problems for children in school and in society at large. Many expressions used by children who speak a variation of English may be foreign to teachers, and many expressions used by teachers may have different connotations for the students. The similarities between the dialects of English and standard English can also cause misunderstandings between students and teachers because both groups may feel they "understand" what the others are saying when, in actuality, they may not.

These "misunderstandings" may be especially true for black English vernacular, which is in the class of nonstandard English. Black English and standard English appear similar, but they are not. Labov's research in the 1980s suggests that the differences between black English and standard English are becoming greater rather than narrower. He states that he would not rule out "the possibility that it is contributing to failure of black children to learn to read. How much a little child has to do to translate!"[14]

Here is a sample summary of some phonological and grammatical interferences between Standard English and Black English that may affect reading.

1. r-lessness. Black English has a rather high degree of r-lessness. The *r* becomes a schwa or simply disappears before vowels as well as before consonants or pauses: *r* is never pronounced in four, Paris becomes Pass, carrot becomes cat.

2. l-lessness. Dropping of the liquid *l* is similar to that of dropping *r* except that the former is often replaced by a back unrounded glide (u) instead of the center glide for *r*. Or the *l* disappears completely, especially after the backrounded vowels. Examples: help = hep, tool = too, all = awe, fault = fought.

3. Simplification of consonant clusters at the end of words. There is a

[12]Ibid., p. 71.

[13]John P. Hughes, *The Science of Language* (New York: Random House, 1962), p. 26.

[14]William Labov, Professor of Linguistics, University of Pennsylvania, January 11, 1990.

general tendency to reduce end consonant clusters to single consonants, particular those ending in /t/, /d/, /s/, or /z/. In approximate order of frequency, the /t,d/ clusters affected are -st, -ft, -nt, -nd, -ld, -zd, -md, thus generating homonyms such as past = pass, meant = men, rift = riff, mend = men, wind = wine, hold = hole. The /s,z/ cluster simplification results in these homonyms: six = sick, box = bock, Max = Mack, mix = Mick. Labov found that the simplification of the /s,z/ clusters is much more characteristic of Black speakers than of White speakers.

4. Weakening of final consonants. This is another example of a general tendency to produce less information after stressed vowels, so that the endings of words (be they consonants, unstressed final vowels, or weak syllables) are devoiced or dropped entirely. Children who possess this characteristic seem to have the most serious reading problems. Most affected by this are the following: boot = boo, road = row, feed = feet, seat = seed = see, poor = poke = pope, bit = bid = big.

5. Possessive deletion. The absence of /-s/ inflection results in: John's cousin = John cousin, whoever's book = whoever book. Deletion of /-r/ makes two possessive pronouns identical to personal pronouns: their book = they book, your = you = you-all.

6. Verb suffix. Labov believes that the third person singular was not present in Black English but imported from standard English in view of the low percentage of use (only 5–15 percent in some cases) and the sharp class stratification between middle and working classes. Some illustrations of the use of the verb suffix in Black English are: Somebody get hurts. He can goes out. He always bes on the beach mosta de time. All our men ares each on side. We goes to church on Sunday. Judy go to school today.

7. Be_2 form. There are two forms of "do" and two forms of "have" in English as in "Does he do it?" and "Has he had any?" In the first question, they could be called Do_1 and Do_2. The second form in each class is a normal main verb. *Be* has a main verb Be_2 which is like other main verbs. The meaning of Be_2 is so versatile that in some instances standard English has no equivalents:

   a) Habitual rather than a temporal or short occurrence. From now on, I don't be playing. He be sad. I be crying. She always be happy. Guys that bes with us.

   b) Repeated occurrence. Wolfram found between 11 to 16 percent of frequency adverbs with Be_2, such as hardly, usually, sometimes, always, mostly, all the time.

   c) Single nonrepeated activity in the future. This practice is used in all cases where *will* is possible or where an underlying *will* could be elicited in tag questions or in negatives: Sometime he don't be busy. He be in in a few minutes. I know he will. Sometime he be busy. I know he do.

d) Deletion of "would." She just be talking, and I wouldn't listen. If he didn't have to go away, he be home.

8. Copulation. Copula deletion is considered basically a phonological process, but it also has strong grammatical constraints which are not random. Deletion may occur with verb following, no vowel preceding, but pronoun preceding. Semantically, deletion occurs most often on short active utterances: Riff eatin. He goin. Ricky too old. Jim goin. She real tired. Carol chairman.

9. Person-number agreement.

a) In Black English, there is a person-number agreement for I am, you are, and he is.

b) There is no third person singular marker, as in most languages around the world. The preferred forms are: He don't. He do. He have. *Does, has,* and *says* are used infrequently.

c) *Was* is the preferred form for past tense of *be.*

10. Past tense. Phonological conditioning weakens the regular past tense as in the reduction of /t,d/ inflection: passed = pass, missed = miss, fined = fine, picked = pick, loaned = loan, raised = raise.

11. Negative forms and negation. In Black English, *ain't* is used as past negative; for example, I told im I ain't pull it; He didn't do nothing much, and I ain't neither. Adults used *didn't* more often than *ain't.* Preteens use *ain't* less often than teenagers. *Ain't* is a stigmatized form but has special social meaning to teenagers.

In negation, Black English seems to carry negative concord principles further than nonstandard Anglo English. Examples: Nobody had no bloody nose or nosebleed. I am no strong drinker. She didn't play with none of us. Down there nobody don't know about no club.

Source: Doris C. Ching, *Reading and the Bilingual Child,* Newark, Del.: International Reading Association, 1976, pp. 15–17.

Some Language Difference Interferences   Teachers need to recognize that students who speak another language will usually try to superimpose what they know intuitively about their language on the new language they are learning. Therefore, teachers would be in a better position to help their students if they knew some of the major interferences between standard English and the nonnative speaker's language. This is not easy because most teachers are not polyglots; however, they could seek help from bilingual or ESL teachers to learn about some of the differences.

Here is a sample of the kinds of problems that Spanish-speaking children have when attempting to learn standard English.

1. Certain vowel sounds will be difficult for the Spanish speaking child: /I/ bit; /æ/ bat; /ə/ but; and /u/ full.

2. English relies on voiced (vocal cords vibrate) and voiceless (vocal cords do not vibrate) sounds to establish meaning contrasts, but Spanish does not: bit-pit; buzz-bus.

3. The Spanish speaker does not use these sounds in his language: /v/ vote; /ð/ then; /z/ zoo; /ž/ measure; /ǰ/ jump. Often the speaker will replace these sounds with sounds he perceives to closely resemble them, or with sounds that frequently occur in similar positions in Spanish.

4. Words that end in /r/ plus the consonants /d, t, l, p/ and /s/ are pronounced without the final consonant: card-car, cart-car.

5. In Spanish the blend of /s/ and the consonant sounds /t, p, k, f, m, n, l/ does not occur, nor does any Spanish word begin with the /s/ + consonant sound. A vowel sound precedes the /s/, and the consonant that follows begins the second syllable of the word. Thus the child has the problem not only of starting the word with the /s/, but also of pronouncing two consonants (star may thus become estar and be pronounced es-tar). The final consonant clusters /sp/ wasp, /sk/ disk, and /st/ last also present problems in consonant pronunciation.

6. Grammatical differences between the two systems may include the following: subject-predicate agreement (The cars runs.); verb tense (I need help yesterday.); use of negative forms (He no go home.); omission of noun determiner in certain contexts (He is farmer.); omission of pronoun forms (Is farmer?); order of adjectives (The cap red is pretty.); and comparison (Is more big.).

Source: Robert B. Ruddell, *Reading-Language Instruction: Innovative Practices*, Englewood Cliffs, N.J.: Prentice Hall, 1974, p. 275.

This summary serves only as an introduction to the teacher to help him [or her] in being alert to the variations between the Spanish and English languages.

A summary of some of the phonological and grammatical variations between Standard English and Chinese is also presented because a large population of children in the United States come from homes where Chinese is the dominant language. The following should help teachers gain a better understanding of some of the difficulties encountered by a number of Chinese-speaking children.

There are many dialects of Chinese with Mandarin, which is spoken by approximately 70 percent of the Chinese people as the national dialect. Cantonese, another major dialect, is spoken by most of the Chinese families that come to the United States from Hong Kong, Kowloon, or Macao. Thus, the Cantonese dialect is the one that is discussed below.

1. English has many more vowels than Chinese; for example, /ay/ buy; /aw/ bough; /ɔ/ bought. There is specific difficulty with production of certain vowels such as the front vowels /iy/ beat, /ey/ bait. This results in homophones for a significant number of English words: beat-bit; Luke-look, bait-bet.

2. A number of English consonant sounds are not in Chinese: /θ/ than / ð/ that; /š/ she; /n/ need; and /r/ rice.

3. Many English words end in consonants, but in Chinese many of the consonants are not used in final positions; for example, /f/ is used only initially in Chinese, and the student has difficulty producing it in a final position. Often an extra syllable will be made of the final /f/; day off becomes day offu.

4. Consonant clusters are nonexistent in Cantonese. Those which occur at the ends of words present difficulty in forming plurals and past tenses using /s, t, d, z/: cap-caps, laugh-laughed, wish-wished, dog-dogs.

5. Most grammatical relationships are indicated by word order and auxiliary words in Chinese: "He gave me two books" becomes "Yesterday he give I two book."

6. Numerical designations or auxiliary words are used to indicate plural forms in Chinese: "two books" is "two book."

7. A time word or phrase indicates the tense of a verb. An action verb followed by the auxiliary word *jaw* indicates past or completed tense: "He go jaw" means "he went."

8. Several English word classes—articles, prepositions, and some conjunctions—are reduced or absent in Chinese.

9. The question form in Chinese does not invert the noun and verb forms. Instead, the order is similar to the statement form but the "empty" words *ma* or *la* are added to the end. For example, "Are you an American?" is "You are American ma?" in Chinese.

10. A subject and a predicate are not required in Chinese when the context is sufficient for understanding. For example, "It rains" may be represented as "Drop rain" in Chinese, while "The mountain is big" may be stated as "Mountain big" in Chinese.

11. Tone or pitch in Chinese distinguishes word meanings, but in English pitch combines with intonation to convey sentence meaning.

Source: Robert B. Ruddell, *Reading-Language Instruction: Innovative Practices*, Englewood Cliffs, N.J.: Prentice Hall, 1974, p. 278.

Special Note:
Idiomatic expressions present a great amount of difficulty for all nonnative speakers because idioms are very culturally loaded. The same is true for figurative language; many nonnative speakers will take these literally. (A person with limited English who sees a sign that says "Chickens sold—dressed and undressed" would have great difficulty understanding its meaning.)

ADOLESCENCE AND INTELLECTUAL DEVELOPMENT

During adolescence, students' thinking ability is capable of maturing fully; it is at this stage of development that students usually are capable of working at hypothetical-deductive reasoning. Students are able to think logically, make hypotheses, verify by experimental means various assertions, and make logical deductions. They are able to work at high levels of abstractions.

Individual differences exist, of course, in adolescent thinking ability, as well as in their rate of physical growth, and the environmental factors that influence young children's intellectual development continue to influence adolescents' intellectual development. During adolescence, however, some students who have not achieved in school become discouraged and disenchanted with intellectual endeavors and feel that they can not achieve in this area. As a result, they begin to pursue other avenues. Many of these students may indeed have the intellectual capability but they lack the desire and the interest to learn. They feel that since they have been unsuccessful in the past, they will continue to be unsuccessful in the future. These students may be having difficulty also because they lack reading or studying skills. Such students in particular would benefit from a directed reading approach to teaching content.

READING AND THINKING

People read, and read, and read, blandly unconscious of their effrontery in assuming that they can assimilate without any further effort the vital essence which the author has breathed into them. They cannot. And the proof that they do not is shown all the time in their lives. I say that if a man does not spend at least as much time in actively and definitely thinking about what he has read as he has spent in reading, he is simply insulting his author. If he does not submit himself to intellectual and emotional fatigue in classifying the communicated ideas, and in emphasizing on his spirit the imprint of the communicated emotions—then reading with him is a pleasant pastime and nothing else.

ARNOLD BENNETT
Literary Taste

Good readers are good thinkers because reading is a thinking act. Students who have difficulty working at different levels of cognition will have difficulty comprehending what they are reading; consequently, they would have difficulty reading their content-area textbooks.

Intelligence deals with thinking; the more intelligent an individual is, the better thinker he or she should be. We often define intelligence as "the ability to do abstract reasoning" or "problem solving ability based on a hierarchical organization of two things—symbolic representations and strategies for processing information." Therefore, individuals who have good strategies for processing information; that is, who know what goes together and what doesn't, will be better thinkers than those who do not have these strategies.

The human brain is actively involved in selecting, transforming, organizing, and remembering information;[15] in many ways it is analogous to a computer's information-processing system. However, the human brain, unlike the computer, is constantly reprogramming itself, generating new strategies, and learning new knowledge. The better strategies a learner has for processing information, the better able the learner is to retain and retrieve the information.

If we look at the learner as an active consumer of information, we give the learner an important, active role and responsibility in learning from instruction and reading. Readers as active consumers of information relate what they are reading to their experiences; they interpret information, draw inferences from it, ignore some information and attend to other information. Good readers are good thinkers. (See "What Are the Characteristics of Good Comprehenders?" in Chapter 3.)

Special Notes:

Although it is stated that good readers are good thinkers, this does not mean that the converse is true, namely, that good thinkers are good readers. It is possible for a student to be a good thinker who has reading difficulties. For example, if a student has difficulty decoding words on a page, he or she will not be able to read the author's message. However, if this same passage were read aloud to the student, he or she could understand it.

It is possible also for students to have been good readers in the elementary grades or in their reading classes but not to be good content-area readers. There could be a number of reasons for this. One reason could be that the student is not interested in the content area. Another could be that the student does not know how to use the material; that is, the student

---

[15]Merlin C. Wittrock, "Education and the Cognitive Processes of the Brain," *The National Society for the Study of Education, Seventy-seventh Yearbook,* Part II (1978): 64.

does not know how to transfer and adapt what he or she has learned in reading classes to the content material. A directed reading approach to teaching content would be especially helpful for these students because teachers using this approach would give those students who need it *direct* help in gaining the skills they need to grasp the concepts of the subject matter they are studying by using relevant content material.

Teachers should recognize also that the more experience students have in doing higher-level thinking, the better able they will be to engage in such activities. (See "What Is Comprehension?" in Chapter 3.)

Intelligence and Reading

Since reading is a thinking process, it seems reasonable to assume that highly able persons, who have the ability to think at high levels of abstraction and the ability to learn, should be good readers. To a degree this assumption is so, and many highly able children do learn to read before they come to school. However, studies have shown that not all highly able children become good readers, and these findings suggest that there are factors besides intelligence that contribute to success in reading and consequently to school achievement.

Studies have also shown that the correlation between intelligence and reading achievement seems to increase as children go through the grades.[16] Such correlations in the first grade are substantial but not high.[17] This is not surprising since mental age, which is the child's present developmental level, is more a determinant of reading success when students are involved with reading for information than with learning to read. (Of course, while learning to read, children are also reading to learn, but the informational load increases as students advance through the grades.) In addition, it is difficult to get a valid IQ score for children seven years old and below.

Most intelligence tests are highly verbal; therefore, it is not surprising that people who do well on vocabulary tests also seem to do well on intelligence tests. Investigators have reported a high positive relationship between reading achievement test scores and intelligence test scores.[18] These findings seem to suggest that reading achievement tests and intelligence tests may be measuring some similar factors. Since vocabulary tests correlate highly with intelligence tests and since reading achievement tests depend highly on vocabulary ability, it seems reasonable to assume that a

[16]Alice Cohen and Gerald G. Glass, "Lateral Dominance and Reading Ability," *The Reading Teacher* 21 (January 1968): 343–348; Dolores Durkin, *Children Who Read Early,* (New York: Teachers College Press, 1966), pp. 20–21.

[17]Albert J. Harris and Edward R. Sipay, *How to Increase Reading Ability,* 9th ed. (New York, Longman, 1990), p. 39.

[18]Keith Raynor and Alexander Pollatsek, *The Psychology of Reading,* (Englewood Cliffs, N.J.: Prentice Hall, 1989), p. 395.

similar and major factor that both kinds of tests have in common is verbal ability. Obviously, reading as a thinking process hinges upon the continuous development of higher levels of verbal ability.

Reading and Thinking: State-of-the-Art

Since 1969, the National Assessment of Educational Progress (NAEP) has done its own national testing and issued periodic reports to Congress on the results of students in various curriculum areas. The good news is that all students seem to be doing well in the lower-level thinking skills and that students in lower socioeconomic levels have made special strides in this area. The bad news is that, nationally, only a small percentage of students do well on higher-order thinking skills. In addition, the average verbal skills scores of students who took the Scholastic Aptitude Tests (SATs) in the spring of 1990 were the lowest in a decade. The emphasis in the 1980s was on basic skills, and some of this appears to be paying off; however, the NAEP report concerning higher-order thinking skills and the dismal showing of students on the SATs is worrisome because schools in the 1980s after *A Nation at Risk* were supposed to be dedicated to helping students gain higher-order thinking skills. The NAEP reports and SAT scores suggest that the schools' efforts were not successful. (See "America's Challenge: A Final Word" in Chapter 1.)

"Television, video games, and teaching quality have all been scolded for contributing to the decline . . ."[19] Even though there is no one cause that we can single out as the villain, "some analysts believe that the main cause of the problem is a self-perpetuating cycle of low expectations and low achievement, rooted in race and class."[20] In other words, they feel that teachers do not expect certain groups of students to do well, so teachers water down the curriculum and "dummy down" the texts to make education less rigorous. This is true not only for minority students and those from low socioeconomic class, but for all students. Thus, we have a vicious cycle.

Special Note:
Teachers must be careful that they do not equate the teaching of content material using a directed reading-thinking approach and the employment of strategies to make the text more enjoyable and readable as "watering down" the curriculum. These are excellent strategies that good teachers use to help their students gain needed concepts and to help them develop skill in higher-level thinking.

[19]William Celis, 3d, "S.A.T. Scores Are In, and All of Education is Judged," *The New York Times*, "The Week in Review," Section 4, Sunday, September 9, 1990, p. 26.
[20]Ibid.

GENDER DIFFERENCES

Teachers should know that although studies do not reveal any significant differences between males and females in general intelligence,[21] studies continue to show differences in specific aptitudes.[22] In the earlier studies, it was reported that in general males are superior in mathematical ability and in science, but females are usually superior in rote memory. It has also been consistently shown that girls usually surpass boys in verbal ability. From infancy to adulthood, females usually express themselves in words more readily and skillfully than males; however, females do not have larger vocabularies than males.[23]

A recent review of the researches on gender differences has reported that even though the data on sex differences studies are inconclusive and contradictory, there are a few generalizations that can be made. The reviewers report that "the largest differences appear in tests of mathematical or quantitative ability, where men tend to do better than women, particularly in secondary school and beyond. In recent years, there is some evidence that the gender gap may be narrowing."[24] What is surprising is that the gap is narrowing between men and women in the area of verbal skills. "Women have tended to do better than men in many tests of verbal skills (particularly writing), but a number of studies indicate that this superiority has diminished since the early 1970s."[25]

In the 1970s and 1980s females made great inroads in male bastions. As a result the latest findings on sex differences may seem confusing because females haven't made the great strides one would have expected. What has happened is that males have gained in verbal skills so that females seem to be losing their edge in this area, and males have continued to maintain their edge in mathematical skills.

Sex Differences and Reading

A review of the national assessments of reading between 1971 and 1988 reveals that even though, as stated earlier, the traditional female advantage in verbal skills seems to be eroding, "females at all three ages (9, 13, and 17)

[21]Scottish Council for Research in Education, *The Intelligence of a Representative Group of Scottish Children* (London: University of London Press, 1939). Scottish Council for Research in Education, *The Trend of Scottish Intelligence* (London: University of London Press, 1949).

[22]Gita Z. Wilder and Kristen Powell, "Sex Differences in Test Performance: A Survey of the Literature," College Board Report No. 89-3, Princeton, N.J.: Educational Testing Service, 1989.

[23]Leona E. Tyler, *The Psychology of Human Differences* (New York: Appleton-Century-Crofts, 1965), pp. 243–246.

[24]"The Gender Gap in Education: How Early and How Large?" ETS Policy Notes, Vol. 2 No. 1, Princeton, N.J.: Educational Testing Service, October, 1989.

[25]Ibid.

outperformed their male counterparts in each of the five NAEP reading assessments . . ."[26]

It should not be surprising then that innumerable studies have found that boys usually outnumber girls in remedial reading classes,[27] and reading disabilities are "from three to ten times more common for boys, depending on how the disability is defined and what population is studied."[28] Researchers have also found "greater variability in reading scores among boys from grades 2 through 7 . . . and boys outnumbered girls among the lowest scores by about 2 to 1 in the lower grades, with the ratio decreasing thereafter."[29]

Both cultural and biological or maturational factors have been put forth as reasons for girls' superior readiness for formal reading. A perusal of the literature seems to lend support to theories suggesting that gender differences in reading may be caused by a combination of both maturational and environmental factors. There are no definitive researches in this area.

It is interesting to note that even though in the past few decades there has been a great emphasis on trying to treat males and females the same, there is "ample evidence that boys and girls are treated differently from birth and perhaps even before, in an age of increasing knowledge about the gender of the unborn child. Parents react more positively toward their toddlers when the children are engaged in gender-appropriate behavior. Moreover, parents' behavior is not always congruent with their stated attitudes."[30]

LEARNING THEORY AND A DIRECTED READING APPROACH TO TEACHING CONTENT

Learning theory studies have shown that persons will retain information over an extended period of time if they are able to make generalizations about the information and if they can see relationships between what they are presently learning and material that they have already learned. Therefore, students who have strategies for processing information will be in a better position to retain and transfer learning than those who do not. Good thinkers have strategies for processing information; they are able to assimilate and accommodate information; they are active consumers of information. As already stated, readers as active consumers of information must

[26]Ina V.S. Mullis and Lynn B. Jenkins, *The Reading Report Card*, 1971–1988, The National Assessment of Educational Progress, Princeton, N.J.: Educational Testing Service, 1990, p. 17.

[27]Norma Naiden, "Ratio of Boys to Girls Among Disabled Readers," *The Reading Teacher* 29 (February 1976): 439–42.

[28]Maccoby and Jacklin, p. 119.

[29]Ibid.

[30]Wilder and Powell, p. 16.

give structure or order to what they are reading. They must relate new experiences to what they already know. No one can do this for the reader; however, the teacher is the facilitator for helping the reader to gain skill in higher cognitive operations. A directed reading approach to teaching content includes strategies and techniques that help those students who need them to gain skill in processing and organizing information; it helps students develop the kind of thinking skills that they need to be effective learners and readers of content material. The technique is an excellent one because students are involved in on-task activities; that is, relevant content material is used to help them gain the skills they need to attain content concepts.

Metacognition and Reading

The term metacognition is omnipresent. It is difficult to pick up an educational journal without seeing this ubiquitous term. Metacognition refers to "both students' knowledge about their own cognitive processes and their ability to control these processes."[31] It literally means "thinking critically about thinking."

Throughout this chapter, we have discussed the importance of students being active consumers of information. Students as active consumers must be involved in their own cognitive processes. Therefore, students who are good readers are engaged in active learning strategies. They use good monitoring strategies whereby they establish learning goals for an instructional activity, determine the degree to which these are being met, and, if necessary, change the strategies being used to attain the goal.[32] Good readers know what to do, as well as how and when to do it; they have the metacognitive abilities that make them active consumers of information.

The "what to do" includes such strategies as "identifying the main idea, rehearsing (repeating) information, forming associations and images, using mnemonics, organizing new material to make it easier to remember, applying test-taking techniques, outlining, and notetaking."[33]

The "how and when" includes such strategies as "checking to see if you understand, predicting outcomes, evaluating the effectiveness of an attempt at a task, planning the next move, testing strategies, deciding how to apportion time and effort, and revising or switching to other strategies to overcome any difficulties encountered."[34]

---

[31]Claire E. Weinstein and Richard E. Mayer, "The Teaching of Learning Strategies," *The Handbook of Research on Teaching*, 3rd ed., Merlin C. Wittrock, ed. (New York: Macmillan, 1986), p. 323.

[32]Ibid.

[33]Anita Woolfolk, *Educational Psychology*, 4th ed. (Englewood Cliffs, N.J.: Prentice Hall, 1990), p. 252.

[34]Ibid.

GRAPHIC SUMMARY OF CHAPTER

Here is a graphic summary of Chapter 2. If you have read the chapter, this graphic illustration should help you remember its main points. Under or beside each heading, you might want to jot down some of the information you recall, as well as some of the key concepts in this chapter. This can act as a good review. You can then check your key concepts against those that follow the graphic summary.

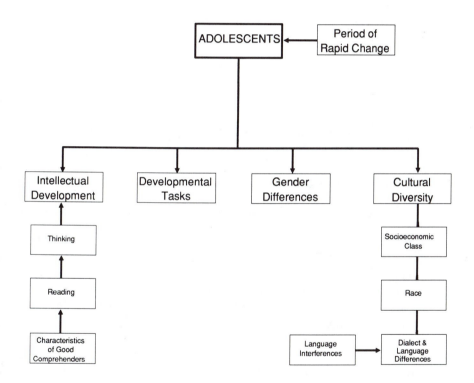

KEY CONCEPTS IN CHAPTER

- Knowledge of the individual differences of students is essential.
- The period of adolescence is filled with contradictions.
- Adolescence is marked by rapid change.
- Adolescents have to successfully accomplish certain developmental tasks to achieve an effective adult role.

- During adolescence, students are capable of the highest level of thinking.
- Reading is a tool to help students cope with their emotional and adjustment problems.
- There appears to be a strong correlation between socioeconomic class and achievement in school.
- A home environment rich with books and where adult figures read is closely related to academic success.
- Teachers usually have a multicultural mix of students in their classrooms.
- Good readers are good thinkers.
- Not all good thinkers are good readers.
- Good readers are active consumers of information.
- There is a high positive correlation between reading achievement test scores and intelligence test scores.
- Boys usually outnumber girls in remedial reading classes.
- Good readers have the metacognitive abilities that make them active consumers of information.

SUGGESTIONS FOR THOUGHT QUESTIONS AND ACTIVITIES

1. You have been asked to give a talk to your local parent-teacher association about adolescence from the viewpoint of a content-area teacher. What would you say?

2. As a content-area teacher, what do you feel is your role in relation to reading? After you finish reading this book, answer this question again. Compare your answers.

3. Ask a number of content-area teachers from different fields who have never had a reading course how they feel about integrating reading into their content areas. Ask the same question of content-area teachers who have had some course or workshops in reading. If possible, visit the classes of both groups of teachers. Make a comparison between the two groups of teachers.

4. Speak to a number of adolescents, and ask them what they see as their most important tasks or goals.

SELECTED BIBLIOGRAPHY

CLARY, LINDA MIXON. "Getting Adolescents to Read." *Journal of Reading* 34 (February 1991): 340–345.

DOLLY, MARTHA R. "Integrating ESL Reading and Writing Through Authentic Discourse." *Journal of Reading* 33 (February 1990): 360–364.

FIELD, MARY LEE, and JO ANN AEBERSOLD. "Cultural Attitudes Toward Reading: Implications for Teachers of ESL/Bilingual Readers." *Journal of Reading* 33 (March 1990): 406–410.

HAVIGHURST, ROBERT. *Developmental Tasks and Education.* New York: David McKay, 1972.

LANGER, JUDITH A., ARTHUR N. APPLEBEE, INA V.S. MULLIS, and MARY FOERTSCH. *Learning to Read in Our Schools: Instruction and Achievement in 1988 at Grades 4, 8, and 12,* National Assessment of Educational Progress. Princeton, N.J.: Educational Testing Service, 1990.

NIELSON, LINDA. *Adolescence: A Contemporary View,* 2nd ed. Fort Worth, Tex: Holt, Rinehart and Winston, 1991.

OSBORNE-WILSON, COLETTE, RICHARD SINATRA, and ANTHONY N. BARATTA. "Helping Chinese Students in the Literacy Transfer Process." *Journal of Reading* 32 (January 1989): 330–336.

RICE, F. PHILIP. *The Adolescent: Development, Relationships, and Culture,* 6th ed. Boston: Allyn & Bacon, 1990.

THONIS, ELENAOR. "Bilingual Students: Reading and Learning." In *Content Area Reading and Learning,* Diane Lapp, James Flood, and Nancy Farnan (eds.). Englewood Cliffs, N.J.: Prentice Hall, 1989, pp. 105–113.

WADE, SUZANNE E., and RALPH E. REYNOLDS. "Developing Metacognitive Awareness." *Journal of Reading* 33 (October 1989): 6–14.

WEBER, ROSE-MARIE. "Linguistic Diversity and Reading in American Society." In *Handbook of Reading Research,* Vol. II. Rebecca Barr, Michael L. Kamil, Peter Mosenthal, and P. David Pearson (eds.). New York: Longman, 1991, pp. 97–119.

Part 2: Reading and Study Skills for Reading in the Content Areas

3

Reading Comprehension

INTRODUCTION: A SCENARIO

Melissa started reading when she was still in diapers, or so it seemed to her parents. She used to carry books to them and say, "Read." She was fascinated with the words and pictures on the pages. It wasn't long before she was retelling the stories her parents had read to her and reading on her

52

own. Her appetite for books has never subsided. She has a broad interest in the world around her and reads to find answers to many of her questions. She also enjoys discussing many of her questions with her parents.

Melissa tries to keep an open mind about things; she tries to hold off making judgments until all the evidence is in. She learned the importance of being as objective as possible from her parents. Fortunately for Melissa, she is in good physical health and has no visual or auditory problems.

What kind of reader would you expect Melissa to be? What kinds of predictions can you make about how well she will do in most of her content-area courses?

Background knowledge of reading comprehension is important for all teachers regardless of what they teach because the development of higher levels of comprehension is closely related to the development of higher-level thinking skills. Also, all teachers are interested in having their students understand what they are reading.

After a general discussion of comprehension and questioning, this chapter will present a number of comprehension skills that students use to master concepts in various content areas. These skills are being presented and emphasized because many preservice teachers may not have acquired them. In order to present a program that advocates a directed reading approach to teaching content, teachers must have these comprehension skills at their fingertips. The foregoing does not imply that the author advocates a separate skills approach or recommends that content-area teachers teach the comprehension skills as ends in themselves. Often, however, when content-area teachers ask their students to draw some inferences from what they have read or to find the main or central idea of text material, their students are not able to do so. The reason for this may be because the students do not know how. Content-area teachers should be careful about the assumptions they make about what their students can or cannot do. If content-area teachers find that their students lack certain reading comprehension skills that they need to understand content material, the content-area teachers should help their students acquire these needed skills by using an integrative approach. This means that the skills needed to understand the content material, as well as the content, are taught together; that is, the specific comprehension skill that is needed to help students learn what is being taught or read is taught by using relevant content material. (See "What Is a Directed Reading Approach to Teaching Content?" in Chapter 1.) A number of chapters in Part 3 will show how teachers can integrate and adapt the comprehension skills presented in this chapter to fit specific content areas illustrating a directed reading approach to teaching content.

KEY QUESTIONS

After you finish reading this chapter, you should be able to answer the following questions:

1. What is reading?
2. What are the components of reading?
3. What is comprehension?
4. What are some relationships between listening and reading comprehension?
5. What are the characteristics of good comprehenders?
6. What is schema theory?
7. How is reading comprehension categorized in this text?
8. What is the role of questioning in stimulating various levels of thinking?
9. What are examples of questions that content-area teachers can ask to stimulate higher-level thinking?
10. What is the role of metacognition in questioning?
11. What are some important reading comprehension skills for content-area students?
12. How can teachers help students find the main idea of a paragraph?
13. What is the central idea of a group of paragraphs?
14. What are some critical thinking skills?
15. What is divergent thinking?
16. What is the creative process?
17. How can teachers foster divergent thinking?

KEY TERMS IN CHAPTER

You should pay special attention to the following key terms:

affective domain
analogies
bias
brainstorming
central idea
cognitive domain
comprehension
creative process
creative reading
critical reading
divergent thinking
interpretation
listening vocabulary

literal comprehension
main idea
perception
perceptual domain
propaganda
Question Answer Relationships
  (QARs)
reading
reading comprehension
reading process
reading taxonomy
schema theory

DEFINING READING

In Chapter 2, the statement "good readers are good thinkers" was made a number of times. In order to help you understand this better it is necessary to attempt to define reading, even though this is a difficult task. (See Special Note that follows this section.)

Which of the following individuals would you consider as reading?

1. Someone is able to pronounce all the words on the page but not able to give you the meaning of what he has read.
2. A person is not able to decode (make the proper grapheme [letter]–phoneme [sound] correspondences) the words on the written page. She cannot answer any of the questions about the passage.
3. An individual's strong feelings are interfering with his getting the author's message. He can't answer any of the questions about the passage.
4. This individual is able to bring her background of experience to the material and extract the author's message. Even though she makes a few decoding errors, these errors do not prevent her from answering all the questions about the passage.

The answer, as to which of the individuals are reading, depends on the definition we choose to use. If we look upon reading as a one-way process, consisting merely of the decoding of symbols from the printed page, then all except individual Number 2 would be considered as reading, and the person in Number 4 would be considered a poorer reader than the one in Example 1. However, if we look upon reading as a dynamic two-way interactive process, then only Number 4 would be considered as reading. Let's discuss this a little more.

There is *no single, set definition of reading.* As a result, it is difficult to define it simply. A broad definition that has been greatly used is that reading is the bringing to and the getting of meaning from the printed page. This implies that readers bring their backgrounds, their experiences, as well as their emotions, into play. Students who are upset or physically ill will bring these feelings into the act of reading, and this will influence their interpretive processes. A person well versed in reading matter will gain more from the material than someone less knowledgeable. A student who is a good critical thinker will gain more from a critical passage than one who is not. A student who has strong dislikes will come away with different feelings and understandings from a pupil with strong likings.

From our broad definition, the getting of meaning from and the bringing of meaning to the printed page, we see that reading is "a process in which information from the text and the knowledge possessed by the reader act together to produce meaning."[1] This has happened only for Number 4.

It is possible that the individual in Number 1 is having difficulty with the presentation of the material. The way the writer presents the information will influence how well the reader will gain the presented concepts. The more clear and logical the presentation and organization of the writing, the easier it is to obtain meaning from the text. It is possible, too, that this student does not have the motivation, skill, or background experience to interpret the text material. Good readers are good problem solvers who must construct "meaning through the dynamic interaction among the reader, the text, and the content of the reading situation."[2]

Special Note:
Many content-area teachers may feel that a definition of reading is important for reading teachers only, but not for them. This is not true. Good content-area teachers who understand what the reading act encompasses and what makes one person a better reader than another will be in a position to help their students get the most from their textbooks and instruction. In other words, knowledge of the reading process helps teachers determine the kind of strategies to use with those students who are having difficulty reading their books, as well as how to help all students get the most from their reading.

Reading as a Total Integrative Act

By using a broad or global definition of reading, we are looking upon reading as a total integrative process that includes the affective, perceptual, and cognitive domains. Even though all three act together as a cohesive whole, for analytical purposes, let's look at each separately.

The Affective Domain Have you ever been so angry with someone or about something that you couldn't see straight? Did your anger interfere with your ability to listen to or read about a topic?

The affective domain includes our feelings and emotions. The way we feel influences greatly the way we look upon stimuli on a field. It may distort our perception. For example, if we are hungry and we see the word *fool*, we would very likely read it as *food*. If we have adverse feelings about certain things, these feelings will probably influence how we interpret what we read. Our feelings will also influence what we decide to read. Obviously, attitudes exert a directive and dynamic influence on our readiness to respond.

---

[1] Richard C. Anderson, Elfrieda H. Hiebert, Judith A. Scott, and Ian A.G. Wilkinson, *Becoming a Nation of Readers* (Washington, D.C.: National Institute of Education, 1985), p. 8.
[2] Karen K. Wixson, Charles W. Peters, Elaine M. Weber, and Edward D. Roeber, "New Directions in Statewide Reading Assessment," *The Reading Teacher* 40 (April 1987): 750.

The Perceptual Domain In the perceptual domain, perception can be defined as giving meaning to sensations or the ability to organize stimuli on a field. How we organize stimuli depends largely on our background of experiences and on our sensory receptors. If, for example, our eyes are organically defective, those perceptions involving sight would be distorted. In the act of reading, visual perception is a most important factor. Readers need to control their eyes so they move from left to right across the page. Eye movements influence what the reader perceives.

Although what we observe is never in exact accord with the physical situation,[3] readers must be able to accurately decode the graphemic (written) representation. If, however, readers have learned incorrect associations, this will affect their ability to read. For example, if a child reads the word *gip* for *pig* and is not corrected, this may become part of his or her perceptions. If children perceive the word as a whole, in parts, or as individual letters, this will also determine whether they will be good or poor readers. The more mature readers are able to perceive more complex and extensive graphemic patterns as units. They are also able to give meaning to mutilated words such as

Perception is a cumulative process that is based on an individual's background of experiences. The perceptual process is influenced by physiological factors as well as affective ones. As already stated, a person who is hungry may read the word *fool* as *food*. Similarly, a person with a biased view toward a topic being read may delete, add, or distort what is being read.

The Cognitive Domain The cognitive domain includes the areas involving thinking. Under this umbrella we would place all the comprehension skills. (See the sections that follow for a discussion of reading comprehension.) Persons who have difficulty in thinking (the manipulation of symbolic representations) would obviously have difficulty in reading. Although the cognitive domain goes beyond the perceptual domain, it builds and depends on a firm perceptual base. That is, if readers have faulty perceptions, they will also have faulty concepts.

Teachers, however, can aid students in developing thinking skills by helping them acquire necessary strategies and by giving them practice in using these strategies in content areas.

[3]Julian E. Hochberg, *Perception* (Englewood Cliffs, N.J.: Prentice Hall, 1964), p. 3.

WHAT IS COMPREHENSION?

Comprehension is a construct; that is, it cannot be directly observed or directly measured. We can only infer that someone "understands" from the overt behavior of the person. *Webster's Third International Dictionary* defines *comprehension* as "the act or action of grasping (as an act or process) with the intellect," and *intellect* is defined as "the capacity for rational or intelligent thought especially when highly developed." Obviously, the more intelligent an individual is, the more able he or she would be to comprehend. This was discussed in Chapter 2. What may not be so obvious is that persons who have difficulty understanding may have this difficulty because they have not had certain experiences that require higher levels of thinking; they may not have learned how to do high-level thinking. Persons who have difficulty doing high-level thinking will have problems in understanding lectures, as well as in reading content-area books, because both listening and reading require reasoning ability.

In 1917, Edward Thorndike wrote the following paragraph, which still seems significant today, especially for teachers using a directed reading approach to teaching content:

> Understanding a paragraph is like solving a problem in mathematics. It consists in selecting the right elements of the situation and putting them together in the right relations, and also with the right amount of weight or influence or force for each. The mind is assailed as it were by every word in the paragraph. It must select, repress, soften, emphasize, correlate, and organize, all under the influence of the right mental set or purpose, or demand.[4]

Thorndike stresses further that the reading of text material requires an active mind and thought. "It thus appears that reading an explanatory or argumentative paragraph in his [the student's] text-books on geography or history or civics, and (though to a lesser degree) reading a narrative or description, involves the same sort of organization and analytic action of ideas as occur in thinking of supposedly higher sorts."[5]

Reading Comprehension and Listening Comprehension

Reading comprehension depends on comprehension of the spoken language. Students who are sensitive to the arrangements of words in oral language are more sensitive to the same idea in written language.

The case in which students can understand a passage when it is orally read to them, but cannot understand it when they read it themselves, indi-

---

[4]Edward L. Thorndike, "Reading as Reasoning: A Study of Mistakes in Paragraph Reading," *The Journal of Educational Psychology* 8, No. 6 (June 1917): 329.
[5]Ibid., p. 331.

cates that the words are in the students' listening vocabulary but that they have not gained the skills necessary for decoding the words from their written forms. It may be that some words are in the students' listening vocabulary (for example, they know the meaning of the individual words when they are said aloud), but they still might not be able to assimilate the words into a meaningful concept.

A person who does not do well in listening comprehension skills will usually not do well in reading comprehension skills. "Good readers tend to be good listeners and, conversely, poor readers tend to be poor listeners."[6] This is especially true at the more advanced levels of reading.[7] Help in one area usually enhances the other because both listening and reading contain some important similar skills,[8] and researchers going as far back as the 1930s seem to support this view. For example, an investigation made in 1936 found that children who did poorly in comprehension through listening were also poor in reading comprehension.[9] Research in 1955 on the relationship between reading and listening found that practice in listening for detail will produce a significant gain in reading for the same purpose.[10] Studies have also found that training in listening comprehension skills will produce significant gains in reading comprehension[11] and that reading and listening have similar thinking skills.[12] Actually, recent investigators have found that "almost all studies of readers beyond the elementary grades report significant correlations between reading comprehension and listening comprehension skill."[13]

Although there are many common factors involved in the decoding of reading and listening—which would account for the relationship between the two areas—listening and reading are, nonetheless, separated by unique factors. The most obvious is that listening calls for *hearing* whereas reading calls for *seeing*. Moreover, in the area of listening, the speakers are doing much of the interpretation for the listeners by their expressions, inflections, stresses, and pauses. Similarly, the listeners do not have to make the

---

[6]Meredyth Daneman, "Individual Differences in Reading Skills," in *Handbook of Reading Research*, Vol. II, Rebecca Barr, Michael L. Kamil, Peter Mosenthal, and P. David Pearson (eds.) (New York: Longman, 1991), p. 526.

[7]Ibid.

[8]Thomas Jolly, "Listen My Children and You Shall Read," *Language Arts* 57 (February 1980): 214-217.

[9]William E. Young, "The Relation of Reading Comprehension and Retention to Hearing Comprehension and Retention," *Journal of Experimental Education* 5 (September 1936): 30-39.

[10]Annette P. Kelty, "An Experimental Study to Determine the Effect of Listening for Certain Purposes upon Achievement in Reading for Those Purposes," *Abstracts of Field Studies for the Degree of Doctor of Education* 15 (Greeley: Colorado State College of Education, 1955): 82-95.

[11]Sybil M. Hoffman, "The Effect of a Listening Skills Program on the Reading Comprehension of Fourth Grade Students," Ph.D. Dissertation, Walden University, 1978.

[12]Thomas Sticht et al., *Auding and Reading: A Developmental Model* (Alexandria, Va.: Human Resources Research Organization, 1974); Walter Kintsch and Ely Kozminsky, "Summarizing Stories After Reading and Listening," *Journal of Educational Psychology* 69 (1977): 491-499.

[13]Daneman, p. 526.

proper grapheme (letter)-phoneme (sound) correspondences because these have already been done for them by the speakers. It is, therefore, possible for students to achieve excellent listening comprehension but not to achieve as well in reading.

Readers must first make the proper grapheme-phoneme correspondences and must then organize these into the proper units to gain meaning from the words. Readers must also be able to determine the shades of meaning implied by the words, to recognize any special figures of speech, and finally to synthesize the unique ideas expressed by the passage.

WHAT ARE THE CHARACTERISTICS OF GOOD COMPREHENDERS?

Reading comprehension is a complex intellectual process involving a number of abilities. The two major abilities involve word meanings and verbal reasoning. Without word meanings and verbal reasoning, there would be no reading comprehension; without reading comprehension, there would be no reading. Most people would agree with these statements; disagreement, however, exists when we ask, "How does an individual achieve comprehension while reading?" In 1917, Edward Thorndike put forth his statement that "reading is a very elaborate procedure, involving a weighing of each of many elements in a sentence, their organization in the proper relations one to another, and the cooperation of many forces to determine final response."[14] He stated further than even the act of answering simple questions includes all the features characteristic of typical reasonings. Today investigators are still exploring reading comprehension in attempts to understand it better, and through the years many have expounded and expanded upon Thorndike's theories.

For more than a quarter of a century, research into the process of understanding has been influenced by the fields of psycholinguistics and cognitive psychology. As a result, terms such as surface structure, deep structure, microstructure, macrostructure, semantic networks, schemata, story grammar, story structure, and so on have invaded the literature. The studies that have been done are not conclusive; that is, from the studies it is not possible to say that if a reader were to follow certain prescribed rules, he or she would most assuredly have better comprehension. Moreover, many of the studies were done with students in the lower grades and dealt with simple stories rather than with more complex content area material. However, some of the studies that have been done do have relevance for content-area readers because they are concerned with the recall or retention of information, which is of great importance to readers of content material.

What seems significant from many of the studies is that attention to

[14]Thorndike, p. 323.

text structure appears to help students recall important text ideas. It follows logically then that techniques such as outlining and noting top-level structure (the way in which the information in the passage is organized) would be helpful to students reading content material.[15] For example, one study in particular trained students to identify main ideas and organizational patterns and found that the quantity and quality of students' recall was enhanced by this procedure.[16] Another study found that poor comprehenders of text material have a processing deficiency; that is, they "do not spontaneously organize paragraph details around main ideas of a passage . . ."[17] Good comprehenders, on the other hand, engage in meaningful learning by assimilating new material to concepts already existing in their cognitive structures;[18] that is, good comprehenders relate their new knowledge to what they already know. They also seem to know what information to attend to and what to ignore; they have good strategies for processing information. A recent study done with high school students suggests that, as the passage difficulty increases, good comprehenders appear to use more types of strategies and to use these more often than poor comprehenders.[19]

Although it is difficult to definitively state how persons achieve comprehension while reading, from the discussion in this chapter and in Chapter 2, we can see that good comprehenders appear to have certain characteristics. It appears that "expert readers use rapid decoding, large vocabularies, phonemic awareness, knowledge about text features, and a variety of strategies to aid comprehension and memory."[20] Novice readers and older, unskilled readers, conversely, "often focus on decoding single words, fail to adjust their reading for different texts or purposes, and seldom look ahead or back in text to monitor and improve instruction."[21]

At this point you should understand better the statement "good readers are good thinkers" and recognize that Melissa (the girl in the introductory scenario) is probably a good reader because of her excellent background of experiences. And Melissa's good reading ability should help her do well in her content courses.

This chapter presents information about the kinds of skills that good

[15]Barbara M. Taylor, "Children's Memory for Expository Text After Reading," *Reading Research Quarterly* 15, No. 3 (1980): 399–411.

[16]B.J. Bartlett, "Top-level Structure as an Organizational Strategy for Recall of Classroom Text." Unpublished doctoral dissertation, Arizona State University, 1978.

[17]John P. Richards and Catherine W. Hatcher, "Interspersed Meaningful Learning Questions as Semantic Cues for Poor Comprehenders," *Reading Research Quarterly* 13:4 (1977–1978): 551–552.

[18]Ibid., p. 552.

[19]Sharon Benge Kletzien, "Strategy Use by Good and Poor Comprehenders Reading Expository Text of Differing Levels," *Reading Research Quarterly* 26 No. 1 (1991): 67–86.

[20]Scott G. Paris, Barbara A. Wasik, and Julianne C. Turner, "The Development of Strategic Readers," in *The Handbook of Reading Research*, Vol. II, Rebecca Barr, Michael L. Kamil, Peter Mosenthal, and P. David Pearson, eds. (New York: Longman, 1991), p. 609.

[21]Ibid.

comprehenders should have and suggests ways for helping students acquire these needed and important skills. (See "America's Challenge: A Final Word" in Chapter 1.)

Special Note:
Schema theory deals with the relations between prior knowledge and comprehension. "According to schema theory, the reader's background knowledge serves as scaffolding to aid in encoding information from the text."[22] From this we can see that a person with more background knowledge will comprehend better than one with less and that the preparation of readers for what they will be reading "by actively building topic knowledge prior to reading will facilitate learning from text."[23]

READING COMPREHENSION TAXONOMIES

A number of reading comprehension taxonomies exist and many appear similar to one another. This is not surprising. Usually the people who develop a new taxonomy do so because they are unhappy with an existing one for some reason and want to improve upon it. As a result they may change category headings, but keep similar descriptions of the categories, or they may change the order of the hierarchy, and so on. Most of the existing taxonomies are adaptations in one way or another of Bloom's taxonomy of educational objectives in the cognitive domain, which is concerned with thinking that students should achieve in any discipline. Bloom's taxonomy is based on an ordered set of objectives ranging from the more simplistic skills to the more complex ones. Bloom's objectives are cumulative in that each one includes the one preceding it. And most taxonomies that have been evolved are also cumulative.

Of the many persons who have tried to categorize reading comprehension, one attempt that is often referred to is Barrett's *Taxonomy of Reading Comprehension*. Barrett's taxonomy consists of four levels; literal comprehension, inferential comprehension, evaluation, and appreciation. In this text, an adaptation of Nila Banton Smith's model is used, and, at first glance, it may appear to be similar to Barrett's. The differences become obvious when we look at the skills subsumed under each of the first three levels. In the model used in this book, literal-type questions are those that require a low-level type of thinking; skills such as the finding of the main idea of a paragraph would not be included under the literal level. However, in Barrett's taxonomy, "recognition or recall of main ideas" is included in his literal level. Finding the main idea of a paragraph is not easy even if it is

---

[22]Steven Stahl, Michael G. Jacobson, Charlotte E. Davis, and Robin L. Davis, "Prior Knowledge and Difficult Vocabulary in the Comprehension of Unfamiliar Text," *Reading Research Quarterly* 24 (Winter 1989): 29.
[23]Ibid., p. 30.

directly stated in the paragraph; students must do more than a low-level type of thinking to determine that something stated in the paragraph is the main idea. In other words, any time that a student must interpret what he or she is reading, the student is required to do reasoning that is beyond merely recalling what is in the text.

Also, in this text, appreciation is not in the hierarchy because appreciation has a hierarchy of its own. It is possible for us to appreciate something we have read or that is read to us at any level of the hierarchy, even though, of course, we would probably have the highest appreciation at the level at which we had the greatest understanding of what we read or heard. (See "What Is Reading for Appreciation?" in Chapter 11.)

Categorizing Reading Comprehension

Comprehension involves thinking. As there are various levels in the hierarchy of thinking, so are there various levels of comprehension. Higher levels of comprehension would obviously include higher levels of thinking. The following model adapted from Nila Banton Smith divides the comprehension skills into four categories.[24] Each category is cumulative in that each builds on the others. The four comprehension categories are (1) literal comprehension, (2) interpretation, (3) critical reading, and (4) creative reading.

Special Note:
In this text an adaptation of Nila Banton Smith's model is used. In her original model, she presented literal-level reading skills as requiring no thinking. In the model used in this book, literal-type questions do require thinking, even though it is just a low-level type of thinking.

Literal Comprehension   Literal comprehension represents the ability to obtain a low-level type of understanding by using only information explicitly stated. This category requires a lower level of thinking skills than the other three levels. Answers to literal questions simply demand that the pupil recall from memory what the book says.

Although literal-type questions are considered a low-level type of thinking, it should *not* be construed that reading for details to gain facts that are explicitly stated is unimportant in content-area courses. A fund of knowledge is important and necessary; it is the foundation for high-level thinking. If, however, teachers ask only literal-type questions, students will not graduate to higher levels of thinking. (See "Questioning: A Key to Higher Levels of Thinking" in this chapter.)

Interpretation   Interpretation is the next step in the hierarchy. This category demands a higher level of thinking ability because the questions in the cate-

[24]Nila Banton Smith, "The Many Faces of Reading Comprehension." *The Reading Teacher* 23 (December 1969): 249–259: 291.

gory of interpretation are concerned with answers that are not directly stated in the text but are suggested or implied. To answer questions at the interpretive level, readers must have problem-solving ability and be able to work at various levels of abstraction. Obviously, children who are slow learners will have difficulty working at this level as well as in the next two categories. (See Chapter 14.)

The interpretive level is the one at which the most confusion exists when it comes to categorizing skills. The confusion concerns the term *inference*. The definition of inference is: Something derived by reasoning; something that is not directly stated but suggested in the statement; a logical conclusion that is drawn from statements; a deduction; an induction. From the definition we can see that inference is a broad reasoning skill involving analysis and synthesis and that there are many different kinds of inferences. All of the reading skills in interpretation rely on the reader's ability to "infer" the answer in one way or another. However, by grouping all the interpretive reading skills under inference, "some of the most distinctive and desirable skills would become smothered and obscured."[25]

Some of the reading skills that are usually found in interpretation are as follows:

> determining word meanings from context
> finding main ideas
> "reading between the lines" or drawing inferences[26]
> drawing conclusions
> making generalizations
> recognizing cause-and-effect reasoning
> recognizing analogies

Critical Reading   Critical reading is at a higher level than the other two categories because it involves evaluation, the making of a personal judgment on the accuracy, value, and truthfulness of what is read. To be able to make judgments, a reader must be able to collect, interpret, apply, analyze, and synthesize the information. Critical reading includes such skills as the ability to differentiate between fact and opinion, the ability to differentiate between fantasy and reality, and the ability to discern propaganda techniques. Critical reading is related to critical listening because they both require critical thinking.

Creative Reading   Creative reading uses divergent thinking skills to go beyond the literal comprehension, interpretation, and critical-reading levels.

---

[25]Ibid., pp. 255–256.
[26]Although, as already stated, all the interpretive skills depend on the ability of the reader to infer meanings, the specific skill of "reading between the lines" is the one that teachers usually refer to when they are teaching *inference*.

In creative reading, the reader tries to come up with new or alternate solutions to those presented by the writer. (A special section, "Divergent Thinking," is presented in this chapter.)

Special Note:
It is at the interpretive level and above that studies suggest students are in the most need of help.[27] Students appear to have difficulty reading analytically and performing well on challenging reading assignments.[28] In addition, students are not performing well in their content-area courses. Certainly, the inability to read well at the interpretive, critical, and creative levels would affect students' performance in all their subjects. (See the integration of reading comprehension skills in specific content areas in Part 3.)

QUESTIONING: A KEY TO HIGHER LEVELS OF THINKING

Read the following:

TEACHER A: Jack, in what year did the battle for Fort Duquesne take place?
JACK: In 1755.
TEACHER A: Good.
TEACHER B: Pat, what are the functions of the skin, skeleton, and muscles of the body?
PAT: They provide the body with protection, support, and movement.
TEACHER C: Dave, can you compare the epidermis with the dermis?
DAVE: The dermis is much thicker than the epidermis. The dermis . . .
TEACHER C: Good.
TEACHER D: Kim, what conclusion can you draw from what you just read?
KIM: Humans are at times inhumane.
TEACHER D: Good.
TEACHER E: Herbert, how do you feel about capital punishment?
HERBERT: I have mixed feelings about this issue because . . .
TEACHER E: Good.
TEACHER F: Sharon, can you come up with an alternate way to solve this problem?
SHARON: Yes, if we were to . . .
TEACHER F: Good.

Although the questions posed by all the above teachers are comprehension questions, there is a wide range of difference in the difficulty of

[27]Ina V.S. Mullis, Eugene H. Owen, and Gary W. Phillips, *America's Challenge: Accelerating Academic Achievement*, National Assessment of Educational Progress (Princeton, N.J.: Educational Testing Service, 1990).
[28]Ibid., p. 9.

their questions. It makes no difference whether teachers are teaching reading skills or content-area courses when it comes to the art of questioning. The teachers who persist in asking only questions similar to Teachers A and B are hindering their students and not helping them reach higher levels of thinking.

All students need help in developing higher-level reading comprehension skills. Unfortunately, much of what goes on in school is at the literal comprehension level. Teachers usually ask questions that require a literal response, and students who answer this type of question are generally looked upon as being excellent students.

The kinds of questions the teacher asks will determine the kinds of answers he or she will receive. Rather than asking questions that would call for literal responses, the teacher must learn to construct questions that call for higher levels of thinking. Some content areas would, of course, lend themselves more to certain kinds of questions than others; however, all lend themselves to higher levels beyond the literal level. For example, students could be asked to find the main or central idea of what they have read; they could be asked to analyze certain events or situations; in mathematics, they could be asked to apply certain formulas, to derive other ways to solve the problem, to make analogies between certain problems; in science, students could be asked to make comparisons, to analyze, to synthesize, to evaluate, to be divergent, and so on.

The key, of course, is in teachers knowing the type of questions to ask to develop higher levels of thinking; however, it is also important for teachers to know what their purposes (objectives) are. The purpose of the teacher's lesson will determine the type of questions he or she will be asking.

A short reading selection[29] follows with four different types of comprehension questions. These are being presented so that you can have practice in recognizing the different types of questions at the four levels.

Vocabulary:

kinetic energy—the energy of a body or a system with respect to the motion of the body; *potential energy*—the energy of a body or a system with respect to the position of the body.

Energy in Other Forms

The two kinds of energy—kinetic and potential—we have spoken of are not the only kinds that occur in nature. Energy in other forms can also perform work. The *chemical energy* of gasoline is used to drive our automobiles; the chemical energy of food enables our bodies and the bodies of domestic animals to perform work. *Heat energy* from burning coal or oil is used to form the steam that drives ships. *Electric energy* and *magnetic energy* turn motors in home and factory. *Radiant energy* from the sun, though man has yet to learn

---

[29]From Konrad B. Krauskopf and Arthur Beiser, *The Physical Universe*, 5th ed. (New York: McGraw-Hill, 1986).

how to harness it efficiently, performs very necessary work in lifting water from the earth's surface into clouds, in producing inequalities in atmospheric temperatures that cause winds, and in making possible chemical reactions in plants that produce foods.

The following are the four different types of comprehension questions:

1. *Literal comprehension:* Name the seven kinds of energy presented in this selection.
2. *Interpretation:* What is the main idea of this selection? What conclusions can you draw about humanity and energy?
3. *Critical reading:* Could we live without the sun? Explain.
4. *Creative reading:* Suppose we were able to harness the sun's energy efficiently. What do you think would be the consequences of this for humanity?

Metacognition and Questioning

The more students understand what they do when they are in the act of answering questions, the better question solvers they can be. As has been mentioned a number of times already, studies have found that students seem to have difficulty working with questions at the interpretive level. (Interpretive questions deal with implied information rather than that which is directly stated.) Teachers may take it for granted that students can differentiate between information they bring to the text and information that is in the text.

Teachers in content-areas could help students gain insight into strategies for answering interpretive-type questions by helping them to "realize the need to consider both information in the text and information from their own knowledge background."[30] In other words, students must be able to differentiate between information that is in the text and information that "they have in their heads."

Here is an example of how content-area teachers can adapt an instructional strategy, Question Answer Relationships (QARs), to help students gain a better understanding of how they go about reading text and answering questions. Let's use the passage "Energy in Other Forms" on page 66 for our example.

Step 1: The students gain help in understanding differences between what is in their heads and what is in the text. The students are asked to read the given passage. The teacher then asks questions that guide them to gain the needed understanding, such as the following:

[30]Taffy E. Raphael, "Teaching Question Answer Relationships, Revisited," *The Reading Teacher* 39 (February 1986): 517.

1. State three kinds of energy discussed in the passage. (Chemical energy, magnetic energy, and electric energy)
2. Which kind of energy is instrumental in producing rain? (Radiant energy)

The students should be helped to see that the first answer is directly stated, whereas the second is not; it is "in their heads."

Step 2: The "In the Book" category is divided into two parts. This step helps students differentiate between information that is directly stated in one sentence in the passage and the piecing together of the answer from information presented in different parts of the passage.

Step 3: This step is similar to Step 2 except that now the "In My Head" category is divided into two parts. The teacher helps students recognize whether the question is text-dependent or text-independent. For example, the answer to the first question requires the student to read the text to answer it, even though the answer would come from the student's background of experiences. However, the student could answer the second without reading the text.

1. What other uses can you give for magnetic energy?
2. How do you think your life will change if the price of oil is so high that gasoline prices go as high as $3 or $4 a gallon?

AN EMPHASIS ON SOME IMPORTANT COMPREHENSION SKILLS FOR CONTENT-AREA READERS

This section presents some comprehension skills that need special emphasis. Although *homographs* (words with multiple meanings) and *context clues* are important comprehension skills, these will be presented in the next chapter, "Vocabulary Expansion." *Finding the main idea of a paragraph* is an especially important comprehension skill for content-area readers. It is also a skill that is many times taken for granted—it is assumed that preservice teachers can find the main idea of a paragraph and that teachers can help their students do the same. This assumption is often not borne out. Other interpretive skills such as inference and analogies will also be presented, as well as some in the critical and creative reading areas. (Before proceeding, it is important to mention again that these skills will be adapted to specific content areas in Part 3.)

Interpretive Reading Skills

Main Idea of a Paragraph   "Fred, could you please state the main idea of the section on the skeletal system?"

"Tara, what do you think is the main idea of the section on forms of energy?"

"John, what is the main idea of the paragraph we just read on computers?"

Do these questions sound familiar? They should because most content-area teachers ask their students to construct the main idea of various passages they are reading.

In reading and writing, finding the main idea is very useful. In reading, the main idea helps students to remember and understand what they have read. In writing, the main idea gives unity and order to their paragraph, and many writing/learning strategies such as summarizing and notetaking require that students be able to state the main idea of passages. (See "Summarizing as a Mode of Learning" and "Notetaking for Studying" in Chapter 6.)

The main idea of a paragraph is the central thought of the paragraph. It is what the paragraph is about. Without a main idea, the paragraph would just be a confusion of sentences. All the sentences in the paragraph should develop the main idea.

Main idea is certainly an essential skill; it is, however, a skill that seems to cause a great amount of difficulty for many students. Students especially find the construction or inventing of the main idea more difficult than selecting the main idea from a given list. This makes sense because the main idea construction process, that is, the coming up with the main idea on one's own, is much more difficult,[31] even if the main idea is directly stated. This is important for content-area teachers to note because students in content-area courses are more involved in inventing the main idea than in choosing one.

Because the task of constructing the main idea is so difficult, sufficient time must be allotted to provide the needed "think time." In addition, research has demonstrated "that if readers' prior knowledge for the text topic is not sufficient, the difficulty of main idea construction is compounded."[32]

Confusion in finding the main idea may exist because it seems to mean different things to different people. One researcher investigating the literature found that "educators have increasingly given attention to main idea comprehension, but with no concomitant increase in the clarity of what is meant by main idea or important ideas. The exact nature of main ideas and the teaching practices intended to help students grasp main ideas vary considerably."[33]

Even though the concept of main idea is nebulous according to some researchers and the "notion that different readers can (and should) con-

---

[31]Peter P. Afflerbach, "The Influence of Prior Knowledge on Expert Readers' Main Idea Construction Strategies," *Reading Research Quarterly* 25 (Winter 1990): 44.

[32]Ibid., p. 45.

[33]James W. Cunningham and David W. Moore, "The Confused World Of Main Idea, *Teaching Main Idea Comprehension,* James F. Baumann, ed. (Newark, Del.: International Reading Association, 1986), p. 2.

struct identical main ideas for the same text has been questioned,"[34] the teaching of main idea is a very important skill for reading, writing, and studying that can and should be taught using relevant content material. It is possible that the skepticism concerning the ability to teach main idea may stem from the "failure to teach students to transfer their main idea skills to texts other than those found in their readers."[35] Some studies have found that "students who have been taught to identify main idea using only contrived texts such as those found in basal reader skill lessons will have difficulty transferring their main idea skills to naturally occurring texts."[36] Based on this information, content-area teachers should not take for granted that their students can construct the main idea and be prepared to model how they go about coming up with the main idea using relevant content material.

Finding the Main Idea   To find the main idea of a paragraph, readers must find what common elements the sentences share. Some textbook writers place the main idea at the beginning of a paragraph and may actually put the topic of the paragraph in bold print in order to emphasize it. However, in literature this is not a common practice. In some paragraphs the main idea is not directly stated but implied. That is, the main idea is indirectly stated, and readers have to find it from the clues given by the author.

Although there is no foolproof method for finding the main idea, there is a widely used procedure that has proved to be helpful. In order to use this procedure readers should know that a paragraph is always written about something or someone. The something or someone is the topic of the paragraph. The writer is interested in telling his or her readers something about the topic of the paragraph. To find the main idea of a paragraph, readers must determine what the topic of the paragraph is and what the author is trying to say about the topic that is special or unique. Once readers have found these two things, they should have the main idea. This procedure is useful in finding the main idea of various types of paragraphs. (See Chapter 10 for more information about finding the main idea of a paragraph.)

Reread the preceding paragraph, and state its main idea. *Answer:* A procedure helpful in finding the main idea of a paragraph is described.

Now read the following passage from "Fight Fat with Behavior Control" by Michael J. Mahoney and Kathryn Mahoney, in *Psychology Today* (May 1976). After you have read the passage, choose the statement that *best* states the main idea.

> In our society, food is often connected with recreation. We go out for coffee, invite friends over for drinks, celebrate special occasions with cakes or big

---

[34]Afflerbach p. 45.

[35]Victoria Chou Hare, Mitchell Rabinowitz, and Karen Magnus Schieble, "Text Effects on Main Idea Comprehension," *Reading Research Quarterly* 24 (Winter 1989): 73.

[36]Ibid., p. 72.

meals. We can't think of baseball without thinking of hot dogs and beer, and eating is so often an accompaniment to watching TV that we talk of TV snacks and TV dinners. Just as Pavlov's dogs learned to salivate at the sound of a bell, the activities we associate with food can become signals to eat. Watching TV becomes a signal for potato chips; talking with friends becomes a signal for coffee and doughnuts; nodding over a book tells us it's time for pie and milk.

1. Watching TV signals a need for food.
2. All persons connect food with recreation.
3. Eating is a social activity.
4. Recreation, in our society, often serves as a signal for food.
5. In all societies food is often connected with recreation.

The answer is statement 4. Statement 1 is a fact in the paragraph, but it is too specific to be the main idea. Statement 2 is too general. The paragraph is not discussing all persons. Statement 3 can be inferred from the paragraph, but it is not the main idea of the paragraph. Statement 5 is too general. Statement 4 is what the paragraph is about. The sentences in the paragraph elaborate this idea by giving examples of various recreations that are connected or associated with food.

Now try this paragraph from a history textbook. Notice how the textbook writers put the topic of the paragraph at the beginning of the paragraph because they want to make sure that readers understand what they are talking about. Read the following paragraph, and state the main idea of it.

Common Sense. Many Americans still remained uncertain as to what stand they should take. Should they remain loyal to Britain or join the patriots? Should they fight for a redress of their grievances or for complete independence? At this time of indecision, Thomas Paine's famous pamphlet, *Common Sense*, struck fire. Thousands of Americans read it, and patriots everywhere agreed with Washington that it contained sound doctrine and unanswerable reason.

Answer: Thomas Paine's pamphlet *Common Sense* helped patriots decide what to do.

The following paragraph is from a high school social science textbook.[37] Note how the author of this book actually puts the main idea of the paragraph in the first sentence.

Poverty is a relative term. That is, it depends on your personal standards. If you have a million dollars in the bank, you might consider someone with only $50,000 poor by comparison. But compared with most people of the world, both you and the person with $50,000 would be considered very wealthy. So

---

[37]John Jay Bonstingl, *Introduction to the Social Sciences,* (Englewood Cliffs, N.J.: Prentice Hall, 1991), p. 310.

would someone earning $10,000 a year, which is below the poverty line in our country. For many poor people on our planet, $1,000 would be a fortune!

Here is a paragraph from a novel. The literary author is usually more concerned with writing expressively than with helping the reader to grasp the main idea of what is being said. The steps that were presented earlier for finding the main idea are especially helpful in such cases.

Read this paragraph.[38] State the topic and what is special about the topic; then state the main idea of the paragraph.

> I keep wishing you were alive, so we could start over. I tell myself that I'd do it differently, be patient with you, try to understand . . . when I guess I'd just act the same way. There aren't many chances in life. You grow up and become what you are without realizing it. I plan to be a better person and find myself repeating all the old patterns, being selfish, not seeing people for what they are. And I don't know how to change that. . . . There are times when I feel beautiful, sexless, light, wanting nothing—but then I crash to earth again and want everything. Myself, most of all.

TOPIC:

WHAT IS SPECIAL ABOUT THE TOPIC:

MAIN IDEA:

Answer:

TOPIC:	Writer's pattern of life.
WHAT IS SPECIAL ABOUT THE TOPIC:	It's difficult to change.
MAIN IDEA:	The writer feels that it's difficult to change one's pattern of life.

Special Notes:

1. Even though the topic of the main idea or central idea is given, it still may not be easy to find the main idea. It may not be easy to find the main idea even if it is explicitly stated because students still need to determine what directly stated information is the main idea. There is no red flag next to the main idea to indicate that it is the main idea.
2. The main idea is a general statement of the content of the paragraph. You must be careful, however, that your main idea statement is not so general that it goes beyond the information that is directly or indirectly given in the paragraph.
3. Chapter 10 presents an in-depth discussion on the supporting details of a paragraph. This information is especially useful because readers use the organization of the paragraph to help them to retain information. Also, teachers using a directed reading approach guide to read-

[38]From Barbara Wersba, *Run Softly, Go Fast* (New York: Atheneum, 1971).

ing content use the structure of the reading material to determine the strategies they will suggest to their students.

Finding the Central Idea of a Group of Paragraphs, an Article, or a Story   We generally use the term *central idea* rather than *main idea* when we refer to a *group* of paragraphs, a story, or an article. The procedure, however, for finding the main idea and for finding the central idea is the same for both.

The central idea of a story is the central thought of the story. All the paragraphs of the story should develop the central idea. To find the central idea of a story, students must find what common element the paragraphs in the story share. The introductory paragraph is usually helpful because it either contains or anticipates what the central idea is and how it will be developed.

Textbook writers are especially interested in students' understanding the topic they are discussing. Usually a chapter is divided into a number of sections, each made up of paragraphs concerned with the topic. To help students more, some textbook writers put the general topic of the section in bold print or in the margins at the beginning of the section with the more specific topics also presented in the margins of the section further on, indented or printed in smaller type.

The technique presented earlier for finding the main idea of a single paragraph also applies to finding the central idea of a group of paragraphs. A section of a textbook, like a single paragraph, is usually written about a particular something or someone. The something or someone is the *topic* of the section. To find the central idea of a section, first find the topic of the section, and then determine what particular point or points the section makes about that topic.

Read the following section from a biology textbook. First state the topic of the group of paragraphs that make up this section. Then state the central idea of the group of paragraphs.

Characteristics of Mammals[39]

You, along with lions, bats, and walruses, belong to a class of chordates called mammals. There are about 4000 species of mammals on the earth and many of them look very different from one another. But all mammals have certain characteristics that set them apart from all other living things.

Mammals are warmblooded vertebrates that have hair and feed their young with milk produced in mammary glands. In fact, the word *mammal* comes from the term **mammary gland.** A mammary gland is a structure in a female mammal that produces milk. Most mammals also give their young more care and protection than do other animals.

At one time during their lives, all mammals possess fur or hair. The fur or hair, if it is thick enough, acts as insulation and enables some mammals to survive in very cold parts of the world. Mammals also can survive in harsh

[39]Wright, Jill, Charles R. Cobie, Jean Hopkins, Susan Johnson, and David LaHart, *Prentice Hall Life Science,* 2nd ed. (Englewood Cliffs, N.J.: Prentice Hall, 1991), p. 252.

climates because, like birds, mammals are warmblooded. The body tempera-ture of mammals remains almost unchanged despite the temperature of their surroundings.

Mammals are believed to be the most intelligent animals on the earth. This intelligence comes from a brain that is better developed than that of any other group of animals.

Answer:

TOPIC: Characteristics of mammals

CENTRAL IDEA: All mammals have certain characteristics that set them apart from all other living things.

Special Note:
It is important to help your students to recognize that the title of a chapter or section in a textbook or the title of a story and the central idea are not necessarily the same. The title of a chapter, section, or story usually merely gives the topic rather than the central idea. The central idea is usually more fully stated than the title of something is.

Visual Representation and Main Idea It is difficult to read a textbook, maga-zine, or newspaper without finding a variety of visual representations in the form of graphs, diagrams, and charts. The sprinkling of these represen-tations gives relief from print; a graphic representation is worth a thousand words. Graphs, diagrams, and charts grab your attention and pack a great amount of information in a small space. For these reasons, *USA Today* uses pictorial representations every day in each section of its newspaper.

Writers use visual representation to convey information, and each one, like a paragraph, has a main idea. To understand the charts, diagrams, and graphs you must be able to get the main idea of them. Not surprisingly, the technique we use to do this is similar to that for finding the main idea of a paragraph. It would probably be a good idea for content-area teachers to model how they go about constructing the main idea of various visual rep-resentations in their specific subject. See page 75 for a visual representation from *USA Today*[40] and how one teacher helps his students get the main idea of it.

1. The teacher tells his students that he first looks at the visual represen-tation to determine its topic. He tells them that writers usually give clues to the topic of their graph or chart, and some writers may actu-ally state it for their readers. He then asks them to write about what they think the topic is, and says that he will do the same.

    He tells his students that for this example, the writer has made it very easy for them because she has stated the topic. Therefore the topic is *Methods used to fall asleep.*

[40]Julie Stacey, *USA Today* "Snapshots," Life Section, September 19, 1990, p. 1D.

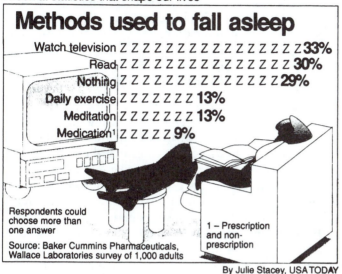

USA SNAPSHOTS®

A look at statistics that shape our lives

Methods used to fall asleep

Watch television Z Z Z Z Z Z Z Z Z Z Z Z Z Z Z Z Z **33%**
Read Z Z Z Z Z Z Z Z Z Z Z Z Z Z Z Z **30%**
Nothing Z Z Z Z Z Z Z Z Z Z Z Z Z Z Z **29%**
Daily exercise Z Z Z Z Z Z Z **13%**
Meditation Z Z Z Z Z Z Z **13%**
Medication[1] Z Z Z Z Z **9%**

Respondents could
choose more than
one answer

1 – Prescription
and non-
prescription

Source: Baker Cummins Pharmaceuticals,
Wallace Laboratories survey of 1,000 adults

By Julie Stacey, USA TODAY

2. Next, he tells his students to look at the graph a little more closely to figure out what is special about the topic. He will also do the same.

He tells them that he sees the writer is comparing various methods to fall asleep. Therefore, the main idea would be *People use a number of different methods to fall asleep.*

Reading Between the Lines Many times writers do not directly state what they mean but present ideas in a more indirect, roundabout way. That is why inference is called the ability to "read between the lines." *Inference* is defined as "understanding that is not derived from a direct statement but from an indirect suggestion in what is stated." Readers draw inferences from writings; authors make implications or imply meanings.

The ability to draw inferences is especially important in reading fiction, but it is necessary for nonfiction, also. Authors rely on inferences to make their stories more interesting and enjoyable. Mystery writers find inference essential to the maintenance of suspense in their stories. For example, Sherlock Holmes and Perry Mason mysteries are based on the ability of the characters to uncover evidence in the form of clues that are not obvious to the others around them.

Nonfiction writers, especially textbook writers, usually present information in a more straightforward manner than fiction writers do; however, even text material includes implied meanings that readers must deduce or infer. For example, when students read about the actions and decisions of some important persons in history, students can deduce something about the characters of the men or women. When people read about a region such as the North Pole, they can deduce the kind of clothing they have to wear, as well as the kind of life they probably have to lead. Readers can also draw inferences about conditions in a region by reading information about the way of life in the region.

Inference is an important process that authors rely on. Good readers must be alert to the ways that authors encourage inference.

Implied Statements As has been said already, writers count on inference to make their writing more interesting and enjoyable. Rather than directly stating something, they present it indirectly. To understand the writing, the reader must be alert and be able to detect the clues that the author gives. For example, in the sentence *Things are always popping and alive when the twins, Herb and Jack, are around,* readers are given some clues to Herb's and Jack's personalities. From the statement readers could make the inference that the twins are lively and lots of fun to have around.

Readers must be *careful,* however, that they *do not read more* into some statements than is intended. For example, read the following statements, and put a circle around the correct answer. *Example:* Mary got out of bed and looked out of the window. She saw that the ground had some white on it. What season of the year was it? (a) winter, (b) summer, (c) spring, (d) fall, (e) can't tell.

The answer is "(e) can't tell." Many persons choose "(a) winter" for the answer. However, the answer is (e) because the "something white" could be anything; there isn't enough evidence to choose (a). Even if the something white was snow, in some parts of the world, including the United States, it can snow in the spring or fall.

In *A Study in Scarlet,* Holmes, upon meeting Watson for the first time, tells Watson that he knows that Watson has been in Afghanistan. Watson is incredulous. He feels that someone must have told Holmes. Following is what Holmes says:

> Nothing of the sort. I *knew* you came from Afghanistan. From long habit the train of thought ran so swiftly through my mind that I arrived at the conclusion without being conscious of intermediate steps. There were such steps, however. The train of reasoning ran: "Here is a gentleman of medical type but with the air of a military man. Clearly an army doctor then. He has just come from the tropics, for his face is dark, and that is not the natural tint of his skin, for his wrists are fair. He has undergone hardship and sickness, as his haggard face says clearly. His left arm has been injured. He holds it in a stiff and unnatural manner. Where in the tropics could an English army doctor have seen such hardship and get his arm wounded? Clearly, in Afghanistan." I then remarked that you came from Afghanistan, and you were astonished.

Holmes is able to correctly identify Watson's former residence. The information is all there, but it is not obvious. It is implied, and Holmes through deduction is able to make the proper inferences.

PEANUTS ® By Schulz

FIGURE 3-1. Lucy doesn't understand the concept of "reading between the lines."

Good readers, while reading, try to gather clues to draw inferences about what they read. Although effective readers do this, they are not usually aware of it. As Sherlock Holmes says in *A Study in Scarlet*, "From long habit the train of thought ran so swiftly through my mind that I arrived at the conclusions without being conscious of intermediate steps."

Instructional Applications Teachers in content area classes can preview the material students will be reading and ask key questions about the material that will encourage students to draw inferences from what they are reading. The students should, also, be asked to supply data from the text that would substantiate their inferences. (See Chapter 1 for two scenarios in which students are involved in drawing inferences about what they are reading. See also "Metacognition and Questioning" for a technique that helps students gain an insight into information that is in the text and information that is implied.) Another technique the teacher could use would be to present certain statements to the students concerning what they have read and have the students use information from their reading to determine whether the statements are true or false. If not enough information exists in the text to state true or false, the students should write, "Can't tell."

Here is an example from a history textbook that illustrates this technique.

Read the following selection[41] carefully. Then read each statement below the selection. Determine whether the statement is true or false. If there is not enough evidence in the selection to determine whether a statement is true or false, write, "Can't tell."

Propaganda and Public Opinion

As hard as it may be to define, public opinion is the most significant long-term force in American politics. Over the long run, no public policy can be followed successfully without the support of a goodly portion of the population. Pressure groups know this and regularly court the public's opinions.

Pressure groups try to create the public attitudes they want with propaganda. **Propaganda** is a technique of persuasion, aimed at influencing individual or group views and actions. It is a vague and somewhat inexact term, much like public opinion. Its goal is to create a particular popular belief. That

[41]*Magruder's American Government*, rev. William A. McClenaghan (Needham, Mass.: Prentice Hall, 1991), p. 283.

belief may be in something "good" or "bad," depending on who makes that judgment. It may be completely true or false, or it may lie somewhere between those extremes. As a *technique*, however, propaganda is neither moral nor immoral; it is amoral. It does not use objective logic; rather it begins with a conclusion and then brings together evidences to support it. Propaganda and objective analysis sometimes agree in their conclusions, but their methods are quite different. In short, propagandists are not teachers. Rather, propagandists are advertisers, persuaders, brainwashers.

Propaganda techniques have been brought to a high level in this country, first in the field of commercial advertising and more recently in politics. . . .

Talented propagandists almost never attack the logic of some policy they oppose. Instead, they often attack it with name-calling; that is, they paint such labels as "Communist," "Fascist," "ultraliberal," "ultraconservative," "pie-in-the-sky," or "greedy," and so on. Or they try to do the same thing by card-stacking—that is, presenting only material that will make something appear to be that which in fact it is not.

Policies they support are given labels that will produce favorable reactions, such glittering generalities as "American," "sound," . . .

Statements:

1. Propaganda is the only technique pressure groups employ.
2. Propaganda can be defined exactly.
3. Propaganda techniques are always negative.
4. Commercial advertising feels that propaganda techniques are effective.
5. Propagandists need buyers.

Answers: (1) can't tell (2) false (3) false (4) true (5) true

Categorizing The ability to divide items into categories is a very important thinking skill and necessary for concept development. (See Chapter 4.) As students advance through the grades, they should be developing the skill of categorizing; that is, students should be able to differentiate and group items into more complex categories; they should be able to proceed from more generalized classifications to more specialized classifications.

When students categorize things, they are classifying things. To be able to classify things, students must know what belongs together and what does not belong together. They must be able to organize information. The ability to classify or organize information is a skill that usually differentiates a good comprehender from a poor one. As stated earlier in this chapter, it was found that the ability to note the organizational structure of the text, as well as outlining, enhances the quantity and quality of a student's recall. (See "SQ3R" in Chapter 5 and sections on outlining in Chapter 6.)

All content areas make use of classification, and teachers in the various content areas usually help their students to classify or categorize things into more general or more specific categories. At a very simplistic level, for example, the category of food is more general than the categories of fruits, vegetables, or nuts; the category of animals is more general than the categories of pets, wild animals, or tame animals. The category of pets is less general than the category of animals but more general than the categories of dogs or cats.

Here is an example of a categorizing activity that draws on a student's knowledge of mathematics, science, and the social studies. Content-area teachers can use such exercises to determine whether students have acquired certain concepts.

Directions: First read the words in each set to see what they have in common; then circle the word in each set that does not belong.

1. Indiana, Connecticut, Seattle, Maine
2. Albany, Harrisburg, San Francisco, Nashville
3. porpoise, shark, whale, dolphin
4. Argentina, Asia, China, Canada
5. spiders, ticks, flies, scorpions
6. frogs, snakes, turtles, lizards
7. mean, median, add, mode
8. 6, 16, 30, 42
9. kilometer, decimeter, centimeter, millimeter

(More will be said about categorizing in upcoming chapters, especially in Chapter 4, when we discuss concepts, and in Chapter 6, when outlining is discussed.)

Categorizing and Semantic Mapping (Graphic Organizer) Semantic mapping is "a graphic representation used to illustrate concepts and relationships among concepts such as classes, properties, and examples."[42] Semantic mapping is a technique for organizing information; it helps to give structure or order. It helps people to see the relationship among concepts, and it shows the various ways that information can be organized or categorized in more general or more specific categories. Using semantic maps to help us to see the relationships between and among ideas is not new; it is an offshoot of diagramming, and it is closely related to outlining. Figure 3-2 is an example of a simplified semantic map of the concept *living organism* going from the most general to more specific. Although a specialized vocabulary exists for semantic mapping, teachers do not really need it in order to help students see how concepts are related and that the more general a category is, the more abstract it is, and the more specific a category is the more concrete it

[42]David P. Pearson and Dale D. Johnson, *Teaching Reading Comprehension* (New York: Holt, Rinehart and Winston, 1980), p. 232.

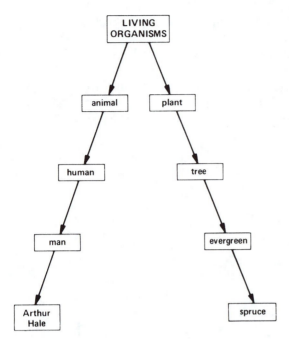

FIGURE 3-2.
Simplified semantic map for living organisms.

is. (See "Semantic Mapping [Graphic Organizer] and Notetaking" in Chapter 6.)

Rather than using semantic maps to help students see the relationships among categories, teachers can use sets such as in Fig. 3-3 (see "Sets and Outlining" in Chapter 6).

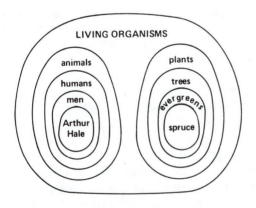

FIGURE 3-3.
The use of sets to illustrate relationships for the universe of living organisms.

Completing Analogies (Word Relationships) Working with analogies requires high-level thinking skills. Students must have a good stock of vocabulary and the ability to see relationships. Students who have difficulty in classification will usually have difficulty working with analogies.

Analogies have to do with relationships. They are relationships between words or ideas. In order to make the best use of analogies or to supply the missing term in an analogy proportion, students must know not only the *meanings* of the words, but also the relationship of the words or ideas to one another. For example, "*doctor* is to *hospital* as *minister* is to _____." Yes, the answer is *church*. The relationship has to do with specialized persons and the places with which they are associated. Let's try another one: *beautiful* is to *pretty* as _____ is to *decimate*." Although you know the meanings of *beautiful* and *pretty* and you can figure out that beautiful is more than pretty, you will not be able to arrive at the correct word to complete the analogy if you do not know the meaning of *decimate*. *Decimate* means "to reduce by one tenth" or "to destroy a considerable part of." Because the word that completes the analogy must express the relationship of more or greater than, the answer could be *eradicate* or *annihilate*, because these words mean "to destroy completely."

Some of the relationships that words may have to one another are similar meanings, opposite meanings, classification, going from particular to general, going from general to particular, degree of intensity, specialized labels, characteristics, cause-effect, effect-cause, function, whole-part, ratio, and many more. The preceding relationships do not have to be memorized. Tell your students that they will gain clues to these from the pairs making up the analogies; that is, the words express the relationship. For example: "*pretty* is to *beautiful*"—the relationship is degree of intensity: "*hot* is to *cold*"—the relationship is one of opposites; "*car* is to *vehicle*"—the relationship is classification.

Teachers could use analogy activities to test students' understanding of concepts in a particular content area. Here is an analogy activity that draws on a student's knowledge in a number of content areas.

Directions: Find the relationship between a pair of words, and then complete each analogy with an appropriate word.

1. Rock is to geologist as bird is to _____. (ornithologist)
2. Distance is to odometer as direction is to _____. (compass)
3. One is to thousand as meter is to _____. (kilometer)
4. Gnu is to antelope as iguana is to _____. (lizard)
5. Kidney is to filter as heart is to _____. (pump)
6. Triangle is to three as hexagon is to _____. (six)
7. Two is to binary as five is to _____. (quinary)
8. Moisture is to rust as fungus is to _____. (mildew)

The activities could be made easier by supplying a word list from which students can choose appropriate answers.

Critical Reading Skills

Distinguishing Between Fact and Opinion The ability to differentiate between facts and opinions is a very important skill of critical thinking that students need to develop. Often opinions are presented as though they are facts. Opinions are not facts. They are based on attitudes or feelings. Opinions can vary from individual to individual; they cannot be conclusively proved right or wrong. Facts, on the other hand, do not change from person to person. Facts are things that exist and can be proved true. Examples of facts: Albany is the capital of New York. Twelve inches equal a foot. A meter equals 39.37 inches. Examples of opinions: That is a pretty dress. He is very smart. It's important to visit museums.

Finding Inconsistencies Good thinkers are logical; that is, they are able to reason correctly. Finding inconsistencies refers to statements that do not make sense—they are illogical; they are not in accord with the given information.

Good readers are alert readers. Teachers need to help their students to recognize that everything that they read is not necessarily true or correct. If they read something that does not make sense, even if it is a textbook written by an authority in the field, they should question it. For example, if in their science book they should find the statement "Humans drink about 1,000 quarts of fluid in a week," should they believe it? Reread it. Does it make sense? Of course not. Think about it. Why doesn't it make sense? Answer: There are only seven days in a week. Even if someone drank four quarts of fluid a day (which is a large amount), that person would still have had only 28 quarts of fluid. The "1,000" is an obvious error. The author probably meant to say ten quarts. (See "Asking Questions of the Textbook and Other Written Material" in Chapter 6.)

Detecting Propaganda Techniques and Bias Students should be helped to detect the presence of propaganda or bias in what they read. This is another essential critical reading skill.

Propaganda is defined as "any systematic, widespread, deliberate indoctrination (the act of causing one to be impressed and eventually filled with some view) or plan for indoctrination." The term *propaganda* connotes deception or distortion. In other words, people who use propaganda are trying to influence persons by using deceptive methods.

Bias refers to a *mental leaning,* a *partiality,* a *prejudice,* or a *slanting of something.*

From the two definitions, you can see that persons interested in propagandizing something have a certain bias. They use propaganda techniques to distort information to indoctrinate people with their own views or bias.

Here are several devices or basic techniques of propaganda that have been identified by the Institute for Propaganda Analysis:

1. Name calling: Accusing or denouncing an individual by using a widely disapproved label such as Red, Fascist, miser, reactionary, radical, and so on.

2. Glittering generalities: Seeking acceptance of ideas by resorting to terms generally accepted, such as freedom, American, Christian, red-blooded, democratic, businesslike, and so on.

3. Bandwagon: Seeking acceptance through appealing to pluralities., For example, an advertisement states: "*Most* persons prefer Dazzles. They know what's good! Do you?" In the "bandwagon" approach, you "go along" because everyone else is doing so.

4. Card stacking: Seeking acceptance by presenting or building on half-truths. Only favorable facts are presented whereas anything unfavorable is deliberately omitted and vice versa.

5. Transfer: Seeking acceptance by citing respected sources of authority, prestige, or reverence such as the home, the Constitution, the flag, the Church, and so on, in such a way as to make it appear that they approve the proposal. For example, in an advertisement, it is stated, "Our forefathers ate hearty breakfasts. Our country is built on strength. Our forefathers would want you to be strong. Eat Product X for strength. Product X will give you a hearty breakfast."

6. Plain folks: Seeking acceptance through establishing someone as "just one of the boys." Example: A presidential candidate is photographed milking cows, kissing babies, wearing work clothes, and so on.

7. Testimonial: Seeking acceptance by using testimonials from famous people to build confidence in a product. For example, in TV commercials, actors, athletes, and famous personalities are used to endorse a product.

Divergent Thinking

Creative reading involves divergent thinking, which has to do with the many different ways of looking at things. Good divergent thinkers are able to look beyond the obvious and come up with new or alternate solutions. Students should be encouraged to try to solve problems in many different ways and try to be intelligent risk-takers or make educated guesses. More will be said about divergent thinking in Chapters 7, 8, and 9. A special section on the creative process follows, which should help teachers gain a better insight into various aspects of creativity.

The Creative Process

Creativity cannot be commanded. It needs time. If teachers want to help students to be creative, they must have an understanding of this process.

According to psychologists, there seem to be four stages to the creative act for most people: (1) preparation, (2) incubation, (3) illumination, and (4) verification.[43]

Preparation involves all the necessary background experience and skills an individual must have in order to be creative in a given area. Knowledge is an important ingredient; the more knowledge people have, the more able they are to be creative. Creativity and knowledge of basic skills are not mutually exclusive. They work hand in hand. The teacher can help students by making sure all are receiving the necessary tools. Those who say, "Let them just create; knowledge gets in the way," and so forth, are not helping to set the proper stage to prepare for creativity. An engineer-lawyer discussing engineering education says:[44]

> Engineering education should encourage students to strive for the mastery of fundamentals, the discovery of the relatedness of things, and the cultivation of excellence. But it should also be a creative experience, stimulating the imagination of students and helping them to prepare themselves for the contests and the challenges of an imperfect world. It should encourage them to believe they can do the "impossible" from time to time, even if it means doing violence to precedent.

The importance of recognizing the tools necessary for creativity has been sidetracked because of the overuse and misuse of the term *creativity*. Persons who have achieved in the creative area usually devote a great portion of their lives to the field in which they work. Competency and creativity demand good preparation.

Incubation is the second step in the creative process. This stage is not visible. It is the time when individuals appear to be thinking about anything but the problem, yet they may actually be mulling it over in their minds.

Illumination is that moment of insight when a spark is lit and a solution seems at hand. A Nobel Prize-winning scientist describes illumination this way:[45]

> . . . I just wander about, without especially clear ideas or preconceived notions so far as I know, and now and then something pops up—boom!—something that is entirely new, that leads to new lines of research.

Verification is the final stage, where the "hunch" (the hypothesis) is subjected to testing and refinement. The same Nobel Prize-winner describes his manner of work:[46]

[43]G. Wallas, *The Art of Thought* (New York: Harcourt Brace, 1926).
[44]Daniel V. DeSimone, "Education for Innovation," *Spectrum* IEEE 5 (January 1968): 83.
[45]Albert Szent-Györgyi, "The Stragegy of Life," *Science and Technology* (New York: International Communications, June 1966), p. 49.
[46]Ibid., p. 49

FIGURE 3-4. The more knowledge and imagination individuals have, the more creative they can be.

But while I am working I usually do not know where I am going. I just follow hunches. I dream up all sorts of theories at night and then disprove them in the laboratory the next day. Checking a hunch, sometimes I see some discrepancy, something unexpected—then I follow it up. Success depends on whether the hunch was good or bad.

Nurturing Creativity Creativity is not something that "just happens." If we want divergent thinkers (persons who can see many different ways to solve problems) and individuals who are and continue to be intelligent risk-takers, we must create an environment that values these traits, and we must involve students in creative experiences. If teachers are not creative—if they are frightened and bothered by divergency—they will be unable to create the proper physical, emotional, and intellectual climate essential for the development of creativity.

A creative atmosphere is one that pervades everything that is done in the classroom. On the first school day the manner in which the students are greeted will determine, to a certain extent, how free students will feel to be different.

Figure 3-5 contains some exercises that have been used with various groups of students on the first few days of class. They help to establish rapport, to awaken many students as to how "set" they are, and also to show how the verbal behavior of the teacher influences students.

In the following line drawing, how many squares do you see?

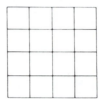

Most people say sixteen. Ask them to look again. They are usually puzzled.

Hint:

What is the definition of a square? Now look again. How many do you see now? At this point some call out seventeen, eighteen, or nineteen. They are getting the idea. They are looking beyond the obvious.

Solution:

There are thirty different squares: sixteen each of 1 x 1; nine each of 2 x 2; four each of 3 x 3; and one of 4 x 4.

How clever are you?
How many know their Roman numerals well? Think of Roman numeral nine, then subtract three. By adding one symbol to Roman numeral nine, you should be able to come up with the answer.
After some time the teacher often has to provide the answer. IX is put on the board, and an "S" is added before the number to produce six.

FIGURE 3-5.　Creative thinking exercises for first day of class.

As an illustration of how rigid many students are and how a teacher's verbal behavior influences students, it can be shown that beginning with the question of how clever someone is can cause anxiety, especially on the first day of class when a student wants to make a good impression. This challenge may bring about less effective functioning. The second question about how well the students know Roman numerals and a repetition of the words can cause students to think about an answer in the area only of Roman numerals, where their minds have been "set."

Another exercise in creative thinking designed to avoid rigidity is to put this dot matrix on the board:

•　　　•　　　•

•　　　•　　　•

•　　　•　　　•

Tell tl e students to connect the dots with four straight lines going through each dot only once and without lifting the pencil from the paper. To solve this new problem, students must use a very important clue, that of *going beyond*. Most people confine themselves to the set of the original square, but the problem can only be solved if one goes beyond.

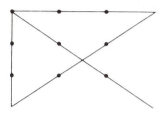

These activities help students recognize how "set" they are and encourage creativity in the class.

Brainstorming Brainstorming (generating many different ideas without inhibition) is a technique that has been popularized in business and industry. It can be used very effectively in the classroom situation to help stretch students' imaginations. The process is an excellent way to break the ice among students on any level. It helps them to work together while creating an atmosphere conducive to creativity.

Certain principles must be followed so that brainstorming will be truly effective:

1. Anything goes.
2. No criticisms.
3. Build on another's ideas.

It has been found that those who generate the most ideas in a brainstorming session most often have the ideas of highest quality.[47]

Before getting students involved in group-brainstorming, they should try self-brainstorming. Students can be given a stimulus to which they must react, "stretching their imaginations" while observing the three principles listed here. They can write down all of their ideas and, after a few minutes, time is called. The student with the greatest quantity of ideas reads his or her list to the whole class. If someone in the class has an idea not on this original list, that idea is added. (This also makes for a very good

47Alex F. Osborn, *Applied Imagination*, 3d ed. (New York: Scribner's, 1963), p. 156.

listening activity for students.) Only after all the ideas have been stated does evaluation take place.

In group-brainstorming students choose one person who is a very fast writer to record oral ideas called out as soon as they are thought up. The same principles prevail for group-brainstorming as for self-brainstorming. But in the group the temptation to criticize must be overcome. These topics could be used for both group- and self-brainstorming sessions:

1. Many different uses of a brick.
2. Many different uses of a pin.
3. Many different uses of a paper clip.
4. Many different uses of a coat hanger.
5. Many different uses of a paper bag.
6. Many different uses of a button.
7. Many different uses of a rubber band.
8. Many different uses of a pencil.
9. Many different uses of a block.
10. Many different uses of a paper carton.
11. State all elements that an "ideal school" would have.
12. State what you would build on the moon, if you were going there on a trip.
13. State all the kinds of automation devices you can think of.

Students should be helped to understand that "different uses" does not include, for example: "A brick can be used to build a house. A brick can be used to build a wall. A brick can be used to build a chimney." It would include such things as: "A brick can be used as a bed warmer, to write with, to carve out and use as an ashtray, to use as a missile," and so on.

GRAPHIC SUMMARY OF CHAPTER

Here is a graphic summary of Chapter 3. If you have read the chapter, this graphic illustration should help you remember its main points. Under or beside each heading, you might want to jot down some of the information you recall, as well as some of the key concepts in this chapter. This can act as a good review. You can then check your key concepts against those that follow the graphic summary.

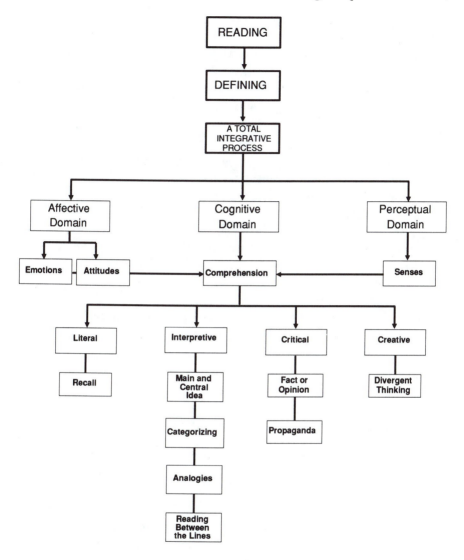

KEY CONCEPTS IN CHAPTER

- Reading is defined as the bringing of meaning to and the getting of meaning from the printed page.
- Reading is a total integrative act.
- Reading as a total integrative act includes the affective, perceptual, and cognitive domains.

- Comprehension is a construct that cannot be directly observed or directly measured.
- Reading comprehension is a complex intellectual process.
- Good comprehenders are active consumers of information.
- Good comprehenders are able to relate present information and experiences to past information and experiences.
- Comprehension involves various levels of thinking.
- The literal, interpretive, critical, and creative comprehension skills are a hierarchy of reading/thinking skills ranging from lowest to highest.
- Literal reading comprehension skills are based on recall.
- Interpretive reading comprehension skills are based on information that is implied.
- Critical reading comprehension skills are based on making a personal judgment on the accuracy, truthfulness, and value of something.
- The creative reading comprehension skills are based on divergent thinking.
- Divergent thinking deals with going beyond the obvious.
- Teachers must learn to ask questions that go beyond the literal level.
- Main idea is an essential skill that is not easy to acquire.
- Content-area teachers must have knowledge of the various comprehension skills to be effective teachers.

SUGGESTIONS FOR THOUGHT QUESTIONS AND ACTIVITIES

1. Choose a selection from a content-area textbook; then construct at least one question for each comprehension level for the selection.
2. Explain the relationship between thinking and comprehension.
3. You have been asked to give a talk to the other content-area teachers in your school concerning how you incorporate reading comprehension skills in your lessons. What will you say?
4. Construct two questions for the literal, interpretive, critical, and creative reading levels that you could use in a content area.
5. Explain to your colleagues how brainstorming can help their students.
6. Prepare some analogy activities using concepts from a specific content area.
7. Prepare some fact or opinion activities using concepts from a specific content area.

SELECTED BIBLIOGRAPHY

AFFLERBACH, PETER P. "The Influence of Prior Knowledge on Expert Readers' Main Idea Construction Strategies," *Reading Research Quarterly* 25 (Winter 1990): 31–46.

DOWNING, JOHN. *Reading and Reasoning.* New York: Springer-Verlag, 1979.

GILLESPIE, CINDY. "Questions about Student-Generated Questions." *Journal of Reading* 34 (December/January 1990/1991): 250–257.

GUZZETTI, BARBARA J. "Enhancing Comprehension Through Trade Books in High School English Classes," *Journal of Reading* 33 (March 1990): 411–413.

HARE, VICTORIA CHOW, MITCHELL RABINOWITZ, and KAREN MAGNUS SCHIEBLE. "Text Effects on Main Idea Comprehension." *Reading Research Quarterly* 24 (Winter 1989): 72–88.

PARIS, SCOTT G., BARBARA A. WASIK, and JULIANNE G. TURNER. "The Development of Strategic Readers." In *Handbook of Reading Research*, Vol. II, Rebecca Barr, Michael L. Kamil, Peter Mosenthal, and P. David Pearson (eds.) New York: Longman, 1991, pp. 609–640.

SINGER, HARRY. "Active Comprehension: From Answering to Asking Questions." *The Reading Teacher* 31 (May 1978): 901-908.

SINGER, HARRY, and STEPHEN SIMONSEN. "Comprehension and Learning from a Text." In *Content Area Reading and Learning.* Diane Lapp, James Flood, and Nancy Farnan (eds.) Englewood Cliffs, N.J.: Prentice Hall, 1989, pp. 43–57.

STAUFFER, RUSSELL. *Teaching Reading as a Thinking Process.* New York: Harper & Row, 1969.

THORNDIKE, EDWARD L. "Reading as Reasoning: A Study of Mistakes in Paragraph Reading." *The Journal of Educational Psychology* 8 (June 1917): 323-332.

4

Vocabulary Expansion

INTRODUCTION: A SCENARIO

Imagine having a six-foot-four-inch sixteen-year-old student say, "Mrs. Regan, I have a great amount of animosity toward you!" It certainly amazed Mrs. Regan because she thought that she had an excellent rapport with Steven, and Steven seemed to enjoy her English class.

The statement somehow didn't ring true, so she decided to probe further. "Steven," she asked. "Is anything wrong? Are you upset about something that I did or said?" Steven looked perplexed. He looked Mrs. Regan right in the eyes and said, "No, I like your class, and I like you." Mrs. Regan replied, "That's what I thought, so why did you say you dislike me?" "I didn't," replied Steven. "I said just the opposite."

At that moment it became clear to Mrs. Regan that Steven obviously didn't know the meaning of animosity. She asked Steven why he used the word animosity if he didn't know what it meant. "Oh," he said with a sheepish grin. "I like the way it sounds, so I use it a lot."

As I said earlier, Steven is six foot four inches tall, so when he would tell someone he has animosity toward them, the other people probably didn't question it. It could also be that the other people to whom he used the word didn't know its meaning either.

Knowledge of word meanings is imperative for communication. Unless individuals know the meanings of the words they are using, the words are merely noises.

A good vocabulary and good reading go hand in hand. Students must know the meanings of words, or they will have difficulty in understanding what they are reading. And the more they read, the more words they will add to their vocabulary. Read the following statement:

The misanthrope was apathetic to the sufferings of those around him.

Do you understand it? Unless you know the meanings of *misanthrope* and *apathetic,* you are not able to read the statement. In order to *read,* you must know the meanings of words and the way words are used in sentences. No one would dispute this statement. However, many teachers may not recognize that a student's problem in a content area may be that he or she does not have the prerequisite vocabulary to understand the concepts that are being presented.

Acquiring word meanings is an important reading skill and one that should continue not only all through school but all through life. Because of its importance, it is being presented in a chapter by itself. One should stress that just knowing the meanings of the words will not ensure that individuals will be able to state the meanings of sentences, nor does knowing the meanings of sentences ensure that readers can give the meaning of whole paragraphs, and so on. However, by not knowing the meanings of the

Berry's World

FIGURE 4-1.
This little girl needs help in vocabulary development.

"I'm collecting for those more than 100 poor helpless <u>lame ducks</u> in Washington that I heard about."

words, the individual considerably lessens his or her chances of being able to read. Without an understanding of words, comprehension is impossible.

As students advance in concept development, their vocabulary development must also advance because the two are interrelated. Students deficient in vocabulary development will usually be deficient in concept development and vice versa. "Numerous researchers have noted that poor readers have smaller vocabularies than good readers. Indeed, vocabulary knowledge is one of the best single predictors of reading comprehension."[1] Because concept development and vocabulary development are dependent on one another, a special section on concept development is presented in this chapter.

KEY QUESTIONS

After you finish reading this chapter, you should be able to answer the following questions:

1. How is concept development related to language and reading?
2. What is a concept?

[1]Meredyth Daneman, "Individual Differences in Reading Skills," in *Handbook of Reading Research*, Vol. II, Rebecca Barr, Michael L. Kamil, Peter Mosenthal, and P. David Pearson eds. (New York: Longman, 1991), p. 524.

3. How are concepts acquired?
4. What is the role of the teacher in concept development?
5. What strategies do students use in acquiring word meanings?
6. What words should be taught in content classes?
7. What is vocabulary consciousness?
8. What are some examples of context clues that students should know about?
9. How does knowledge of context clues help students figure out meanings of homographs and other words?
10. How can knowledge of word parts help students expand their vocabulary?
11. How can teachers help students expand their vocabulary?

KEY TERMS IN CHAPTER

You should pay special attention to the following key terms:

accommodation	context clue
affixes	homographs
analysis	phonics
antonyms	structural analysis
assimilation	synonyms
combining forms	synthesis
concept	vocabulary consciousness
connotative meaning	word recognition
context	

LANGUAGE DEVELOPMENT, CONCEPT DEVELOPMENT, AND READING

Language development depends on the interrelationships of such factors as intelligence, home environment, cultural differences, gender differences, and so on. The factors that influence language development also influence concept development. And students who are more advanced in language development also tend to be better readers than those who are not as advanced. For example, in Chapter 3, the introductory scenario presents a student who has had many advantages because of her home environment, and you probably had little difficulty making predictions about how well you feel she would do in school. Her family reads, so she reads. The more she reads, the better reader she becomes; the better reader she becomes, the more information she gains; the more information she acquires, the better prepared she is for reading her textbooks, and so on. Yes, it appears that success breeds success. The importance of a student's home background in determining school success is enormous. However, teachers cannot change their students' home environment or lift them from one socioeconomic class to another.

Teachers, nevertheless, must be able to help all students, regardless of socioeconomic class, attain the concepts they need in order to gain the most from their textbooks. It's not an easy task, but it can be done. To accomplish this goal, teachers must know as much as possible about how concepts are acquired, as well as what a concept is.

WHAT IS A CONCEPT?

Read the following statements. Do they sound familiar? They should because teachers every day in almost every classroom probably make statements similar to these:

"We're working with the concept of _____."

"Students don't understand the concept of _____."

"Jerome's concept on _____ is erroneous."

"I'm teaching the concept of _____."

Teachers use the term *concept* very often, but is it understood? Unless it is, teachers will usually have difficulty helping students correct or acquire certain concepts.

Is Julia Smith a concept? Is animal a concept? Is my pet canary, Sheshe, a concept? Is New York a concept? Is war a concept? What about peace? (If you said animal, war, and peace are concepts, you are correct.) Stop reading for a moment, and state how you would define concept.

A concept is a group of stimuli with common characteristics. These stimuli may be persons, objects, or events. Terms, such as peace, game, book, poem, human, animal, pet, teacher, coach, and so forth, are concepts. All these concepts refer to classes or (categories) of stimuli. Particular stimuli, such as Ms. Smith; Mr. Johnson; the Persian Gulf War; Miss Green, the lawyer; Stephen King, the writer; the Rose Bowl; and Emily Dickinson's poem "There's No Frigate Like a Book" are not concepts.

Concepts are needed to reduce the complexity of the world. When children learn that their shaggy pets are called dogs, they tend to label all other similar four-footed animals as "dogs." This is because young children overgeneralize, tending to group all animals together, and have not yet perceived the differences between and among various animals. Unless children learn to discern differences, the class of words that they deal with will become exceptionally unwieldy and unmanageable. However, if children group each object in a class by itself, this too will bring about difficulties in

FIGMENTS

FIGURE 4-2. Language development and concept development are closely related. Not understanding that words may have different meanings, the child incorrectly interprets adult speech.

coping with environmental stimuli, because it will also be such an unwieldy method.

Piaget and Concept Development

Concept development is closely related to cognitive (thinking) development. Jean Piaget, a renowned Swiss psychologist, has written on children's cognitive development in terms of their ability to organize (which requires conceptualization), classify, and adapt to their environments.

According to Piaget,[2] the mind is capable of intellectual exercise because of its ability to categorize incoming stimuli adequately. Schemata (structured designs) are the cognitive arrangements by which this takes place. As children develop and take in more and more information, it is necessary to have some way to categorize all the new information. This is done by means of schemata, and, as children develop, their ability to categorize grows too. That is, children should be able to differentiate, to become less dependent on sensory stimuli, and to gain more and more complex schemata. Children should be able to categorize a cat as distinct from a mouse or a rabbit. They should be able to group cat, dog, and cow together as animals. Piaget calls the processes that bring about these changes in children's thinking *assimilation* and *accommodation*.

Assimilation does not change an individual's concept but allows it to grow. It is a continuous process that helps the individual to integrate new, incoming stimuli into existing schemata or concepts. For example, when children tend to label all similar four-footed animals as dogs, the children are assimilating. They have assimilated all four-footed animals into their existing schemata.

If the child meets stimuli that cannot fit into the existing schema, then

[2]Jean Piaget, *The Origins of Intelligence in Children* (New York: International Universities Press, 1952).

the alternative is either to construct a new category or to change the existing category. When a new schema or concept is developed or when an existing schema is changed, this is called accommodation.

Although both assimilation and accommodation are important processes that the child must attain in order to develop adequate cognition, a balance between the two processes is necessary. If children overassimilate, they will have categories that are too large to handle and, similarly, if they overaccommodate, they will have too many categories, as we have already seen. Piaget calls the balance between the two *equilibrium.* A person having equilibrium would be able to see similarities between stimuli and thus properly assimilate them and would also be able to determine when new schemata are needed for adequate accommodation of a surplus of categories.

As children develop cognitively they proceed from more global (generalized) schemata to more particular ones. For the child there are usually no right or wrong placements, but only better or more effective ones. That is what good education is all about.

Instructional Implications

Concepts are necessary to help students acquire increasing amounts of knowledge. For example, in school, as one proceeds through the grades, learning becomes more abstract and is expressed in words, using verbal stimuli as labels for concepts. Many teachers take for granted that those spoken concept labels are understood by their students, but this is not always so. Many times these concepts are learned either incompletely or incorrectly. This example illustrates incomplete concepts for the tourist and immigrant.[3]

> All tourists may be obviously American whereas all the immigrants may be obviously Mexican. The tourists may be well dressed, the immigrants poorly dressed, and so on. If the natural environment is like a grand concept-formation experiment, it may take a child a long time to attain the concepts *tourist* and *immigrant;* indeed, the environment may not be as informative as the usual experimenter since the child may not always be informed, or reliably informed, as to the correctness of his guesses. No wonder a child might form the concept that a tourist is a well-dressed person who drives a station wagon with out-of-state license plates!

When children come to school, the teacher must assess their concept-development level, then help them to add the attributes necessary and relevant for the development of particular concepts while aiding them to delete all those concepts that are faulty or irrelevant.

[3]John Carroll, "Words, Meanings and Concepts" in *Thought & Language: Language and Reading,* ed. Maryanne Wolf et al. (Cambridge, Mass.: *Harvard Educational Review,* 1980), p. 42.

THE ROLE OF CONTENT-AREA TEACHERS IN CONCEPT DEVELOPMENT

Content-area teachers cannot assume that students will automatically master the concepts that they need to learn the content of a subject area. They must help their students to discard faulty concepts, to acquire new ones, and to expand old ones.

The first step in acquiring concepts concerns vocabulary. Teachers must help their students to expand vocabulary and to be more precise in their use of language so that they can distinguish subtle differences in word meanings. Vocabulary development, as already stated, is closely related to concept development because concepts are based on word meanings. Without vocabulary, there would be no concepts because there would be no base for the development of concepts.

The second step in acquiring concepts involves reading to gather data, that is, specific information about the concept to be learned. While reading, students must notice the way that the specific information is related, that is, how it is organized. This is important because it enables students to categorize those items that belong together and those that do not. Concepts are formed when the data are organized into categories. For more information on concept development, see sections on outlining in Chapter 6 and the section on categorizing in Chapter 3.

VOCABULARY IN CONTENT-AREA COURSES

If students are to gain key concepts in content areas, they usually have to acquire a specialized and technical vocabulary. Many textbook writers in recent years recognize that this may put a strain on many students, so a number of writers make special provisions in their chapters for vocabulary study and, wherever possible, use context clues to help students gain word meanings. (See the sections on context clues.) For many students, this is ample, but there are a number of students who need more help. For such students, vocabulary study must be integrated with the content lesson and be an important part of it rather than be incidental to it. (See Chapter 1 for special guides and Chapters 7, 8, and 9 for the integration of vocabulary in content-area lessons.)

There is no set formula or prescription for determining what words should be chosen from each content area to be taught. The decision as to which words to choose would depend on the technical or specialized vocabulary unique to the particular content course and on the ability levels of the students. Even when these factors are taken into account, teachers cannot predict all the words that will cause difficulty for their students.

The most effective approach would be for the teacher to choose those key words that students need to acquire the particular content-area concepts and to present these in strategies that will help make students become more independent in vocabulary development. The content-area teacher is thus helping students gain necessary vocabulary while teaching content material and, at the same time, is helping students acquire skills to make them more independent learners. This chapter presents many word meaning strategies that content-area teachers should use to help their students become more independent learners of vocabulary.

Which Vocabulary Words Deserve Treatment?

The previous section touched on the problem that teachers have in determining which words to select for special emphasis. Teacher judgment plays an important role in this area; the number of words, the kinds of words, and the methods of presentation will vary based on the subject matter and the level of the students. Each subject area usually has a specialized vocabulary that is essential to the understanding of what is being read, and many textbook writers put in bold print those words that they feel are important to gaining key concepts. Teachers could peruse their students' reading assignments and select all those key words that they feel are necessary for students to understand what they are reading. Even if these words are defined in the textbook, it would be a good idea for the teacher to present these words before their students read them in print. If students have met a number of key words beforehand, they will be reinforced when they meet the words in their reading, and this should help to improve their reading comprehension.

Teachers should especially be on the lookout for words with multiple meanings that are used often in everyday language but that have special or unique meaning for the subject matter area because such words can cause difficulty for students. For example, the terms *heat, force,* and *work* are words in students' everyday vocabulary; however, in physics these terms have very specific and precise meanings. It would probably be a good idea for the teacher to select all such words, and, depending on his or her purpose, either highlight the words or give direct explanations for them.

The teacher should also carefully check his or her students' reading assignments for other important words to present to students. Although these are not key words, the author uses them to develop the understanding of key concepts, and the teacher feels that these words may not be in his or her students' reading vocabulary.

After the word selection process, the teacher must still decide whether the words will be directly explained or merely highlighted. Teacher purposes, as well as textbook material and student ability, will determine whether the words the teacher has chosen should be highlighted or directly explained. If the teacher feels that the author has done an excellent job in explaining the key terms or if the teacher wishes the students to gain skill in inferring the meanings from their textbook, the teacher may just highlight the words; that is, he or she may call attention to the words and tell students that these are important terms that they should note in their reading. On the other hand, if the teacher feels that certain terms are critical to understanding key concepts in the unit and this unit is an exceptionally important one, the teacher may decide to directly explain a number of terms, even though they are explained very well in the textbook.

Vocabulary Aids in Textbooks   Teachers should help acquaint students with the many aids that textbook writers provide for their readers. At the beginning of the term teachers should spend time with students to discuss the various techniques used in their textbooks to help students acquire vocabulary; nothing should be taken for granted. Most textbook writers use a combination of aids such as the following: context clues, marginal notes, footnotes, parenthetical explanations, illustrations, glossaries, pronunciation keys, word lists, italicized words, bold print, and so on. Teachers should familiarize students with each of the aids to make sure that students can use them effectively. (The rest of this chapter helps readers gain insight into word recognition strategies and gives numerous examples of how teachers can present vocabulary to their students, as well as help students expand their vocabulary.)

WORD RECOGNITION STRATEGIES

Content-area teachers feel the most insecure when it comes to word recognition skills. This makes sense. Content-area teachers are generally not expected to teach students to learn to read, and word recognition skills are associated with learning to read. Even though content-area teachers will not be teaching students such skills as phonics, it would be helpful for them to have some background regarding how students recognize words so that they can identify those students who may have difficulty reading their textbooks. Also, content-area teachers frequently employ such word recognition strategies as context clues, structural analysis, and the dictionary to help their students gain word meanings. What follows should help content-area teachers gain a better understanding of how students gain word recognition skills as well as the kinds of word recognition skills students should have.

Word Recognition Strategies for Pronunciation

Word recognition is necessary to be able to read. No one would disagree with that statement; however, persons do disagree on what word recognition encompasses. In this book, word recognition is looked upon as a twofold process that includes both the identification of printed symbols by some method so that the word can be pronounced and the attachment or association of meaning to the word after it has been properly pronounced.

When we read, we are intent on getting the message and appear to do so automatically and in one step. We don't notice the individual letters, groups of letters, or even every word. If we are good readers, this is what should be taking place. It isn't until we stumble on an unfamiliar word that we become aware of the individual letters that are grouped together to form a word. The reason we stopped reading is because the word we stumbled on has interfered with our getting the message. The question is: Do you remember what you did when a word interfered with your understanding of what you were reading? To understand better the concept that word recognition is a twofold process, that there are a number of strategies that can be used to figure out how to pronounce a word as well as strategies that can be used to determine the meaning of a word, and that these strategies are not necessarily the same, we will be involved in a number of exercises involving nonsense and actual words.

As already stated, the strategies for determining how to pronounce a word are different from those that are used to unlock the meaning of the word. Read the following sentence:

The clake looks funny.

You should have stumbled on the nonsense word *clake*. Imagine that you do not know that *clake* is a nonsense word. Let's look at the kinds of strategies we could and could *not* use to help us to gain the pronunciation of a word *independently*.

STRATEGY 1:   Phonic analysis and synthesis

DEFINITION: Phonics is a decoding technique that depends on students' being able to make the proper grapheme (letter)—phoneme (sound) correspondences. *Analysis* has to do with the breaking down of something into its component parts. *Synthesis* has to do with the building up of the parts of something into a whole.

ANALYSIS: Break down *clake* into the blend *cl* and the phonogram *ake*. We have met the blend *cl* before in such words as *climb* and *club*.
We have met the phonogram *ake* before in such words as *bake* and *lake*.
We, therefore, know the pronunciation of *cl* and *ake*.

SYNTHESIS: Blend together the *cl* and *ake*.

Using this technique, we should be able to pronounce *clake*, or at least gain an approximation of its pronunciation.

STRATEGY 2:   Whole word or "look and say" method

DEFINITION: The whole word or "look and say" method, which is also referred to as the sight method, has to do with the teach-

er's or any other individual's directing a student's attention to a word and then saying the word. The student
must make an association between the oral word and the
written word, and he or she shows this by actually saying
the word.

This technique is a useful word recognition strategy that helps us to
learn to pronounce words, but it will not help us to figure out the pronunciation of unfamiliar words independently.

STRATEGY 3:   Ask someone to pronounce the word for you.

This could be done, but it would be similar to the "look and say"
method, and it would not help us to figure out the word independently.

STRATEGY 4:   Context clues
DEFINITION: By *context* we mean the words surrounding a word that
can shed light on its meaning. When we refer to context
clues, we mean clues that are given in the form of definitions, examples, comparisons or contrasts, explanations,
and so on, which help us figure out word meanings.

This is a word recognition technique, but it is not one that helps us to
figure out the pronunciation of words. It is one that is used for helping us to
gain the meaning of a word.

STRATEGY 5:   Structural analysis and synthesis (word parts)
DEFINITION: Structural analysis and synthesis have to do with the
breaking down (analysis) and building up (synthesis) of
word parts such as prefixes, suffixes, roots (bases), and
combining forms.

Structural analysis is most often used in conjunction with phonic
analysis. Knowledge of word parts such as prefixes, suffixes, and roots
helps us to isolate the root of a word. After the root of a word is isolated,
phonic analysis is applied. If the word parts are familiar ones, then we can
blend together the word parts to come up with the pronunciation of the
word.

Structural analysis is a helpful word recognition technique that can
aid with the pronunciation of words, but it will not help us to figure out the
pronunciation of *clake* unless we apply phonic analysis to *clake* because *clake*
as a nonsense word is an unfamiliar root (base) word.

Structural analysis is especially helpful in figuring out the pronunciation of an unfamiliar word if the word is composed of familiar word parts
such as prefixes, suffixes, and roots. The technique to use is similar to that
used with phonic analysis and synthesis. For example, let's see how we

would go about figuring out how to pronounce the italicized word in the following sentence using structural analysis and synthesis.

The salesperson said that the goods were not *returnable*.

STRUCTURAL ANALYSIS: Break down the word into its parts to isolate the root.

re turn able

If we had met *re* before and if we had met *able* before, we should know how to pronounce them. After we have isolated *turn*, we may recognize it as a familiar word and know how to pronounce it.

STRUCTURAL SYNTHESIS: Blend together *re*, *turn*, and *able*.

If *turn* is not a familiar root word for us, then we could apply phonic analysis to it and after that blend it together with the prefix *re* and the suffix *able*.

STRATEGY 6: Look up the pronunciation in the dictionary.

This is a viable method, but you may not have a dictionary handy, and by the time you look up the pronunciation of the word, you may have lost the trend of what you were reading.

Let's list those techniques that can help us to figure out the pronunciation of words:

1. Phonic analysis and synthesis
2. Whole word or "look and say."
3. Ask someone.
4. Structural analysis and synthesis.
5. Looking up the pronunciation in the dictionary.

FIGURE 4-3. Linus needs some more help in pronunciation; however, the pronunciation of the names is not vital to comprehending the story he is reading.

© Copyright 1975, United Feature Syndicate, Inc.

Word Recognition Strategies for Word Meanings

Being able to pronounce a word is important, but it does not guarantee that we will thereby know the meaning of the word. Word recognition is a two-fold process; the first involves the correct pronunciation, and the second involves meaning. After we have pronounced a word, we have to associate the word with one in our listening vocabulary in order to determine the meaning of the word; that is, we need to have heard the word before and know what the word means. Obviously, the larger our stock of listening vocabulary, the better able we will be to decipher the word. However, even though we can pronounce a word such as *misanthropic*, it doesn't mean that we can associate any meaning to it. If we have never heard the word before, it would not be in our listening vocabulary; therefore, the pronunciation would not act as a stimulus and trigger an association with a word that we have stored in our memory bank. Let's see the techniques that we can use to help us unlock words that we have never heard of or met before.

STRATEGY 1:   Context

By *context* we mean the words surrounding a particular word that can help shed light on its meaning. (Context clues are especially important in determining the meanings of words, and because of their importance, special emphasis is given to this area in this chapter.) Read the following sentence:

Even though my *trank* was rather long, I wouldn't take out one word.

From the context of the sentence you know that the nonsense word *trank* must somehow refer to a sentence, paragraph, paper, or report of some sort. Even though you had never met *trank* before, the context of the sentence did throw light on it. You know from the word order or position of the word (syntax) that *trank* must be a noun, and words such as *word* and *long* give you meaning (semantic) clues to the word itself. There are times, however, when context is not too helpful so that other strategies must be used.

STRATEGY 2:   Structural analysis and synthesis for word meaning

Read the following sentence:

We asked the *misanthrope* to leave.

From the position of the word *misanthrope* in the sentence, we know that it is a noun; however, there is not enough information to help us figure out the meaning of *misanthrope.* Structural analysis could be very useful in situations where there are insufficient context clues, and the word consists of a number of word parts.

ANALYSIS: Break down *misanthrope* into its word parts.

Mis means either "wrong" or "hate," and *anthropo* means "mankind."

SYNTHESIS: Put together the word parts. It doesn't make sense to say, "Wrong mankind," so it must be *hate* and *mankind.* Since *misanthrope* is a noun, the meaning of *misanthrope* would have to be "hater of mankind."

Structural analysis is a powerful tool, but it is dependent on your having at your fingertips knowledge of word parts and their meanings. If you do not have these at hand, you obviously need another strategy. (More will be said about structural analysis later on in this chapter.)

STRATEGY 3:   Ask someone the meaning of the word.

This at times may be the most convenient if someone is available who knows the meaning of the word.

STRATEGY 4:   Look up the meaning in the dictionary.

If you cannot figure out the word independently rather quickly so that your train of thought is not completely broken, the dictionary is a valuable tool for word meanings.

Let's list those techniques that can help us figure out the meaning of words:

1.   Context of a sentence.
2.   Structural analysis and synthesis.
3.   Asking someone.
4.   Looking up the meaning in the dictionary.

There are times when it is possible for context clues to help with the correction of mispronounced words that are in the listening vocabulary of the reader but not yet in his or her reading vocabulary. Here is such an example. A student is asked to read the following sentence:

The horse pulled the sleigh in the snow.

The student reads the sentence as follows:

The horse pulled the *sleege* in the snow.

The reader then self-corrects himself, and he rereads the sentence correctly. What has taken place? The first pronunciation of *sleigh* was obtained from graphic clues. As the student continued to read, the context of the sentence indicated to the student that the mispronounced word should sound like *slay* rather than *sleege*. Since *sleigh* was in the listening vocabulary of the student, he was able to self-correct his mispronunciation. In this case, the context clues helped the reader to correct his mispronunciation of *sleigh*.

It is important to state that the reader would not have been able to self-correct his mispronunciation if the word *sleigh* had not been in his listening vocabulary and if he had not heard it correctly pronounced. In addition, readers usually use a *combination* of word recognition strategies.

The sections that follow will expand on what has been presented in this section that relates to gaining word meanings.

Special Note:
Many foreign students who are learning English as a second language or students who speak nonstandard English may pronounce a number of words incorrectly because they have heard them pronounced that way or because they have difficulty producing the sounds, but they may know the meanings of the words. It could also be that the words are not in their listening vocabularies, and they do not know the meanings of the words. Content-area teachers should be on the lookout for this and try to discern whether the mispronunciation is due to a pronunciation problem or a comprehension problem.

VOCABULARY CONSCIOUSNESS

When students recognize the power of words and that many words have different meanings based on surrounding words, they are beginning to build a vocabulary consciousness. This vocabulary consciousness grows and matures when students independently search out word meanings. Teachers can help awaken this vocabulary consciousness in students by helping them to acquire tools besides the dictionary to expand their vocabulary.

Vocabulary consciousness grows when students do the following:

1. Become aware of words they do not know.
2. Try to guess the meaning from the context and their knowledge of word parts.
3. Learn the most-used combining forms.
4. Jot down words that they do not know and look them up in the dictionary later.

5. Keep a notebook and write down the words they have missed in their vocabulary exercises, giving them additional study. Learn to break words down into word parts in order to learn their meanings.
6. Maintain interest in wanting to expand vocabulary.

LEVELS OF WORD MEANING KNOWLEDGE

All of us usually have three levels of word meaning knowledge: unknown, acquainted, and established.[4] Words at the unknown level are obviously unfamiliar words; words we do not know the meanings of. Words with which we are acquainted are those that we have met at one time or another, but we cannot easily figure out their meanings. Often, we may be able to determine their meanings after a great amount of effort. Words at our established level are those for which we can very easily state meanings.

Throughout the term, teachers should help their students expand their vocabulary to increase their established level of word meaning knowledge. Teachers need to do this by using direct instruction in vocabulary rather than depending completely on incidental learning. Often incidental learning of vocabulary increases our acquaintance level, but it does not ensure that the words will become part of our established level of word knowledge. Words that are at our established level are those that we have usually overlearned. In other words, we have made a concerted effort to learn the meanings of the words and have continued practice beyond the point at which we thought we needed the practice. Here is a scenario that shows how one teacher raises his students' consciousness level to the various types of word meaning knowledge they have.

Scenario: A Vocabulary Lesson in Mr. Jones's Ninth Grade English Class at the Beginning of the Term
Mr. Jones has always had a very strong vocabulary program in his English classes, and this year would be no exception. He believes in helping his students learn how to use a number of vocabulary expansion strategies and especially emphasizes a combination of word parts and context clues. Before he shows his students the power of having these strategies, he likes to raise their consciousness levels to the various word meaning knowledge levels they have. And that is the objective of this lesson.

Mr. Jones puts the following sentence on the board and asks his students to write the meaning of the underlined word.

That is an apocryphal story.

---

[4]See Michael F. Graves, Wayne H. Slater, and Thomas G. White, "Teaching Content Area Vocabulary," in *Content Area Reading and Learning*, eds. Diane Lapp, James Flood, and Nancy Farnan (Englewood Cliffs, N.J.: Prentice Hall, 1989), pp. 216–17.

He then asks if someone would tell him the meaning of the underlined word. No one volunteers. A number call out that they had never met the word before. Mr. Jones explains that he deliberately chose a word he thought would be unfamiliar to them to illustrate the various levels of word knowledge we have. Obviously, any word we have never met in our listening or reading experiences would be an unfamiliar word. These words would be at our lowest level of word knowledge.

Mr. Jones explains the meaning of *apocryphal* to his students and has them put the word in a sentence. He tells them that they are now at the second level of word knowledge; that is, they are now acquainted with the word. Therefore, if they were to meet the word in their reading, they might be able to figure out the meaning especially if there were good context clues. However, in order for words to be in their established vocabulary, which is at the highest level of word meaning knowledge, they would have to be able to quickly state the meaning of the word whenever they heard it or saw it in writing.

Mr. Jones then gives them a few sentences to illustrate words with which they are probably acquainted and those which most had at their established word meaning level. He presents them with the following two sentences and has them state the meanings of the underlined words.

1. The papers were of doubtful authenticity.
2. It is fictitious.

The students immediately stated the definition of *fictitious:* however, many said they had seen and heard the word *authenticity,* but they weren't sure of the meaning.

When Mr. Jones expanded sentence 1 by adding an independent clause to it, all the students were able to determine the meaning of *authenticity.*

The papers were of doubtful authenticity, but he swore they were not fake.

Mr. Jones tells his students that we all have word meaning knowledge at all three levels, and that his goal is to increase their established word meaning level, and to help them gain various strategies that will help them figure out unfamiliar words and words with which they are acquainted.

VOCABULARY LEARNING: A SPECIAL NOTE

The studies done on the acquisition of word meanings have not been conclusive. That is, one cannot point to a specific technique or strategy and say that it is the best way to promote vocabulary learning. "And, indeed a vari-

© 1963, United Feature Syndicate, Inc.

FIGURE 4-4. Lack of word meanings can be painful.

ety of positions has been taken by different researchers."[5] However, "none of these positions is espoused to the exclusion of others, but the degree of emphasis among various researchers is quite different."[6]

Some researchers' feelings that students can learn vocabulary from context "has led to a laissez-faire view of instruction."[7] Rather than instruction in vocabulary, this group has advocated wide reading. Another group also believes in context as a strong factor in vocabulary learning, but this group recommends giving students instruction in gaining word meaning from context. Another group prefers the dictionary over context, and still another group feels that "no matter what context contributes, direct instruction can play an important role in vocabulary development."[8]

In this book, direct instruction using a combination of strategies is advocated to promote vocabulary expansion. The rest of this chapter is primarily concerned with techniques that help students expand their vocabulary and stir their vocabulary consciousness. In Part 3 you will see how vocabulary expansion is integrated in content-area lessons.

GAINING WORD MEANINGS THROUGH CONTEXT

In 1918, Chief Justice Oliver Wendell Holmes said the following concerning a word:

> A word is not a crystal, transparent and unchanged; it is the skin of a living thought and may vary greatly in color and content according to the circumstances and the time in which it is used.

Because many words have more than one meaning, the meaning of a particular word is determined by the position (syntax) of the word in a sen-

[5]Isabel Beck, and Margaret McKeown, "Conditions of Vocabulary Acquisition," in *Handbook of Reading Research*, Vol. II, p. 809.
[6]Ibid.
[7]Ibid.
[8]Ibid.

tence and from meaning (semantic) clues of the surrounding words. By *context* we mean the words surrounding a word that can shed light on its meaning.

Although investigators do not agree on the best way to help students derive word meanings, common sense dictates that students learn unfamiliar words best when the new word is presented in a meaningful, familiar context so that the learner can see how the word is used, as well as when the word is used. The student can then assimilate the new information into his or her existing schemata or categories. The ability to relate the word to what is already known aids the learner in retaining the word's meaning.

When the content-area teacher presents vocabulary in context to students, he or she should also point out the context clues that the writer uses. The sections that follow should help teachers in doing this.

Context Clues

A context clue is the specific item of information that helps the reader to figure out the meaning of a particular word. Context clues can be in the form of definitions, descriptions, comparisons, contrasts, examples, and so forth. The following examples display different kinds of context clues that writers frequently use.

1. If a writer wants to make sure that the reader will get the meaning of a word, he or she will define, explain, or describe the word in the sentence. For example, in the preceding section, the term *context clue* has been defined because it is a key term in that section. In the following examples the writer actually gives us the definition of a word. (Sentences such as these are generally found in textbooks or technical journals.)

    Examples:
    A. An *axis* is a straight line, real or imaginary, that passes through the center of rotation in a revolving body at a right angle to the plane of rotation.
    B. In geometry, a plane figure of six sides and six angles is called a *hexagon.*

2. Notice how the writer in the next example gives the reader the meaning of the word by using a synonym. (A synonym is a word that has a similar meaning to another.) Notice also how this makes his writing more expressive and clear and avoids repetition.

    Example:
    Although Senator Smith is *candid* about his drinking problem, he is less *frank* about his investments.

3. In the next examples, notice how the writer *describes* the words that she wants the reader to know.

Examples:
A. Although my *diligent* friend works from morning to night, he never complains.
B. Interior paints no longer contain *toxic* materials that might endanger the health of infants and small children.
C. The *cryptic* message—which looks as mysterious and secretive as it is—is difficult to decode.

Special Notes:

1. The word *or* may be used by the writer when he or she uses another word or words with a similar meaning. Example: John said that he felt ill after having eaten *rancid* or *spoiled* butter.
2. The words *that is* and their abbreviation *i.e.,* usually signal that an explanation will follow. Example: Man is a biped, that is, an animal having only two feet, or Man is a biped, i.e., an animal having only two feet.

4. Many times an author helps us get the meaning of a word by giving us examples illustrating the use of the word. An example is something that is representative of a whole or a group. It can be a particular single item, incident, fact, or situation that typifies the whole. In the following sentence notice how the examples that the writer gives in his sentence help us determine the meaning of the word *illuminated*.
   Example:
   The lantern *illuminated* the cave so well that we were able to see the crystal formations and even spiders crawling on the rocks. (From the sentence you can determine that *illuminated* means "lit up.")
5. Another technique writers employ that can help us gain the meaning of a word is *comparison*. Comparison usually shows the similarities between persons, ideas, things, and so on. For example, in the following sentence notice how we can determine the meaning of *passive* through the writer's comparison of Paul to a bear in winter.
   Example:
   Paul is as *passive* as a bear sleeping away the winter. (From the sentence you can determine that *passive* means "inactive.")
6. *Contrast* is another method writers use that can help the reader to figure out word meanings. Contrast is usually used to show the differences between persons, ideas, things, and so on. In the following sentence we can determine the meaning of *optimist* because we know that *optimist* is somehow the opposite of "one who is gloomy or one who expects the worst."

Example:

> My sister Marie is an *optimist,* but her boyfriend is one who is always gloomy and expects the worst to happen. (From the sentence you can determine that *optimist* means "one who expects the best" or "one who is cheerful.")

Special Notes:

1. The writer may use the words *for example* or the abbreviation *e.g.* to signal that examples are to follow. *Example: Condiments,* e.g., pepper, salt, and mustard, make food taste better. (From the examples of condiments we can determine that condiments are seasonings.)

2. Many times such words as *but, yet, although, however,* and *rather than* signal that a contrast is being used. Example: My father thought he owned an *authentic* antique chest, but he was told recently that it was a fake. (From the sentence the reader can tell that *authentic* is the opposite of fake; therefore, *authentic* means "not false but genuine or real.")

Here are examples of sentences from various content areas. Notice how the underlined word is usually a key word in the sentence; that is, if the readers do not know the meaning of the underlined word, they would probably have difficulty determining the author's message. If teachers give students sentences such as these and have them try to figure out the meanings of the underlined words by using context clues, they will come to see how helpful context clues are.

1. I play a dual role in the play. In the first act I'm a teenager, and in the second act I'm middle-aged.
2. In the alphabet the letter "a" precedes the letter "b."
3. Jane is the recipient of three science awards. She received the awards because of her work in controlling air pollution.
4. John is a very conscientious person; i.e., he is very particular, thorough, and careful about everything he does.
5. My friend is very diligent, but her brother never finishes anything he starts.
6. My English instructor said that we could use short quotations in our papers but not long excerpts.
7. The desolate town looked like a ghost town from a Western movie.
8. It's interesting that the same parents can produce siblings who are so different from one another.
9. When you pilfer something, you steal in small quantities or amounts.
10. Years ago in England, children worked in coal mines clad only in over-

alls. One book states that they wore only canvas trousers and that they had an iron chain attached to a leather belt and passing between their legs.

11. The child looked as <u>fragile</u> as delicate chinaware.

12. Before the Massachusetts Act of 1642, the first law making education <u>compulsory</u>, children did not have to attend school.

13. The Massachusetts Act of 1642 was a <u>significant</u> event in the history of education in the United States because it led the way for other states to pass similar important laws.

14. A set in mathematics may be referred to as an <u>aggregate</u>.

15. Science and technology are <u>cumulative</u>; that is, the work of one scientist is built onto another's.

16. Isaac Newton was a shy man who very much disliked the <u>controversy</u> on which Galileo thrived.

17. The federal <u>fiscal</u> year, which used to begin July 1, has been extended to October 1 so that Congress and the administration can have more time to consider the <u>succeeding</u> year's budget.

18. <u>Evaporation</u>, or the change from liquid to gas, requires heat.

19. The ability of seeds to germinate is called <u>viability</u>.

20. A <u>force</u> is a physical quantity that can affect the motion of an object.

21. In science a <u>law</u> (or principle) is a statement that describes a natural phenomenon.

22. A <u>scale drawing</u> is an accurate drawing of an object.

23. If there is no middle number in a set of data, the <u>median</u> is midway between the two middle numbers.

24. The distance around a figure is its <u>perimeter</u>.

25. Maps give a <u>scale</u> that shows how the map distance compares to the actual distance.

Context Clues (An Emphasis on Synonyms) Often a word can be defined by another, more familiar word having basically the same meaning. For example, *void* is defined as *empty*, and *corpulent* is defined as *fat*. The pairs *void* and *empty* and *corpulent* and *fat* are synonyms. Synonyms are different words that have the same or nearly the same meaning. Writers use synonyms to make their writing clearer and more expressive. Although the term *synonym* was presented in the preceding section, it is being presented again because many writers use this strategy, and it is an effective technique for teaching word meanings. Teachers can present sentences such as the following to students to illustrate the use of synonyms by authors.

1. Many cities are <u>razing</u> old buildings in the belief that demolishing them is the only way to begin to rebuild their communities.

2. The infamous Al Capone was most notorious for his cruelty.
3. The exhausted man was so tired he could not move another step.
4. Although we hold equivalent job titles, our wages are not equal.
5. We did not have sufficient capital to start a business, nor were we able to borrow enough money from the bank.
6. The immense truck was too big to pass under the archway of the old inn.
7. She is a virtuoso in French, and I am an expert in Spanish.
8. The spy said that the perilous mission was too risky for him.
9. I am always looking for a quick remedy, but I guess fast cures aren't really much good.
10. After his or her appointment, the civil servant must serve a period of probation, that is, a trial period.
11. Among these other forces, several demographic factors—that is, population characteristics—are quite important.
12. This means that $3x + 5 = 38$ and $x = 11$ must have exactly the same solution set, namely, $\{11\}$; that is, they are equivalent equations.

Context Clues (An Emphasis on Antonyms) Antonyms, which are words opposite in meaning to each other, are used often by writers and, like synonyms, are an effective strategy to teach word meanings. In an earlier section, it was also stated that authors use contrast to help make their sentences clearer and more informative. Antonyms are used to show contrast. Here are some examples of sentences in which the author uses antonyms to make his or her writing clearer and more expressive. Teachers can present examples such as the following to their students and have them try to determine the meaning of the underlined word using their knowledge of context clues.

1. My sister is an optimist and can see a good side to everything, unlike my brother, the pessimist.
2. You are so trusting and naive, yet your friends are all so sophisticated.
3. I prefer studying ancient rather than modern history.
4. My friend is so vindictive that he will not forgive his brother for a wrong done ten years ago.
5. Make your flattery and compliments subtle instead of obvious.
6. How is it possible for the same family to include one brother robust enough to play semiprofessional hockey and another so frail as to collapse in a game of Twenty Questions?
7. I always seem to make innumerable mistakes in my themes, but my friend Jack makes very few.

Determining Meanings of Homographs (Words with Multiple Meanings) from Context Clues   Many words that are spelled the same have different meanings. These words are called *homographs*. The meaning of a homograph is determined by the way the word is used in the sentence. For example, the term *run* has many different meanings. (One dictionary gives 134 meanings for *run*.) In the listed sentences, notice how *run*'s placement in the sentence and the surrounding words help readers figure out the meaning of each use.

1. Walk don't <u>run</u>.
2. I have a <u>run</u> in my stocking.
3. Senator Jones said that he would not <u>run</u> for another term.
4. The trucker finished his <u>run</u> to Detroit.
5. She is going to <u>run</u> in a ten-mile race.
6. The play had a <u>run</u> of two years.

> In sentence 1, *run* means "go quickly by moving the legs more rapidly than at a walk."
> In sentence 2 *run* means "a tear or to cause stitches to unravel."
> In sentence 3 *run* means "be or campaign as a candidate for election."
> In sentence 4 *run* means "route."
> In sentence 5 *run* means "take part in a race."
> In sentence 6 *run* means "continuous course of performances."

From these, we can see that the way the word is used in the sentence will determine its meaning. As already stated, words that are spelled the same but have different meanings are called *homographs*. Some homographs are spelled the same but do not sound the same. For example, *refuse* means "trash," but it also means "to decline to accept." In the first sentence, *refuse* (ref' use) meaning "trash" is pronounced differently from *refuse* (re fuse') meaning "to decline to accept" in the second sentence. In reading, we can determine the meaning of *refuse* from the way it is used in the sentence (context clues). For example:

1. During the garbage strike there were tons of uncollected *refuse* on the streets of the city.
2. I *refuse* to go along with you.

As already shown, readers should be able to grasp the meaning of homographs from the sentence context (the words surrounding a word that can shed light on its meaning). Here are some other examples. Note the many uses of *capital* in the following sentences.

THE BORN LOSER

© 1975 by NEA, Inc.

FIGURE 4-5. When words have more than one meaning, people may get the wrong meaning.

1. That is a <u>capital</u> idea.
2. Remember to begin each sentence with a <u>capital</u> letter.
3. The killing of a policeman is a <u>capital</u> offense in some states.
4. Albany is the <u>capital</u> of New York State.
5. In order to start a business, you need <u>capital</u>.

Each of the preceding sentences illustrate one meaning for *capital.*

In sentence 1 *capital* means "excellent."
In sentence 2 *capital* means "referring to a letter in writing that is an uppercase letter."
In sentence 3 *capital* means "punishable by death."
In sentence 4 *capital* means "the seat of government."
In sentence 5 *capital* means "money or wealth."

Teachers must help students to be careful to use correctly those words with many meanings. (See "Which Vocabulary Words Deserve Treatment?" in this chapter.)

Special Note:
Confusion may exist among the terms *homonym, homophone,* and *homograph* because some authors are using the more scientific or linguistic definition for the terms and others are using the more traditional definition. *Homonyms* have traditionally been defined as words that sound alike, are spelled differently, and have different meanings; for example, *red, read.* However, many linguists use the term *homophone* rather than homonym for this meaning. Linguists generally use the term *homonym* for words that are spelled the same, pronounced the same, but have different meanings; for example, *bat* (the mouselike winged mammal) and *bat* (the name for a club

used to hit a ball.) *Bat* (baseball bat) and *bat* (animal) would traditionally be considered a homograph (words that are spelled the same but have different meanings), but linguists usually define *homographs* as words that are spelled the same but have *different pronunciations* and *different meanings;* for example, *lead* (dense metal) and *lead* (verb).

The teacher should be aware that different English textbooks may be defining the three terms somewhat differently and should be familiar with the various systems and definitions in use.

In this book the generic definition of *homograph* is used; that is, homographs are words that are spelled the same but have different meanings, and the words may or may not be pronounced the same.

THE CONNOTATIVE MEANING OF WORDS

Teachers need to help students recognize that the author's purpose for writing will greatly influence what he or she has to say and how he or she says it. Just as our past experiences influence our feelings about what we read, so will the author's past experiences influence what he or she writes. Teachers must alert students to the fact that writers can sway unsuspecting or uncritical readers. One of the best defenses against this is to have a good understanding of the connotative meanings of words.

Many words have connotative meanings. They have meanings beyond the denotative meanings, which are the direct, specific meanings. When we speak or write, we often rely more on the connotative meanings of words than on their denotative meanings to express our true position. The connotative meaning includes all emotional senses associated with the word; it is the suggestive meaning of the word based on the individual's past experiences. The connotative use of a word, therefore, requires an understanding of more than a simple definition. Teachers must help students recognize that when they respect a word's connotative meanings, they will use the word precisely and effectively.

Here is what one teacher does to help students better understand the connotative meanings of words. Mrs. Smith has her students read the following two sentences written by two different writers about the same person:

Writer A: Mrs. Davis is a very trusting person.

Writer B: Mrs. Davis is very credulous.

She then asks them to look up the meanings of *trusting* and *credulous* in the dictionary. The students find that both words have a similar denotative meaning: ready to believe or have faith in. Next, Mrs. Smith asks her students if they feel the two sentences mean the same. The students feel they do not mean the same. She asks them what is different about the sentences. The students state that they feel the one with the word *trusting* seems more positive than the other one. The one describing Mrs. Davis as *credulous* seems negative.

Mrs. Smith compliments the students and says she agrees with them. She says further that if you refer to someone as *trusting*, you are saying he or she has the admirable trait of believing the best of someone or something. If you refer to the same person as *credulous*, you are saying that he or she lacks judgment, that he or she foolishly believes anything. Although both words have the same denotative meaning, in their very different connotative senses one is complimentary and the other is belittling or insulting. Connotative meanings are obviously vital to saying the right thing the right way.

Mrs. Smith tells students that some words often have different overtones or associations for different people. For example, the term *mother* can bring forth images of apple pie, warmth, love, and kindness to one person whereas for another it can mean beatings, hurt, shame, fear, and disillusionment. She also states that some words lend themselves more readily to emotional overtones or associations than others. For example, the term *home* can bring forth good or bad associations based on the past experiences of an individual. However, the term *dwelling*, which has the same specific definition as *home*, does not have the emotional overtones that *home* does.

She then tells them that a number of words have substitutes that more aptly express a particular meaning and puts the following sentences on the board:

1. The <u>conservative</u> man saves his money.
2. The <u>miserly</u> man saves his money.
3. The <u>economical</u> man saves his money.

She then asks the students to tell her what is different about the sentences. They state that sentence 1 is more or less neutral; it probably does not evoke any emotional response; whereas in sentence 2, the term *miserly* is a negative term. Mrs. Smith agrees. She says further that the derogatory term *miserly* is considered a pejorative term because it has strong negative overtones. She then questions them about sentence 3. Everyone agrees that the term *economical* is a positive term.

Mrs. Smith then challenges her students to generate some other adjectives with positive and negative overtones in place of *economical* and *miserly*. Her students had no difficulty stating such adjectives as *stingy* and *cheap* for *miserly* and *thrifty* and *prudent* for *economical*.

VOCABULARY EXPANSION USING WORD PARTS

Context clues are a viable means in helping students figure out the meaning of an unfamiliar word in a passage so that a reader's train of thought is not lost. However, the ability to use context clues does not ensure that the reader will remember the term if he were to meet it in another context, and it is probably unlikely that it will become part of the reader's established vocabulary. In addition, there may not be enough context clues to help the reader figure out the meaning of the unfamiliar word, which may hinder comprehension of the passage.

Knowledge of word parts is an excellent means of helping students to expand their vocabulary quickly and effectively.[9] Knowledge of this effective word expansion strategy, combined with context clues, can give students vocabulary power.

Before discussing word expansion instruction as an aid in helping students increase their vocabulary, we should define some word part terms.

Defining Word Part Terms

In order to help students to use word parts as an aid to increasing vocabulary, we should define some terms. There are a great number of words in our language that combine with other words to form new words, for example, "grandfather" and "policeman" (compound words). You may also combine a root (base) word with a letter or a group of letters, either at the beginning (prefix) or end (suffix) of the root word, to form a new, related word, for example, "replay" and "played." *Affix* is a term used to refer to either a prefix or a suffix.

In the words *replay* and *played, play* is a root or base, *re* is a prefix, and *ed* is a suffix. A *root* is the smallest unit of a word that can exist and retain its basic meaning. It cannot be subdivided any further. *Replay* is not a root word because it can be subdivided to *play. Play* is a root word because it cannot be divided further and still retain a meaning related to the root word.

Derivatives are combinations of root words with either prefixes or suffixes or both. *Combining forms* are usually defined as roots borrowed from another language that join together or that join with a prefix, a suffix, or both a prefix and a suffix to form a word. Many times the English combining form elements are derived from Greek and Latin roots. In some vocabulary books, in which the major emphasis is on vocabulary expansion rather than on the naming of word parts, *combining forms* are defined in a more general sense to include any word part that can join with another word or word part to form a word or a new word.[10] The latter definition is the one most used in this book because the emphasis is on vocabulary expansion.

---

[9]See Thomas G. White, Michael A. Power, and Sheida White. "Morphological Analysis: Implications for Teaching and Understanding Vocabulary Growth," *Reading Research Quarterly* 24 (summer 1989): 283–304.

[10]Dorothy Rubin, *Vocabulary Expansion*, 2nd ed. (New York: Macmillan, 1991).

VOCABULARY EXPANSION INSTRUCTION USING WORD PARTS

Vocabulary expansion instruction depends on the ability levels of students, their past experiences, and their interests. If they are curious about sea life and have an aquarium in the classroom, this could stimulate interest in such combining forms as *aqua* meaning "water," and *mare* meaning "sea." The combining forms *aqua* could generate such terms as *aquaplane, aqueduct,* and *aquanaut.* Since *mare* means "sea," students could be given the term *aquamarine* to define. Knowing the combining forms *aqua* and *mare,* many will probably respond with "sea water." The English term actually means "bluish-green." The students can be challenged as to why the English definition of aquamarine is bluish-green.

A *terrarium* can stimulate discussion of words made up of the combining form *terra.*

When discussing the prefix *bi,* students should be encouraged to generate other words that also contain *bi,* such as *bicycle, binary, bilateral,* and so on. Other suggestions follow.

Write the words *biped* and *quadruped* in a column on the board, along with their meanings. These words should elicit guesses for groups of animals. The teacher could ask such questions as: "What do you think an animal that has eight arms or legs would be called?" "What about an animal with six feet?" And so on. When the animals are listed on the board, the students can be asked to look them up in the dictionary so that they can classify them.

The students can also try to discover the combining forms of the Roman calendar.[11]

Martius	Sextilis
Aprilis	September
Maius	October
Junius	November
Quintilis	December

Students should discover that the last six months were named for the positions they occupy.

Another set of words made from combining forms describing many-sided geometric figures (polygons) are:

3 sides	trigon
4 sides	tetragon

---

[11]See Loraine Dun, "Increase Vocabulary with the Word Elements, Mono through Deca," *Elementary English* 47 (January 1970): 49–55.

5 sides	pentagon
6 sides	hexagon
7 sides	septagon
8 sides	octagon

When presenting the combining forms *cardio, tele, graph,* and *gram,* place the following vocabulary words on the board:

cardiograph	telegraph
cardiogram	telegram

After students know that *cardio* means "heart" and *tele* means "from a distance," ask them to try to determine the meaning of *graph,* as used in *cardiograph* and *telegraph.* Have them try to figure out the meaning of *gram,* as used in *telegram* and *cardiogram.* Once students are able to define *graph* as an instrument or machine and *gram* as message, they will hardly ever confuse a *cardiograph* with a *cardiogram.*

When students are exposed to such activities, they become more sensitive to their language. They come to realize that words are human-made, that language is living and changing, and that as people develop new concepts they need new words to identify them. The words *astronaut* and *aquanaut* are good examples of words that came into being because of space and undersea exploration.

Students come to see the power of combining forms when they realize that, by knowing a few combining forms, they can unlock the meanings of many words. For example, by knowing a few combining forms, students can define correctly many terms used in the metric system, as well as other words. (See Chapter 9.)

Teachers should caution their students that many times the literal definitions of the prefixes, suffixes, or combining forms may not be exactly the same as the dictionary meaning. For example, *automobile.*

Special Note:
Many teachers ask the question: What combining forms should be presented? The combining forms that are presented would depend on the specific content area being taught, as well as on the individual differences of the students. In Part 3 many of the chapters integrate the study of vocabulary by using a combining forms approach with particular content areas.

Vocabulary Expansion Instruction for Students Weak in Vocabulary

Working with students who are especially weak in vocabulary requires a relatively structured approach, one that emphasizes the systematic presentation of material at graduated levels of difficulty in ways somewhat similar to those used in the teaching of English as a second language. Each day roots, combining forms, prefixes, and suffixes should be presented with a list of words made up from these word parts. Emphasis is placed on the meanings of the word parts and their combinations into words rather than on the naming of the word parts. For example, *bi* and *ped* are pronounced and put on the chalkboard. Their meanings are given. When *biped* is put on the board, the students are asked by the teacher if they can state its meaning.

The terms presented for study should be those that students will hear in school, on television, or on radio, as well as those they will meet in their reading. The word parts should be presented in an interesting manner, and those that combine to form a number of words should be given. When students see that they are meeting these words in their reading, they will be greatly reinforced in their learning.

To provide continuous reinforcement, daily "nonthreatening" quizzes on the previous day's words may be given. Students should receive the results of such quizzes immediately, so that any faulty concepts may be quickly corrected. The number of words that are presented would depend on individual students.

The possibilities for vocabulary experiences in the classroom are unlimited. Teachers must have the prefixes, suffixes, and combining forms at their fingertips in order to take advantage of the opportunities that present themselves daily. Table 4-1 provides a list of some often used word parts and vocabulary words derived from these word parts.

Sample Vocabulary Activities Using Word Parts

Sample exercises that teachers should find helpful for stimulating interest in learning new words through word parts follow.

Directions: Master some useful combining forms. From the words on each line, figure out the meaning of the combining form or forms. Write the meaning. Think of other words with the same combining form or forms.

1. geo—geology, geography

---

2. anni, annu, enni—annual, biannual, biennial, anniversary

---

3. bio—biology, biography

---

4. scope—microscope, telescope

---

5. cent, centi—century, bicentennial, centennial

Table 4-1 Some Often Used Word Parts and Vocabulary Derived from Them.

Prefixes	Combining Forms	Vocabulary Words
a—without	anthropo—mankind or human	anthropology, apodal
ante—before	astro—star	astronomy, astrology
arch—main, chief	audio—hearing	audiology, auditory, audition, audible, archenemy
bi—two	auto—self	automatic, biped, binary
	archy—rule	autocracy
cata—down	bene—good	benefit, catalog
circum—around	bio—life	biology, biography, autobiography
hyper—excessive	chrono—time	chronological, hypertension
hypo—under	cosmo—world	microcosm, cosmology
in—not	gamy-marriage	monogamy, bigamy, polygamy
inter—between, among	geo—earth	interdepartmental, geology
mis—wrong, bad	gram—written or drawn	telegram, mistake
mono—one, alone	graph—written or drawn, instrument	telegraph, monarchy
post—after	logo—speak	theology, logical, catalog
re—backward, again	macro—large	macrocosm, macron
trans—across	micro—small	microscope, transatlantic
	mis—hate	misanthrope, misogamist
	poly—many	polyglot
	retro—backward	retrorocket
Suffixes	ped, pod—foot, feet	pseudopod, apodal, podiatrist
able—able to	scope—instrument for seeing	microscope
ible—able to	phobia—fear	monophobia
ology—the study of	theo—god	theocracy, theology
tion—the act of	pseudo—false	pseudoscience

6. auto—autograph, autobiography

---

7. graph—autograph, biography

---

8. ped, pod—pedestrian, pedal, peds, biped

---

9. dic, dict—dictation, diction, dictator

___

10. spect-spectacle, spectator, inspect

___

Directions: Choose a word from the word list that *best* fits the blank in each sentence. Use the word parts and their meanings to help you.

Word Parts and Meanings: grat = pleasing; in = not; con = with, together; ous = full of, having; jud, judi, judic = judge; pre = before

Word List: gratuity, ingrate, gratuitous, gratitude, congratulated, gratified, judicious, prejudiced

1. It _____ her to have her friend wear her gift.
2. _____ persons are usually not interested in looking at all the evidence.
3. Everyone _____ him when he made the final point that won the game.
4. The decision was a(n) _____ one, and it was bound to be hailed as a step forward in bettering employer-employee relations.
5. We couldn't believe our ears when we were told that our _____ was not enough.
6. As I am not used to receiving _____ services, I insisted on paying something.
7. The _____ that the parents felt toward the doctor who had saved their child's life could not be put into words.
8. What a(n) _____ he is to behave in such a manner after we did so much for him.

SUBJECT-MATTER GLOSSARIES

One way to encourage students to learn new words and to help them recognize how important vocabulary expansion is is to have them keep their own subject-matter glossaries. In each area, students should have a special part of their notebook just for vocabulary. The page should be divided in half. On the left side should be the vocabulary word presented in a sentence, and on the right side should be the meaning of the word with examples. At the beginning of each period, students should be asked to review the words in their glossary. Also, new words may be added to the glossary at that time. Of course, any time during the lesson, when it is applicable, new words could be added.

Table 4-2. Comparison of the Pronunciation of Three Words in Five Different Dictionaries.

Word	Webster's New Twentieth Century Dictionary	Webster's Third New International Dictionary	Random House Dictionary of the English Language	The American Heritage Dictionary of the English Language	Funk & Wagnalls Standard College Dictionary
1. coupon	çou'pon	'k(y)ü, pän	ko͞o'pon	ko͞o'pŏn	ko͞o'pon
2. courage	çour'age	'kər • ij	kûr'ij	kûr'ĭj	kûr'ij
3. covet	çov'ĕt	'kəvət	kuv'it	kŭv'ĭt	kuv'it

THE DICTIONARY AND VOCABULARY EXPANSION

Even though the dictionary is a necessary tool and one with which all students should be familiar, it should not be used as a crutch; that is, every time students meet a word whose meaning is unknown to them, they should first try to use their knowledge of combining forms and context clues to unlock the meaning. If these techniques do not help and the word is essential for understanding the passage, then they should look up the meaning.

Teachers should also help students to recognize that the purpose of dictionaries is not to prescribe or make rules about word meanings and pronunciations, but only to describe. Difficulties exist because persons in different parts of the country often pronounce words differently. For example, pronunciations in the East are often different from those in the South or Midwest. As a result, the pronunciation of a word in a dictionary may not agree with its pronunciation in a student's region.

Teachers should help their students to recognize that different dictionaries use different pronunciation keys and to be on the lookout for this. The pronunciation key is composed of words with diacritical marks. To know how to pronounce a word in a particular dictionary, students must familiarize themselves with the pronunciation key in that dictionary. For example, look at the way that five different dictionaries present a few similar words in Table 4-2.

If your students had no knowledge of the pronunciation key of the specific dictionary, they would have had difficulty in pronouncing the word. Pronunciation guides are generally found at the beginning of dictionaries. Many dictionaries also have a simplified pronunciation key at the bottom of every page.

FUN WITH WORDS IN CONTENT AREAS

Content-area teachers could use stimulating word activities to reinforce their students' vocabulary learning. These activities should feature either specialized words from a specific subject area or general words that the teacher feels are important for students to know. Teachers could also challenge their students to create their own enjoyable word activities that could be presented to the class.

Some samples of vocabulary activities follow, which can be adapted for any content area. These are merely springboards to stimulate teachers to create their own to suit the needs of their students.

Several ways to use a single word follow. Find the right word for each group of meanings.

1. Assault; the guns of a warship; a combination of apparatus for producing a single electrical effect.
2. A one-room dwelling; smallest unit capable of independent life.
3. Cultivation; expert care and training; cultivation of living material in prepared nutrient media.

Answers: 1. battery 2. cell 3. culture

Find the six words in the word rectangle that share a common meaning. Hint: one of the words means "force times distance."

P	U	L	S	A	T	E	D
T	R	A	V	A	I	L	O
I	K	B	W	O	R	K	D
R	T	O	I	L	E	E	O
E	G	R	I	N	D	R	R
D	R	U	D	G	E	R	Y

Answers: 1. travail 2. work (meaning given above) 3. toil 4. grind 5. drudgery 6. labor
Shared Meaning: activity involving effort or exertion

The following word scramble is based on words from Chapter 3 in your textbook. The meanings are your clues to arranging the letters in correct order. (This refers to a hypothetical assignment.)

1. xat — a charge laid by government upon persons or property to meet the public needs
2. eeessrrivg — decreasing in rate as the base increases
3. eeiautblq — dealing fairly and equally with all concerned
4. ylve — to collect by legal authority

Answers: 1. tax 2. regressive 3. equitable 4. levy

Here are five clues for five words that you have met this term. If you fill in the blanks correctly, you will have the word that means "the difference between the largest and smallest numbers in a set of numbers." To get the word, put the circled letters together.

1. ⊖ _ _ _ _ _ _ _ _   a four-sided plane figure whose opposite sides are parallel and whose angles are right angles

2. _ ⊖ _ _ _   a pair of numbers that expresses a comparison

3. _ ⊖ _ _ _ _ _ _   all whole numbers and their opposites

4. _ _ ⊖ _ _   two rays with a common endpoint

5. _ _ ⊖ _   the measure, in square units, of the region enclosed by a plane closed figure

Answers: 1. rectangle 2. ratio 3. integers 4. angle 5. area

Word: RANGE

Six pairs of words follow. Some pairs are the same or nearly the same in meaning, and some pairs are opposite in meaning. If a pair is opposite in meaning, write *O* in the blank. If a pair is similar in meaning, write *S* in the blank.

1. enervated   exhausted   _____
2. regressive   progressive   _____
3. tariff   tax   _____
4. obese   corpulent   _____
5. starved   satiated   _____
6. mean   average   _____

Answers: 1. S 2. O 3. S 4. S 5. O 6. S

A word and a number of phrases follow. Choose all those phrases that when combined with the word would be true statements. Support each true statement.

Energy

1. comes from coal.
2. comes from wood.
3. comes from oil.
4. comes from water.
5. comes from the moon.

6. comes from the sun.

7. comes from outer space in the form of cosmic rays.

8. comes from all rocks.

9. comes from the air.

There are convergent answers and not so obvious answers in this activity. The acceptability of each answer is left to the content-area teacher depending on the level of the students and the reasoning given for the answer.

Here are samples of other fun vocabulary exercises that are good brain teasers. Again, these examples can be adapted for any content area and students can be challenged to generate their own brain teasers.

1. Present students with a number of sentences that have a few blanks. Have them find a word for each sentence that fits all of its blanks. Tell them that the word is spelled the same but it may or may not be pronounced the same.

   Examples:

   a. Jane started to _____ on the _____ scheme she devised to outwit her opponent.

   b. Mr. Brown, who helped write our club's _____, has an excellent _____ because he never gets sick and can eat anything.

   c. Our teacher asked us to write an _____ of a very _____ article.

   Answers: a. elaborate b. constitution c. abstract

2. Present students with a number of word riddles to solve.

   Examples:

   a. I'm a member of the rodent family; add two letters to me, and I'll become angry.

   b. I'm a five-letter word meaning a single-celled organism; switch the first two consonants, and you will have someone who wanders.

   c. I'm extremely modest; take away one of my letters, and I'll become impolite.

   Answers: a. rat—irate b. monad—nomad c. prude—rude

GRAPHIC SUMMARY OF CHAPTER

Here is a graphic summary of Chapter 4. If you have read the chapter, this graphic illustration should help you remember its main points. Under or beside each heading, you might want to jot down some of the information you recall, as well as some of the key concepts in this chapter. This can act as a good review. You can then check your key concepts against those that follow the graphic summary.

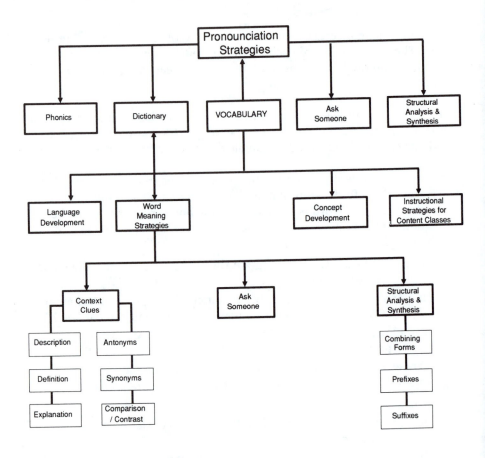

KEY CONCEPTS IN CHAPTER

- Knowledge of word meanings is essential for comprehension.
- Knowledge of word meanings does not guarantee comprehension.
- Vocabulary development should continue all though school and beyond.
- The factors that influence language development also influence concept development.
- A concept is a group of stimuli with common characteristics.
- Assimilation is a continuous process.
- Assimilation helps individuals integrate new, incoming stimuli into existing schemata or concepts.

- Accommodation takes place when a new schema or concept is developed or when an existing schema is changed.
- Equilibrium is the balance between assimilation and accommodation.
- Vocabulary and ability to categorize are necessary for concept development.
- Content-area teachers need to directly help students acquire the general and technical vocabulary they need to read their textbooks.
- Word recognition is a twofold process that includes both the identification of printed symbols in some way so that the word can be pronounced and the attachment of meaning to the word after it has been properly pronounced.
- Content-area teachers are responsible for helping their students expand their vocabulary in the content area.
- There are a number of pronunciation strategies.
- There are a number of word meaning strategies.
- The three levels of word meaning knowledge are the unknown, acquainted, and established.
- Vocabulary consciousness grows when students independently search out word meanings.
- To best understand a word, students must also be aware of its connotative meanings.
- The connotative meaning of a word includes all the emotional senses associated with the word.
- Context refers to the words surrounding a word that can shed light on the particular word's meaning.
- A context clue is the specific item of information that helps the reader figure out the meaning of a particular word.
- There are a number of context clues that help students figure out word meanings in connected text.
- Knowledge of word parts is a viable method to help students figure out word meanings and expand their vocabulary.
- Teachers should have a number of word parts and their meanings at their fingertips.
- The dictionary is an important tool.
- Dictionaries do not prescribe or make rules about word meanings and pronunciation; their purpose is only to describe.

SUGGESTIONS FOR THOUGHT QUESTIONS AND ACTIVITIES

1. Develop a lesson in a specific content area that creatively incorporates vocabulary expansion skills.

2. Construct a few creative vocabulary activities that you could use in a content-area course.

3. You have been put on a committee to develop a special vocabulary course at the secondary school. What suggestions would you make to the committee about this course?

4. Explain the relationship between vocabulary development and concept development.

5. Peruse some content-area textbooks. Select a number of sentences in which the writer uses good context clues to help students gain word meanings.

6. Choose a particular content area; then write all those combining forms that would relate to the content area and help students figure out word meanings.

SELECTED BIBLIOGRAPHY

BECK, ISABEL, and MARGARET MCKEOWN. "Conditions of Vocabulary Acquisition." In *Handbook of Reading Research*, II. Rebecca Barr, Michael L. Kamil, Peter Mosenthal, and P. David Pearson (eds.) New York: Longman, 1991, pp. 789–814.

CHASE, ANN C., and FREDERICK A. DUFFELMEYER. "VOCAB-LIT: Integrating Vocabulary Study and Literature Study." *Journal of Reading* 34 (November 1990): 188–193.

JENKINS, JOSEPH R., BARBARA MATLOCK, and TIMOTHY A. SLOCUM. "Two Approaches to Vocabulary Instruction: The Teaching of Individual Word Meanings and Practice in Deriving Word Meaning from Context." *Reading Research Quarterly* 24 (spring 1989): 215–235.

NAGY, WILLIAM, RICHARD C. ANDERSON, MARLENE SCHOMMER, JUDITH ANN SCOTT, and ANNE C. STALLMAN. "Morphological Families and Word Recognition." *Reading Research Quarterly* 24 (summer 1989): 262–279.

RUBIN, DOROTHY. *Vocabulary Expansion.* New York: Macmillan, 1991.

RUBIN, DOROTHY. *Gaining Word Power.* New York: Macmillan, 1986.

RUBIN, DOROTHY. *Vocabulary Expansion II.* New York: Macmillan, 1982.

WHITE, THOMAS G., MICHAEL A. POWER, and SHEIDA WHITE. "Morphological Analysis: Implications for Teaching and Understanding Vocabulary Growth." *Reading Research Quarterly* 24 (summer 1989): 283–304.

ITTZÉS, KATA. "Lexical Guessing in Isolation and Context." *Journal of Reading* 34 (February 1991):360–366.

5

Reading and Study Skills I

INTRODUCTION

How many times have you heard students make the following statements?

> "I spent all night studying, but I did very poorly on my exams."
> "I reread the chapter ten times, but I still don't understand it."
> "I reread the chapter about fifteen times, and I don't even remember what I read."

"I always listen to music when I study."
"I like to be relaxed when I study."
"I don't need to study."
"I don't know how to study."

And so it goes . . .

Many students do poorly in school because they have never learned how to study. Elementary school teachers usually do not spend time in helping children to acquire study skills because they themselves may lack the skills,[1] and because they feel that this is the job of high school teachers, and many high school teachers do not spend time in this area because they make the assumption that their students have already acquired the study skills they need. As a result, many students may go through the grades without ever having been helped to acquire study skills. This is a mistake. Students should be helped to acquire good study habits as soon as possible before they develop either poor study habits or erroneous concepts concerning studying. Students should be helped to learn that, with good study habits, they could spend less time in studying and learn more. The next chapter and this one are concerned with helping teachers gain the information and skills that are necessary to help students to become better learners.

KEY QUESTIONS

After you finish reading this chapter, you should be able to answer the following questions.

1. What does studying require, and what is the key to building good study habits?
2. What is SQ3R?
3. What is the role of concentration in studying?
4. How do attitudes influence studying?
5. What is skimming?
6. What is the role of skimming in studying?
7. What kinds of activities would help students be better direction followers?
8. What should students know about their textbooks?
9. What are the purposes of maps, charts, and graphs?
10. What are examples of some reference books that can help students?
11. What should students know about the dictionary?
12. How can teachers help students organize their time better?

[1]Eunice N. Askov et al., "Study Skill Mastery Among Elementary Teachers," *The Reading Teacher* 30 (February 1977): 485–488.

KEY TERMS IN CHAPTER

You should pay special attention to the following key terms:

concentration   SQ3R
overlearning   study procedures
recite or recall   survey
skimming

CONTENT-AREA TEACHERS AND STUDY SKILLS

Susan is a tenth grader who, up to now, has done exceptionally well in school even though she has spent very little time studying. This year things are not going as well. Her teachers are requiring her to do a vast amount of independent work that requires a great deal of out-of-class reading and writing. Susan is just not prepared to do this kind of independent work. Although she is putting in a lot of time studying this school year, she is not learning. Susan is frustrated because she has been able to "sail through her courses" before by just attending class every day and doing the few out-of-class assignments that were not very time-consuming and that were clearly spelled out for her.

Although Susan is putting more time than she ever has before into studying, she is not learning because she has poor study habits. With good study habits, Susan could spend *less* time in studying and learn more. Should Susan's teachers have to help Susan and others like her to acquire study skills? If so, what is the role of the content-area teacher in providing study skills help for those students who need it?

Throughout this book it is stressed that the content-area teacher's main goal is in having students master the content material of the course. As a means of doing this effectively, a directed reading approach to teaching content has been advocated. This approach integrates the skills that students need to acquire the content with the subject matter of the course to achieve the required content. Since study skills techniques are essential in helping students learn and retain information, these must also be considered part of the directed reading approach to teaching content, and teachers need to provide help in this area for those students who need it. Teachers must directly teach any needed study skill using content material.

The Integration of Study Skills in Content-Area Classes

In Chapter 1 two guides were presented for using a directed reading approach in content-area courses; one guide was for preparing students to read assignments, and the other was for teaching a lesson. Both guides provide interest, direction, and organization for what is to be read or taught. An essential part of both guides is the step that gives special strategies for acquiring the content material.

The strategies include *insights into the organization of the material* and *provide the tactics that the students should use to gain the most from what is being taught or read.* The category of *tactics* would include study skills techniques, which are drawn from learning theory studies.

The study skills tactics that teachers choose to present to their students would depend on the uniqueness of the content-area material being presented and teacher purposes, as well as on the ability levels of the students in the class. Obviously, the amount and type of information and help students will need will vary from class to class; some teachers will need to spend more time in some areas than in others. The strategies, which are integrated with the content material being taught, should not only help students master content material, but they should also help students become more independent learners.

Content-area teachers at the beginning of the term can discuss with students the unique requirements of the course and the kinds of assignments they will have. Teachers can then also discuss with students the skills they will need to do the specific course's assignments. If the course is one that requires a great amount of reading and studying, the teacher may want to give the students some general information on building good study habits. By doing this at the beginning of the term, students will know what is expected of them, and it will help students plan their study schedule. It will also help students realize that the teacher is concerned about their getting the content material and that he or she is *serious* in this intent. It will, at the same time help to set an atmosphere in the classroom that is conducive to learning; genuine enthusiasm, interest in subject, and a desire to help students will provide a good affective environment.

Giving students general information about good study habits is only the first step. Throughout the term, the teacher should present whatever study skills techniques he or she feels students will need to learn certain content-area concepts being taught or studied at the time. The sections that follow will present the kind of study skills and learning information that teachers need to help their students gain content-area material, as well as to help students become independent learners.

BUILDING GOOD STUDY HABITS

Although there is no simple formula of study that will apply to all students, educational psychologists have found that some procedures help all students. The key is in building good habits, devising a system that works for the individual student, and keeping at it.

A person cannot relax and study at the same time. Studying requires a certain amount of tension, concentration, and effort in a specific direction. Of course, the amount of tension varies with different individuals. The point is that studying is hard work, and students who are not prepared to make a proper effort are wasting their time.

As discussed in an earlier section, teachers will probably want to share some of the information on building good study habits with students at the beginning of the term. The amount of information given will, of course, depend on the individual differences of the student. Teachers should recognize, however, that even highly able students may not have good study habits. Some teachers may present their students with a questionnaire such as the one on page 139 to gain information about their students' study habits. It is important that students know the purposes of the questionnaire and that they cooperate; otherwise, they will answer in the expected direction; that is, they will answer in the way they think the teachers want them to. Some mathematics teachers may have students prepare charts showing the amount of time they study. (See "Charts and Graphs" in this chapter.) Some teachers may wish to present students with a list of helpful hints or tips about studying, and some may want to add information about studying on the study guide, whereas others may wish to discuss these in class. Whatever technique the teacher chooses, it should be related to the course content and in particular to what is being studied at the time.

Special Note:
Teachers should be careful not to intimidate students concerning study time requirements. They should also be reasonable in time expectation based on course and credit load and take into account the nature of the course. Teachers should recognize that students have other courses and responsibilities besides their particular course.

Steps in Building Good Study Habits

1. The first step in building good study habits is to determine *when to study*. Some students study only just before an announced test. Some may even stay up until all hours and cram. All of us have probably done this once or twice. However, if this is a student's normal way of doing things, he or she will not do well in school. Cramming does not bring about sustained learning. It can be justified only as a last resort. To be a good student, the student must plan his or her study time and spread it out over a period of time. Students must be helped to realize that a regular plan will prevent confusion and help them to retain what they are studying. Students, even in the elementary grades, should be helped to plan an overall time schedule in which they allow for social and physical activities. It is to be hoped that their time schedule also allows for some recreational reading. (See Chapter 11 entitled "Reading for Appreciation: Gaining a Lifelong Habit.") Stu-

dents must recognize that a rhythm of activities is important. It does not matter whether they study in the evening, before or after dinner, or right after class during free periods. The important thing is for the student to follow a schedule and spread out the studying over the week.

2. The second step in building good study habits is to determine *where to study*. Some students are able to study well in a school or public library, but there are others who cannot. Most school students study at home. Regardless of where the student studies, he or she should choose a place that is comfortable and convenient, has enough light, and is *free from distractions*. Consistency is important.

    To help students to establish a comfortable, convenient, and suitable place for study at home, the teacher and the students can design such a place at school in the classroom. A special area in the classroom can be set aside as a study area. The area should be one that is as free from distractions as possible, comfortable, and well-lighted. Students should be free to go to this area whenever they wish to study. If a student is in this area, other students should recognize this as "off bounds"; that is, other students should respect the student's desire to study and not interrupt or bother the student.

    Teachers must recognize that there are some students in class who may not have a place at home to study. There may be many children in the house and not enough rooms, so that the only place to study may be in the kitchen. This place, however, is not very good because it usually has too many distractions. Teachers should try to be aware of the home situations of their students and try to help them as much as possible without embarrassing them. One thing the teacher could do would be to discuss the possibility of the student's studying at the library or at a friend's house. If these are not feasible and if the student does not have to ride a school bus to school, the teacher might make some arrangements whereby the student can study in the school. A teacher must be sensitive to the fact that students who do not have a place to do homework or study at home are actually being penalized twice—once because they do not have a place to study and twice because they will probably be penalized for not doing the homework, and they will also probably not do well in school.

3. The third step in building good study habits is to determine the *amount of time* to spend in studying. Teachers must help students to recognize that the amount of time they spend in studying will depend on the subject and how well they know it. It is unrealistic for teachers to set a hard-and-fast rule about the amount of time students should study in a specific subject because the amount of time will vary. In some subjects a student may need to spend a lot of time studying because he or she is weak in that area whereas in others the student

may have to spend only a short time studying. Teachers should help students to understand the concept of *overlearning* because some students feel that if they know something, they do not have to study it at all. In order to overlearn something, students must recognize that they must practice it even after they feel they know it. *Overlearning* is not bad like *overbaking* the roast. It helps people retain information over a period of time. Overlearning happens when individuals continue practice even after they think they have learned the material.

Teachers can learn about their students' study habits by asking them to fill out the following short questionnaire:

Study Habits Questionnaire

Name_____

Grade_____

Subject_____

This questionnaire will not be used to determine your grade in this course. Please try to answer the questions as honestly as you can. If you do not want to give your name, you do not have to do so.

1. How much time do you usually spend a week in studying?
2. How much time do you expect to spend in studying this course?
3. Where do you study?
4. Do you have the radio on when you study?
5. Do you have the television on when you study?
6. Would you like help in gaining study skills?
7. Do you use any special technique when you study? If so, please explain.

Teachers are again cautioned that many students may answer in the expected direction, that is, provide answers that they feel their teachers want them to provide. Therefore, teachers must emphasize strongly to their students the purpose of the questionnaire.

Organizing a Weekly Schedule

Students today have so many activities that vie for their time and attention that many may feel overburdened. Teachers can help students recognize hat good students are generally good planners, who make effective use of their time. They set short- and long-term goals for themselves and attempt to accomplish these goals by organizing their time realistically. The term *realistically* is important. There are only so many waking hours in a day. Teachers can brainstorm with students the kinds of items they should include in their weekly plan. Here are some items that teachers should help students recognize are important to include if their schedule is to be a realistic one:

1. Sleep—It is not possible to function well over an extended period of time without adequate sleep, which is about seven or eight hours.
2. Meal Time—Students cannot do well without adequate nourishment.
3. Class time—Class attendance is imperative.
4. Employment—Even though studies show that employment does interfere with students doing well in school, there are a number of teenagers who hold part-time jobs. Employment does cut heavily into time allotments for social activities and studying time.
5. Study time—Students must include adequate time to study all their subjects. Special papers or projects that are due must also be included.
6. Leisure time—Everyone needs time to just mull things over, listen to music, watch a TV show, go to a movie, read a newspaper, book, or magazine, go out with friends, or do whatever else makes that individual relax.
7. Physical activity time—Students need to allow time for daily physical exercise. Of course, if a student is in a special athletic program, he or she must include playing and training time, as well as traveling time to games.
8. Commuting time—Travel time to and from school must be included.
9. Miscellaneous things—Students must also include many mundane things such as taking care of their personal needs, shopping for clothing, going to the dentist, and so forth.

Obviously, students' schedules will vary from week to week based on their individual responsibilities.

Teachers need to help students recognize the importance of organizing a weekly schedule. However, students must also realize that the schedule is merely a tool and as such should be used as a means to an end and not an end in itself. In other words, students must learn to follow their schedule but to be flexible.

Teachers could have students fill out a weekly schedule and report on how effective it is. Many students may find that they probably have more time than they think they have.

STUDENT ACHIEVEMENT AND HOMEWORK

Studies show that the investment of significant amounts of time in homework is related to students' success in school. "Extra studying helps children at all levels of ability and homework can boost the time spent studying."[2] The National Assessment of Educational Progress in a summary of findings states that "homework gives students experience in following directions, making judgments, working through problems alone, and developing responsibility and self-discipline."[3] Unfortunately, teachers are not requiring students to do much homework: "the startling fact remains, however, that more than two-thirds (71 percent) of the high-school seniors typically do one hour or less of homework each day."[4]

Earlier in this chapter, we discussed the importance of teachers recognizing that students will spend different amounts of time on studying based on their backgrounds and therefore absolutes cannot be made concerning studying time for students. However, teachers must make sure they do indeed give students meaningful and challenging homework based on their ability levels and show students they feel that the homework is important by going over it in class.

The homework should supplement the work students are doing in class and provide the added practice students need to overlearn the material. Teachers should prepare students for the homework and provide direct help based on the needs of their students (see "A Guide for Using a Directed Reading Approach in Reading Content Material" in Chapter 1).

HOW TO STUDY

After teachers have discussed with their students the need to attain positive attitudes toward their learning tasks and have helped them to recognize that they must exert effort to study, find a suitable place to study, and spend time in studying, teachers must still help them learn *how to study*. There are a number of study techniques; however, SQ3R[5] will be presented rather than some of the others because it is a widely used study technique that has proved helpful to many students.

One procedure the teacher can use is to give students a sheet listing the five steps of SQ3R. The five steps should be discussed and then practiced on an actual assignment. Students can be told that they will be given a

[2]Ina V.S. Mullis, Eugene H. Owen, and Gary W. Phillips, *America's Challenge: Accelerating Academic Achievement*, The National Assessment of Educational Progress, (Princeton, N.J.: Educational Testing Service, 1990) p. 74.
[3]Ibid.
[4]Ibid.
[5]Adapted from Francis P. Robinson, *Effective Study*, 4th ed. (New York: Harper & Row, 1970).

mock test (one that does not count) after the activity to see how well they did.

SQ3R

Here are the five steps in the SQ3R technique:

1. *Survey*—First get an *overall* sense of your learning task before proceeding to details. Skim the whole assignment to obtain idea(s) about the material and how it is organized.
2. *Question*—Check section headings, and change these to questions to set your purposes for reading.
3. *Read*—Read to answer the questions that you have formulated for yourself. While reading, notice how the paragraphs are organized because this will help you to remember the answer.
4. *Recite*—*This step is very important.* Without referring to your book, try to answer the questions that you formulated for yourself. (Writing down key ideas will provide necessary notes for future review.)
5. *Review*—Take a few moments to review the major headings and sub-headings of what you have just finished studying before starting to study a new part or assignment. (How well you are able to combine or incorporate the new learning with your previous learning will determine how well you will remember the new material.)

Teachers should make sure students understand that they can survey a reading assignment to determine its organization and to obtain some ideas about it, but they cannot study unfamiliar material by skimming or reading rapidly. Teachers should emphasize to their students that the key factor in remembering information is recall or recitation and not the immediate rereading of their assignment. The time students spend answering the questions that they have formulated is crucial in learning. (See "Note-taking and Study Guide" on page 174 in Chapter 6 for a study technique that does not use questions to set purposes for reading.)

Here is an example of how teachers can help their students to adapt the SQ3R technique to suit their personal needs. The following should be done in class as a class activity.

Example: Assignment—Reading a chapter in a textbook

STEP 1:   Students quickly look over the entire chapter to get an overview of the whole chapter and to see the organization and relationships. In doing this it's a good idea for students to read quickly the first sentence of each paragraph because textbook writers generally put the topic sentence at the beginning of the paragraph. (Students should notice section headings and author's margin notes.)

STEP 2:   Students should choose a part of the chapter to study. (The

FIGURE 5-1. Linus has a lot to learn about studying.

amount of material they choose will depend on their concentration ability and their prior knowledge in the area. [See section on concentration in this chapter.])

STEP 3: Students should look over the first part of the chapter that they have chosen to study and formulate questions on it. (Most textbooks have section headings that are very helpful for formulating questions.)

STEP 4: Students should read the material to answer their questions. While reading, they should keep in mind the way that the author has organized his or her details.

STEP 5: Students should attempt to answer questions formulated before reading.

STEP 6: Students should go on to the next section of their chapter and follow the same steps. After they have finished their whole assignment, they should review or go over *all* that they have studied. (When they review, they should go back to the beginning of the chapter, look at each section heading, and try to recall the main idea of each paragraph in the section.)

(See "Adapting SQ3R in Science Reading" in Chapter 8.)

Activities Some sample activities teachers can give students to practice in using the SQ3R technique follow.

1. Choose a selection from their textbook that your students have not read before, and have them do the following:
   a. Survey the selection to determine what it's about.
   b. Use the given six questions to set purposes for reading.
   c. Read the selection carefully.
   d. Without looking back at the selection, try to answer the questions. (Prepare six questions that can be used to set purposes for reading.)
2. Choose a selection from their textbook that your students have not read before, and have them formulate questions that could help them in studying.

Special Note:
The selections that teachers choose for their students should be those that the teachers would normally assign for reading. The intent is to master content material using study techniques to facilitate the mastery of the content.

CONCENTRATION

Teachers need to help students to recognize that even though they are acquiring some good study habits, they may still have difficulty studying because they can not *concentrate*. Concentration is necessary not only for studying but also for listening in class. Concentration is sustained attention. If students are not feeling well, if they are hungry or tired, if they are in a room that is too hot or cold, if their chair is uncomfortable, if the lighting is poor or if there is a glare, if there are visual or auditory distractions, they will not be able to concentrate.

Skill in concentration can be developed, and teachers should plan to have their students spend time in this area, which is essential for both reading and listening skills. Concentration demands a mental set or attitude, a determination that learners will block everything out except what they are reading or listening to. For example, how many times have you looked up a phone number in the yellow pages of your telephone directory and forgotten the number almost immediately? How many times have you had to look up the *same* number that you had dialed a number of times? Probably very often. The reason for your not remembering is that you did not *concentrate*. In order to remember information, you must concentrate. Concentration demands active involvement; it is hard work. Teachers must, therefore, help students to recognize that it is a contradiction to say that they will concentrate and relax at the same time. Concentration demands wide-awake and alert individuals. It also demands persons who have a positive frame of mind toward their work. Teachers must have a good affective environment in their classrooms and be encouraging because the student's attitude or mental set toward what he or she is doing will greatly influence how well he or she will do. Obviously, if students are not interested in the lecture or reading assignment, they will not be able to concentrate. Teachers should, therefore, try to make the lectures and assignments as interesting as possible.

Teachers should also help their students recognize that they cannot listen to the radio or watch television and study at the same time; the combination of these activities tends to overload the brain's central processing capacity; that is, it interferes with the individual's ability to take in information.

Researchers have found that human central processing resources are limited and that extra demands on attention, such as watching TV or having the television on when students are involved in tasks that require con-

FIGURE 5-2.   These students are concentrating on what they are doing.

centration such as reading or studying, may interfere with their getting the most from their primary task.[6] This certainly makes sense; therefore it should not be surprising that researchers have found that background TV has adverse effects on activities such as reading comprehension, complex problem solving, and creative thinking.[7]

It is, of course, necessary to help students understand that paying attention does not guarantee that they will comprehend what they have read or heard, but it is an important first step. Without concentration, there is no hope of understanding the information.

FOLLOWING DIRECTIONS

Being able to follow directions is an important skill that we use all our lives. Scarcely a day goes by without the need to obey directions. Cooking, baking, taking medication, driving, traveling, repairing, building, planning,

---

[6]G. Blake Armstrong and Bradley S. Greenberg, "Background Television as an Inhibitor of Cognitivce Processing," *Human Communication Research* 16 (Spring 1990): 375.
[7]Ibid.

taking examinations, doing assignments, filling out applications, and a hundred other common activities require the ability to follow directions.

Following directions is especially important in content-area courses because, in practically all of these courses, students are required to do tasks that include following directions, for example, taking examinations, doing assignments, reading maps, reading charts, reading diagrams, and so on. Students who have difficulty following directions are at a disadvantage in any course. It may be that a student does poorly on an examination because he or she has misinterpreted the questions and not because this student does not know the content material. The reason for the misinterpretation may be because the student has read the question too quickly and, in doing so, has left out a key word. This is possible because good readers usually do not read every word; however, in reading directions, students must read every word. The strategy for reading discourse material is different from that of reading directions for an examination or for any other purpose. (See "Test Taking" in the next chapter.) And there is hardly anything more disconcerting for a student than to realize that he or she knew the answer to the question but had misinterpreted the question; the realization has made many a student want to "kick himself or herself."

Teachers can help students be better direction followers. At the beginning of the term teachers can present the students with the following list of pointers and the mock test at the end of the list.

1. Read the directions *carefully.* Do *not* skim directions. Do not take anything for granted and, therefore, skip reading a part of the directions.
2. If you do not understand any directions, do not hesitate to ask your teacher and/or another student.
3. Concentrate! People who follow directions well have the ability to concentrate well.
4. Follow the directions that *are* given, not the ones that you think ought to be given.
5. Reread directions if you need to, and refer to them as you follow them.
6. Remember that some directions should be followed step by step.
7. Practice following directions. Try this activity, which will give you experience in following directions.

Directions: Read carefully the entire list of directions that follows before doing anything. You have four minutes to complete this activity.

1. Put your name in the upper right-hand corner of this paper.
2. Put your address under your name.
3. Put your telephone number in the upper left-hand corner of this paper.

4. Add 9370 and 5641.
5. Subtract 453 from 671.
6. Raise your hand and say, "I'm the first."
7. Draw two squares, one triangle, and three circles.
8. Write the opposite of *hot*.
9. Stand up and stamp your foot.
10. Give three meanings for *spring*.
11. Write the numbers from one to ten backward.
12. Write the even numbers from two to twenty.
13. Write the odd numbers from one to twenty-one.
14. Write seven words that rhyme with *fat*.
15. Call out, "I have followed directions."
16. If you have read the directions carefully, you should have done nothing until now. Do only directions 1 and 2.

Answer: The directions stated that you should read the entire list of directions carefully *before doing anything*. You should have done only directions 1 and 2. When you take timed tests, you usually do *not* read the directions as carefully as you should.

The preceding mock test usually dramatizes the need for students to read directions *carefully* before taking any test; it helps raise students' consciousness level for the need to do this. If teachers discover that their students are misinterpreting their test questions, they should check to see whether their test questions are ambiguously stated. If the problem is not the test question but the misinterpretation of the test question, teachers should give students practice in interpreting different kinds of questions. (See "Test Taking" in the next chapter.)

In those content-area courses that require map reading and the interpretation of charts, diagrams, and various tables, teachers should not assume that their students can automatically do these tasks; teachers should give students direct instruction in reading map legends and in interpreting various symbols, as well as in reading charts, diagrams, and tables. (See sections later on in this chapter for more information on these areas.)

In science classes that include laboratory experiments, direction-following ability is especially essential. Teachers at the beginning of the term should set up simple exercises or experiments as a means of teaching students the importance of following directions to attain desired results. To dramatize this fact, the teacher can show, for example, how the improper mixing of certain chemicals could result in disaster. (This would, of course, be done under very controlled conditions by the teacher.) Teachers should also impress students with the importance of following directions exactly in replication experiments to reproduce results.

In this computer age, students who have difficulty in following directions will be at a disadvantage in working with computers. If students can't follow directions, they will find it difficult to get on or off the computer or to call back their own program on the computer. In computer science classes or any other classes that use computers, teachers could demonstrate this at the beginning of the term.

Also, at the beginning of the term, it would be a good idea for content-area teachers to supply students with sample study guides, assignments, and tests. Teachers should have students read these, and then the teacher should go over the instructions with the students. A discussion should follow on the importance of following directions, and the teacher should clear up any confusions that students may have concerning the directions.

SKIMMING

Setting purposes for reading is a crucial factor in reading. Students need to learn that they read for different purposes. If they are reading for pleasure, they may either read quickly or slowly based on the way they feel. If they are studying or reading information that is new to them, they will probably read very slowly. If, however, they are looking up a telephone number, a name, a date, or looking over a paragraph for its topic, they will read much more rapidly. Reading rapidly to find or locate information is called *skimming*. All skimming involves fast reading; however, there are different kinds of skimming. Skimming for a number, a date, or name can usually be done much more quickly than skimming for the topic of a paragraph or to answer specific questions. (Some persons call the most rapid reading *scanning* and the less rapid reading *skimming*.) Teachers should help students recognize that they read rapidly to locate some specific information, but that once they have located what they want, they may read the surrounding information more slowly.

Teachers should also make sure that students do not confuse skimming with studying. Although skimming is used as part of the SQ3R technique when students survey a passage, skimming material is not the same as studying. Studying requires much slower and more concentrated reading. Skimming is an important skill because it is used so often throughout one's life, and it is many times the only way to get a job done in a reasonable amount of time.

Teachers can help students to recognize that skimming is an important skill by having them read the following list and then checking those items that apply to them. Teachers can ask students also to supply more items to add to the list.

_____ 1. Skim newspaper headlines.

_____ 2. Skim the movie ads.

_____ 3. Skim tape or record catalogs.

_____ 4. Skim the yellow pages of the phone book for some help.

_____ 5. Skim the television guide to find a particular show.

_____ 6. Skim the dictionary to find the syllabication, spelling, meaning, or history of a word.

_____ 7. Skim the want ads.

_____ 8. Skim the clothing ads.

_____ 9. Skim the index of a textbook.

_____ 10. Skim the telephone directory.

Teachers should impress upon students that they can skim material most rapidly when it is clearly organized according to some logical system: alphabetically in telephone books and dictionaries, topically in catalogs, and chronologically or numerically or geographically in charts, tables, and schedules.

Special Note:
Obviously, students must know the alphabet in order to use the many sources of information that are arranged in alphabetical order.

Example:
Very quickly skim Table 5-1 (an excerpt from a finance table) to find the finance charge for $423.00 and the monthly payments.

Table 5-1. Finance Table

If Cash Price (Including any sales tax and shipping charge), less Down Payment If Any Amounts to	We Shall Add for FINANCE CHARGE	Amount Payable Monthly Is
$100.00 to $110.00	$ 15.30	$ 5.00
110.01 to 120.00	19.10	5.00
120.01 to 130.00	23.20	5.00
130.01 to 140.00	27.70	5.00
140.01 to 150.00	32.65	5.00
150.01 to 160.00	38.00	5.00
160.01 to 170.00	38.40	5.50
170.01 to 180.00	41.90	5.75

Table 5-1. Finance Table (Continued)

If Cash Price (Including any sales tax and shipping charge), less Down Payment If Any Amounts to	We Shall Add for FINANCE CHARGE	Amount Payable Monthly Is
180.01 to 190.00	43.20	6.25
190.01 to 200.00	45.60	6.50
200.01 to 210.00	49.30	6.75
210.01 to 220.00	50.40	7.25
220.01 to 230.00	52.80	7.50
230.01 to 240.00	55.20	8.00
240.01 to 250.00	57.60	8.25
250.01 to 260.00	60.00	8.50
260.01 to 270.00	62.40	9.00
270.01 to 280.00	64.80	9.25
280.01 to 290.00	67.20	9.75
290.01 to 300.00	69.60	10.00
300.01 to 310.00	72.00	10.25
310.01 to 320.00	76.45	10.50
320.01 to 330.00	81.05	10.50
330.01 to 340.00	85.80	10.75
340.01 to 350.00	90.65	10.75
350.01 to 360.00	95.65	11.00
360.01 to 370.00	100.80	11.00
370.01 to 380.00	106.05	11.00
380.01 to 390.00	111.45	11.25
390.01 to 400.00	114.40	11.50
400.01 to 410.00	120.00	11.50
410.01 to 420.00	125.70	11.75
420.01 to 430.00	128.20	12.00
430.01 to 440.00	134.70	12.00
440.01 to 450.00	140.80	12.00
450.01 to 460.00	144.00	12.50
460.01 to 470.00	150.25	12.50
470.01 to 480.00	156.65	12.50
480.01 to 490.00	160.00	12.75
490.01 to 500.00	169.85	12.75
500.01 to 510.00	176.65	12.75
510.01 to 520.00	183.60	12.75
520.01 to 530.00	187.20	13.00
530.01 to 540.00	197.85	13.00
540.01 to 550.00	201.60	13.25

Answer: $128.20; $12.00

Students need to learn that they skim less rapidly when they are look-ing for more than just a word or group of words. Looking for the topic of a paragraph or for specific details abut the topic of a paragraph requires rela-tively slow skimming. (Remember: The topic of a paragraph is not its main idea. See "Main Idea" in Chapter 3.)

Example:

Skim this paragraph and state its topic:

Turn on the TV and almost immediately you are greeted with the omnipresent commercial. At times it is difficult to tell the commercial from the program. However, there is one tell-tale sign—the volume. Have you noticed how it is significantly louder for the commercial?

Answer: The omnipresent commercial on TV

Students need to learn that when they skim, they pass over many words and phrases. In many informative passages the message of each par-agraph will reveal itself even if the minor words and phrases are left out. Following is a paragraph that has a number of words and phrases omitted. Quickly skim the skeleton message and then, without looking back, an-swer the true/false questions on it. Compare your answers with those given.

Example:

_____ kids _____ sissies _____ nature; I was _____ sissy

_____ conviction. I _____ _____ intelligent, rational child,

_____ _____ see _____ myself _____ not _____ was fighting

sinful; _____ _____ _____ dangerous.

True/False Questions:

_____ 1. The child was unhappy about being a sissy.

_____ 2. The child had a poor opinion of himself.

_____ 3. The child consciously became a sissy.

_____ 4. The child disapproved of fighting.

_____ 5. The child purposefully avoided fighting.

Answers: 1. F 2. F 3. T 4. T 5. T

Here are samples of some other practices that teachers can give students. Very quickly skim this list of names to supply the requested information.

Sample Telephone Directory:

Smith D.	Old Haven Rd.	372-4401
Smith Davis	Broad St.	420-7713
Smith Donald	John St.	651-7801
Smith Douglas	5 Connor Rd.	491-3270
Smith Dudley	24 Stuart Rd.	659-4590
Smith E.	113 13th St.	862-7321
Smith E.	14 Nassau St.	937-6542
Smith E.	91 Arlington Rd.	420-5143
Smith E.	27 Roger Lane	862-9450
Smith E. P.	Cherry St.	659-7700
Smith Earl lawyer	1012 Terry St.	491-4420
Smith Edgar	987 Delaware Ave.	651-3157
Smith Edw. L.	56 Lover's Lane	372-7011
Smith Edw. M.	Skillman Rd.	428-1276
Smith F. Rev.	9 Morris Ave.	937-5520
Smith Frank	25 Mead St.	651-4376
Smith Fred	457 Province Rd.	659-7701
Smith G.	11 Jackson St.	372-1113
Smith G. R.	101 Bank St.	372-5012
Smith George M.D.	Merry Lane	862-9901
Smith Gerald	Clark Rd.	651-4403
Smith Harry	Laurel St.	491-3598
Smith Henry	Old York Rd.	420-7011

Questions:

1. What is the first name of the Smith living on Delaware Ave.?
   _____

2. What is the phone number of Dr. Smith? _____

3. What is the address of Rev. Smith? _____

4. What is the first name of the Smith who is a lawyer? _____

5. What is the phone number of Harry Smith? _____

6. Where does Edward L. Smith live? _____

7. What is the phone number of Dudley Smith? _____

8. What is the first name of the Smith with the phone number 651-4403?
   _____

9. What is the address of the Smith with the phone number 862-9450?
   _____

10. What is the first name of the Smith with the phone number 420-7011?
   _____

Skim the train schedule (Figure 5-3, on page 154) to answer the questions.

Questions:

1. What is the name of the train that leaves Washington D.C., at 1:05 P.M. daily? _____

2. How many miles is it from Washington to New Haven? _____

3. What is the number of the connecting train that leaves Providence, R.I., at 2:50 P.M. Monday through Friday?_____

4. What time will you get into New York if you leave Washington at 9:05 A.M.?_____

5. What time will you get into New London if you leave New York, N.Y. (Penn. Sta.), at 11:10 A.M.?_____

(See the next section, "Knowing the Textbook," for more skimming activities.)

KNOWING THE TEXTBOOK

Helping students to know about the various parts of their textbooks is an important studying skill that can save students valuable time and effort. Here are some things that teachers should have students do at the beginning of the term after they have acquired their textbooks.

1. *Survey the textbook.* This helps students to see how the author presents the material. Students should notice whether the author presents topic headings in bold print or in the margins. Students should also notice if there are diagrams, charts, cartoons, pictures, and so on.
2. *Read the preface.* The preface or foreword, which is at the beginning of the book, is the author's explanation of the book. It presents the author's purpose and plan in writing the book. Here the author usually describes the organization of the book and explains how the book either is different from others in the field or is a further contribution to the field of knowledge.
3. *Read the chapter headings.* The table of contents will give students a

Kilometers	Miles	Train Number →	180	168	170	172	174	150		176	142	178	162	60	66
		Train Name →	The Pilgrim	The Benjamin Franklin	The Minute Man	The Patriot	The Colonial	The Flying Yankee		The Senator	The Bankers	The Merchants Limited	The Bostonian	The Montrealer	The Night Owl
		Frequency of Operation →	Daily	Daily	Daily	Daily	Daily	Daily		Daily	Daily	Daily	Fr and Su Only	Daily	Daily
		Type of Service →	⊠	Amclub	Amclub	Amclub	Amclub	⊠		Amclub	Amclub	Amclub	⊠	✕	Sleeping Car
0	0	WASHINGTON, DC .... Dp			7 05 a	9 05 a	11 05 a	12 00 n		1 05 p	2 05 p	3 10 p	4 05 p	6 05 p	10 30 p
14	9	Beltway Station (Lanham), MD			R 7 18 a	R 9 18 a	(21)11 18 a	|		(21)1 18 p	R 2 18 p	|	R 4 18 p	R 6 18 p	R10 43 p
64	40	BALTIMORE (Penn. Sta.)			7 49 a	9 45 a	11 46 a	12 38 p		1 49 p	2 49 p	3 50 p	4 44 p	6 49 p	11 15 p
113	70	Aberdeen, MD ● ☆			8 18 a	|	|	|		|	|	|	|	|	|
174	108	WILMINGTON, DE			8 49 a	10 45 a	12 49 p	1 18 p		2 49 p	3 49 p	4 51 p	5 46 p	7 49 p	12 25 a
216	134	PHILADELPHIA, PA (30th St. Sta.)		AMFLEET SERVICE 7 15 a	AMFLEET SERVICE 9 15 a	AMFLEET SERVICE 11 15 a	AMFLEET SERVICE 1 17 p	METROLINER 1 42 p	2 18 p	3 15 p	4 15 p	5 18 p	6 16 p	8 15 p	AMFLEET COACHES 12 55 a
222	138	North Philadelphia, PA		7 24 a	|	|	|	↓	2 25 p	|	4 25 p	|	|	|	1 10 a
267	166	TRENTON, NJ		(7 52 a) Su Only	9 52 a	11 51 a	1 52 p	↓	2 53 p	3 52 p	4 52 p	5 51 p	6 53 p	8 55 p	1 39 a
282	175	Princeton Jct. (Princeton) ⊕		↓	↓	↓	↓	↓	↓	↓	↓	↓	↓	↓	↓
307	191	New Brunswick		↓	↓	↓	↓	↓	↓	↓	↓	↓	↓	↓	↓
320	199	Metropark (Iselin)		↓	↓	↓	↓	↓	↓	↓	↓	↓	↓	↓	↓
344	214	NEWARK, NJ (Penn. Sta.)		8 36 a	10 40 a	12 36 p	2 40 p	↓	3 40 p	4 40 p	5 40 p	6 32 p	7 40 p	9 40 p	2 27 a
360	224	NEW YORK, NY (Penn. Sta.) .... Ar		8 50 a	10 55 a	12 51 p	2 55 p	3 01 p	3 55 p	4 55 p	5 55 p	6 47 p	7 55 p	9 55 p	2 45 a
360	224	NEW YORK, NY (Penn. Sta.) .... Dp	7 10 a	9 10 a	11 10 a	1 05 p	3 10 p	4 10 p		5 10 p	6 15 p	7 00 p	8 05 p	10 10 p	3 10 a
404	251	Rye, NY	(1)7 48 a	(1)9 48 a	|	(1)1 43 p	|	↓		↓	|	|	|	(1)10 48 p	(1)3 50 a
418	260	Stamford, CT	(1)8 00 a	(1)10 00 a	(1)12 00 n	(1)1 55 p	(1)4 00 p	↓		↓	(1)7 03 p	(1)7 46 p	(1)8 55 p	(1)11 00 p	(1)4 03 a
454	282	Bridgeport	(1)8 25 a	(1)10 25 a	(1)12 25 p	(1)2 20 p	(1)4 25 p	↓		↓	(1)7 28 p	(1)8 10 p	(1)9 20 p	(1)11 25 p	(1)4 28 a
481	299	NEW HAVEN .... Ar	8 45 a	10 45 a	12 45 p	2 40 p	4 45 p	5 38 p		6 42 p	7 50 p	8 28 p	9 40 p	11 45 p	4 45 a
		Connecting Train Number →	↓	404	406	408	410	↓		↓	↓	↓	↓	↓	400
		Connecting Train Frequency →	↓	Daily	Mo thru Fr	Daily	Daily	AMFLEET SERVICE		AMFLEET SERVICE	AMFLEET SERVICE	AMFLEET SERVICE	↓	↓	Mo thru Fr from New Haven
481	299	Inland Route: NEW HAVEN .... Dp	↓	11 00 a	1 20p	3 20p	5 20 p	↓		↓	8 00 p	↓	↓	11 55 p	6 50 a
502	312	Wallingford ⊕	↓	11 19 a	1 39p	3 39p	5 39 p	↓		↓	8 19 p	↓	↓	|	7 09 a
512	318	Meriden	↓	11 31 a	1 51 p	3 51p	5 51 p	↓		↓	8 29 p	↓	↓	12 20 a	7 20 a
523	325	Berlin (New Britain)	↓	11 42 a	2 02p	4 02p	6 02 p	↓		↓	8 39 p	↓	↓	12 30 a	7 31 a
541	336	HARTFORD	↓	11 55 a	2 15p	4 15p	6 16 p	↓		↓	8 52 p	↓	↓	12 45 a	7 46 a
550	342	Windsor ●	↓	E12 05 p	E 2 25p	E 4 25p	E 6 26 p	↓		↓	|	↓	↓	↓	7 55 a
560	348	Windsor Locks ●	↓	12 14 p	2 34p	4 34p	6 36 p	↓		↓	D 9 07 p	↓	↓	↓	8 04 a
568	353	Thompsonville, CT ● (Enfield)	↓	12 22 p	2 42p	4 42p	6 42 p	↓		↓	|	↓	↓	↓	8 12 a
581	361	SPRINGFIELD, MA	↓	12 40 p	3 00p	5 00p	7 00 p	↓		↓	9 30 p	↓	↓	1 20 a	8 30 a
481	299	NEW HAVEN, CT .... Dp	8 55 a	10 55 a	12 55 p	2 50 p	4 55 p	5 53 p		6 52 p		8 38 p	AMFLEET SERVICE 9 50 p	Thru train to Montreal	5 05 a
534	332	Old Saybrook	9 29 a	11 29 a	1 28 p	3 23 p	5 28 p	|		7 25 p		9 11 p	10 23 p		E 5 39 a
563	350	New London	9 50 a	11 50 a	1 48 p	3 44 p	5 50 p	6 45 p		7 45 p		9 30 p	10 41 p		6 02 a
578	359	Mystic, CT ● (Mystic Seaport)	10 02 a	E12 02 p	2 00 p	3 57 p	6 01 p	|		7 56 p		9 41 p	11 02 p		E 6 15 a
592	368	Westerly, RI	10 12 a	12 13 p	2 10 p	4 10 p	6 11 p	|		8 06 p		9 51 p	11 12 p		E 6 27 a
620	385	Kingston	10 26 a	12 29 p	2 24 p	4 26 p	6 24 p	↓		8 22 p		10 07 p	11 28 p		E 6 47 a
663	412	PROVIDENCE, RI ⊕	10 54 a	12 57 p	2 50 p	4 54 p	6 50 p	7 41 p		8 50 p		10 32 p	11 55 p		(S)7 25 a
715	444	Route 128, MA	11 27 a	1 29 p	3 21 p	5 24 p	7 20 p	D 8 23 p		9 20 p		D11 02 p	12 25 a		D 8 03 a
732	455	BOSTON (Back Bay Sta.) .... Ar	D11 45 a	D 2 00 p	D 3 50 p	D 5 56 p	D 7 52 p	D 8 43 p		D 9 52 p		D11 31 p	D12 41 a		D 8 20 a
734	456	BOSTON, MA (South Sta.) .... Ar	11 50 a	2 07 p	3 57 p	6 06 p	8 00 p	8 50 p		10 00 p		11 40 p	12 48 a		8 25 a

FIGURE 5-3. Train Schedule.

good idea of what to expect from the book. Then when they begin to study, they will know how each section they are reading relates to the rest of the book.

4. *Skim the index.* The index indicates in detail what material students will find in the book. It is an invaluable aid because it helps students find specific information that they need by giving them the page on which it appears.

5. *Check for a glossary.* Not all books have a glossary; however, a glossary is helpful because it gives students the meanings of specialized words or phrases used in the book. If a glossary exists, teachers should go over the glossary's pronunciation legend with the students and give them practice in finding and pronouncing some of the listed terms.

Special Note:
The sections that follow on charts, maps, and graphs are especially essential areas that should be stressed by teachers because they help students learn about their textbooks and how they can get the most from their textbooks. (See also "Vocabulary Aids in Textbooks" in Chapter 4.)

Figures 5-4 and 5-5 are excerpts from textbooks that illustrate the kinds of helpful techniques that textbook writers incorporate because textbook writers are particularly interested in having students acquire the information that they present. Note especially the use of italics and bold print to emphasize special words and key concepts, the use of diagrams, marginal notes, and vocabulary hints. (See Appendix A for a "General Checklist for Textbook Readability.")

Activities Teachers can have students skim to answer the following:

1. Using the index of one of the students' textbooks, have them state the pages on which they would find various topics.

2. Using one of their textbooks, have the students give the meaning or meanings of some of the terms that are presented in the glossary of one of their textbooks.

3. Using the table of contents of one of their textbooks, have the students state the pages on which some chapters start.

READING MAPS, CHARTS, AND GRAPHS

Many textbook writers employ charts, graphs, and maps to make their ideas clearer. A number of teachers use these techniques also because they have learned from experience that "a picture is usually worth a thousand words." Not only are charts, graphs, and maps used in school; they are used also outside school, and persons who have difficulty understanding these will be at a disadvantage in our society.

Teachers should help students to gain facility in interpreting and us-

FIGURE 5-4. Sample excerpt from a history textbook to illustrate writers' helpful techniques.

Popular Sovereignty Means the People Rule[8]

The first three words of the Constitution, "We the people," express the principle of popular sovereignty. According to this principle, the people rule. They hold the final authority, or ruling power, in government.

CHART SKILL The right to vote has expanded since the Constitution first went into effect. Who could vote in 1789? In 1971? Which amendment granted women the right to vote?

The Right to Vote

Year	People Allowed to Vote
1789	White men over age 21 who meet property requirements (state laws)
Early 1800s–1850s	All white men over age 21 (state laws)
1870	Black men (Amendment 15)
1920	Women (Amendment 19)
1961	People in the District of Columbia in presidential elections (Amendment 23)
1971	People over age 18 (Amendment 26)

A contract with the government. The Constitution is a contract, or formal agreement, between the people and their government. In it, the people grant the government the powers it needs to achieve its goals. At the same time, they limit the power of government by spelling out what the government may not do.

The people vote. How does popular sovereignty work? In a large society, people cannot always take part directly in government. Instead, they exercise their ruling power indirectly. The people elect public officials to make laws and other government decisions for them. This practice is called *representative government.*

The people elect public officials by voting in free and frequently held elections. Americans today have the consitutional right to vote for members of the House of Representatives (Article 1, Section 2) and for members of the Senate (Amendment 17). The people also elect the members of the electoral college, who, in turn, choose the President (Article 2, Section 1).

The right to vote has been gradually expanded over time. When the Constitution was *ratified,* or approved, only white men over age 21 who owned property could vote. As the chart at left shows, other Americans have won the right to vote since then. Today, if you are a citizen, you are eligible to vote at age 18.

---

[8]James West Davidson and John E. Batchelor, *The American Nation.* 3rd ed. (Englewood Cliffs, N.J.: Prentice Hall, 1991), p. C6.

FIGURE 5-5. Sample excerpt from a science textbook to illustrate writers' helpful techniques.

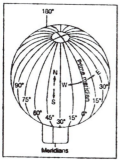

Figure 9-12 *Meridians are lines running north to south on a map or globe. What are meridians used to measure?*

Sharpen Your Skills

Mapping Your Neighborhood

1. Draw a detailed map of your neighborhood. Streets, houses, and other important features should be represented.

2. Be sure to draw the map to scale. At the bottom of the map, place a scale that compares distance on the map to actual distance on the earth's surface. For example, 1 cm might equal 100 m.

3. Use different colors for buildings, industrial areas, crop fields, and bodies of water.

4. Make a legend that includes the symbols in the map and their meanings.

Meridians[9]

When you look at a globe or a map, you see many straight lines on it. Some of the lines run between the points that represent the geographic North and South poles of the earth. These lines are called **meridians** (muh-RIHD-ee-uhnz).

Each meridian is half of an imaginary circle around the earth. Geographers have named the meridian that runs through Greenwich, England, the **prime meridian**. The measure of distance east or west of the prime meridian is called **longitude**. Meridians are used to measure longitude.

The distance around any circle, including the earth, is measured in degrees. The symbol for degree is a small circle written at the upper right of a number. All circles contain 360°. Each meridian marks 1° of longitude around the earth. But not all meridians are drawn on most globes or maps.

The prime meridian is labeled 0° longitude. Meridians to the east of the prime meridian are called east longitudes. Meridians to the west of the prime meridian are called west longitudes.

Meridians of east longitude measure the distance halfway around the earth. Meridians of west longitude measure the distance around the other half of the earth. Because half of the distance around a cirlce is 180°, meridians of east and west longitude go from 0° to 180°.

Time Zones

As you know, a day is 24 hours long. During these 24 hours, the earth rotates a total of 360°. So the earth rotates 15° every hour. The earth is divided into 24 zones of 15° of longitude each. These zones are called **time zones.** A time zone is a longitudinal belt of the earth in which all areas have the same local time.

---

[9]Charles R. Coble, Dale R. Rice, Kenneth J. Walla, and Elaine G. Murray, *Prentice Hall Earth Science*, 2nd ed. (Englewood Cliffs, N.J.: Prentice Hall, 1991), p. 222.

ing maps, graphs, and charts. If students are given opportunities to work with various types of illustrative materials, they will be in a better position to decipher these when they are reading. Unfortunately, much important information is lost because many students do not pay attention to textbook writers' charts and graphs. Often students skip completely over the author's illustrative materials. The reason for this may be because teachers have not taken the time to stress their value, so students may feel that they are merely space fillers, and, therefore, not too important, or it may be that students do not know how to interpret them. Whatever the reasons are, students need to gain skill in interpreting illustrative materials.

Content-area teachers should not assume that their students are able to interpret illustrative materials. They should make the interpretation of illustrative materials part of their instructional program, and time should be set aside for students to gain experience in working with illustrative materials. It is usually best to present the lessons on interpreting charts, graphs, or maps when students are meeting these in their readings. In practically all subject areas, students will have to be able to interpret various types of charts and graphs; maps are a vital part of social studies.

Maps

A map is a means of communicating information. Teachers must help students learn how to read and interpret maps correctly. Students need to recognize that a map is a representation of a flat surface of a whole or part of an area and that it is not an exact replica of an area because it is difficult to portray the round earth on a flat surface. Teachers should help their students recognize the limitations of maps and that relationships are only approximations. There are many different types of maps, and each stresses a particular feature of an area. For example, there are street maps, road maps, political maps, physical maps, relief maps, vegetation maps, land-use maps, product maps, pictorial maps, population maps, historical maps, war maps, weather maps, and so on. All maps have a legend or key that needs to be interpreted; different types of maps require different types of coding. For example, political maps use color coding and definite boundary lines to indicate political divisions; consequently, the map's legend would present a key indicating what various colors represent. A rainfall and temperature map uses a combination of color coding and special type lines. The color coding is used to represent the amount of rainfall, and the special lines are used to indicate the average temperature in an area. Legends may vary from map to map; the clue lies in being able to interpret the particular legend for a particular map.

Road maps are the ones with which students are probably the most familiar and which they will use the most often. Road maps indicate road and distance information and help persons choose travel routes on land. Teachers could use road maps in class to help students to gain facility in map reading and to acquaint them with map scales, which show how the

FIGURE 5-6. This fifth-grade teacher meets individually with her students to help clear up any erroneous concepts they may have.

map distances compare to the actual distances. (Any map scale is a ratio between whatever the map is measuring and its corresponding measurement on earth.) Teachers can stimulate students' interest in map reading by using activities such as the following:

1. Teachers could have students bring in a road map of the community in which they live and then have them challenge one another to find the shortest distance to get to a certain destination.
2. Another activity would be for teachers to bring in maps of foreign countries and challenge students to find certain locations or the distance between two different locations.
3. Teachers could have students prepare their own maps of regions they are studying. Practice in constructing maps is probably one of the best ways to have students gain an appreciation of their importance, as well as to help students understand maps better.

Charts and Graphs

As there are a number of different types of maps, so are there various types of charts and graphs. The ones that are presented are those that students will meet most often in their textbooks. Charts and graphs are used to display data. Most of us have at one time or another prepared a chart to display some information. Students can be asked to construct a chart showing the amount of time they study during the week in a particular content area or in a number of areas. For example:

Table 5-2. A Student's Study Pattern.

Day	Amount of Time	Subject
Monday	1½ hours	algebra
Monday	½ hour	English
Monday	1 hour	history
Tuesday	½ hour	French
Tuesday	2 hours	chemistry
Wednesday	1 hour	chemistry
Wednesday	½ hour	English
Thursday	2 hours	algebra
Thursday	½ hour	French
Friday	0	
Saturday	0	
Sunday	2 hours	chemistry
Sunday	3 hours	algebra
Sunday	1 hour	English

(An analysis of Table 5-2 could help students gain some insight into their studying patterns.)

The kinds of information that can be charted are too numerous to state. Practically anything that can be tallied or quantified can be displayed on a chart. Graphs are more limited in what they can illustrate than charts because they are usually more structured, but they, too, can display many different kinds of information. The three graphs that students will meet most often in their readings are the bar graph, the line graph, and the circle graph.

An example of a bar graph is shown in Figure 5-7. A bar graph is used to show comparisons between or among the quantity or measures of something or of qualities. Bar graphs are generally used when we wish to compare more than six items or categories. The bar graph shown in Figure 5-7 compares the amount of time the student spent studying during the week.

The line or profile graph is helpful in showing the direction of change that has taken place over a period of time; it shows whether there has been an increase or decrease in something. This type of graph is useful in showing trends. The circle graph is used to illustrate parts of a whole; it shows how a total amount of something has been divided. The entire graph is equal to 100 percent, and each segment or part is a fraction of the 100 percent.

In the courses that require that students decipher pictorial aids, it would probably be a good idea for teachers to have their students create

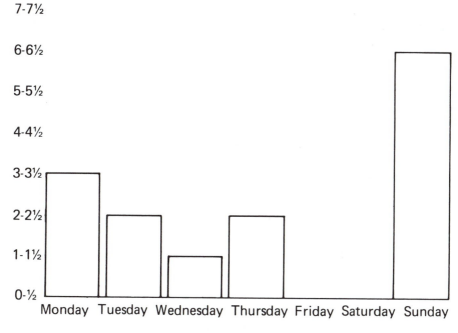

FIGURE 5-7. Bar Graph of a Student's Study Pattern

such aids. For example, social studies teachers could have students chart the composition of Congress according to party affiliation at a particular time in history, transportation trends, Federal expenditures for transportation, and so on, based on what students are studying in class. Science teachers could have students explain the results of their experiments using graphs. Actually, an excellent way to get students to gain experience in reading and constructing pictorial aids is for content-area teachers to require pictorial aids, where applicable, for students' oral and written reports.

REFERENCE SOURCES

Teachers should help students to understand that it is impossible for one person to know everything today because of the vast amount of knowledge that already exists, compounded each year by its exponential growth. However, a person can learn about any particular area or field if he or she knows what source books to go to for help. For example, the *Readers' Guide to Periodical Literature* will help one to find magazine articles written on almost any subject of interest. There are reference books on language and usage, such as Roget's *Thesaurus of English Words and Phrases*, which would help students in finding synonyms and less trite words to use in writing. There are reference books available that can supply information about a famous writer, baseball player, scientist, celebrity, and so forth. The key factor is knowing which reference book to go to for the needed information. Here is a list of some selected reference sources:

Biography (indexes)
Biography Index
New York Times Index
Readers' Guide to Periodical Literature

Book reviews (indexes)
Book Review Digest
Book Review Index
Education Index
Humanities Index
New York Times Index
Social Science Index

Encyclopedias
Afro-American Encyclopedia
Encyclopedia of American Facts and Dates
Encyclopedia of Education
Encyclopedia of Psychology
Encyclopedia of Science and Technology
Encyclopedia of World History
The New Encyclopaedia Britannica

Teachers can help their students by acquainting them with the various reference books that are particularly germane to their content area. Then they could supply students with certain questions or assignments related to their content area and ask them which books they would go to for assistance.

The Dictionary: A Special Emphasis

A special section is being presented on the dictionary because it is probably the most used of all reference sources. Teachers should help their students recognize that the dictionary supplies a great amount of information besides word meanings and pronunciation. (The amount of information varies according to the dictionary.) Here is an outline of some items frequently found in a dictionary.

Uses of the Dictionary

A. Information concerning a word
1. Spelling.
2. Definitions.

FIGURE 5-8. This student knows the librarian is a good resource person.

    3. Correct usage.
    4. Pronunciation.
    5. Syllabication.
    6. Antonyms.
    7. Synonyms.
    8. Parts of speech.
    9. Idiomatic phrases.
   10. Etymology—history of the word.
   11. Semantics—analysis of the word's meanings.
  B. Other useful information
    1. Biographical entries
    2. Lists of foreign countries, provinces, and cities with population estimates.
    3. Charts of other geographical data.
    4. Air distances between principal cities.
    5. Listing of foreign words and phrases.
    6. Complete listing of abbreviations in common use.
    7. Tables of weights and measures.
    8. Signs and symbols.
    9. Forms of address.

In those content courses in which students will need to consult the dictionary regularly, it might be a good idea for the teacher to emphasize that students should pay attention to the pronunciation legend that usually is given at the beginning of the dictionary. (See "The Dictionary and Vocabulary Expansion" in Chapter 4.) The teacher might also want to present the students with a number of questions related to their particular content area and have them find the answers in the dictionary. Here are examples of the

FIGURE 5-9. This student uses many reference books for her reports.

type of questions from various content areas that teachers can use to heighten students' awareness of the amount of information they can gain from the dictionary.

1. Is *litter* a term in the metric system?
2. Is haiku a Hawaiian mountain?
3. What is a centaur?
4. What is a centipede?
5. What are the parts of a bird?
6. Is a margay a flower?
7. How many inches is a meter?
8. What system of money is used in Hungary?

GRAPHIC SUMMARY OF CHAPTER

Here is a graphic summary of Chapter 5. If you have read the chapter, this graphic illustration should help you remember its main points. Under or beside each heading, you might want to jot down some of the information you recall, as well as some of the key concepts in this chapter. This can act as a good review. You can then check your key concepts against those that follow the graphic summary.

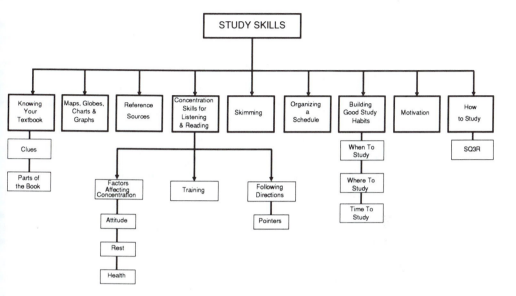

KEY CONCEPTS IN CHAPTER

- Students need to build good study habits.
- Building good study habits deals with where to study, when to study, and how much time to spend on studying.
- Content-area teachers should integrate study skills with content material.
- A weekly schedule helps students apportion their time more effectively.
- The SQ3R technique is a viable study method.
- Concentration is sustained attention.
- Individuals cannot concentrate and be relaxed at the same time.
- Following directions is an essential skill.
- Setting purposes for reading is a crucial factor in reading.
- Knowledge of textbooks is important in studying.
- Graphs, charts, and maps help make ideas clearer.
- Graphs, charts, and maps are a means of communication.
- Students should know how to use various reference sources.
- The investment of significant amounts of time in homework is related to students' success in school.

SUGGESTIONS FOR THOUGHT QUESTIONS AND ACTIVITIES

1. You have been put on a committee to help develop a reading and study skills program in your school. What suggestions would you make?

2. Choose a content area; then choose a textbook from this area, and develop some skimming activities for students from this textbook.

3. Develop some concentration activities for secondary school students that are related to what the students are studying.

4. Prepare a lesson on helping students become acquainted with a specific content-area textbook.

5. Prepare a lesson on map reading for a particular content area.

6. Plan a lesson in which students must use at least three different reference sources.

7. Construct some questions in a specific content area that require the students to use the dictionary.

8. Make some suggestions on how you would help students become better direction followers in a particular subject area.

SELECTED BIBLIOGRAPHY

ARMSTRONG, G. BLAKE, and BRADLEY S. GREENBERG. "Background Television as an Inhibitor of Cognitive Processing." *Human Communication Research* 16 (spring 1990): 355–386.

McCLAIN, LESLIE J. "Study Guides: Potential Assets in Content Classrooms." *Journal of Reading* 24 (January 1981): 321–325.

McCULLOUGH, BARBARA, and GENE TOWERY. "Your Horoscope Predicts: You Can Teach Students to Follow Directions." *Journal of Reading* 19 (May 1976): 653–659.

MOORMAN, GARY B., and WILLIAM E. BLANTON. "The Information Text Reading Activity (ITRA): Engaging Students in Meaningful Learning." *Journal of Reading* 34 (November 1990): 174–183.

RUBIN, DOROTHY. *Reading and Learning Power,* 3rd ed. Needham Heights, Mass.: Ginn Press, 1990.

WADE, SUZANNE, WOODROW TRATHEN, and GREGORY SCHRAW. "An Analysis of Spontaneous Study Strategies." *Reading Research Quarterly* 25 (spring 1990): 147–166.

6

Reading and Study Skills II

OVERVIEW

INTRODUCTION

"I feel like an idiot whenever I ask a question in that class."
"If you don't ask any questions, our teacher thinks you know the material."
"Everyone laughs when someone asks a question in my classes."
"I never know what to put down when I take notes. It seems as though every-
  thing is important."
"I really wouldn't mind school if it weren't for tests. I just can't take tests."
"Writing papers are the worst, especially reports that require notetaking."

Are any of the preceding remarks that were made by these students familiar ones? Probably. This chapter, which is a continuation of Chapter 5, will present information that should enable teachers to rid students of their insecurities when it comes to the art of asking questions. It should also help students gain skill in both notetaking and test taking. It is important, however, before we begin, to state again what has been stated at the beginning of Chapter 5, namely, that the study skills that are presented in these two chapters should be integrated with the content material that students are studying and that teachers should directly teach any skill that students need to master certain concepts if it is necessary to do so. The skills that are taught should be taught by using the content material that is being studied in class.

KEY QUESTIONS

After reading this chapter, you should be able to answer the following questions:

1. Why should students be good askers of questions?
2. How can students become good askers of questions?
3. What is the role of outlining?
4. How is outlining related to studying?
5. How can semantic mapping be used for studying?
6. How do you summarize a paragraph?
7. How can the teacher help students to be better notetakers?
8. How can the teacher help students to be better test takers?

KEY TERMS IN CHAPTER

You should pay special attention to the following key terms:

buzz words
graphic summary
objective tests
outlining
questions

semantic mapping (graphic organizer)
subjective tests
summary
telegraphic writing

ASKING QUESTIONS IN CLASS

A section on asking questions in class is presented because this is an area in which students need special help. Many students become intimidated early in school about asking questions and as a result hardly ever ask any. Asking questions is an important part of learning! Students must be helped to recognize this, and teachers must provide an environment that is nonthreatening so that students will feel free to ask questions. Knowing how and when to ask questions helps students to gain a better insight into a subject, gives the teacher feedback, and slows the teacher down if he or she is going too fast. Unfortunately, as has already been stated, many students are afraid to ask questions. Sometimes their fear may be due to a teacher's attitude; however, often it's because a student doesn't know how to formulate the question or is "afraid of looking like a fool."

Here are some pointers that teachers at the beginning of the term should convey to their students.

1. Persons who ask the best questions are usually those who know the material best.
2. Asking questions is not a substitute for studying the material.
3. Questions help to clarify the material for students.
4. Teachers usually want and encourage questions.
5. The questions that students ask will probably help a number of other students.

After content-area teachers have conveyed the preceding information to their students, they could present students with a guide on asking questions. The guide would contain suggestions on the kind of questions students should ask about examinations, as well as on how these should be asked. (An example of such a guide is on page 170).

If some teachers feel that their students need more than the guide to help them, they should construct questions for their particular content area as examples for their students. Another technique the teacher could use is to have students either individually or in groups formulate questions for an upcoming test. Teachers could also ask students at the end of a lecture or discussion to construct two questions on the lecture or discussion.

An activity that is especially helpful in teaching students the value of asking good questions is called "The Question-Only Strategy."[1] This has four mandatory steps and one optional step. Step 1 prepares the students for the activity; the teacher states a topic and explains the rules of the interaction. The students are the question askers and the teacher is the answerer. The teacher will answer only those questions that the students ask; then a test will be given that will cover all the material that the teacher feels is important about the topic whether the students have asked the questions or not. Step 2 is the interaction between the students and the teacher. Step 3 is the test. After the test, there is a discussion about the questions that were asked and those that should have been asked. Step 4 requires the

[1]Anthony D. Manzo. "Three 'Universal' Strategies in Content Area Reading and Languaging," *Journal of Reading* 24 (November 1980): 148.

students to read their textbooks or listen to a short lecture to acquire the information they failed to attain through their questions. The last step, which is optional, is a follow-up test.

Suchman's inquiry method is also a good technique to make students better question-askers. Even though this technique is generally used in science classes with experiments, it can be adapted to other subject areas. This technique requires students to ask questions in the form of hypotheses. The teacher only answers "Yes" or "No." If students formulate enough correct question hypotheses, they will subsequently arrive at the correct conclusion or solution.

STUDENT GUIDE FOR ASKING QUESTIONS IN CLASS

Here are suggestions on the kind of questions you should ask about examinations:

1. What kind of test will it be? Will it be an objective or subjective test?
2. How long will the test be? (This will help you to know whether it's a quiz [a minor exam] or a test [one that usually counts for more than a quiz]).
3. Will dates, names, formulas, and other such specifics be stressed? (This is important for you to know because it will influence the type of studying that you will do.)
4. Will it be an open-book or closed-book exam? (This is important because it will influence the type of studying you will do.)
5. What chapters will be covered?

Other kinds of questions you should ask might be these:

1. In going over an examination, you should ask general questions or those that relate to everyone's papers. If you have specific questions on your paper, you should ask the teacher this question in private.
2. You should not hesitate to ask questions about the marking of your paper if you do not understand it. You should especially ask the teacher about a comment on your paper that you do not understand. You should also recognize that you learn from the knowledge of results and from understanding your mistakes.

Now some suggestions on how you should ask questions follow.

1. Be as specific as possible.
2. State the question clearly.
3. Do not say, "I have a question," and then go into a long discourse before asking the question. (The question may be forgotten.)
4. Make sure that the question is related to the material.

FIGURE 6-1.   Does this complaint sound familiar?

ASKING QUESTIONS OF THE TEXTBOOK AND OTHER WRITTEN MATERIAL

Students not only should be adept at asking questions in class, but they should also ask questions about the material they are reading. In the section on SQ3R in Chapter 5, students use questions to set their purposes for reading. This helps give direction and organization to what they are reading; students, however, in order to be actively involved in what they are reading, as well as problem solvers, should ask questions about the text during and after their reading. These are usually other types of questions. The questions the students ask could be triggered by a number of factors. For example, it may be that the student finds some inconsistencies in his or her reading or feels that the author has misplaced emphasis; that is, the writer either presents too much or too little on a topic. The student may be confused about the author's presentation because the writing is ambiguous; the student may find some errors in the text or find material that does not seem relevant. It may be that the author presents opinions as if they were facts or does not substantiate what he or she says. It may also be that the student is confused about the purpose, bias, or stance of the writer.

Teachers can encourage students to ask questions about text material by asking students to be good critical thinkers and to evaluate what they have read. For example, teachers can ask students to read an article or a section of their textbook and to read the material as though they were investigative reporters. What kinds of questions would they ask? Why would they ask such questions? This should stimulate a lively discussion. Some teachers may need to give more guidance to their students. These teachers, during a discussion of a reading assignment, may ask students if there were any questions that came to their minds while they were reading the material or after they had completed their reading. The teachers could then tell the students that a number of questions had come to their minds and then share the questions with the students. A further discussion should follow concerning the importance of asking questions of the text material while reading the content material.

Asking questions about text material is consistent with viewing reading as problem solving, as well as with helping students gain skill in thinking like scientists, social scientists, or mathematicians. (See Chapters 7, 8, and 9 for sections on asking questions.)

READING AND WRITING AS MODES OF STUDYING

There are a number of reading and writing strategies teachers can help students acquire that would help their students learn better. Teachers should share with their students that notetaking is an effective learning tool that they can combine with SQ3R (see Chapter 5) to help them in their studying. Other helpful strategies include summaries, outlining, and graphic organizers. Teachers should introduce each strategy using relevant content material.

Notetaking for Studying

Notetaking is a very important tool; it is useful not only in writing long papers but also in studying. Students are usually not concerned with note-taking until they begin writing long reports or papers; at that time, students need to learn how to take notes. If notetaking is a technique the teacher feels will help students learn better the content material of his or her course and if the teacher suspects or finds that students do not know how to take notes, the teacher should convey important information about notetaking to the students and give them practice in taking notes.

Notes consist of words and phrases that help persons remember important material. They do not have to be complete sentences; however, unless an individual's notes are clear and organized, he or she will have difficulty in using them for study purposes.

Teachers can get these important concepts across to students by putting a set of notes, related to the topics they are studying, on an overhead projector and asking the students to organize the notes according to some given topics. A discussion could then take place concerning notetaking procedures. For example, a teacher could have students examine a set of notes and have them try to fit the notes into the given main topics. (Teachers would, of course, use an example of notes from their own content areas.) Here is a scenario that illustrates what one teacher does.

Scenario: Notetaking Procedure
Mr. Jackson presents the following notes to his students on a transparency. (He tells them that the notes do not belong to anyone in the class. Nevertheless, the notes are on a topic they are studying.) He asks the students to examine the notes carefully.

Notes:

1. skin
2. epidermis
3. influenced by age
4. outer layer
5. influenced by gender
6. thin
7. thicker than epidermis
8. dermis
9. touch
10. stores fat
11. several layers

List of Main Topics:

I. Age of skin
II. Layers of skin
III. Skin

He then asks his students their opinions about the notes. He also asks whether the notes are representative of what they studied and whether the notes help "jog their memories." He says further that refreshing memories is one of the main purposes of notes and good notes do this. He then discusses with his students why the notes were not very helpful. Here are some of the things they said:

1. It is difficult to make sense of these notes because the main topics are either vaguely stated, too general, or too specific.
2. The items in the list of notes can fit under more than one main topic; they are not precise enough; that is, they do not contain enough information to unmistakingly identify or distinguish them.

Mr. Jackson then presents his students with some notetaking techniques that would aid them. He also tells them that notetaking for studying can be combined with the SQ3R study technique that he had previously introduced. Next, he gives each student the following special notetaking and study guide which combines notetaking with studying and SQ3R.

NOTETAKING AND STUDY GUIDE

1. Read the whole selection to get an overview of what you have to study. A preliminary reading helps you to see the organization of the material.
2. Choose a part of the selection to study, basing your choice on your concentration ability.
3. Survey the part chosen, and note the topic of the individual paragraph or group of paragraphs. Write the topic or topics in your notebook instead of the questions you would write in a normal SQ3R procedure.
4. Read the part.
5. After you finish reading each paragraph, state its main idea. Put down only important supporting details under the main idea.
   a. Although you do not have to use a formal outline for your notes, you should *indent* your listing so that the relation of supporting material to main ideas is clear.
   b. Try not to take any notes until after you have finished reading the whole paragraph. Remember, *recall* is the essential step in the SQ3R technique. By not taking notes until you have finished reading, you are more actively involved in thinking about the material as you try to construct notes.

Special Note: Good notes are very helpful for review purposes, and they can save you a great amount of time.

Teachers should help their students recognize that for study purposes, if the material is new to the students, it's usually a good idea to write the topic for each paragraph unless the paragraph is a transitional one. As already mentioned in an earlier chapter, teachers should tell their students that textbook writers sometimes list the topics of their paragraphs in the margin and that they should be on the lookout for these helpful clues.

Here is an example of notetaking using the section "Notetaking for Studying" as the source:

I. Notetaking
  A. A helpful tool
     1. Writing
     2. Studying
  B. Notes must be clear and organized
     1. Whole sentences not needed
     2. Topics should be clearly distinguished
  C. Correlated with SQ3R
     1. Follow steps in SQ3R
     2. Note topics—not questions
     3. After reading, recall main idea
     4. Insert details under main idea
  D. Useful for review

From this example, you can readily see the four important ideas presented in this section; namely, *notetaking is a helpful tool, notes should be clear and organized, notetaking is correlated with SQ3R,* and *notetaking is useful for review.*

A discussion of underlining textbook passages is not being presented because this is a technique that students do not generally engage in until they enter college; public school students do not own their textbooks, so they cannot write in them.

Semantic Mapping (Graphic Organizer) and Notetaking

A number of students find that a visual representation of the material helps them to remember information they have studied. Here is a scenario of how Mr. Jackson presents this technique to his students.

Scenario: Semantic Mapping (Graphic Organizer), Notetaking, and Studying

Mr. Jackson tells students that rather than taking notes using an informal outline of what they have studied, they could make a graphic illustration of what they are studying and combine this with the SQ3R technique. Mr. Jackson tells his students he will model what he would do if he were constructing a semantic map to help him in studying. What follows are the steps Mr. Jackson models for his students:

Step 1: Mr. Jackson tells his students that, as in SQ3R, he chooses the amount of information he will be studying. (This is usually more than a paragraph.) He asks his students to look over their assignment and do the same.

Step 2: He then tells them he sets purposes for reading. He asks them to do the same.

Step 3: "Now," he says, "we have to read the material. Let's all do that now."

Step 4: After reading the material, Mr. Jackson tells his students that they are now ready to construct their semantic map. "First," he says, "we have to determine the central idea of what we have read and put that in the center of a blank sheet of paper."

Step 5: "Next, we have to reread each paragraph, state the main topic of each, and append it to the central idea."

Step 6: "For the last step, we go over the material once again and append the important supporting details to its main topic."

(Figure 6-2 is an example of the semantic map that Mr. Jackson did with his class.)

FIGURE 6-2. Graphic Organizer as an Aid to Studying

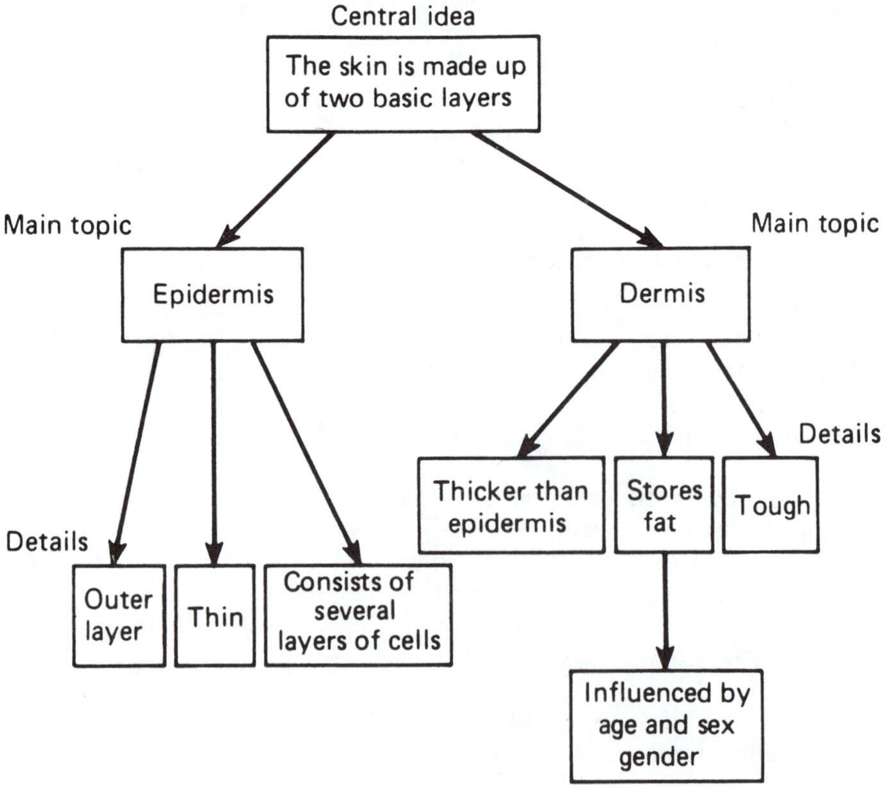

Central idea

The skin is made up of two basic layers

Main topic

Epidermis

Main topic

Dermis

Details

Thicker than epidermis

Stores fat

Tough

Details

Outer layer

Thin

Consists of several layers of cells

Influenced by age and sex gender

Special Note:
Rather than stating the topic of every paragraph, teachers could have the students state the main idea of each one and append supporting details to each main idea. There really is no correct way to construct a graphic illustration. The test is whether it helps students recall a significant amount of information. In this text, graphic summaries are used at the end of each chapter for this purpose. (See section on "Graphic Summary: A Special Review Study Aid.")

Summarizing as a Mode of Learning

Many teachers help their students learn how to summarize passages because they recognize this as a viable means of having students gain essential information. Summarizing material is a mode of learning that helps persons to retain the most important concepts and facts in a long passage. It forces students to think about what they have read and to identify and organize the essential information. Also, if the summary is a written summary, it helps to integrate the reading and writing process. (See Chapter 10.)

Teachers can help their students learn how to summarize by having students begin with summarizing single paragraphs and then working up to longer passages. Teachers should inform students that a good summary ought to be brief and ought to include only essential information. The main idea of the paragraph (if only a paragraph is being summarized) or the central idea of an article and the important facts should be stated but not necessarily in the sequence presented in the passage. The sequence in the paragraph or article must be followed in the summary *only if* that sequence is essential. Teachers need to help their students to include only the information stated in the paragraph or article and not their opinions or what they think should have been included.

Before teachers work with summaries, it might be a good idea for them to review with their students how to find the main or central idea of passages. (The passages that are used should be content material that the students are studying.)

Teachers can also convey to their students that in the writing of a summary, it is sometimes a good idea to begin with the writer's conclusion and work backward to pick out essential points leading to that conclusion.

After teachers have conveyed pertinent information about summaries to their students, they should give students practice in writing summaries, using content material the students are studying. One technique the teacher could use might be to have the students read a paragraph or a section from the textbook that they are presently studying and then have them write a summary of it in class. After they have written their summaries, they could read some of them and discuss which are good summaries and why they are good. Another technique is to have students read a selection from their textbook and then to present them with a few summaries on the selection and have them determine which is the best summary and then explain why. Still another technique the teacher could use would be to have students write a summary of a selection they have read and then to have them compare their summary with a sample summary that is shown on the overhead projector.

Some teachers may want to have students write a summary together before having them write one individually. Some teachers may merely present students with a sheet that contains tips on how to write a summary, as well as two sample summaries of a section from their textbook. As has been stated many times in this text, what tactics teachers employ will depend on the uniqueness of the subject matter, as well as on the individual differences of the students and their past experiences.

Some teachers may give their students a mock test after they have written their summary to illustrate to them how helpful the writing of summaries is in retaining and explaining information. (See "Incorporating Summarizing and Studying in Social Studies" in Chapter 7 for a scenario showing how one teacher integrates summaries into his social studies class.)

Teachers may find useful the following samples of two articles and very brief sample summaries of them.

Example 1:
This is a selection on Roberto Clemente from *Roberto Clemente: Batting King* by Arnold Hano. Roberto Clemente was a baseball star who died a hero's death while flying supplies to victims of a Nicaraguan earthquake in the 1970s.

Roberto Clemente did not spend his usual winter after the 1957 season had ended. Instead of going home to Puerto Rico for another go at winter-league baseball, Clemente went back for a brief rest, and returned to the United States.

He had a date. With the Marines.

For six months, Clemente fulfilled his obligation to the country of his citizenship—the United States of America—by training at Parris Island Marine Corps Recruitment Depot, in South Carolina.

It is said the Marines will make a man out of a boy. Roberto Clemente has insisted that he has been a man ever since the age of seventeen, when he put away his schoolbooks to enter a full-fledged profession.

Still, the Marines nearly always leave their particular mark on those men or boys who pass through the corps. Roberto Clemente was no exception. He went into the corps with an aching back. He came out a reasonably well man.

When asked how this extraordinary change occurred (men with strong sacroiliac-lumbar regions go into service and often come out with the famous "aching backs," but seldom does it work the other way). Clemente answered tersely:

"I worked like hell."

That sums it up. A Marine recruit works long hours on arduous tasks. Clemente threw himself into the routine. The rhythm of the work smoothed out the crazy-jig spasms that for so long had seized his back ever since the day he picked up a too-light bat and swung it too hard.

When Roberto Clemente reported to the Pirate camp at Fort Myers, he was a different man. Which is not to say he would always be well again.

The sight of a once-again strong-backed Roberto Clemente meant more than just a healthier right fielder. Players reacted positively to the new Clemente. The whole team took on a healthier air. Not since 1949 had a Pirate club finished better than last or next to last, and that Pittsburgh team of nine years before had ended sixth. Not in a decade had a Pirate team finished in the first division.[2]

Sample Summary: Roberto Clemente fulfilled his obligation to the United States by entering the Marine Corps for a six-month training period after the 1957 season had ended. This strenuous training corrected Roberto's back problem. A strong-backed and healthier Roberto led his team to great success.

Example 2:

This is a selection on the life and works of Martin Luther King, Jr. from *The Life and Words of Martin Luther King, Jr.* by Ira Peck.

Early in the evening of April 4, 1968, a rifle bullet ended the life of Martin Luther King, Jr., in Memphis, Tennessee. His death plunged the nation into gloom, just as President John F. Kennedy's death had a few years before.

King was only thirty-nine when he was killed, but he had already been the foremost Negro civil rights leader in the United States for more than twelve years. King became the leader of that movement late in 1955, when he was chosen by Montgomery, Alabama, Negroes to lead a boycott against the city's bus lines. At the time, King was the pastor of a fairly well-to-do Baptist Church in Montgomery. He might have done little more and still led a very useful life. But some people "have greatness thrust upon them," and King was one of these.

When he was elected to lead the boycott, he really didn't want the job. But, once chosen, he felt that he couldn't refuse to serve his people in their cause. King led the Negroes' cause in Montgomery against segregated buses, and overcame every kind of obstacle. Even the danger of violence against himself didn't cause him to flinch. From then on King felt he had to lead the Negro people to freedom, not only in Montgomery, but wherever there was a racial injustice. When he left his church in Montgomery to return to his home in Atlanta, Georgia, he told his people:

"History has thrust something on me which I cannot turn away."

King never flinched from what he thought was his duty. Some people said that he went too far, that he was a "troublemaker." Others said that he did not go far enough, that he was, in fact, an "Uncle Tom." King always said that he was a middle-of-the-road man. Some Negroes, he said, wished to do nothing about segregation and injustice, and just let things go on as they were. Others

[2]New York: G. P. Putnam's Sons, 1973.

were full of hatred and talked of using violence against white people. His way, non-violence, King said, was the best way—the only way—for the Negro in the United States to win equality and dignity. King warned that if white people did not support his non-violent movement, many Negroes would turn to "black nationalism" and hatred of all things white. This, he said, would lead to a racial nightmare. The ghetto riots of the summers of 1965–67 seemed to bear him out.

After many attempts on his life, King, the man of nonviolence, finally met a violent death. King knew that he might meet death almost any day after he became a civil rights leader. But at the end he was no longer afraid of dying. The day before he was killed he said:

It (death) really doesn't matter with me now. Because I have been to the mountaintop. And I've looked over, and I've seen the promised land. I may not get there with you. But I want you to know tonight that we as a people will get to the promised land. So I'm happy tonight. I'm not worried about anything. I'm not fearing any man. Mine eyes have seen the glory of the coming of the Lord![3]

Sample Summary: Martin Luther King, Jr., was the foremost civil rights leader in the United States. Chosen by his people to lead them, he accepted his duty and never turned back. He was an unswerving middle-of-the-road man who believed in the inevitable and enduring victory of nonviolence but met his death by violence when he was only thirty-nine.

Graphic Summary: A Special Review Study Aid

The saying "A picture is worth 1,000 words" is well-known and true for many people, and because of this, each chapter of this book ends with a graphic summary, which is a visual representation of the material presented in the chapter. The graphic illustration should help you recall the information you have studied because it organizes the major points in a logical way. It is an excellent review.

Teachers can help students gain skill in using this technique for study purposes by having their students do the following:

Step 1: Choose a short selection from the students' textbook.

Step 2: Use the SQ3R technique on the short selection; however, tell students to omit the last step of SQ3R, which is the review.

Sample Selection:

States and Properties of Matter

Our present understanding of the changes we see around us, like the melting of ice and the burning of wood, is intimately tied to our understanding of the nature and composition of matter. Matter is the physical material of the universe; it is anything that occupies space and has mass.

[3]New York: Scholastic Book Services, 1974.

Matter exists in three physical states: gas (also known as vapor), liquid, and solid. A gas has no fixed volume or shape. It takes the volume and shape of its container. A gas can be compressed to fit a small container, and it will expand to occupy a large one. A liquid has a definite volume but no specific shape. It assumes the shape of the portion of the container that it occupies. A solid is rigid. It has both a fixed volume and a fixed shape. Neither liquids nor solids are compressible to any appreciable extent.

Step 3: After they have done all the steps in SQ3R except the last one, have them make a semantic map of what they have read. (See "Semantic Mapping [Graphic Organizer] and Notetaking.")

Sample Semantic Map:

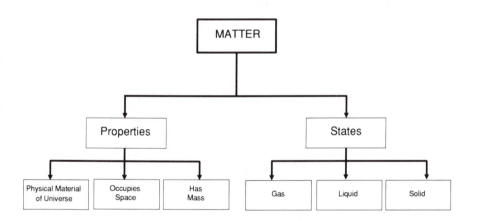

Step 4: Now, have them look at the graphic summary of their selection. They should note that the illustration organizes the material presented in the selection, and the main topic is in the center of the illustration with related material appended to it. Without looking back at their selection, have them use the graphic summary to help them recall the material in the selection.

NOTETAKING FOR WRITING A PAPER

Many students of the intermediate-grade level and higher are beginning to write reports and papers. Teachers should help these students to acquire some good notetaking skills at this time because notetaking is helpful in writing reports and long papers. Good notes save time and effort, and they should begin when the paper is begun. Here is some important information that teachers should convey to their students concerning notetaking:

1. The notecard is an essential aid in recording notes for papers. The size of card that the student chooses should be based on his or her style of writing. If the student writes large and intends to use some long quotes, a larger size (5-by-7-inch cards) is better than smaller sizes (3-by-5- or 4-by-6-inch cards). Whichever size card the student chooses, he or she should be consistent; that is, he or she should use cards of only one size. Next, the student should use one card for each note. Teachers should help their students to learn not to record two different ideas on the same card.

   Notecards are better than slips of paper because they are easier to handle. They are superior to regular notepaper not only because they are easier to handle but also because they are more convenient to organize, store, and edit.

2. To avoid problems when they write papers, students should acquire good habits.

   a. The notecard should contain the topic they are writing on or that topic and the subtopic to which the particular note applies. (If the student doesn't know this information for certain when he or she begins to take notes, he or she should leave room to fill it in later.)

   b. Students should make sure that they write down the exact source of their information at the bottom or top of the card. Bibliographical forms vary, but by fourth grade students usually use the following form: the author's last name is written first, a comma separates the last name from the first name, and the title of the book is capitalized and underlined. A comma and page numbers follow the title. For example:

   Wiese, Kurt, *You Can Write Chinese*, pages 45–50.

   By sixth grade the bibliography also includes the date of publication. The teacher should initiate a discussion on the importance of knowing this factor. The teacher should also tell the students that they only have to record the author's last name and the page from which the information was obtained if they have used the source before. They should, of course, include the first name if there are two authors with the same last names. (Teachers should give students information and examples on the bibliographical form they want their students to use.)

   c. Students should record the information as clearly as possible. The information may be a summary in their own words, figures or statistics, definition, a direct quotation, or some other bit of relevant information.

Sample Notecard:

Topic	The Protection of Leopards
Main idea	Leopards are now widely protected because they play an important part in maintaining nature's balance.
Important details	Leopards used to kill thousands of baboons every year, until the leopard was virtually wiped out. Leopards are now needed to control the baboon population problem.
	Hunter, J.A., *African Hunter*, Harper & Brothers, 1952, p. 52.

(Notecard contains a summary of the following paragraph.)

In many parts of Africa, the use of traps, poisons, and dogs has virtually exterminated the leopard. In my youth, we thought that the only good leopard was a hide stretched out for drying. But now we are discovering that the leopard played an important part in maintaining nature's balance. Leopards used to kill thousands of baboons every year, and now that the leopards have been largely wiped out baboons are proving to be a major control problem in many parts of the colony. The perfect way to keep them in check is by allowing their natural enemy, the leopard, to destroy them. So leopards are now widely protected and allowed to increase in numbers. Such is the strange way that man works—first he virtually destroys a species and then does everything in his power to restore it.[4]

3. Teachers should impress upon students the importance of writing each note as clearly as possible so that they will not have difficulty understanding it or why they wrote it. See the sample guide on page 184 for writing notes on cards that teachers can give their students.

Activities

1. Teachers present a number of notecards to their students that do not have topic headings. Students have to read each card and determine the author's topic and also whether a source has been used before.
2. Teachers present a number of notecards to their students without topic headings, and students have to state the idea or ideas recorded. If more than one idea is recorded, students have to write or state that this is so.
3. Teachers present a number of notecards to their students that have

---

[4]J.A. Hunter, *African Hunter* (Harper & Brothers, 1952), p. 52.

GUIDE FOR WRITING NOTES ON NOTECARDS

Each note that you take should be so clearly written that you have no difficulty understanding it or why you wrote it.

1. If you are quoting an author's exact words, make sure you put them in quotation marks.
2. Try to summarize what you have read but be careful that you are stating facts, not opinions.
3. If you are giving your or someone else's opinion, make sure you record this on your card so that you will not confuse the opinion with fact.
4. Do not take notes on matters of common knowledge.
5. Do not take notes on the same information twice. If two or more sources give the same facts or ideas, note the idea only once. This rule should *not* be followed, however, if you are collecting evidence to prove or disprove something. The more evidence you can uncover that points to a single conclusion, the better you will be able to defend your position on the question.

enough information for one or two paragraphs and students have to use the notecards to write the paragraph or paragraphs.

NOTETAKING FOR LISTENING TO LECTURES

Research has shown that children in the elementary grades spend at least 57.5 percent of class time in listening;[5] this percentage rises to about 90 percent in high school. Obviously, students who have difficulty listening will be at a disadvantage in school, but even good listeners may be at a disadvantage if they are not also good notetakers.

It is not too soon for intermediate-grade level students to learn how to listen and take good notes while listening; however, many times such students are not given instruction in these areas. Because of this, content-area teachers should not assume that their students are gaining the information that they are disseminating in their talk or lecture. Teachers need to help their students recognize that listening to a talk or lecture requires an active thinking mind, listening ability, and notetaking skill; and many teachers present material in their talks that simplifies, clarifies, and otherwise highlights the key points of the information that students have read in their textbooks.

Many students in content-area courses have probably learned from

[5]Miriam E. Wilt, "A Study of Teacher Awareness of Listening as a Factor in Elementary Education," *Journal of Educational Research* 43 (April 1950): 626–636.

experience that it is more difficult to take notes while listening to someone talk than it is to take notes while reading a textbook. These students should be especially receptive to help in this area. One way to help students gain insights into how they can be better listeners and notetakers is to present students with a guide stating some general and specific information that the students need. This guide can be distributed at the beginning of the term or whenever the teacher feels is the time to do so in his or her class. The teacher should have the students read the guide, and then a discussion should take place concerning the points made on the guide.

An example of the type of guide a teacher may want to distribute to his or her students follows; however, as already stated, this guide is merely an example. The amount and type of information that the teacher would include in his or her guide would have to depend on the individual differences of the students, the grade level, and the content area. Some teachers, rather than give students a complete guide on notetaking for listening to a talk, may incorporate helpful hints about notetaking before a talk or in their introduction to the lesson.

GUIDE FOR NOTETAKING DURING A LECTURE

1. Although there is no single lecture-notetaking technique that is best for everyone, there are a number of basic principles that do apply for most students.

   a. Come to a lecture prepared to learn something; that is, come with a positive attitude. This does not mean that you should not be a good critical thinker. It does mean that you should listen to a talk with an open mind and with the desire to learn something.

   b. Come to a lecture well rested and well fed.

   c. Sit in a seat where you can see as well as *hear* the speaker. The speaker's facial gestures and body movements help give meaning to what he or she is saying. Try to sit as close to the front as possible. Make sure that you can see the chalkboard. Try not to sit near students who distract you. Avoid sitting near a door or window.

   d. Come prepared with notepaper and pencils or pens.

      (1) A looseleaf notebook is better than a notepad because the pages are usually larger. You can easily take notes out and reorder them or insert other materials. (When you take a page out of a notepad, the whole business may fall apart.)

      (2) An inexpensive mechanical pencil is superior to a regular wooden pencil, if you use a pencil, because it always has a sharpened point.

2. The speaker will usually give you a number of helpful clues. Here are some things to listen or look for during a lecture:

   a. Emphasis announced with the words "This is a key point," "This is very important," "This is vital information," and so on. Write these points down and underline them.

b. Emphasis implied by time spent on a subject. Obviously the speaker feels something is important if he or she dwells on it. Underline or box your notes on the topic explained at length.

c. Announcements that you need *not* take notes. Perhaps the topic is a digression, a sideline of discussion; perhaps the speaker knows that the matter is covered thoroughly in your text. Don't tire yourself with needless recording of a lecture.

d. Outlines of the lecture written up on the chalkboard. Copy them and leave room to insert additional points that arise in the lecture.

e. Guides in the form of main ideas listed on the chalkboard. (Sometimes only the main topic of the lecture is given.)

f. Handouts containing points to be covered in the lecture. (Be sure to insert these in your notebook.)

3. The teacher's quizzes and tests give you vital information, especially the first quiz. You should use the quiz as a learning experience. From it you can find out what the teacher feels is important. After a quiz you should go over your lecture and text notes to compare them with what was on the quiz.

4. Ask questions. This is essential in helping you to understand something better. Don't hesitate to ask a question if you haven't understood a point. Asking a question slows down the teacher, gives you a chance to catch up, and gives the teacher some clue as to whether he or she is getting his or her material across to the students.

5. Before a lecture, *review* your notes from the previous lecture to set up continuity between the old and new material. In reviewing your notes, look at the "buzz" words (see item 6) and try to *recall* the key ideas presented in the last lecture. Remember, you learn more from recall than from just rereading your notes.

6. The notes that you take during a lecture must make sense to you when you read them later, and they should be organized. You do not have to use a formal outline, nor do you have to write in sentences.

   Here are some suggestions on the technique of taking notes during a lecture:

   a. Do not attempt to write every word the instructor says. Use "buzz" words and "telegraphic writing" instead. "Buzz" words (words that sound a buzzer in the mind) are any words that take on particular importance in the discussion of a topic. Often they are technical terms or words used in a special way to explain or define a professional or academic subject. The great virtue of buzz words is that they are reminders of a wide range of facts, associations, and concepts in very small packages. Advertisers find them invaluable for getting ideas across in a few words. Listen for the buzz words in the subject at hand. You can usually spot them because they are unfamiliar and crop up often. Be sure you note them and learn what they stand for. "Telegraphic writing" involves the use of one or two words to recall a complete message. The words that are used are content words, that is, words that contain significant information. Economy of writing is important in taking lecture notes, but the notes should not be so bare-boned that you have difficulty remembering what you "meant" to say. (Example of this paragraph reduced to telegraphic writing: Use buzz words; use telegraphic writing: Buzz words—words used in special way—recall sizable amount of knowledge; Telegraphic writing—one or two significant words—recall lecture.)

    b. Concentrate on making generalizations (statements or conclusions based on an accumulation of specific data); to do this, you must be actively thinking. Indent important details under your generalizations. Leave some lines blank under each idea in case the speaker returns to an idea to emphasize or embellish it. Good notetakers space out notes so that they can add material if necessary.

    c. It's sometimes a good practice to divide your page in half. Put your generalizations and supporting details on the right-hand (or left-hand) side; put the buzz words, comments, dates, questions (to ask when you can), and names on the other—as closely parallel as you can with the generalizations they refer to. If the teacher provides an outline of the lecture on the chalkboard, do not immediately copy the whole outline and then try to "squeeze" in the lecture. It's better to write the teacher's main topics and subtopics one at a time as the teacher comes to them and then fill in the details. You can still divide your paper with your outline on one side and your buzz words, comments, dates, and so on, on the other. Remember to use the teacher's clues in your notes. These help you know what to emphasize when studying for a test.

7. After a lecture, go over your notes to see if they make sense to you. If anything is confusing to you, don't hesitate to ask the teacher to clarify a point for you.

Special Note:
It's a good idea to date your notes. If you go over them and find that something is confusing, it is helpful to have a reference point for the notes. That way it's easier for another student or the teacher to help you.

An example of a student's lecture notes follows. (Some teachers may want to include a sample of lecture notes from their content area in the guide that they distribute to students.)

Jan. 15	Few absolutes in mythology, if any
	What the word "Myth" means: (Greeks have other meanings)
Many diff.	Mythology—body of myths or collection of all myths of
meanings of myth:	God; Mythology of God; collection; (no complete def., because of diverse uses)

	Mythology—"other people's religion"
	myths—used to mean a lie, untruths, but not simply untruths, fables, stories, etc.
	myths aren't really true or untrue for people who tell them
Myths used to structure reality:	Myths can be valid or invalid, in sense that interpret experience—genuine myths are narratives that tend to provide structure or order, every person's order is not the same, but each has some system of order
	Myths—explain how world came into being, provide structure
	If can't prove something, categorize it as "myth"; examples: 1. botany/zoology structure of classifying plants and animals; 2. the idea that you can look at world objectively—can't prove or disprove myths

Teachers should caution their students not to expect to find someone else's notes helpful if they did not attend the lecture. The sample lecture notes are composed mostly of generalizations. When students read them, if they attended the lecture, the notes should bring forth a great amount of other information.

Activities

1. Practice notetaking with your students in a specific content area. Present a lecture to your students on a specific topic that they are studying. Have them take notes on the talk. After they have finished, ask various students to give a summary of the talk, using their notes as a guide.

2. Have your students practice notetaking with a partner. Have each take turns reading a short excerpt from their content-area textbook and taking notes on it. After they have both had a chance doing this, they could compare their notes.

3. Present a lecture to your students, and have them take notes on it. After they have finished, give them a quiz on the lecture. (The students can use their notes while taking the quiz.)

4. Present a lecture to your students, and have them take notes on it. Tell them beforehand that they will have a quiz on the lecture and that they will be able to use their notes to take the quiz. See if they do better on the quiz when they know beforehand that they will have a quiz on the material.

OUTLINING

Outlining, which is closely related to categorizing and classification, helps students organize long written compositions or papers. An outline is useful also for studying purposes because it serves as a guide for the logical arrangement of material. (See "Notetaking for Studying" in this chapter.) Developing skills in outlining should begin early in the grades and should continue throughout the grades.

Outlining readiness begins in the primary grades when students work with categorizing. Beginning with about grade 4, students often need to use and make outlines for reporting information found in reading a variety of references; listening to tape recordings, radio, and television; experimenting to find answers to questions; observing; and interviewing people who can help with the question at hand. *As the need for making an outline arises*, pupils may consult their English books to find out about the rules involved. In the upper elementary grades and even higher ones, such suggestions as the following can be kept on a chart for reference:

Use Roman numerals for the main topics, putting a period after each Roman numeral.

Use capital letters for subtopics, with a period after each capital letter. Indent the subtopics.

Use ordinary (Arabic) numerals for details under subtopics and small letters under the details for less important points. Put a period after each number and letter.

Begin each topic with a capital letter, whether it is a main topic, a subtopic, or a detail. Do not put a period after a main topic, a subtopic, or a detail. Do not put a period after a topic unless it is a sentence.

Keep Roman numbers, capital letters, ordinary numbers, and small letters in straight vertical lines.

Topics are usually phrases, sometimes sentences. Do not mix phrases and sentences in the same outline.

An example of an outline that conveys some pertinent information about outlines follows:

I. Main topic
  A. Prime importance
    1. Joins everything under it
    2. Signaled by a Roman numeral (I, II, III, and so on)
    3. Begins with a capital letter
  B. Example: I. The main topic in an outline

II. Subtopics
   A. Grouped under main topics
   B. Related to main topics
      1. Indented under main topic
      2. Signaled by a capital letter (A, B, C, D, and so on)
      3. Begin with a capital letter
   C. Example: I. The relationship of subtopics to main topics
                    A. How related
                    B. How written

III. Specific details
   A. Grouped under appropriate subtopics
   B. Represented by Arabic numerals (1, 2, 3, 4, and so on)
   C. Example: I. The dictionary
                    A. An important reference tool
                    B. Uses of dictionary
                       1. Information concerning a word
                       2. Other useful information

IV. More specific details
   A. Grouped under appropriate Arabic numerals
   B. Represented by lowercase (small) letters (a, b, c, d, and so on)
   C. Example: I. The dictionary
                    A. An important reference tool
                    B. Uses of the dictionary
                       1. Information concerning a word
                          a. Spelling
                          b. Definitions
                          c. Correct usage
                          d. Syllabication, and so on
                       2. Other useful information
                          a. Biographical entries
                          b. Signs and symbols
                          c. Forms of address, and so on

V. Types of outlines
   A. Topic outline
      1. Consists of phrases
      2. Useful in preparing either short or long papers
   B. Sentence outline
      1. Consists of complete sentences
      2. Used primarily in planning long papers

Special Notes:

1. The main idea of a paragraph and the main topic in an outline of that paragraph are closely related, but they are not necessarily worded the same. The outline is drawn up before the paragraph is written, and its main topic will almost certainly be stated less fully than the main idea will be.

2. Outlines are used most often to sketch the contents of long, complex papers before the actual writing begins. They are, however, equally useful aids in the development of shorter papers and even of paragraphs. An outline forces you to stop to think about the way you will

organize your ideas, and it will control any urge to follow a train of thought beyond the limits of the paper or paragraph you are working on. *Example:* The main idea of this paragraph is as follows: Outlines are useful in long or short writing projects. The main topic in the outline of the paragraph may have been as follows: I. The uses of outlines.

Teachers can give students practice in working with outlines by giving students activities from their content areas such as the following:

1. From the given words or phrases, choose your title, main topics, subtopics, and specific details; and arrange them in outline form to fit the given skeleton outline.

Big Bear	location
Native Americans	animals
the constellations (groups of stars)	humans
ancient Greeks and Romans	attitudes toward constellations
seasons	Greek and Roman gods
northern hemisphere	Greek and Roman heroes
examples of constellations	factors influencing the viewing of stars
southern hemisphere	Leo
Little Bear	familiar objects
Gemini	

Title: _____

   I. _____

      A. _____

         1. _____

         2. _____

      B. _____

         1. _____

         2. _____

         3. _____

  II. _____

      A. _____

      B. _____

         1. _____

         2. _____

 III. _____

      A. _____

      B. _____

C. _____

D. _____

2. Write, in topic outline form, the main topic and subtopics of each given paragraph.

   a. A bird is a warm-blooded animal with a vertebral column (backbone) that is descended from reptiles. It differs from its ancestral reptiles by possessing a covering of feathers instead of scales, a completely fourchambered heart, fully separate systemic and pulmonary circulations, a warm-blooded metabolism, and hard eggs with hard calcareous (containing calcium carbonate) shells. Birds subsist on insects (such as caterpillars and gnats), insect larvae, worms, and seeds.

   Main topic: I. _____

   Subtopics: A. _____

   B. _____

   b. *Erosion* is the term used to explain the transportation of rock and soil particles from one place to another by natural processes. The agents of erosion are water, ice, and air. The greatest dislocation of rock and soil fragments is affected by water and air, for water and air are constantly circulating. The motion of these two agents causes other materials to move with them.

   Main topic: I. _____

   Subtopics: A. _____

   B. _____

   C. _____

Another effective technique that teachers can use is to give students a partially completed outline of a chapter from one of their textbooks and have them complete it. As students advance through the book, the teacher can present students with outlines that have less and less information until the students can produce an entire outline on a complete chapter on their own.

Sets and Outlining

An exercise involving sets can be used with students to help them recognize that outlining and classification are closely related. First, teachers should ask students to think of the set of all the books in the library. This is a very general set:

Next they should ask students to state the kinds of books one would find in the library. By doing this we are becoming less general:

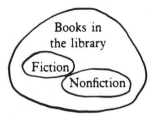

Now the teacher should ask students to state what kinds of books they would find in the set of fiction books and what kinds of books they would find in the set of nonfiction books:

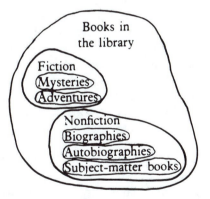

At this point the teacher should ask the children to name a particular mystery or adventure book. Here we are becoming very specific:

Finally, the teacher should ask the students to put this information in outline form.

TEST TAKING

The term *tests* seems to make most students shudder. However, tests are necessary to help students learn about their weaknesses so that they can improve and to learn about their strengths; they help give students a steady and encouraging measure of their growth. Tests are also helpful for review.

The more students know about tests, the better they can do on them. Educational Testing Service in Princeton, New Jersey, has stated that students can do better on the SATs if they practice on old ones. Also, most published tests have practice tests, which are designed to ensure that students know how to mark an answer *before* they take the actual test. Many teachers may feel that their students are test-wise because they have taken so many tests; most students, however, usually are not.

Teachers can and should help their students to be better test takers because this will ensure that the test measures what students know and not their familiarity with test taking procedures. In the content areas, if teachers find that their students should be doing better than they are on the tests they are taking, some teachers may want to discuss this with their students and try to give them some helpful guides in test taking. The amount of time that teachers spend in this area and the amount of information that teachers present to their students would depend on the content area, the grade level of the students, and their ability levels.

If teachers decide to present some test-taking techniques to their students, they should convey to them beforehand that there are no shortcuts to studying and that the best way to do well on a test is to be *well prepared.* However, research has shown that persons do better on tests if they know certain test-taking techniques and if they are familiar with the various types of tests.

Teachers could acquaint students with the various kinds of tests they give by giving them sample questions and discussing with them how they would answer the questions. Then the teacher could read aloud sample answers that he or she has prepared in advance or that he or she has from previous years. The teacher should present a number of samples so that students can see those that the teacher considers excellent as well as those that he or she considers poor or unsatisfactory. Another technique the teacher could use would be to present a lecture to the students and then give them a mock test on the lecture, that is, a test that does not count. The students are told in advance that they will get a test on the lecture after it is over, but they are not told that it is a mock test. After the students have taken the test, the teacher explains to them that it is a mock test and that one of the prime purposes of the test is to give students practice in test-taking procedures. Students discuss the answers to the questions. The teacher then collects the papers and begins to read aloud some of the answers. (To avoid any embarrassment, no names are disclosed.) The students are encouraged to analyze the various answers. The teacher also gives his or her comments concerning the answer, as well as the probable grade that the student would have received if it had been an actual test. This technique is especially helpful for students because they can see how well they would have done in relation to others in the class if the test had been graded, and they are gaining information about what to expect on future tests.

As in the area of notetaking, teachers can present students with guides that contain test-taking information, and after students have read the information, the teacher and students could discuss what they have read. Teachers could refer students to the guides when a test is announced, as well as when going over tests. At times, a teacher may want, in private, to refer a student only to a specific part of the guide because the student seems to have a particular test-taking problem. Some teachers may have a number of guides available and give different ones to different students based on need. A number of test-taking guides that teachers can use to convey important test-taking information to their students, as well as other information on tests, are presented in the remainder of this chapter.

TEST-TAKING GUIDE I

This guide contains some general test-taking principles.

1. *Plan* to do well. Be prepared. Have a *positive attitude.*
2. Be *well rested.* (Don't stay up the whole night before a test.) Research has shown that sleep after studying, even a few hours, will help you to retain the information better.
3. Be prepared. The better prepared you are, the less nervous and anxious you are. (A small amount of tension is usually necessary to activate you to do your best.)
4. Look upon tests as a learning experience. Plan to learn from them.
5. Look over the whole test before you begin. Notice the types of questions asked and the points allotted for each question. (Do not spend a long time on a one- to five-point question that you know a lot about. Answer it and go on.)
6. Know how much time is allotted for the test. Allot your time wisely. Remember to check the time.
7. Concentrate!
8. Read instructions very carefully. Do not read anything into them that is not there. If a question asks for a description and examples, do not forget to give the examples. If you do not understand something or if something does not make sense, ask the instructor about it. There may be an error on the test. Do not dwell on the point of confusion before you ask the instructor.

9. Begin with the questions you are sure of. This will give you a feeling of confidence and success. However, as already advised, do not dwell on these at length.

10. If you do not know an answer, make an intelligent guess. As long as the penalty for a wrong answer is the same as for no answer, it pays to take a calculated guess. (Of course, if your guess is wrong, you do not get any points for it.)

11. After you answer the questions you are sure of, work on those that count the most, that is, that are worth the greatest number of points.

12. Allow time to go over the test. Check that you have answered all the questions. Be leery about changing a response unless you have found a particular reason to while going over the test. For example, you may have misread the question, you may have misinterpreted the question, or you may not have realized that it was a "tricky" question. If the question is a straightforward one, it's probably better to leave your first response.

13. After the test has been graded and returned, go over it to learn from the results. Unless you find out why an answer is wrong and what the correct answer is, you may continue to make the same mistake on other tests.

Objective Tests

An objective test is any test involving short answers, usually one or two words. Among the variety of objective test questions are true/false, multiple choice, matching items, completion or fill-in, and short answers. As there is only one correct answer for a given question, objective tests are, on the whole, easier to take and easier to grade. They can cover a good deal of subject knowledge but not in the depth a subjective test permits. One system of study preparation is appropriate for objective tests and another for subjective tests.

Teachers should convey to their students the type of test they intend to give and give them some information about preparing for the test. Some content-area teachers also share with students examples of the types of objective questions that they will ask on the test.

Because an objective test is comprehensive and aimed at discovering powers of *recognition* and *recall*, teachers should help students prepare for it by concentrating on details. Teachers should also tell students to review important definitions, principles, concepts, formulas, names, dates, and terms that relate to the material to be covered on the test. As students *go over the details*, they should *be sure to review the relation of the details to the whole*. Unless the students know their facts and how the facts relate to the general content of the subject, they will find any examination difficult, if not bewildering.

The information that follows is for the content-area teacher so that he or she will be able to help students be better test takers. The individual teacher will have to determine the amount of aid and information that he or she will give to students.

Studying for Objective Tests   True/false, multiple choice, and matching tests call for *recognition*. Fill-in or completion tests call for *recall*. Recall tests are usually more difficult than recognition tests because students have to produce the answer from memory. Recognition tests are usually easier because students have answers from which to choose. However, research has shown that students who do best on recognition tests also do best on recall tests. Presumably, those who know how to distinguish between items in a list also know the material thoroughly enough by memory to recall the right choices.

Although objective tests deal with recognition and recall, test questions can be devised to look for such things as students' ability to think critically, to solve new problems, to apply principles, and to select relevant facts. To do well, students need a *fund of knowledge* and *reasoning ability*. If students have the reasoning ability but no fund of knowledge, they either have not studied the material or have not approached their studying from the right angle; the students will probably not do well.

Research has shown that students *remember* generalizations longer than material memorized by rote with no attempt to make associations. Research has indicated also that people forget information mainly because, in learning new information, they put the old mentally to one side. If students *overlearn* the old material, learn the new material *and its relation to the old,* and continue to use the old as they work with the new, they are less likely to confuse the old with the new or forget the old altogether. Overlearning (continuing of practice after students feel they know the material) the basic information in a field is essential. For example, in some subjects certain definitions, formulas, axioms, or concepts that are often used are worth overlearning.

Studying for generalizations does not mean that students should not memorize certain definitions, formulas, principles, and so on. The key thing is for students to understand how to use the material they memorize and to see its relationship to the whole. The following steps are helpful in memorizing material:

1. Students should read through the whole passage they wish to memorize. It's important to see the relationship of the parts to the whole and to make associations.
2. If it's a long selection, students should break it up into manageable parts and memorize each part, but students should always remember to relate the part to its whole.
3. As students learn a new part, they should go back over the old part and relate it to the new.
4. Students should go over the whole selection a number of times. They

should remember that to *overlearn* something means that they should practice it beyond the point when they feel they know it. Students should remember also that they should distribute their practice over a period of time.

5. Students should use mnemonic devices. A mnemonic device is a memory association trick that helps students to recall material. For example: HOMES is a mnemonic device to help students to remember the five Great Lakes. Each letter of HOMES is the first letter of one of the Great Lakes—Huron, Ontario, Michigan, Erie, and Superior. Students should be careful not to use a mnemonic device that's more complicated than the fact to be remembered. "Thirty days hath September, April, June, and November" is adequate. Who knows all of this?

> Thirty days hath September,
> April, June, and November;
> All the rest have thirty-one,
> Excepting February alone,
> and that has twenty-eight days clear
> and twenty-nine in each leap year.

And who needs it? Help your students to remember that the best way to commit information to memory is to learn generalizations and to look for relationships within the material they are studying.

Special Notes:

1. Although an objective test question is usually supposed to have only one answer, it's possible that there may be more.

2. Completion and short answer tests lend themselves to more subjectivity than the other types of objective tests because students' recall responses may be worded in many different ways. The teacher must interpret whether the response is the desired one or not. Whenever there is interpretation there is usually some subjectivity.

TEST-TAKING GUIDE II

This guide contains information on taking true/false tests.

True/False Tests

1. Do not leave a true/false question unanswered. You have a 50 percent chance of getting the answer correct just by guessing. (You may be penalized; that is, more points may be deducted for an incorrect answer than for no answer on some standardized tests.)

2. *Always* read carefully any true/false question that says *always, never, all, none, impossible, nothing,* and so on. These are usually giveaways that the

answer is false. Almost every rule has exceptions. Of course, there are times when inclusive categories such as *all, no, always* or *never* are accurate. *Examples:* All humans are mortal. (T); No human is without vertebra. (T); Children always learn to speak. (F); All people who study do well on exams. (F); All true/false tests are objective (T); All children need ten hours of sleep. (F). Notice that when the answer is true for such categories as *all, no, always* or *never* the statement is usually a definition or a rule.

3. Rather than use giveaways such as *always* or *never,* teachers usually make true/false questions more difficult by stating only part of a definition or by inserting something incorrect in a definition; that is, part of an accurate definition is given but the other part is left out or misstated. Obviously, you should be *well prepared* on details such as definitions for true/false tests. You should be very alert. Examples: (1) Language is defined as a shared, learned system used for all communication. (True or <u>False</u>) (Although what is said is correct, the statement is not complete enough to be marked true. The complete definition is *Language is a learned, shared, and patterned, arbitrary system of vocal sound symbols with which people in a given culture can communicate with one another.*) (2) An amoeba is a single-celled plant. (True or <u>False</u>) (An amoeba is single-celled, but it is an animal, not a plant.)

4. Statements that use words such as *sometimes, often, usually, many, generally, frequently, as a rule, some,* and so on are usually true. Examples: Usually children learn to speak. (<u>True</u> or False) As a rule, small children need ten hours of sleep. (<u>True</u> or False)

Special Note:

Make your T's and F's very clear. It may be a good idea to write out *true* or *false* so that there is no question of misinterpretation. If the T or F is not clear, the instructor may mark it wrong.

© 1965 United Feature Syndicate, Inc.

FIGURE 6-3. Poor Linus! When will he learn that studying helps you pass true/false tests?

TEST-TAKING GUIDE III

This guide contains information on taking multiple-choice tests.

1. Multiple choice tests are not as easy to guess on as true/false tests are. But even on a multiple choice test if you have only four answers from which to

choose for each question, you have a 25 percent chance of being correct by guessing. Therefore, attempt to answer each question.

2. When taking a multiple choice test, read the statement or question and then before reading the choices think for a moment about what you feel the answer should be. Read the choices carefully to determine if one matches.

3. Read the complete or incomplete question or statement to be answered very carefully. If a negative is contained in the question or statement, note it. It may help to mentally check off each item in the positive. Example: Which of the following is *not* an example of a prime number: (1) 7 (2) 13 (3) 21 (4) 11?

   In your mind you could very quickly say the following: 7 is a prime number, 13 is a prime number, 21 is not a prime number, and 11 is a prime number. The answer is 21. Here are examples of some numbers. Choose the one that is a *prime number:* (1) 9 (2) 51 (3) 73 (4) 63.

   In this example three are incorrect, and only one is correct. Although you feel that you know your prime numbers and you can come to the correct one quickly, take a moment to look at the others to make sure that you do indeed have the correct answer.

4. Look for teacher's clues in multiple choice tests. Here are some give-aways: (1) a choice that is much longer and more detailed than the others is usually the correct answer; (2) a word in a choice that also appears in the statement or question usually implies that the choice is the correct answer; (3) ridiculous choices among the items allow you to arrive at the answer by elimination (usually, you can easily eliminate two items, but then you are left with a choice between the two remaining items); (4) a special part of speech required in the answer will identify the correct choice. Example: The definition of *optimist* is: (a) cheerful (b) looking at the bright side (c) one who looks at the bright side of things (d) being cheerful. The answer must be (c) because *optimist* is a noun.

TEST-TAKING GUIDE IV

This guide contains information on matching items tests, fill-in or completion tests, and short answer tests.

Matching Items Tests.

1. In a matching items test you must usually match the items in one column with the items in another. Teachers commonly use this kind of test to match the following elements: words with their meanings; dates with historical events; persons with their achievements; authors with their books; rules with their examples; and so on.

2. If the teacher uses a variety of material on the same matching test, you have a better chance of doing well. For example, if authors are matched with titles of books, wars or major events with dates, terms with defini-

FIGURE 6-4. When you're not prepared, all tests are "mystical."

tions, and rules with examples on the same matching test, your choices are more limited.

3. It is often useful to use the process of elimination to help you solve difficult matches. That is, once you have completed all matches you are certain of, you will have a much smaller list to choose from.

Fill-in or Completion Tests.

1. The fill-in or completion test is one in which you receive a statement that omits a key word or phrase. You must produce from memory the missing item. Example: The sixteenth President was _____.

2. The fill-in or completion test is one in which you must *recall* the correct answer. Recall items, like recognition items, can test either for simple facts or for more complex understandings. For such a test, you should concentrate on details, but you should understand how the details are organized, that is, how they are related to what you are studying. Memorizing isolated details will not help you to retain the information or help you to understand it.

3. Sometimes the teacher intentionally or unintentionally gives you grammatical clues. Be on the lookout for these. Examples: A person of high birth is called *an* _____. A man who has many wives is called *a* _____. (Here the indefinite article *an* is a clue that the answer begins with a vowel and the indefinite article *a* is a clue that the answer begins with a consonant.) Example: The authors of the paper describing the first transistor were _____. (Here the plural noun and verb tell you that the answer must be in the plural; that is, there is more than one author involved.)

Short Answer Tests.

The short answer test is very similar to the completion or fill-in test. It is similarly based on recall, and the correct answer is usually a word or phrase. However, in the short answer test a question or a simple statement is used rather than a statement with a blank for a missing word or phrase. Examples: Name the sixteenth President of the United States. What is the capital of California?

Special Note:
If you feel that a recall or recognition test item can be answered by more than one answer, bring this to the attention of your teacher. It may be that the test question was incorrectly written. If the teacher tells you that the question *is* correctly written, try to choose the best answer. However, you might write a note in the margin of your paper (if there is time) explaining why you think it could be the other answer, also. Then when you go over the test in class, bring this question up, or discuss this point after the exam with the teacher.

Subjective Tests (Essay Tests)

Essay tests are usually given when a teacher wants to see that the students know the material thoroughly enough to organize it and use it to draw conclusions, which is something more than merely knowing material well enough to recognize it. Subjective tests are more difficult to take and to grade than are objective tests. Their answers are not merely right or wrong but are demonstrations of reasoning, thought, and perception.

Often teachers share with their students examples of essay tests to illustrate to students the kinds of responses they consider good ones, and they analyze the reasons for this. Some teachers give students practice in taking essay tests and give students examples of some of the different ways that essay questions can be worded. Here are some of these:

1. Give the reasons for . . .
2. Explain how or why . . .
3. Present arguments for and arguments against . . .
4. Compare the poem _____ to the poem _____ in terms of the author's ability to portray fatalism.
5. Analyze the male character in _____.
6. Give the events that led to the _____ War.

Comparison of Essay Tests to Objective Tests   On an essay test students spend most of their time thinking and writing whereas, on an objective test, they spend most of their time reading and thinking. Students are more free to express their ideas and be creative on an essay test than on an objective test. A drawback to essay tests is that they may encourage bluffing; a drawback of objective tests is that they allow students to guess at an answer. Both essay and objective tests can measure simple and complex concepts and knowledge if properly constructed.

TEST-TAKING GUIDE V

This guide contains information on studying for essay tests.
    Essay tests require you to recall material and to be able to express your ideas logically. Here are some study suggestions:

1. Look for broad, general concepts (ideas) and for relations between concepts. Study for main ideas and generalizations. Note the organization of details that develop the main ideas.
2. Distribute your studying time.
3. Study in particular the material your teacher emphasized or spent much time on in class.
4. Try to anticipate some of the essay questions. It may be a good idea to work up one or two essays answering questions that you think your instructor is likely to ask (See Special Notes.) Also, your text may contain "questions for discussion" at the end of each chapter. These questions are usually subjective questions. Go over them because they may appear on the test as they are or thinly disguised. If they are not given on the test, your study of them will at least have prepared you for the *kind* of question given.

Special Notes:

1. Although it may be a good idea to try to anticipate essay questions and prepare one or two in advance, be careful! Do not spend a great amount of time doing this. It's better to spend more time on studying generalizations and relations between concepts.
2. If the essay you prepared in advance is not related to the question that is asked, *do not* give your prepared essay answer as the answer on the test. Answer the question. Perhaps you can use a small part of your prepared essay. (After the test, study the essay questions asked on the test and compare these with your text and lecture notes to try to determine why your instructor asked these questions. This will help you anticipate questions better next time.)

TEST-TAKING GUIDE VI

This guide contains information on taking essay tests.

1. Read the question. Make sure you understand it. Do not read into it what is *not* there. Check to see if examples or illustrations are asked for. Check to see if your opinion is asked for. If you are asked to list, name, or identify, do exactly that. Do not give more information than is asked for. If you are asked to summarize, give an overview. If you are asked to analyze, you must break down the question into its parts. The most general type of question is one that asks you to discuss or explain. In a comparison/contrast question, you must give similarities, differences, or both. If you are asked to evaluate, you must make a value judgment. This type question is the most difficult to answer because it requires that you know a great amount of information on the topic to determine what is best or correct.
2. Put down on a scrap sheet of paper any special formulas, principles, concepts, or buzz words that you have memorized and that you think will be

relevant to the question. Do this immediately so that you will not forget to include the important details that you have memorized.

3. *Think* about the question.
4. Plan your answer. (Again, make sure that you are answering the question.)
5. Prepare an outline for your answer.
6. Write out your answer. Use lists where applicable.
7. Check the time available to you.
8. Do not spend all your time on a single essay if there is more than one question.
9. Reread your essay to make sure that your ideas are clearly and logically stated. Make sure that you have used complete sentences and that each of your paragraphs expresses one main idea.

Special Note:

Although it's usually permissible to list items in an essay test, some teachers frown on your writing your complete essay in outline form. Be sure to check with your teacher whether you can answer by outline *before* you proceed to do so. However, if you are pressed for time, and you have no choice, it's a good idea to present your essay in outline form.

TEST-TAKING GUIDE VII

This guide contains information on taking a combination essay and objective test.

Many tests are composed of both objective and subjective test items. On such tests you must plan your time especially wisely. Here are some suggestions:

1. Read the whole test through.
2. Notice how many points each part of the test is worth.
3. Put down any special formulas, principles, ideas, or other details you have memorized that you think may be relevant to your essay question.
4. Do the objective part first. It may give you clues for your essay question. The objective part of the test usually takes less time than the essay part. If

FIGURE 6-5. Peppermint Patty is learning that studying is the easy way to do things.

you do it first you will be more at ease, more accustomed to the test, when you begin work on the essay questions. You will also be relieved to know part of the test is behind you.

GRAPHIC SUMMARY OF CHAPTER

Here is a graphic summary of Chapter 6. If you have read the chapter, this graphic illustration should help you remember its main points. Under or beside each heading, you might want to jot down some of the information you recall, as well as some of the key concepts in this chapter. This can act as a good review. You can then check your key concepts against those that follow the graphic summary.

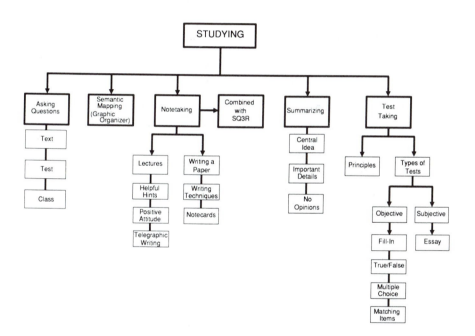

KEY CONCEPTS IN CHAPTER

- Asking questions in class is important for learning.
- Asking questions of what one is reading helps individuals be active consumers of information.
- Asking questions of what one is reading is consistent with viewing reading as problem solving.
- Asking questions helps slow teachers down.
- Asking questions helps students gain a better insight into the subject.

- Reading and writing are important modes of learning.
- Notetaking is a tool that can be used for studying.
- Visual representations can help students organize and remember information.
- Summarizing is an excellent mode of learning that helps students retain the most important concepts and facts in a selection.
- Good summaries usually include the central idea and important details.
- Notecards should be clearly written.
- Notetaking can be used for writing long papers, listening to lectures, and studying.
- Outlining helps students retain and organize information.
- Students should learn test-taking procedures.
- Tests help students learn about their strengths and weaknesses.
- Being well-prepared is the best way to do well on a test.

SUGGESTIONS FOR THOUGHT QUESTIONS AND ACTIVITIES

1. You have been appointed to a committee to help set up a program in your school that will help students gain notetaking and test-taking skills. What notetaking and test-taking skills do you feel should be taught? What suggestions will you make?
2. Brainstorm a number of questions that you think are good ones that students should ask about tests.
3. Prepare a lesson, and present the main points of the lesson in an outline that you could give to students.
4. Brainstorm techniques for presenting notetaking techniques to students in a content area of your choice.
5. Choose a topic from a content area and construct a semantic map that would help students see the interrelationships of ideas in relation to this topic.
6. Explain how summarizing helps students retain information.
7. Brainstorm techniques for presenting test-taking guides to your students.

SELECTED BIBLIOGRAPHY

DAVEY, BETH. "Active Responding in Content Classrooms." *Journal of Reading* 33 (October 1989): 44–46.
GILLESPIE, CINDY. "Questions about Student Generated Questions." *Journal of Reading* 34 (December/January 1990/1991): 250–257.

HAYES, DAVID A. "Helping Students GRASP the Knack of Writing Summaries." *Journal of Reading* 33 (November 1989): 96–101.

HELFELDT, JOHN P., and WILLIAM A. HENK. "Reciprocal Question-Answer Relationships: An Instructional Technique for At-Risk Readers." *Journal of Reading* 33 (April 1990): 509–514.

HUNKINS, FRANCIS P. *Involving Students in Questioning.* Boston: Allyn & Bacon, 1976.

McPHAIL, IRVING P. "Why Teach Test Wiseness?" *Journal of Reading* 25 (October 1981): 32–38.

MICCINATI, JEANNETTE L. "Mapping the Terrain: Connecting Reading with Academic Writing." *Journal of Reading* 31 (March 1988): 542–552.

RUBIN, DOROTHY. *Reading and Learning Power,* 3rd ed. Needham, Heights, Mass.: Ginn Press, 1990.

SPIRES, HILLER A., and P. DIANE STONE. "The Directed Notetaking Activity: A Self-Questioning Approach." *Journal of Reading* 33 (October 1989): 36–39.

Part 3: Integrating Reading and Study Skills Approaches into Specific Content Areas

7

Integrating Social Studies and Reading/Study Skills Instruction

OVERVIEW

Introduction
Key Questions
Key Terms in Chapter
Central Idea and Social Studies
Critical Comprehension and Social
  Studies
    The Teacher's Role in
      Developing Critical Thinking
      Skills
    Bias and Political Cartoons
    Detecting Fallacious Arguments
Interpretive, Critical, and Creative
  Comprehension Questions for
  Social Studies
    Student Questions in Social
      Studies
    Simulated Activities: Insight
      into the Nature and
      Methods of History
Vocabulary Development in Social
  Studies

The Connotative Meaning of
  Words
Context Clues
Combining Forms
Correlating Social Studies with
  Vocabulary Study and Other
  Areas
Incorporating Summarizing and
  Studying in Social Studies
Sample Social Studies Activities
Computer Software and Social
  Studies
    Database Management Systems
    Computer-Assisted Instruction
Graphic Summary of Chapter
Key Concepts in Chapter
Suggestions for Thought Questions
  and Activities
Selected Bibliography

The present is only a fleeting instant, and everything we are conscious of is already in the past, has already become a part of history.
Robert Daniels
STUDYING HISTORY: HOW ANᴰ WHY

INTRODUCTION

Read the following headlines that seemed to be omnipresent in the 1980s and early 1990s.

STUDENTS LACK BASIC HISTORY AND GEOGRAPHY
KNOWLEDGE
ONLY 5 PERCENT OF STUDENTS CAN INTERPRET COMPLEX
HISTORICAL INFORMATION AND IDEAS

The National Assessment of Educational Progress (NAEP) has reported on the dismal performance of our students in history, geography, and civics. The *Summary of Findings from 20 Years of NAEP,* states: "The truth may be that relatively few children are receiving the education they need for life in the 21st century. There is considerable evidence that large numbers of students graduate from school lacking the skills needed by employers and expected by college professors."[1] The report states further that "the problem, however, is much larger than simply a lack of basic skills."[2] The concern appears to be as to how well prepared our students are to compete in the world market and how knowledgeable they are about the major issues and debates confronting society today. There is great concern about the mounting evidence that the "typical high school student is not knowledgeable enough to appreciate what these issues or debates are all about, let alone to participate creatively and effectively in making decisions about the salient issues."[3]

In the area of history and civics, in general, "students' performance can be described as indicating a moderate understanding of some historical events, but far from displaying a coherent grasp of how these events interacted to shape our nation. Evidence of this lack permeated the assessment results."[4] In other words, students seem to be able to answer questions at a literal level but not at an interpretive level. For example, 56 percent of the fourth graders knew the names of Columbus's ships, but only 36 knew why he sailed to America.

---

[1]Ina V.S. Mullis, Eugene H. Owen, and Gary W. Phillips, *Accelerating Academic Achievement: A Summary of Findings from 20 Years of NAEP,* The National Assessment of Educational Progress (Princeton, N.J.: Educational Testing Service, September 1990), p. 6.
[2]Ibid., p. 7.
[3]Ibid.
[4]Ibid., p. 23.

Students fared no better in geography; that is, they were able to locate major countries on a world map, but they had difficulty answering questions that required them to make inferences or interpretations based on presented information. For example, "when twelfth graders were presented with two maps of the same area—one showing amount of rainfall and the other showing elevation—only 27 percent of the students put the sets of information together to identify areas of likely soil erosion."[5] The NAEP report goes on to say that, "high school seniors demonstrated generally low performance across all four areas emphasized in the geography assessment—location and place, skills and tools, cultural geography, and physical geography."[6]

What is devastating is that "fewer than 10 percent appear to have both an understanding of the specialized material and ideas comprising the curriculum and the ability to work with these to interpret, integrate, infer, draw generalizations, and articulate conclusions."[7] Students who have difficulty thinking clearly and doing higher-level thinking will definitely have difficulty in reading their social studies textbooks. It is not surprising then that these students "in reading, have difficulty identifying the global messages and purposes of text and even greater difficulty articulating evidence to support their understanding."[8]

Based on what has been said, it seems almost ludicrous to have a special chapter devoted to a discussion of how reading comprehension can and should be incorporated in the teaching of social studies. The teaching of social studies is still largely dependent on the ability to gain information from reading, and students who lack high-level comprehension skills will be at a decided disadvantage in any social studies course. However, what seems clearly obvious is many times not obvious until it is brought to view. As in the tale "The Emperor's New Clothes," it wasn't until the little boy said aloud that the emperor was naked that the people recognized that this was so and stopped deluding themselves. According to Santayana, "those who cannot learn from history are doomed to repeat it." It may be that the reason we have so much conflict and misunderstanding in the world is because people do not have the critical comprehension skills that they need to interpret past and present events properly. Without critical comprehension skills, they can be easily deluded. This chapter will show how reading comprehension skills are used to gain social studies concepts, and how a directed reading approach can enhance the teaching of social studies.

[5]Ibid., p. 27.
[6]Ibid.
[7]Ibid., p. 29.
[8]Ibid., p. 28.

KEY QUESTIONS

After you finish reading this chapter, you should be able to answer the following questions:

1. Why do students need critical thinking skills when they are reading social studies material?
2. What is the teacher's role in helping students develop critical thinking skills?
3. How can teachers enhance students' critical thinking ability?
4. What are some critical comprehension skills that students need to be effective readers?
5. What are the purposes of political cartoons?
6. What should students know about political cartoons?
7. What should students know about fallacious arguments?
8. What kinds of questions can stimulate higher-level responses?
9. What techniques will enhance vocabulary development in social studies?
10. How do the connotative meanings of words influence readers?
11. How can teachers correlate social studies lessons with other areas?
12. How can teachers incorporate summarizing and study skills techniques in social studies lessons?
13. How can some social studies computer programs enhance the teaching of social studies?

KEY TERMS IN CHAPTER

You should pay special attention to the following key terms:

appeal to inappropriate authority
appeal to pity
argument from ignorance
attacking the person
complex question
database management systems

fallacies
fallacious arguments
false cause
irrelevant conclusion
political cartoons
special circumstance of person

CENTRAL IDEA AND SOCIAL STUDIES

Autonomy of the mind, that is, independence of thought, is necessary to maintain a free society. Unless individuals are able to figure out information for themselves, our freedom is at great risk. Social studies teachers cannot take for granted that their students have the skill to figure out the essence of what they are reading. One way to help would be to model how to attain the main or central idea of written material. Here is what one social studies teacher does at the beginning of the term.

Scenario: Central Idea and the Reading of the Social Studies Textbook
When students receive their textbook, Mrs. Johnson has them go through the book to get an overview of what it covers. She asks them to note the kinds of tactics that the writer uses to help them gain the most from their reading. They spend some time looking at such items as the running glossary, which is in the margins, terms that are in italics or bold print for emphasis, and the kinds of section headings the author uses to give readers an idea of what the sections are about.

After the students are acquainted with the textbook, she tells them that they must be able to get the central idea of what they are reading and to help them she will demonstrate how she does this.

She has her students turn to a page toward the beginning of the book and tells them that she will share with them how she goes about constructing the central idea of the section on that page. She then takes them through the procedure step by step.

First, she tells them she surveys the section to note the section head, the terms in the margins, and any other helpful hints the writer may use. Mrs. Johnson asks her students to do the same. She tells her students that the section head gives her a good idea of what the section is about and what to anticipate. The section head usually contains the topic of the central idea. Now she has to read the section to determine what is special about the topic that helps pull everything in the section together. She asks her students to read the section also and try to construct its central idea.

After she finishes reading the section, she waits for the students to finish also. She then verbalizes for them her thoughts as to how she constructs the central idea. She tells them that the section head gives her the topic, so her job is to read carefully to figure out what is special about the topic and helps pull everything together. She then gives them her central idea statement and shows them how all the paragraphs help develop the central idea of the section. Next, she presents her students with examples of central idea statements that are incorrect and challenges them to state why. (See sections on main and central idea in Chapter 3.)

CRITICAL COMPREHENSION AND SOCIAL STUDIES

We are living at a time when individuals from early childhood onward are daily exposed to a plethora of news, advertisements, and information from the mass media. From past experiences we have learned that what is presented as fact may actually be suspect. One way that teachers can help to lessen the impact of propaganda or half-truths is to emphasize critical thinking. Critical thinking is the high-level thinking skill needed to do both critical reading and critical listening. Critical thinking has to do with the ability to detect bias, propaganda, and so on. It is a high-level thinking skill because it demands that individuals make judgments. Critical thinking has been discussed as an important skill in a number of chapters in this book; however, it is especially essential in the social studies program because objectivity is the handmaiden of social studies.

Humans are responsible for recording the events of the past and present. The events that are chosen, the persons who are chosen, and the manner of presenting these will all influence our perception of them. The same event reported by two different reporters will usually result in two different reports based on each writer's bias. It used to be thought that history never changes; however, we now know that past events are reinterpreted in the light of current events. Many times terrible things are buried and tend to be forgotten or are assumed to have never taken place, and leaders who were thought to be monsters become heroes because of a reinterpretation of past events. Truth is truth as seen in the eyes of the beholder. If facts are not available and if only half-truths and partial data are given, how can we judge what had taken place? Even with the advent of the mass media, it is difficult in this day and age to find out what is taking place in some totalitarian regimes. Imagine then how difficult it must be to get any semblance of reality from the past because most regimes prior to 1776 were authoritarian in one manner or another.

The purpose of presenting the prior information is not to discourage students from reading social studies books but to encourage them to check their sources, to be alert to propaganda techniques, and to be cautious about making inferences from sparse data. It is still mostly through reading that we can gain information of the past as well as of the present. It is through reading that we can gain sufficient, needed details for clarification and verification. Information can, of course, be gained from listening, but this avenue is fraught with even more possibilities of misinterpretation than reading. In listening to a speaker, the listener must contend not only with the speaker's voice, expressions, mannerisms, and so on, which impede critical listening, but he or she must contend with the tyranny of the audience. Speakers may be able to sway even antagonistic audiences to a one-sided view, and individuals caught up in this soon lose their objectivity and succumb to the mob view. An example would be the almost hypnotic effect that Adolf Hitler had on his German audiences at mass meetings during the 1930s.

The Teacher's Role in Developing Critical Thinking Skills

The teacher is the key person in the class who can help students be alert to the need for objectivity, the need to see all sides, and the need to suspend judgment until all the evidence is seen. First, it is imperative that teachers themselves behave in an objective and unbiased manner in the classroom. "Learning by example" is still a valid adage. If teachers present or at least attempt to the best of their ability to present all sides of an issue, if they avoid giving opinions as if they were facts, and if they suspend making judgments until sufficient data is available, they will be helping their students to do the same. Of course, the teacher's role in helping students to develop critical thinking skill, which is essential for critical comprehension, does not end there. The teacher's behavior is only the beginning. Next, the teacher must develop a program so that students recognize what propaganda techniques are and how to counteract them. One way to do this is to use a directed reading approach. For example, if students are to read material that requires them to know how to detect bias and propaganda, the teacher should go over propaganda techniques with students, using content material, and discuss the role of bias in propaganda so that students can understand the important content concepts. If the teacher feels that some students need more help, he or she should prepare a special guide for these students. (See Chapter 1 for information on using a directed reading approach.)

Activities to Enhance Critical Thinking   The Institute for Propaganda Analysis has identified several devices or basic techniques of propaganda (see Chapter 3 for these). In courses on subjects like American government or political science, in which students are analyzing the wheels of government, teachers could have students read and listen to politicians' speeches and have them determine what tactic or tactics are being used. (See Chapter 14 for a propaganda learning center that social studies teachers can adapt for use in their classes.) Teachers could also have students read different reporters' reports of the same politician's speech and have them try to determine the position of the reporter. (See the section in this chapter on connotative meanings.) A discussion should also take place concerning the role of the reporter, who is charged with reporting the news and only the news without bias or opinions. A comparison between the role of the editorial and the straight news story should be made, and then students should be asked to read a number of editorials related to government and try to determine the writer's bias. Another activity could involve the writing of a paper on a specific issue related to what is being discussed in class at the time. The students are told to choose an issue, to research it, and try to report on it in as objective a manner as is possible. The teacher tells students that they should check their sources and make sure that the information is relevant. Students should also check the "newness" of the material if this is vital to the topic being written on and maintain a position of objectivity. To make this assignment more interesting, the teacher might ask a few persons to report on the same issue. Perhaps the issue that is chosen should be a controversial one. Here is a scenario showing how one teacher helped her students to recognize the power of propaganda.

Scenario:

(A ninth-grade class in American Government. The students have been studying about municipal governments. A mayoralty race is in progress at the time, so the teacher, Mrs. Thompson, decides to use this as a focal point of her unit. She wants to help her students not only to learn about how the municipal government functions but also to learn how pervasive propaganda can be even in a democracy and how students must be good critical thinkers to be able to recognize this.)

Mrs. Thompson has been teaching social studies for ten years. She can't believe that a decade has already gone by, but it has, and this fact is sharply brought home when some of her former students come to visit her. Mrs. Thompson had been known as a dreamer and an idealist when she was in college. She was also exceptionally creative. Mrs. Thompson may not be as idealistic as she was when she was in college, but she is just as creative, and this creative ability has made her into an exceptional teacher, who is much admired by her students. Mrs. Thompson has the following epigram written in bold print in the center of one of the bulletin boards, and on the first day of class she brings her students' attention to it. She explains how vitally important it is for students of government to have sufficient data before making judgments.

> A little learning is a dangerous thing;
> Drink deep or taste not the Pierian spring;
> There shallow draughts intoxicate the brain,
> And drinking largely sobers us again.
> ALEXANDER POPE

Mrs. Thompson is known as a teacher who tries to be objective and who stresses critical thinking. These attributes have remained constant throughout the ten years, and Mrs. Thompson's feelings toward these attributes haven't changed. Moreover, she uses her creative teaching ability to help students gain skill in critical thinking in a number of different ways. The following scenario illustrates one of these ways.

Mrs. Thompson's students have been reading about municipal governments, and she thinks that it would be a good idea for the students to learn about the government of their own local municipality in a personal way and at the same time learn how to be good critical thinkers. She has decided to have a mayoralty election within her own class. The timing for this is perfect because there is one taking place within their municipality. Mrs. Thompson also thinks that it would be an excellent idea to see if the media people in the school district would tape the debate and discussion that would take place. In that way, the students could view themselves and analyze their behavior more objectively; that is, if the students were confused about what took place, they could go back to the videotape rather than depend on their memories. From this, the students should also learn how fickle their memories could be.

To initiate this project, Mrs. Thompson asks the students the names of the candidates for mayor in their local community. She asks them their views about the candidates and where they got their views. The class has been studying about politicians and the kinds of propaganda tactics that many politicians resort to. Mrs. Thompson tells her students that they will have an opportunity to learn firsthand about how local governments function in a democracy. They, the students, will hold their own election. She further states that this may sound easier than it is; however, to simulate the actual process, the students will have to do a great amount of reading to determine how a person is nominated and what the primary election does and how it is set up. After persons from the class have been nominated and elected in the primary election, they will need to read to find out what takes place next. Also, the chosen nominees will be responsible for presenting their views on a number of issues. The audience will have to be well read to know about the issues so that they can vote intelligently. The audience will also have to be alert to any propaganda tactics that the chosen nominees may use. The chosen nominees can choose campaign managers who will conduct the campaign for them. On a certain day that will be appointed, the candidates will debate one another; the audience will consist of all the ninth-grade classes in the school. After the debate, which will be videotaped, the audience will vote to elect the person they feel should be mayor. After the election, the class will view the videotape to analyze what has taken place.

Mrs. Thompson's class is so excited about the project that they can hardly wait to begin. Mrs. Thompson cautions her students again about the fact that this project demands a great amount of research. In addition, all persons must be actively involved in the project. Actually, the audience's role is the most important because they must make a judgment, and, to do this effectively, they must be knowledgeable about all the issues and be able to weed out propaganda when they see or hear it.

In Mrs. Thompson's class the wheels of government are in motion.

FIGURE 7-1. Lucy doesn't understand the role of the political cartoonist.

1960 United Feature Syndicate, Inc.

Bias and Political Cartoons

Junior high and secondary school students, as well as a number of upper-elementary grade level students, are ready to be introduced to the political cartoon, which is the political cartoonist's vehicle for propaganda. Teachers can use political cartoons to advance the students' critical thinking. The ability to interpret political cartoons helps make students more sophisticated readers.

Political cartoonists use satire to ridicule and hold up to contempt what they feel are vices, follies, stupidities, abuses, and so on. From the presentation of the subject matter in the cartoon, the reader can usually detect the cartoonist's bias (mental leaning, slanting, or partiality).

Here is a political cartoon that teachers could use with their students to give them experience in interpreting the meaning of the cartoon. Questions that teachers can use to ask about the cartoon follow.

"It Shrunk"

By John Riedell, Courtesy of Peoria Journal-Star

Questions: What is the cartoonist commenting on?
What is he satirizing?

Answer: The cartoonist is commenting on inflation. He is satirizing the decline in the value of the dollar.

Teachers could also present students with a political cartoon such as the one on page 218 and have them construct questions about the cartoon.

Students could be encouraged to draw their own political cartoons based on what they are studying. Teachers could have the students scan the various newspapers for political cartoons that would apply to topics that are being studied. These cartoons could be brought to class and students could challenge one another to interpret the cartoons.

Political Cartoon   By David Seavey, USA Today

Detecting Fallacious Arguments

In social studies, many writers try to sway readers to their point of view. This point has been made a number of times already in this chapter, information on propaganda and bias has been presented, and it has been stressed that teachers should make a concerted effort to help their students to be good critical thinkers. This section is also concerned with the development of good critical thinking. In the secondary school it is not too soon for teachers to begin to help their students to be able to detect fallacies in arguments. The information that follows will enable teachers to help their students become good critical readers. The amount of information on detecting fallacies that teachers decide to present to their students will, of course, depend on the ability levels of their students, as well as on what they are studying.

Fallacies are false beliefs or mistaken ideas about something. Logicians (experts in correct reasoning) refer to fallacies as "incorrect arguments." Fallacious arguments are *incorrect* but may be psychologically or structurally persuasive—in other words, arguments that seem to be correct. Often propaganda techniques are employed to make arguments more persuasive. (See the section on propaganda in Chapter 3.)

There are a number of fallacies that persons commit. Following are examples of some of these.[9]

1. *Irrelevant Conclusion*—The fallacy of irrelevant conclusion consists of directing attention to something else, something irrelevant (not applicable) to the matter in question. For example, someone proposes that a new school building be built and argues the case by discussing how important an education is for all children. Hardly anyone would disagree that an education is important, but this has nothing to do with the need or lack of need for a new school building.

2. *Attacking the Person*—The fallacy of attacking the person consists of directing attention to the person instead of trying to disprove the truth of what is said. The person who made the statement is attacked. The character of the person making the statement does not prove or disprove the statement. However, someone who attacks the person and not the argument is directing attention away from the issues. For example, a witness in a murder trial has stated that he saw the defendant with the murder weapon, a knife, a number of times. He also claims that he heard the defendant threaten the victim many times. The defendant's lawyer says, "I understand that you have been in jail. What were you in for?" Rather than disproving the statements, the lawyer is attacking the character of the person making the statement. (See Name Calling in section on propaganda in Chapter 3.)

3. *Special Circumstance of Person*—The fallacy of special circumstance of person is similar to the fallacy just discussed. However, rather than attacking the character of the person, the acceptance of something is urged *because* of the person. The person doesn't attempt to establish the truth or falsity of something but rather attempts to convince others to accept the statement because the person making it is in a *special circumstance*. For example, if a clergyman has put forth a certain argument for something, one might, instead of examining the merits of the argument, say that it should be accepted because it is made by a

[9]Adapted from Irving M. Copi and Carl Cohen, *Introduction to Logic*, 8th ed. (New York: Macmillan, 1990), pp. 91–107.

clergyman, and its rejection would not be in agreement with the Bible. In other words, nothing is proved or disproved; acceptance of a proposal is urged merely because it is associated with someone in a special circumstance.

4. *Argument from Ignorance*—In the fallacy of argument from ignorance, people attempt to prove their argument by stating that no one has ever disproved it. The opposite is also true; that is, people try to disprove something by saying that no one has ever proved it. For example, people will say that spirits must exist because no one has proved spirits can't exist. Not being able to prove something does not establish whether the argument is true or false.

5. *Appeal to Pity*—The fallacy of appeal to pity consists of asking that a proposal be accepted on the grounds of feeling sorry for someone rather than establishing the truth or falsity of something. For example, a defense attorney, rather than proving the innocence of a client, says, "This poor young man comes from a situation in which he is greatly needed. He helps to support his old grandmother and crippled mother. . . ."

6. *Appeal to Inappropriate Authority*—In the fallacy of appeal to inappropriate authority, people attempt to prove or disprove their argument by referring to well-known individuals, who are not authorities on the matters in question. This belies objectivity. We must be very careful whether the person referred to as an authority is one in the situation under question. For example, Einstein was an authority in matters relating to physics, but he was not an authority in psychology. Therefore, saying that according to Einstein a certain psychological theory is true would be a faulty argument. An appeal to inappropriate authority is being made in advertising when a famous person endorses a product that is outside his or her field of competence.

7. *False Cause*—In the fallacy of false cause, people try to convince others that a preceding event causes an event that follows. Just because an event occurs before another does not mean that the first event causes the second. For example, if every time you take a shower, the phone rings, this does not mean that your taking a shower causes the phone to ring. That the two events occur simultaneously or one after the other is merely a coincidence.

8. *Complex Question*—The fallacy of complex question refers to questions that cannot be answered with a simple yes or no. For example, if you were to ask someone, "Have you given up your bad habits?" the assumption (something taken for granted) is that the person *has* had bad habits. You cannot make that assumption. The question that you are asking is not a simple one but a complex one. Another example would be when someone asks a question such as "Are you for Demopluts and law and order or not?" You can be for law and order but not necessarily for the Demopluts, and vice versa.

Special Note:
Appeal to inappropriate authority and special circumstance of person are closely related. In appeal to inappropriate authority, you refer to a *well-known authority* in some area regardless of whether he or she is an authority on the matter in question. In special circumstance of person, you use the *position* of the person to convince others to accept it. The person used is usually one who is in a highly respected position such as a clergyman, judge, or congressman. A clergyman, judge, or congressman need not be an authority in any particular area. Each is used because of his or her position and association with a respected field. For example, a judge is associated with justice, and a clergyman is associated with the Scriptures and the church.

INTERPRETIVE, CRITICAL, AND CREATIVE COMPREHENSION QUESTIONS FOR SOCIAL STUDIES

The emphasis in social studies, as in the other content areas, is to develop students' high-level thinking skills. The teacher's role is important in doing this because it is generally the teacher who sets the purposes of the direction of learning in the content area, and the purposes are usually determined by the type of question that is asked. Here is a list of sample questions that could be used to elicit responses that require high-level thinking ability.

Samples of Interpretive Comprehension Questions

1. What is the main or central idea of the selection you just read?
2. How does this writer's views compare to the other writer's views?
3. Can you draw any analogies about what we just finished reading and what we studied previously? If so, what are some analogies?
4. What are some generalizations you can make about what we have just read?
5. What are some inferences you can make about their lives based on what we have just read?

Samples of Critical Comprehension Questions

1. What do you think was the author's intent in writing this article?
2. What propaganda techniques does this writer use?
3. How would you go about determining whether this writer is being dogmatic?
4. How would you go about determining the authenticity of this writer's statements?
5. Given what we now know, do you feel that the President acted in the best interests of the country? Explain your answer.

6. How would you determine whether a newly discovered document is actually as old as it is claimed to be?

Samples of Creative Comprehension Questions

1. Choose a period in history. Project yourself into that period, and then explain what you would do that would change the course of history.
2. If you could be any famous person in history, whom would you choose to be? Explain why you chose the person you did.
3. Choose a famous person about whom we have studied; then write a dialogue between him or her and some other famous person concerning an issue of some importance.
4. If you could change any events in history, what event or events would you change? Explain why you chose the events you did.
5. What predictions can you make about life in the twenty-first century?
6. Imagine that you had the opportunity to establish a whole new civilization. What kind of civilization would you establish?

Student Questions in Social Studies

Student questions play a significant role in helping students to gain insights into what they are reading—and throughout this book it is stressed that students should ask questions of what they read—as well as to use questions to set purposes for their reading. Student questions can also help students gain insights into how historians think, and this would make them more effective readers in the social sciences.

Teachers can help students to think like historians by involving students in various simulated situations that require that the students be historians, act like historians, and consequently ask questions like historians. For example, students can be told that they will be responsible for writing the history of their school. Students have to decide what information they need to do this; whom they should interview; how they should go about getting the information they need; and the kinds of questions they should ask to determine the kinds of information they need, as well as the questions they should ask of the persons they will interview. Another device the teacher could use could be called the "island game."[10] The "island game" also involves students in a situation that requires them to think like historians. The teacher sets the scenario; the students are the role players. The teacher tells the students that they are a team of historians (or political scientists or economists) who have volunteered to go to a newly discovered civilization on an island off the coast of Africa. Their assignment is to generate a list of questions to ask the leaders of the new society from the standpoints of their respective disciplines. These questions and those of other

[10]The "island game" was suggested by Edward V. Jones, in-service education coordinator, George Mason University.

student groups representing different social sciences are then discussed in class. After the questions that students had formulated have been analyzed and refined, they could be used to set purposes for reading in the different social sciences.

Simulated Activities: Insight Into the Nature and Methods of History

Teachers can use simulated activities such as those presented in the preceding section to help students gain insights into the nature and method of a discipline, as well as its conceptual framework, if they challenge students to go beyond question asking. Teachers could ask students to determine how they would go about answering their questions by making use of the advances of different sciences. Students should learn from this that historians make use of means such as chemical tests to establish the genuineness of documents and statistical methods to present economic trends. Students should learn also that "history, like the physical sciences, is an empirical discipline and shares with them many methods of inquiry such as observation, classification and the framing and testing of hypotheses."[11]

VOCABULARY DEVELOPMENT IN SOCIAL STUDIES

The acquisition of vocabulary is as important in the area of social studies as in any other subject matter field. Social scientists, like other scientists, have a specialized vocabulary that students need to acquire, and teachers should use a number of techniques to help students gain the necessary vocabulary. The field of social studies, moreover, seems to have many writers that often depend on the connotative meaning of words rather than on their denotative meaning to express themselves. This can cause difficulty in the interpretation of what is being read. Because of this, a section on the connotative meaning of words follows.

The Connotative Meaning of Words

The author's intent will greatly influence what he or she has to say and how he or she says it. The reader must be able to determine whether the author has some kind of vested interest in saying what he or she does. Just as our past experiences will influence our feelings about what we read, so will the writer's past experiences influence what he or she writes. Two persons reporting the same event can write two very different versions. Consider the much quoted story in which one man says, "It's half empty" and the other says, "It's half full."

The way the writer presents information can sway us unless we are

---

[11]Wilhelm Dilthey, *Pattern and Meaning in History: Thoughts on History and Society*, ed. H.P. Rickman (New York: Harper & Brothers, 1961), pp. 33–34.

alert. For example, read the following two sentences, and try to detect the writer's feelings in each.

1. Ms. Jones, the white-haired grandmother newly elected to the House of Representatives, grasped the meaning of the resolution slowly.
2. Ms. Jones, a newly elected but well-informed member of the House of Representatives, carefully thought through the meaning of the resolution.

The person writing statement 1 has a low opinion of Ms. Jones's ability, as evidenced by the use of the terms *white-haired, grandmother,* and *grasped slowly.* The person writing statement 2 has a high opinion of Ms. Jones's ability. This writer avoids any reference to age but emphasizes Ms. Jones's past experience and careful thought. So it is clear that the way the writer uses words is meant to influence the reader. Teachers must help their students to understand this and give students practice in detecting the bias of writers.

Here is what one teacher does to help students better understand the connotative meanings of words.

Scenario: Mrs. Smith's Lesson on the Connotative Meanings of Words
Mrs. Smith, throughout the term, has tried to impress upon her students the importance of being good critical thinkers and avoid "swallowing whole" everything they read. She has discussed with them the importance of knowing the source of their information and the particular bias of the writer, because the writers' bias will influence what he or she will write.

For the past week her tenth grade social studies class has been reading various reports about the Vietnam War. They have also read a number of newspaper articles written by different journalists about the same topic. It has been an eye opener for many of the students.

Mrs. Smith started her unit by presenting her students with two different accounts written by two different writers on the same topic, "The American People's Attitude Toward the War." She asked her students to state the writers' biases based on reading the accounts. She then asked them to analyze the accounts and tell her what the writers did; that is, how did the writers try to persuade us to their views. Mrs. Smith then discussed with her students the connotative meanings of words. After this, she broke her class into groups and gave each group a different topic. She asked the students in each group to write three headlines for their specific topic. She told them that when they were finished they would read their headlines to the class and state which one was positive, negative, or neutral. (See Chapter 4 for a discussion on the denotative and connotative meaning of words.)

Context Clues

In Chapter 4, emphasis was given to the many context clues that textbook writers use to help students acquire word meanings. Social studies teachers should review the various context clues with their students and give them practice in figuring out unfamiliar words. Here are a number of sentences that have been selected from some social science textbooks. Teachers may want to use these or other examples similar to these to illustrate how effective context clues can be in figuring out word meanings. Teachers should help their students to notice that many times writers give clues to word meanings in the next sentence or sentences.

Some examples follow:

1. The great bulk of <u>transients</u> roam from one city to another in pursuit of food and shelter.

2. While new millionaires occasionally <u>flaunted</u> their wealth with huge and costly parties in New York, many dirt farmers in the Middle West and South could scarcely <u>wrest</u> a bare <u>subsistence</u> from the soil, and many factory workers could not earn enough to support their families.

3. Nevertheless, in a world <u>beset</u> with <u>grave</u> international perils and the continuous tensions of a cold war, diplomacy is not enough. It is necessary to maintain armed forces sufficiently powerful to <u>deter</u> any would-be <u>aggressor</u>. In such a world, military readiness and military policy become tools of foreign policy.

4. During adolescence the percentage of <u>obese</u> children increases. Studies show that girls <u>react</u> more strongly to being very fat than boys.

5. Like the blind men and the elephant, each <u>specialist</u> views <u>humanity</u> from a different position; as a result certain elements are <u>overemphasized</u> and others ignored or <u>diminished</u>.

6. As women assume a larger number of positions of responsibility, ulcers may be more <u>equitably</u> distributed among males and females.

7. Had agriculture and industry <u>expanded</u> rapidly, Russia would have been, even today, far from becoming a "<u>saturated</u> area" in which the increase of population is <u>inhibited</u>.

8. The <u>wily</u> foreign minister easily outplayed the other statesmen.

9. Social punishment by <u>peers</u> in the form of <u>ostracism</u> is a powerful means of control. Children do not like to be excluded by their classmates.

10. The agricultural problem in Russia presented a <u>paradox</u>. A country of <u>boundless</u> territory, with a <u>sparse</u> population, suffered from a shortage of land.

Combining Forms

Many words in the social sciences are derived from combining forms. Teachers can use Table 7–1 with its list of combining words and the words derived from these to illustrate to their students how a knowledge of combining forms is effective in vocabulary expansion.

Table 7-1.[12]

Combining Forms	Words Derived from Combining Forms
a—without	agnostic, anarchy
agog, agogue—leading, directing, inciting	demogogue
animus—spirit, mind, soul	animosity, magnanimous
anthrop, anthropo—mankind, man, human	anthropology
anti—against	antiwar
arch, archy—rule, chief	monarchy, democracy
archae—ancient	archaeology
auto—self	autocracy
belli, bello—war	belligerent
cide—murder	homicide
civis—citizen	civilization
bi—two	bigamy
cor, corp, corpor—body	corporation
cap, capit—head	capitalism
demo—the people	democracy
fic, fid, fide—trust, faith	fidelity
gnosi, gnosis—knowledge	agnostic
gen, geno—kind, race, descent	genocide
gamy—marriage	polygamy, misogamist
graph—something written, machine	geography
leg, legis, lex—law	lexical, legal
ology—the study of, the science of	anthropology
pac—peace	pacifist
geo—earth	geography
inter—between, among	interstate
intra—within, inside of	intrastate
magna—great, large	magnanimous
nasc, nat—born	nation, nationality
mono—one	monogamy
poly—many	polygamy
tele—from a distance	telegraph
pop—people	population

Special Note:
As already stated in Chapter 4, a combining form is usually defined as a root borrowed from another language that joins with another combining form or that joins with a prefix, a suffix, or both a prefix and a suffix to form a word. Because the emphasis in Part 3 of this book is on the building of vocabulary meanings rather than on the naming of word parts, prefixes, suffixes, English roots, and combining forms will *all* be referred to as combining forms. In Part 3 of this book a combining form is defined as any word

[12]See Dorothy Rubin, *Vocabulary Expansion* (New York: Macmillan, 1991).

part that can join with another word or word part to form a word or a new word.

Correlating Social Studies with Vocabulary Study and Other Areas

Even though teachers of students in the intermediate and lower grades can correlate social studies and vocabulary study with other subject areas better than teachers who teach a specific content area, content-area teachers can use this approach also. Two scenarios follow that demonstrate this. The first takes place in a fifth grade class, and the second takes place in a high school social studies class.

Scenario: Fifth-Grade Social Studies Lesson
Each week Mr. Jones chooses a certain number of words from his students' various content-area books and highlights these as the words of the week. When he presents the words to his students, he pronounces each word, puts it into a sentence, and then challenges the students to use their knowledge of context clues and combining forms to figure out the word. If they can't figure out the word, he gives them the definition of it. During the week students can use these words to make up word riddles and challenge their classmates to answer the riddles. The words become part of the week's spelling words, and students are asked to put the words into sentences that show the students understand the meaning of the words, or Mr. Jones presents the words in sentences to the students and asks them to define the word as used in the sentence. Here is an example of how he correlates social studies to vocabulary, spelling, and other language arts areas.

Mr. Jones's students in his social studies unit are working with famous people from other continents. The spelling and vocabulary words for the students include three sets of words:

General Words	Continents	Countries
continent	North America	Brazil
globe	South America	Canada
atlas	Africa	India
hemisphere	Asia	Japan
meridian	Australia	Israel
latitude	Europe	France
longitude		England
		Argentina
		Algeria
		China
		United States

Mr. Jones tells the students that the words on the board are words that they will meet when they read their social studies assignment. He points to the globe and atlas and says that students have probably seen these, but they may not have worked with them. Today they will. First he will pronounce each general word, put it into a sentence, and explain certain of the terms. After that he will pronounce each continent and country that is listed on the board. Then he will have some students look at the map, some at the globe, and some in the atlas to find the continents and countries that are listed on the board.

During the lesson Mr. Jones asks a question concerning two leaders whom they have read about and about whom the class has already talked.

A discussion ensues about why the leaders have been in the news so much. Mr. Jones then asks the name of another famous leader who has been in the news. A girl is called on and answers correctly. He says, "Good. You really seem to know your world affairs and your countries. Let's see how good you are in categorizing countries according to their continents. I have an outline map for each one of you, and I'd like you to see if you can put the continents in the right areas and then insert the countries that I have listed on the board. Does anyone have any questions? Let's do one together to make sure everyone understands."

Mr. Jones points to an area on one of the outline maps and asks, "Can everyone see where I am pointing? Okay, what is this continent?"

Almost everyone calls out, "North America!"

"Correct," says Mr. Jones. "Looking at the list on the board, which country would you place in this continent and approximately where would you put it?"

Many of the children call out one of the correct answers.

"Good. Let's see how many of you can finish this on your own."

The children start working, and Mr. Jones walks around checking their papers and stopping to help those who need it. After some time has elapsed, the teacher goes over the correct answers with the group to give them feedback on the results. He helps students summarize what they have done and asks them to check the news for exciting things that are happening in other areas of the world so that they can add those to their list.

"Tomorrow," Mr. Jones says, "we're going to be combining outlining with our study of continents and countries. Then we're going to use the outline as a guide to learn more about the country we choose to study. I would like you to think about which country you want to get to know better. At your seats, review some of the things we talked about concerning outlines. This sheet should help you."

Commentary:

Mr. Jones is not only helping his students to expand their vocabulary; he is helping them to see how skills such as categorizing and outlining are related and how these skills can help students learn and retain information. If students are given opportunities to work with categorizing and other important thinking skills, they will be more prone to use these skills when they are reading alone.

Scenario: Ninth-Grade Class in American Government
The students have been learning about their government and the capacity of the citizens to make wise decisions and govern themselves. The teacher, Ms. Smith, at the beginning of each unit presents the objectives of the unit so that students will know what they are supposed to have accomplished when the unit is completed. Ms. Smith also presents any words that she feels may cause some difficulty for the students when they read their textbook or when they discuss certain issues. Here is an example of how Ms. Smith correlates her lessons with vocabulary study, English, study skills, and current events.

Ms. Smith asks the students if they know what had taken place in a certain theocracy that would offend people living in a democracy. She tells them that if they know the meaning of theocracy, that would narrow the choices and help them to come up with the country she is thinking of. She says further that the country is not only a theocracy but it is headed by an autocrat, who is also a demagogue. Many people were assassinated because they dared to speak against the person in power. An uprising put the nation in anarchy. Ms. Smith tells the students that the reason they are having difficulty coming up with the answer is that they probably do not know key words in the sentences. Ms. Smith puts the following combining forms with their meanings on the board:

theo—God   auto—self
arch—rule, chief a—without
mono—one   agogue, agog—leading, directing, inciting
demo—people

Ms. Smith then tells her students that she will show them how useful combining forms are in helping them expand their vocabulary. She repeats the question that she had asked earlier and puts the following words on the board:

theocracy   democracy
demagogue   autocrat
anarchy

Next, Ms. Smith tells her students that the words on the board can be derived by using their knowledge of combining forms as well as context clues. She also puts the words in sentences. Here they are:

1. Theocracies may still exist but not to the same extent as centuries ago, when the Church ruled a large part of Europe.

2. Hitler is a good example of a <u>demagogue</u> because he could stir persons' emotions and get them to do what he wanted them to.

3. In a state of <u>anarchy</u> there is confusion because there are no laws.

4. In our <u>democracy</u> all persons over eighteen have the right to vote, and the government is ruled by the people through elected representatives.

5. An <u>autocrat</u> has absolute power.

The students are able to come up with the meanings of the words listed on the board. Ms. Smith says, "Good," and asks them to answer the question concerning what had taken place in a certain theocracy. A number of students are able to answer this question. Ms. Smith now tells her students that today they will begin comparing the democratic form of government as it is conducted in the United States with other forms of government. She asks the students to list some other forms of government. A number of students raise their hands to give other forms of government.

Ms. Smith explains to her students that their answers are not all forms of government. She says that in order for them to be able to make a comparison between or among different types of governments, they first have to know what the forms of government are, and then something about the various types of governments. In the new unit they will be learning about various forms of government. They will see that a monarchy may or may not be an autocracy and that an autocracy is always a totalitarian form of government. This unit should help them to clear up a number of misconceptions that they have concerning forms of governments. She states further that many people are confused about forms of government. A key factor in this unit is terminology. Many persons use similar terms in different ways; this can and does lead to confusion. "When we describe the various forms of governments," says Ms. Smith, "we will try to be as accurate as we possibly can. For this unit we will use many different sources besides our textbook. What are some of the sources that we can use?"

A discussion takes place concerning the various sources that the students will be using to get the information they need. Ms. Smith tells the students that she will review some notetaking skills with them so that they will be able to record the information that they need. She also tells them that she would like them to write a summary of what they have found on each form of government, and she will review with them the techniques for writing summaries.

In this unit, Ms. Smith wants her students to learn concepts such as the following:

1. Governments are the products of human beings.

2. No two governments are exactly alike.

3. A government may be classified in terms of one or more of its basic features.

INCORPORATING SUMMARIZING AND STUDYING IN SOCIAL STUDIES

Most social studies courses require a great amount of reading. Students must not only read their textbooks, but they usually also have a lot of other reading that they must do. Many social studies teachers ask their students to write summaries of what they have read, and many test questions may have students writing summaries. Teachers can help their students by giving them helpful pointers on how to study and how to write summaries. Actually, the two are closely interrelated.

Writing a summary is an excellent way for students to review what they have read because to write a good summary, students need to be able to state the main idea of the paragraph or the central idea of a group of paragraphs, as well as the key details. Teachers should give students practice in writing summaries of articles and different material and show them how this will help them retain information over an extended period of time. Here is the way one teacher does this.

Mr. Trent at the beginning of the term usually discusses with his students the kinds of assignments that they will be getting. He tells them he will require that they do quite a bit of summarizing of material because he has found from past experiences that the summarizing of material helps students remember better what they have read. Mr. Trent tells his students that he will prove this, but first he has to help students learn how to write summaries. He explains to his students procedures for summarizing information. He reviews with them a technique for finding the main or central idea of selections because this information is necessary for writing a good summary. He gives each student the same selection from the textbook they will be reading and tells them that they will practice writing a summary together, and after they have written the summary, he will give them a quiz on the selection. He tells the students also that he has selected some words from the passage and defined them at the top of the page because some of these words may be unfamiliar to them. He pronounces each of the words. Mr. Trent then tells his students to read the selection to find its central idea. After they have finished reading the selection, they go over the selection's central idea. Mr. Trent writes this on the board; then he asks the students to try to recall the key details in the selection. He puts these on another board. After the students have finished listing these key details, Mr. Trent asks them to see whether there are some details that they feel are not key ones. After a while a few of the listed details are erased. Mr. Trent then asks the students to put the key details that are left on the board into sentences. Under the central idea, he writes the sentences that are given to him. After the students have finished this activity, Mr. Trent takes back the paper with the selection on it and gives the students a quiz on the material. When the students see how well they have done on the quiz, this usually reinforces many to use summarizing as a viable studying technique.

SAMPLE SOCIAL STUDIES ACTIVITIES

1. In one junior high school class, students were studying the Renaissance. Each student was responsible for a special activity related to the Renaissance. A number of students decided to produce a newspaper, which was to be a replica of events that might have taken place at that time. Figure 7-2 is the front page of a paper produced by a highly able student. There is humor, knowledge, organizational ability, and handiwork in its production.

2. One teacher in an American government class had her students survey various newspapers to find letters to the editor that discussed issues related to what they were discussing in class. Students were then asked to write their own letter to the editor concerning a specific issue under study.

3. One teacher had students write a script on a particular happening in history about which they had studied. Students then acted out the script.

4. In one class the teacher would have students role play historical figures who had a significant part in shaping events. To role play their part effectively, students had to read about the life of the character whom they were acting out.

5. At the beginning of every social studies class, the teacher would have a student present some information about a person whom they had or were still studying about. (Each student in the class was responsible for reading about the life of some famous person.)

6. One teacher presents her students with passages that have certain inconsistencies and challenges her students to find them. Here is an example of one such passage.

> Regardless of the merits of claims that Norsemen discovered Europe before Columbus, nothing came of their efforts. They erected many permanent settlements. Whether explorers of North America a few thousand years later had used Viking knowledge of the area no one knows. When Christopher Columbus set out from Spain on his eastward voyage in 1429, he seemed to have had no notion of any land lying to the west between Europe and China and Japan.

Answers: *Europe*—America; *many*—no; *thousand*—hundred; *eastward*—westward; 1429—1492.

COMPUTER SOFTWARE AND SOCIAL STUDIES

In 1986, the National Assessment of Educational Progress (NAEP) conducted the first nationwide survey of computer competence. The assessment showed that computers are seldom used to teach subject-matter

Investigation Uncovers Cardplayers

THE RENAISSANCE CHRONICLE

Weather
Summers-Hot
Winters-Cold

First and Only Edition

Columbus Gives Details Of Journey

Pope Accepts Illegal Money —People Riot

Augsburg Confession Becomes Official Lutheran Creed

The Religious Situation -1560

FIGURE 7-2.   A highly able student produced this front page.

courses. "Computers are used almost exclusively to teach about computers."[13]

This is too bad because computers can help to individualize instruction in the classroom and act as an important tool for both teachers and students. Let's look at some of the ways computers can enhance instruction.

Database Management Systems

Database management systems (DBMs) are exactly what the phrase states they are. They are ways to manage or classify data. Students or teachers can store information on a disk and can then easily add, delete, or change any of the information. The data is easily accessible.

In social studies classrooms, students can store any data they wish about anything they are studying or researching. They can then use this information to analyze the data, discern similarities and differences about the data they have stored, discover trends, use it to infer hypotheses, deduce assumptions about their data, and even to test their hypotheses.[14] For example, they could collect data on the backgrounds of all the Presidents of the United States and wars in which the United States has engaged. They could then make the following hypothesis: More presidents over sixty have engaged in wars than those under sixty years of age.

Their database system could then check for all presidents under and over sixty, as well as the wars in which the United States has engaged. A cross check could then be done on the terms of presidents over sixty and wars during their terms, as well as those of presidents under sixty and wars occurring during their terms.

SAMPLE DATABASE: PRESIDENTS

NAME:
BIRTH AND DEATH:
MARRIED: SINGLE: DIVORCED:
NUMBER OF CHILDREN:
POLITICAL PARTY:
YEARS IN OFFICE:
MAJOR ACCOMPLISHMENTS:

---

[13]Michael E. Martinez and Nancy Mead, *Computer Competence: The First National Assessment* (Princeton, N.J.: Educational Testing Service, 1988), p. 3.

[14]Carla Mathison and Linda Lungren, "Using Computers Effectively in Content Area Classes," in *Content Area Reading and Learning* (eds.) Diane Lapp, James Flood, and Nancy Farman (Englewood Cliffs, N.J.: Prentice Hall, 1989), p. 307.

FIGURE 7-3.   These students use the computer to help them overlearn certain concepts.

Computer-Assisted Instruction

Computer-assisted instruction (CAI), which is not new, is an excellent management tool if used properly. These computer programs are usually used to dispense information to students, and to give them added practice so that they can overlearn certain content material. When the computer is used in a tutorial or one-on-one situation with the student, the student knows the results in a friendly, nonthreatening way.

Computers can also be used to give teachers information about students' levels of knowledge in a specific area. For example, during a social studies lesson, students could read a passage, and then the computer could question each student simultaneously through his or her own terminal. The students could then answer by menu selection, whereby only a single letter or number needs to be pressed to indicate the answer. The teacher's result is immediate feedback of all students' responses. This type of questioning and feedback can be repeated for however much depth and breadth of coverage the teacher requires. The teacher can not only receive immediate feedback but can also see a pattern of the answers. This pattern would help the teacher immediately discern those questions that caused the most or the least difficulty for the students. The computer could also display for the teacher a pattern of an individual's responses or compare what an individual student has done over an extended period of time. The possibilities are limitless.

GRAPHIC SUMMARY OF CHAPTER

Here is a graphic summary of Chapter 7. If you have read the chapter, this graphic illustration should help you remember its main points. Under or beside each heading, you might want to jot down some of the information you recall, as well as some of the key concepts in this chapter. This can act as a good review. You can then check your key concepts against those that follow the graphic summary.

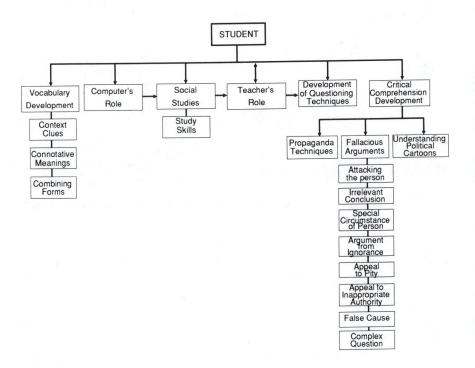

KEY CONCEPTS IN CHAPTER

- Students need help in developing higher level thinking in social studies.
- Social studies teachers are key persons to help students develop critical thinking.
- Social studies teachers must emphasize critical thinking because many writers attempt to delude unsuspecting readers and sway them to their views.
- In social studies, writers' biases can interpret history in many different ways.

- Humans are responsible for recording the events of the past and present.
- Critical thinking has to do with the passing of personal judgment on the accuracy, truthfulness, and value of something.
- Teachers can use a directed reading approach to help students recognize propaganda techniques.
- Teachers can use political cartoons to advance students' critical thinking.
- Connotative meanings are important in recognizing writers' biases.
- Students' knowledge of combining forms can help them figure out the meanings of many words in their social studies textbooks.
- Computers can help individualize instruction in social studies classrooms.

SUGGESTIONS FOR THOUGHT QUESTIONS AND ACTIVITIES

1. You have been asked to speak to your local parent-teacher association about the teaching of critical thinking skills in the social studies program. What will you say?
2. Develop a number of questions in a specific social studies unit that demand higher-level critical thinking.
3. Prepare a lesson in which social studies, vocabulary study, and other curriculum areas are correlated.
4. Brainstorm some creative social studies activities that require critical comprehension.
5. Peruse a number of newspapers to find examples of writers' use of the connotative meanings of words.
6. Prepare a social studies lesson in which students must detect propaganda techniques that writers use.
7. Make a list of all the combining forms that you can think of that will help students in expanding their social studies vocabulary.
8. State the characteristics of computer software you would like to see made available to social studies teachers.
9. Review some of the social studies computer software currently on the market. Note whether they contain the characteristics you stated in number 8.

SELECTED BIBLIOGRAPHY

DILTHEY, WILHEIM. *Pattern & Meaning in History.* New York: Harper & Brothers, 1961.
HAMMACK, DAVID C., et al. *The U.S. History Report Card,* National Assessment of Educational Progress. Princeton, N.J.: Educational Testing Service, 1990.

HAYES, BERNARD, and CHARLES PETERS. "The Role of Reading Instruction in the Social Studies Classroom." In *Content Area Reading and Learning.* Diane Lapp, James Flood, and Nancy Farnan (eds.) Englewood Cliffs, N.J.: Prentice Hall, 1989, pp. 152–178.

KRATZNER, ROLAND R., and NANCY MANNIES. "Building Responsibility and Reading Skills in the Social Studies Classroom." *Journal of Reading* 22 (March 1979): 501–505.

MULLIS, INA V.S., EUGENE H. OWEN, and GARY W. PHILLIPS. *Accelerating Academic Achievement: A Summary of Findings from 20 Years of NAEP.* National Assessment of Educational Progress. Princeton, N.J.: Educational Testing Service, 1990.

SANACORE, JOSEPH. "Creating the Lifetime Reading Habit in Social Studies." *Journal of Reading* 33 (March 1990): 414–418.

8

Integrating Science and Reading/Study Skills Instruction

OVERVIEW

Science taught as a process of enquiry and as a mode of thinking provides
the best means so far discovered to enable young people to participate in
both the world of today and the world of tomorrow.
Paul deHart Hurd
SCIENCE TEACHING FOR A CHANGING WORLD

INTRODUCTION

"It is widely believed that the condition of science education in this country needs improvement and the results of the National Assessment of Educational Progress's (NAEP) 1986 science assessment do not assuage this concern."[1] What is devastating is that "only 7 percent of the nation's 17-year-olds have the prerequisite knowledge and skills thought to be needed to perform well in college-level science courses. Since high school proficiency is a good predictor of whether or not a person will elect to pursue post-secondary studies in science, the probability that many students will embark on future careers in science is very low."[2]

The NAEP report also shows that "despite recent gains, the average proficiency of 13- and 17-year-old Black and Hispanic students remains at least four years behind that of their White peers."[3]

The report also shows that "while average science proficiency for 9-year-old boys and girls was approximately the same—except in the physical sciences—a performance gap was evident at age 13 and increased by age 17 in most content areas. At age 17, roughly one-half of the males but only one-third of the females demonstrated the ability to analyze scientific procedure and data."[4]

The reasons given for this large gender difference is that teachers usually have higher expectations for their male students than for their female students and ask them higher-level questions. In addition, females report that they are less likely to engage in out-of-school science activities and experiences.[5]

Science touches each of our lives; it enriches, enhances, and empowers all of us. It is necessary for the advancement and survival of our nation. Because of its importance, teachers must make a concerted effort to present science subject matter in such a way that it captures the minds of all students and helps them realize its impact on their lives.

The teaching of science stresses the acquisition of concepts through the scientific method. It is concerned with helping students become aware of the world around them and curious enough regarding their environment to start asking questions about problems that exist. Once students' sense of curiosity is aroused to the existence of problems, they can be initiated into the investigative skills of inquiry used by scientists—the scientific method. The scientific method is a technique that scientists use in research ex-

[1]Ina V.S. Mullis and Lynn B. Jenkins, *The Science Report Card: Elements of Risk and Recovery.* The National Assessment of Educational Progress (Princeton, N.J.: Educational Testing Service, 1988), p. 5.

[2]Ibid., p. 6.

[3]Ibid., p. 7.

[4]Ibid.

[5]Ibid., p. 8.

periments, which consists of a number of steps. A scientist usually must first survey the literature relating to the problem. He or she then identifies and defines the problem. After this, the scientist comes up with a problem hypothesis, which is a possible solution to the problem. From the hypothesis, the scientist deduces certain consequences. He or she then constructs an experimental plan, conducts the experiment, and determines whether the results are significant or not.

The scientific method that is associated with the sciences can be adapted to life situations on a daily basis because it is a way of thinking. To use the scientific method effectively, students must have the literal, interpretive, critical, and creative thinking skills that are found in reading comprehension. This chapter will show how interrelated the skills of scientific inquiry and reading comprehension are and how teachers can use knowledge of reading comprehension and a directed reading approach to enhance their teaching of science.

Let us hope that more effective science teaching will translate into students feeling more positively toward science and, as a result, pursue more work in this area.

KEY QUESTIONS

After you finish reading this chapter, you should be able to answer the following questions:

1. What is the scientific method?
2. What skills do students need to develop their investigative ability?
3. What is the place of reading in the science program?
4. How are the investigative skills necessary to be a good scientist related to reading skills?
5. How are reading and the scientific method related?
6. Why must scientists have good reading skills?
7. Why must teachers behave in a scientific manner when teaching science?
8. What are some examples of teaching science scientifically?
9. How can teachers encourage students to be good critical thinkers?
10. How can teachers encourage students to do higher-level thinking in the sciences?
11. How can teachers encourage students to be divergent thinkers?
12. What are some techniques the teacher can use to expand students' science vocabulary?
13. How can the teacher adapt SQ3R to help students read their science assignments?
14. What is the place of computers in the science classroom?

KEY TERMS IN CHAPTER

You should pay special attention to the following key terms:

hypothesis   scientific method
reading in a scientific manner

THE IMPORTANCE OF READING IN THE SCIENCES

Reading is necessary to absorb the knowledge of what has occurred before in order to be on an equal standing and to move forward. It is through reading that individuals are able to stand on the shoulders of the intellectual giants of humankind (to paraphrase the great seventeenth-century scientist Sir Isaac Newton) and study the physical reality of earth. From reading, we are able to gain information in a relatively short time—information that it has taken scientists centuries to accumulate. It is from reading that we recognize that bigotry and dogma are the enemies of science and that openmindedness, inquiry, and the suspension of judgment are its handmaidens. It is from reading about men such as Copernicus, Galileo, Newton, and Pasteur that we learn that it is not until we are ready to give up our preconceived ideas that we are ready and able to go beyond into new vistas of knowledge. From reading about such men, we are able to take giant steps forward because we gain insights into the scientific mind. We learn that scientific laws pervade all of nature; all the universe moves according to scientific laws. Reading about what has taken place in the past helps us to dispel bigotry and helps us to recognize that successful scientists are those with a bold imagination who are able to employ precise measurement to verify their theories. We learn also that successful scientists are those who are able to accept uncomfortable facts even if these facts do not agree with their preconception of things.

INVESTIGATIVE SKILLS OF GOOD SCIENTISTS

Teachers should be aware of the attributes that good scientists possess so that they can help their student scientists attain those that they may be lacking, as well as provide an environment that is conducive to scientific thought and growth. What follows is a description of many important traits that are necessary ingredients of good scientists.

Good scientists are *curious*. They want to know why things happen; they want to know how things happen. They are keen *observers* of their environment, and they use all their senses to help them become aware of the existence of a problem. Then their sharp observational ability helps them to gather the data necessary for the solution of the problem. Working hand in hand with the skill of observation is that of *estimation* and the abil-

FIGURE 8-1. The students in this high-school science class are reading carefully the lab manual to prepare for their next experiment.

ity to use instruments to make scientists' observations of scientific phenomena more accurate.

The ability to *categorize* or *classify* is another important skill that good scientists possess. They are able to compare likenesses and differences and determine to what group an object belongs. After an object has been categorized, a scientist can make inferences about the particular object based on the group to which it belongs because the characteristics of the object are known. Therefore, good scientists also have good *inference* ability. Inference is necessary to formulate hypotheses. For example, when a student scientist classifies copper as a metal, he or she can use his or her reasoning ability to infer that, as a metal, it will be a good conductor of heat or electricity. Also, when the student scientist sees moisture on the outside of his or her glass of cold milk, an inference could be made that it comes from the air.

At this point readers should begin to recognize that the skills that good scientists possess are those that we have been emphasizing throughout this book because they are also the skills that good readers possess. (See the following section.) Let's look at a few more skills that good scientists have. They have the ability to make *predictions* and recognize that predictions vary based on conditions; that is, good scientists change their predictions if the given set of conditions change. They also use their fund of concepts to predict outcomes. For example, student scientists have learned that fire needs air to burn. If they want to extinguish a fire, they must smother or suffocate it; consequently, they use sand to smother the fire. Another skill that good scientists have is being able to *test* or *verify* their hypotheses. Good scientists can deduce consequences from their hypotheses and then test the consequences. They are also good critical thinkers who can suspend judgment until all necessary data have been tested, and they can report their results in an accurate, concise, and complete manner.

READING AND THE SCIENTIFIC METHOD

Good readers are good thinkers. This statement has been made innumerable times in this book because it is an exceedingly vital one. Persons who are able to read at high levels of comprehension will be better able to solve problems that require a high level of thinking. If students have experience using the scientific method and are challenged to answer questions that require interpretive, critical, and creative thinking, they will be better able to do this kind of thinking when they are reading their science textbooks. However, the science teacher, like other content-area teachers, cannot take for granted that students have the skills necessary to read in a scientific manner. Science teachers must also guide and direct their students' learning and help them acquire any of the reading and study skills that they may need to read required materials. Science teachers should present the reading skills important in science through reading materials being studied in class.

Reading comprehension includes many skills similar to those that good scientists need. For example, good readers are good inferential thinkers. They have to be able to gain information from writers' clues and use this information to make generalizations. Good readers can make deductions from information that is not explicitly stated but implied or suggested. They also need to be able to categorize the information that they are reading; they must be adept at extracting meaningful information from confusing data. Moreover, good readers can make predictions about what they are reading. (Predictions are synonymous with hypotheses.) The better readers we are, the better our predictions will be. Scientists verify their predictions by experimentation; readers confirm their predictions by continuing to read to determine whether their predictions are correct or not.

Reading in a Scientific Manner

In science, students must read a great deal to gain information. Teachers can help their students to read scientifically if they give them some techniques that incorporate the scientific method with some study skill method. The SQ3R technique that is presented in Chapter 5 is one that teachers can introduce to their students to help them gain needed information. Teachers, however, want students to do more than gain information;

they want students to be able to determine whether the information is reliable or unreliable or requires further verification. Teachers should help students see the relationship between being a good reader and the scientific method. Students, while reading, must be alert and scientific; that is, students must not blindly accept everything that is presented; they should read critically, and they should question what does not make sense to them. Teachers should also help students recognize that reading to collect data is part of the scientific method and an important part of research. If students approach their reading in a scientific manner, they will be good readers, as well as on the road to becoming good scientists.

TEACHING SCIENCE SCIENTIFICALLY

Science, of all the content areas, should especially be taught in such a way so that it does not violate logic and reason, which is an integral part of the scientific method. It would be a paradox to teach science unscientifically, that is, to have teachers resort to teaching tactics that emphasize the memorization of arbitrary rules and formulas and to have students do these without question. Authorities on science teacher education state that "more important than the information a teacher acquires about science is a teacher's knowing how to inquire, how to find answers, how to use material and human resources, and how to model these in a science classroom."[6]

Good science teachers should behave in a scientific manner and help students to gain insights from what they read and learn. They should help students to deduce these insights from existing facts or combinations of facts, from theories, or from facts embodied in laws or theories. They also should encourage student questions, and all facts that are not clearly understood should be explained. If a statement in a textbook is confusing to students, the teacher should not say, "If it's in the book, it must be correct." The teacher should try to help the students understand what the author is saying and challenge the students to try to figure out the author's meaning. For example, here is a statement that appeared in a science textbook that seemed to confuse a number of students.

On the average, we use about 247 gallons of water a day.

After reading this statement in their textbook, a few students started to total up the amount of water they used in a day. This amount was obviously miniscule in relation to the number given in the book. These students then totaled up the amount that their whole families used in a day. This was still too small. At this point the students were confused; they asked the teacher for an explanation. How a teacher handles such a question will determine

6Robert E. Yager, and John E. Penick, *Science Teacher Education,"* in *Handbook on Research in Teacher Education,* W. Robert Houston, ed. (Macmillan: New York, 1990), p. 663.

whether students will ask other questions and maintain the mode of inquiry that is essential for any science program.

Fortunately for these students, their teacher was knowledgeable not only in the subject matter of science but also in teaching techniques and learning theory. The teacher, rather than immediately giving the students the answer or explanation, asked the students to try again to see if they could figure out what was behind the writer's statement. She further told the students that the statement was not an erroneous one; that is, it was correct. She told them that she wanted them to read between the author's lines. First, of course, they should reread the statement to try to pick out key words that are clues. The key words in the sentence are *on the average*. The author has made the assumption that students will realize that this refers not to each person's own personal use but to the use that is needed for the economy to function effectively. The number 247 refers to industrial and agricultural usage as well as personal usage. The search for what is behind the statement involves inferential reasoning and is part of the scientific method. Good scientists as good readers must be alert to the clues that authors give.

In Figure 8-2 is an example of the type of activity the teacher can use to encourage students to do inferential thinking. The teacher asks the students to read the statement in Figure 8-2. She then asks them to analyze it carefully and then to state what inferences can be deduced from the state-

FIGURE 8-2. Deducing Inferences from a Statement

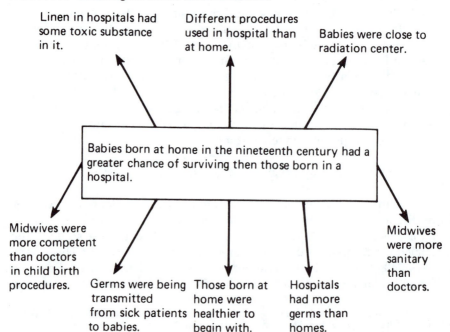

ment. As the students give their inferences or deductions, the teacher appends them to the original statement.

CRITICAL THINKING IN SCIENCE

As stated in an earlier section, good scientists must be open-minded and be able to suspend judgment until all data are collected; they must be as objective as possible so as not to contaminate their results. Even though good scientists follow hunches, they arrive at these hunches based on some scientific evidence, and then they evaluate what they have done to determine whether it does verify their hypothesis beyond a doubt.

Evaluation has to do with the ability to pass personal judgment on something; it has to do with the ability to examine material by using objective means, with comparing what was done to some established criteria, and with then acting on the judgment that has been made. Evaluation requires good critical thinking, which is at the heart of science.

Teachers can help their students to develop critical thinking skill if they present students with many opportunities that require critical thinking and if they themselves behave in a manner that shows they respect and value critical thinking. For example, teachers can encourage critical thinking if in their teaching they always make it clear when they are giving their opinion and when they are giving facts. Also, when they are teaching, they should try to be as objective as possible and not allow their emotions to interfere with their better judgment on some issues; they should be willing to suspend judgment until all the evidence is in.

Teachers can encourage critical reading comprehension by asking questions that demand critical thinking responses. These questions should be asked before students begin their reading assignment and should act as advance organizers or objectives for the reading assignment. (See section entitled "Interpretive, Critical, and Creative Comprehension Questions for Science" for a list of the type of questions teachers can ask to stimulate critical thinking.) Also, for those students who need more help in critical reading, the teacher using relevant material should directly teach those skills the students need to prepare them for their reading assignment. (See "Adapting SQ3R in Science Reading" in this Chapter.)

THE SCIENTIST, THE TEACHER, AND CREATIVITY

The comprehension area that is probably the most neglected is that of creative comprehension, but for scientists this area is probably one of the most important. In Chapter 3, some quotes are given from Albert Szent-Györgyi, a well-known scientist and Nobel Prize-winner. These quotes give an insight into the creative scientist's mind and his or her manner of thinking and working. According to Szent-Györgyi, "the great scientists were those who were at home in the unknown and left their footsteps there, the dreamy fellows moving about with hands in pockets, who suddenly came up with something new."[7]

Although teachers cannot command creativity or with the swish of a magic wand make students into creative thinkers, they can do many things to encourage and stimulate divergent thinking in students. A number of the things that teachers can do were discussed in Chapter 3. Some of the points will be reiterated here because they are essential ones for the science teacher. Teachers are role models for students. If they behave in a creative and scientific manner, their students will be more likely to do so too. Teachers can encourage creativity by having an inquiring mind themselves and by allowing students to question and to be intelligent risk-takers. Teachers can stimulate divergent thinking by encouraging students to look at alternate ways to solve problems and to try to go beyond the known into the vast unexplored terrains. Teachers can encourage creativity in their students by using creative teaching techniques and by having a stimulating, encouraging, and nonthreatening atmosphere in the classroom.

Teachers can encourage students to read creatively if they ask questions that stimulate divergent thinking. Teachers who have as one of their objectives divergent thinking and who ask questions that demand this type of thinking show that they feel that creative comprehension is important. For example, when students read a description of an experiment, teachers can challenge their students to think of other ways the researcher could have conducted the experiment.

INTERPRETIVE, CRITICAL, AND CREATIVE COMPREHENSION QUESTIONS FOR SCIENCE

The kinds of questions that teachers ask will determine the kinds of thinking that students will need to do to answer the questions. Throughout this book emphasis is given to the art of questioning. The reason for this is that questioning is a technique that practically all teachers engage in, and it can be an especially effective procedure for stimulating students to do high-level thinking if the right questions are asked. Unfortunately, the right questions often are not asked. Obviously, the key is in formulating types of questions that stimulate the kinds of thinking that we wish students to engage in. Examples of these types of questions follow.

Interpretive Comprehension Questions

1. What is the main or central idea of what you have read?
2. What consequences can you deduce from this hypothesis?

[7]Albert Szent-Györgyi, "The Strategy of Life," *Science and Technology* (New York: International Communications, June 1966), pp. 49–50.

3. What are some hypotheses that you can infer, based on the given evidence?
4. Based on the given evidence, what do you predict will take place?
5. How would you go about solving this problem?
6. How is this related to the other problem we just discussed?
7. How would you categorize this problem?
8. How would you illustrate the information that you have gathered?
9. What generalization can you make from these data?
10. How would you go about proving your hunch?
11. How would you compare the work of this scientist with the work of this other scientist?
12. How can you explain the author's statements?
13. Why did that happen?
14. What would happen if we changed this?

Critical Comprehension Questions

1. How would you verify your results?
2. Do the authors of this book or article have any particular biases? If so, what are they?
3. Can you discern the author's attitude? If so, what is it?
4. How do you feel about this?
5. What would you have done if you were the scientist?
6. After looking at all the evidence that the author has presented, do you agree with his or her conclusions? Why or why not?
7. Is the evidence that is being presented sufficient to draw the conclusion that is drawn?
8. Would you have continued with the experiment, even though it might be dangerous?
9. If you were the scientist, would you have used human subjects to test a controversial and experimental drug? Explain your position on this.
10. Knowing what you now know about the subject, how would you have conducted the experiment to arrive at the results?

Creative Comprehension Questions

1. How else can you solve this problem?
2. Given everything that the scientist knows, can you come up with an alternate solution?
3. What do you think might be the ramifications of this discovery?

FIGURE 8-3. This fifth-grade science teacher stimulates her students to think.

SCIENTIFIC VOCABULARY

The science textbooks that students are required to read are replete with technical terms that students must master in order to understand what they are reading. Textbook writers are aware of this, and many try to make a concerted effort to present key terms in such a way that students can gain their meanings. Textbook writers usually explain, describe, or define the word, using context clues. (See section on "Context Clues" in Chapter 4.) Many times, however, there are a number of nontechnical words that writers assume students know. Teachers should be on the lookout for these words because they can cause just as much difficulty for students as some technical words. Students may misinterpret the meaning of what they are reading if they are not precise in their definitions of all terms. Teachers can present a number of key words in the context of what the students are studying and have them try to figure out the meanings. Here are some examples:

1. To test this idea, we must first look at a system we can see. Scientists call such a system a *model* or an *analogy*. (The context clue is a synonym.)
2. Here are two *quantitative* ways that scientists use to communicate a regularity. The first is the listing of the experimental data in a table. The second is the visual representation of the data in a graph. (Context clues are examples.)

3. The particles making up gas are called *molecules*. (The context clue is a definition.)

Expanding vocabulary by using word parts or combining forms is a technique that the science teacher can also employ. (See Chapter 4.) Here are examples of some combining forms that would help students in figuring out word meanings in science:

anthropo = man, human	con = with
bio = life	geo = earth
de = away; from; off; completely	in = into; not
duc = lead	ology = the study of; the science of

Here are some words derived from these combining forms:

anthropology	induction
geology	deduction
biology	conduction

The combining forms should be presented when the students' readings employ words that are derived from these combining forms. As is suggested in the next section, the teacher could survey the students' readings beforehand to note any words that might cause difficulty for the students when they are reading their assignment. While doing this, the teacher could also pick out those words that are derived from combining forms. The combining forms and the words derived from them should be presented to the students with the other words that are selected for presentation to the students.

A short selection from a typical biology textbook and a list of combining forms that were chosen from the selection are presented to illustrate the power students have if they possess knowledge of combining forms. The words underlined in the selection are derived from the list of combining forms.

Combining Forms

sym = same	bi = two
a = without	latus = side
pseudo = false	dors, dorsi, dorso = back
ped, pod = foot	ante = before
loc, loco = place	post = after
mob, mov, mot = move	in = not
meter = measure	sphere = ball

Symmetry and Similarities

Similarity of structure is important in classification. The general form of each organism is called its symmetry. The ameba has no definite shape, so it is said to be asymmetrical. It orients itself to the environment by moving in any direction with its pseudopods. Most sponges grow in colonies without a definite shape. They also may be thought of as asymmetrical. An organism with spherical symmetry meets the environment on all its surfaces. Organisms with spherical symmetry often have no effective method of locomotion, and they float on or near the water's surface.

Most organisms are affected by gravity, however. The sea anemone, for example, has tentacles at one end and a basal disk for attachment at the other. The sea anemone has radial symmetry. Its tentacles radiate like spokes of a wheel from a central disk. Imagine a line drawn right through the mouth and the center of the body. This line would be the central axis of the sea anemone. Some sponges, most coelenterates (hydra, anemones), and most adult echinoderms (sea urchin, sand dollar) are radially symmetrical.

Actively moving organisms are better adapted for their way of life by having bilateral symmetry, which means "two-sided shape." Animals with this kind of symmetry are similar on two sides. They can be divided in half by a plane passing through a longitudinal axis, from the center of the upper surface, to the center of the lower surface. The two halves of a bilaterally symmetrical animal are the right side and the left side. One side is the mirror image of the other. The upper surface of the animal is dorsal, the lower surface is ventral. It also has a definite front, or anterior end, and a hind, or posterior, end. All vertebrates and many invertebrates have this kind of symmetry. In humans, dorsal is your "back," ventral is your "front."

Many organisms with bilateral symmetry have a concentration of nerves and sense organs at the anterior end.

Some science textbook writers feel that knowledge of word parts (combining forms) is so important that they present special information on word parts early in their books (see Figure 8-4).[8] This is good; however, teachers still must make a concerted effort to directly teach these important word parts and not take for granted that their students will learn the word parts and their meanings just because they are presented in the textbook.

Special Note:
The terms *word parts* and *combining forms* are used interchangeably. In Chapter 4, it is stated that the general definition of combining forms is being used in this book when the emphasis is on vocabulary expansion (see Chapter 4).

ADAPTING SQ3R IN SCIENCE READING

Throughout this chapter, stress has been given to having teachers behave and teach in a way that does not violate the scientific method. Emphasis was given also to the types of thinking that good scientists need to be able to do. It was further stated that teachers can help their students to develop these kinds of thinking if they give students the opportunities to engage in activities that require higher-level comprehension skills using materials re-

[8]Jill Wright, Charles R. Coble, Jean Hopkins, Susan Johnson, and David LeHart, *Prentice Hall Life Science*, 2nd ed. (Englewood Cliffs, N.J.: Prentice Hall, 1991), p. 12.

FIGURE 8-4. The writers of this science textbook recognize the importance of word parts in vocabulary expansion.

Sharpen Your Skills

What's the Word?

Use the prefixes and suffixes in Figure 1-7 to determine the meanings of the following words.

biology	exostosis
gastropod	exoskeleton
hemostasis	epidermis
homeostasis	cytology
photometer	

Figure 1-7 *Learning the meanings of these prefixes and suffixes will make learning new science terms easier. What is the meaning of the word arthropod?*

Life science can be divided into a number of specialized branches. One branch of life science is **zoology** (zoh-AHL-uh-jee). Zoology is the study of animals. Another branch of life science is **botany** (BAHT-uh-nee), which is the study of plants. A third branch of life science is **ecology**, or the study of the relationships between living organisms and their environment. Still another branch of life science is **microbiology**. Microbiology is the study of **microorganisms**, or microscopic organisms.

Just like any branch of science, life science has many special terms that may be unfamiliar to you. The chart in Figure 1-7 gives the meanings of some prefixes and suffixes that are commonly used in science vocabulary. If you learn the meanings of these prefixes and suffixes, learning new science terms will be easier. For example, suppose you are reading a magazine article and you come across the term *osteology*. You know that the prefix *osteo-* means bone and the suffix *-logy* means study. By joining the meanings of the prefix and suffix, you learn that osteology is the study of bones.

Prefix	Meaning	Prefix	Meaning	Suffix	Meaning
anti-	against	herb-	pertaining to plants	-cyst	pouch
arth-	joint, jointed	hetero-	different	-derm	skin, layer
auto-	self	homeo-	same	-gen	producing
bio-	related to life	macro-	large	-itis	inflammation
chloro-	green	micro-	small	-logy	study
cyto-	cell	multi-	consisting of many units	-meter	measurement
di-	double	osteo-	bone	-osis	condition, disease
epi-	above	photo-	pertaining to light	-phase	stage
exo-	outer, external	plasm-	forming substance	-phage	eater
gastro-	stomach	proto-	first	-pod	foot
hemo-	blood	syn-	together	-stasis	stationary condition

quired in the course. This section will present a scenario to show how teachers can prepare students for their reading assignments.

Scenario

Mr. Johnson has been teaching science for twenty years. He has met a great number of students in his day, but most of the students whom he has had were those who were interested in science and who wanted to study science as their lifework. In the past few years, Mr. Johnson has been asked to teach less advanced science courses. The students in these courses were taking the science course because it was required either for graduation or for college admission. Mr. Johnson realized early that his teaching tactics would have to be modified somewhat to accommodate these students. Oh, by no means, would he compromise his basic approach, which stressed doing things in a scientific manner and the development of critical and creative thinking in his students. What would change would be his approach in presenting the material and the emphasis he would give to vocabulary development. Mr. Johnson, from listening to some students read aloud, recognized that a number of students had word recognition problems and could not pronounce a number of the technical words. Mr. Johnson is certainly not a reading teacher, but he is an excellent science teacher, who takes great pride in his profession. He knew that the only way that he could be successful with the groups of students he was now asked to teach would be to help them gain skill in reading their textbook. He knew that it was just not possible to present everything orally. (Mr. Johnson's school district had required that all content-area teachers take two reading courses to update their certification. He remembers how he resented this and how he complained about the unfairness of it all; however, he was now grateful that he had had these courses.)

Mr. Johnson now prepares the students to read the material on their own. Here is the procedure he follows:

1. Mr. Johnson first surveys the material the students will be reading. He selects all those terms he feels might cause difficulty for his students. Scientific vocabulary as well as nontechnical vocabulary is selected. Mr. Johnson puts the words on a special guide sheet that students will get. On the guide sheet the words are presented in context and defined. Mr. Johnson pronounces each word for the students beforehand, puts it in a sentence, and then either challenges students to figure out the meaning or states the meaning. For certain technical terms, he will often spend more time on the words, especially if they are key words that are germane to understanding the material to be studied.

2. Mr. Johnson sets purposes for the students' reading of the material. These are given in the form of questions. Mr. Johnson gives students questions at all comprehension levels. These are also stated on the students' guide sheets.

3. Mr. Johnson introduces the students to the material. He explains the SQ3R method to them and tells them that they can still set questions for themselves while reading but that they should also keep in mind the questions that he would like them to answer. When they review, they should see whether they can answer the questions he has asked. He also says that a good way to review is to go back to the beginning and see whether one can give the main idea of each of the paragraphs studied.

Commentary

It should be stated that Mr. Johnson does not give his students a guide sheet for everything they will be reading in their textbook because the textbook writers of the book he has chosen for his students emphasize vocabulary development and make a concerted effort to use context clues to help students acquire the specialized vocabulary they will need to read their books. The book also has an excellent glossary. Here is a sample guide sheet that Mr. Johnson would prepare in advance for his students. Note that the guide sheet also gives the steps in the SQ3R method.

SAMPLE GUIDE SHEET

Course: Modern Biology

Reading Assignment: How Pathogenic Organisms Attack the Body pp. 214–226

Review Combining forms: anti = against; bio = life; patho = disease; gen, geno = race, kind, descent; tox = poison; micro = very small.

Words derived from combining forms: antibiotic = germ killing substance; antitoxin = a substance in the blood that acts against a specific toxin (poison); pathogenic = disease-causing; genus = class, kind, or group; antibodies = immune substances in the blood and body fluids; microorganism = an organism so small that it can be seen only under a microscope.

Other words: hostile = unfriendly; immune = free from, exempt from; contaminated = infected by contact or association; penetrate = to pass into or through; devour = eat up greedily.

Key Questions: How is disease caused?
Why do immune carriers cause problems for humans?
How do microorganisms damage our bodies?
What lines of defense do we have?
How do cells within the body devour bacteria?
What chemical defenses do we have against disease?
What medical defenses do we have against disease?

Write a summary of this section. Remember to include in your summary the central idea of this section and the key details.

Special Note: As you study this section, the following study technique should help you.

---

1. Survey the complete section before beginning to read. In surveying the section, note the main topic of the section and the subtopics.
2. Use the given questions to set your purposes for reading.
3. Read the selection. You do not have to read the whole selection at one sitting. Choose a part that will answer each question.
4. After you have finished reading the part you have chosen, try to answer the question on it. *This part of your studying is very important.* Follow the same procedure for each question.
5. After you have finished reading the whole selection, review what you have read. A good way to do this is to start at the beginning of the selection, look at each paragraph, and try to state the main idea of it.

SAMPLE READING/SCIENCE ACTIVITIES

Here are some examples of science activities that should be challenging for students because they demand more than literal comprehension ability.

Activity 1 Directions: Find the word from the word list that makes each sentence *always* true and that makes sense. More words are given in the word list than you need for answers, and a word may be used once only.

Word List

animals	polygons	ounce
box	oval	fluids
moisture	onion	herbivorous
cherry	tomato	carnivorous
ten	solids	air
rectangles	pound	sun
five	quart	moon
twenty	gallon	snakes
humans	half-pound	squares

1. A pound of ice weighs the same as a(n) _____ of water.

2. No _____ have limbs.

3. All four-sided figures are _____.

4. Many _____ are quadrupeds.

5. Every millennium has _____ centuries.

6. All _____ are bipeds.

7. All horses are _____.

8. All planets have a(n) _____.

9. All gases are _____.

10. Hygrometers measure _____ in the air.

Answers: 1. pound 2. snakes 3. polygons 4. animals 5. ten 6. humans 7. herbivorous 8. sun 9. fluids 10. moisture

Activity 2 Directions: Choose the word from the word list that belongs to each set.
Word List

squids	turtles	decimeter
sharks	larva	decade
dogs	million	salamanders
ticks	decameter	asps
butterflies	kilometer	

1. egg, _____, pupa, adult

2. one, _____, century, millennium

3. meter, _____, centimeter, millimeter

4. scorpions, _____, mites, spiders

5. louse, _____, bee, termite

6. snakes, _____, lizards, crocodiles

7. frogs, _____, toads, newts

8. adders, _____, cobras, rattlers

9. clams, _____, snails, oysters

10. whale, _____, porpoise, walrus

Answers: 1. larva 2. decade 3. decimeter 4. ticks (eight-legged)
5. butterflies (insects) 6. turtles (reptiles) 7. salamanders (amphibians)
8. asps (snakes) 9. squids (shellfish) 10. seal (aquatic mammal).

Activity 3: Fitting the Word to Meanings and Characteristics Choose a word that fits the meaning(s) and characteristics in each set.

1. This is the basic unit of life; it is composed of a membrane, nucleus, and cytoplasm; it is capable of functioning independently.

2. The substance of which a physical object is composed; the element in the universe that undergoes formation and alteration; it may be solid, liquid, or gas.

3. These organisms contain chlorophyll; they have no true roots, stems, or leaves.

4. These are very small microorganisms; they are found everywhere; they reproduce asexually; they are beneficial as well as harmful.

5. This is the functional unit of the nervous system; there are millions of these.

Answers: 1. cell 2. matter 3. algae 4. bacteria 5. neuron

Activity 4: What Are We? or What Am I? Use the given clues to figure out the plants or animals to which they refer.

1. We are small, herblike plants; some of us resemble trees; we are found in most parts of the world, and there are about 9,300 species of us. What are we?

2. I am constantly changing my shape; therefore, I have no definite shape. I am a one-celled animal. What am I?

3. Lizards, snakes, and turtles all belong to my class. The dinosaur is one of our ancient ancestors. What are we called?

4. We are very quiet because we are voiceless; persons hardly notice us; we live in or near water. Most of us become active at night. We are amphibians. What are we?

Answers: 1. ferns 2. amoeba 3. reptiles 4. salamanders

Activity 5 Present students with the following problem. Have them read the problem very carefully to gather all clues; then have them try to solve the problem, using an inquiry technique. Have the students compose questions in the form of hypotheses to gain information. The teacher answers only "yes" or "no" to each question that is asked. The students need to ask pertinent questions to gain enough information to arrive at the correct solution.

> Three murderers killed their victim in a sauna. They left the sauna without the weapon. The police came and found no trace of the weapon. How was the victim killed, and what was the weapon used? There is enough evidence to solve this mystery.

Answer: The victim was stabbed with an icicle.

Ideas for Activities

1. Present students with a list of plants and animals, and have them classify these into various categories.
2. Present students with a hypothesis. Have them read it carefully, and then have them explain how they would go about proving or disproving it.
3. Give students a list of facts. Have them draw inferences from these.
4. Give students a hypothetical problem. Ask them how they would go about solving it.
5. Ask students to keep a diary of their behavior for a week. Ask them to analyze their behavior to see how many times they used scientific techniques to solve their everyday problems.
6. Assign students a short library research project so that they can have some experience in working with science journals.
7. Have students write three questions that they feel would be good test questions. The questions should be based on their readings.
8. Have students write a summary of an article that they have read in a science journal.
9. Present students with a problem that does not have enough information. Ask students to try to determine what information is needed to solve the problem.

COMPUTERS IN SCIENCE

Computers play a significant role in all the sciences. Many of the major advances in science have been facilitated by computers because computers allow for the access and analysis of large amounts of data.

Scientists primarily use computers to solve complex mathematical models of physical systems, chemical actions, biological systems, drug absorption in the body, the effectiveness of vaccines, the efficacy of new drugs, and so forth.

In the classroom, teachers must help students recognize that the computer is an essential tool of the scientist; however, it is only as good as the person programming it. And to use the computer effectively in the sciences, students must have good reading skills. The teacher should prepare students by introducing them to the special science vocabulary and building topic knowledge. Of course, in order to adequately access computer programs, students need knowledge of computer language, and they must be able to follow directions.

Computer-assisted instruction (CAI) is a viable use of computers in the science classroom. Here, as in other content areas, CAI can be used for drill and practice so that students can overlearn important concepts and information. Demonstrations help give students insights into concepts, and tutorials help give students added practice and help in understanding information. Simulation activities require students to be active participants and to make predictions based on given data. Instructional science games can also help students gain information in an enjoyable way.

GRAPHIC SUMMARY OF CHAPTER

Here is a graphic summary of Chapter 8. If you have read the chapter, this graphic illustration should help you remember its main points. Under or beside each heading, you might want to jot down some of the information you recall, as well as some of the key concepts in this chapter. This can act as a good review. You can then check your key concepts against those that follow the graphic summary.

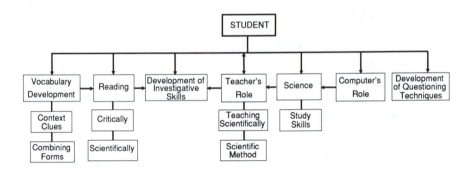

KEY CONCEPTS IN CHAPTER

- Reading helps students gain information about what has taken place in the past.
- Reading helps students gain insights into the scientific mind.
- Reading is closely related to the scientific method because both emphasize reasoning ability and critical thinking.
- Students must have literal, interpretive, critical, and creative thinking ability to be good scientists.
- Student scientists need to develop good investigative skills.
- Investigative skills include such abilities as categorizing or classifying, inference, prediction, and evaluation.
- The teacher plays a crucial role in helping students read in a scientific manner.
- Students in science classes must learn the technical vocabulary.
- Teachers should use a number of approaches to help students acquire

the vocabulary they need to understand the concepts they are learning.

- Combining forms is a viable approach to help students learn many scientific terms.
- Computers play a significant role in all the sciences.

SUGGESTIONS FOR THOUGHT QUESTIONS AND ACTIVITIES

1. You have been asked to speak to your local parent-teacher association about the role of reading in the sciences. What will you say?

2. Prepare some activities related to what students are studying that will stimulate students to use divergent thinking.

3. You have been asked to give a talk to your colleagues on how you teach science scientifically. What will you say?

4. Prepare a list of combining forms that you can use to help students expand their science vocabulary.

5. Prepare a guide sheet for a group of students that will help them read their science textbook.

6. Discuss those teaching tactics that you feel will help teachers to teach scientifically.

7. Prepare some science activities that stress classification.

8. State the characteristics of the kinds of computer software you would like to see made available to science teachers.

9. Review some of the computer software on the market for science classes. Note whether they contain the characteristics you stated in number 8.

SELECTED BIBLIOGRAPHY

DOLE, JANICE A., and VIRGINIA R. JOHNSON. "Beyond the Textbook: Science Literature for Young People." *Journal of Reading* 24 (April 1981): 579–582.

GUERRA, CATHY L., and DELORES B. PAYNE. "Using Popular Books and Magazines to Interest Students in General Science." *Journal of Reading* 24 (April 1981): 583–586.

LLOYD, CAROL V., and JUDY NICHOLS MITCHELL. "Coping with Too Many Concepts in Science Texts." *Journal of Reading* 32 (March 1989):542–545.

MALLOW, JEFFREY. "Reading Science." *Journal of Reading* 34 (February 1991): 324–338.

MULLIS, INA V.S., and LYNN B. JENKINS. *The Science Report Card: Elements of Risk and Recovery.* The National Assessment of Educational Progress. Princeton, N.J.: Educational Testing Service, 1988.

MULLIS, INA V.S., EUGENE H. OWENS, and GARY W. PHILLIPS. *America's Challenge: Accelerating Academic Achievement.* The National Assessment of Educational Progress. Princeton, N.J.: Educational Testing Service, 1990.

SANTA, CAROL, LYN HAVENS, and SHIRLEY HARRISON. "Teaching Secondary Science through Reading, Writing, Studying, and Problem Solving." In *Content Area Reading and*

Learning. Diane Lapp, James Flood, and Nancy Farnan (eds.) Englewood Cliffs, N.J.: Prentice Hall, 1989, pp. 137–151.

THELAN, JUDITH. *Improving Reading in Science.* Newark, Del.: International Reading Association, 1976.

YAGER, ROBERT E. "The Importance of Terminology in Teaching K–12 Science." *Journal of Research in Science Teaching* 20 (1983): 577–588.

YAGER, ROBERT E., and JOHN E. PENICK. "Science Teacher Education." In *Handbook of Research on Teacher Education.* W. Robert Houston (ed.) New York: Macmillan, 1990, pp. 657–673.

9

Enhancing Mathematical Learning Through Reading/Study Skills

> There exists a passion for comprehension just as there exists a passion for music. That passion is rather common in children, but gets lost in most people later on. Without this passion, there would be neither mathematics nor natural science.
>
> ALBERT EINSTEIN

INTRODUCTION

"Despite concentration on the fundamentals of mathematics in elementary schools, only 21 percent of the 9-year olds and 73 percent of the 13-year olds displayed a firm grasp of the four basic operations and of beginning problem solving. Without a foundation in problem-solving skills and basic numerical understanding, it may not be surprising that only half the high-school students displayed success with moderately challenging material."[1] Apparently, mathematics does not fare any better in the schools than science or social studies.

However, hardly a day passes without our having to do some kind of mathematical computation. Cooking, baking, driving, shopping, sewing, repairing, gardening, reading newspapers, analyzing reports and bank statements, paying the mortgage, and so on require the use of mathematics at various levels of difficulty. With the advent of calculators, quantitative operations have become relatively easy, and even primary-grade level children are able to use some calculators to do some basic operations. These calculators are omnipresent, and they have revolutionized the world of mathematics. However, these calculators can only do mathematical operations; they cannot yet interpret the kinds of operations that need to be done—that require mathematical reasoning. They cannot yet read the word problem to determine what the problem is. (In the future, however, computer scientists hope to be able to develop language translation programs for use by computers in directly translating word problems into succinct mathematical statements that can then be solved by computer operations.)

In the world of numbers, we still must be able to read. We need to learn the language of mathematics and recognize that numerals, as well as letters, are symbolic representations. We need to be able to decode these symbols and associate meaning with them. We need to be able to read the explanatory sections, as well as the word problems. We need to be able to work at high levels of comprehension because mathematics demands individuals who are good thinkers.

KEY QUESTIONS

After reading this chapter, you should be able to answer the following questions:

1. How are mathematics and reading interrelated?
2. What could be causes of students' mathematics problems?
3. Why do word problems in mathematics cause difficulty for some students?
4. How is the English language related to mathematics?

---

[1]Ina V.S. Mullis, Eugene H. Owen, and Gary W. Phillips, *America's Challenge: Accelerating Academic Achievement—A Summary of Findings from 20 Years of NAEP,* (Princeton, N.J.: Educational Testing Service, 1990), p. 20.

5. How can teachers through teaching mathematics help students to be more precise in their communication?
6. What are examples of interpetive, critical, and creative comprehension questions that mathematics teachers can ask?
7. How can teachers help students solve mathematics word problems by using a guided approach? How can teachers help students expand their mathematics vocabulary?
8. What are some mathematics activities that teachers can construct?
9. What is the role of computers in mathematics classes?

KEY TERMS IN CHAPTER

You should pay special attention to the following key terms:

mathematics	set theory
set	word problem in mathematics

MATHEMATICS AND READING

Mathematics is the science of numbers. It demands persons who are able to reason at various levels of abstraction; it demands logical thinkers. Reading comprehension and mathematics are related in that they both emphasize thinking skills. As stated earlier in this textbook, the reading teacher is primarily concerned with the development of reading skills whereas the content-area teacher is primarily concerned with the development of concepts in a specific content area. However, even mathematics teachers may need to give their students direct instruction in those reading/thinking skills that they need to solve mathematical problems; even mathematics teachers can use a directed reading approach to teaching content.

A student may be able to do quantitative reasoning or basic mathematical operations but still have difficulty in mathematics. It may be that the student has a reading problem; that is, the student cannot read the explanatory material or interpret the so-called mathematical word problem. In a word problem, the problem is not stated in its most succinct mathematical form, which is a set of equations with all variables defined. In a word problem, the English language paragraph is used to describe the problem, and from the description, the students must extract the correct mathematical description of the problem. This involves comprehension skill at the interpetive and critical reading levels. Students must sift through the given data to determine the following:

1. What is the problem?
2. What are the variables?

3. What information should be discarded; that is, what information is extraneous?

4. How will the given information help to solve the problem?

The student must use comprehension skill plus mathematical ability to solve word problems. These problems are different from the ones in which students are given an equation and told to crank out the answer. In many textbooks, interestingly, problems may not require much thought because they are artificial ones whose purpose is to give students practice in manipulating equations; however, in real-life situations, problems are not usually defined succinctly and convergently, and there often is extraneous information. In these situations, it is rare that individuals are given the derived equation and have merely to compute the answer. For example, here is a seemingly simple problem that many suburbanites face: How many pounds of fertilizer should they buy to fertilize their lawns? Let's see how involved this seemingly simple problem is.

To determine how many pounds of fertilizer to buy, we must first determine the area of our lot that we want fertilized. As our lot is not an exact rectangle and as we have a house area, a driveway area, a garden area, and so on, we will have to figure out all these areas piecemeal. Then we will have to use geometry formulas to calculate the various geometric areas. The second part has to do with determining proportions. Fertilizer is usually composed of a mixture of chemicals. The important chemical is that of nitrogen (different fertilizers have different percentages of this element), and we should put down one pound of actual nitrogen for each 1,000 square feet of lawn. Different bags of fertilizer not only have different percentages of nitrogen, but they also have different costs. We, therefore, have to be able to compute amounts from percentages to determine the amount we need, as well as our best buy.

The problem becomes even more complex because the deed to the property says that the lot is $2/3$ of an acre in area for the lot we own; however, there is a 15-foot wide strip that belongs to the Township that we would like to fertilize, so. . . . Yes, the problem goes on. We can see why this seemingly simple problem has baffled many a homeowner. It's really not the mathematics because we are not dealing with high-level mathematics. The problem has to do with reasoning ability. It involves problem-stating skills and the ability to break the problem down into its essential and manageable, calculable elements. It involves high-level thinking without high-level quantification.

Here is another rather simple problem, which is precisely stated, yet a number of students have difficulty solving it because they misinterpret the problem.

Divide 30 by $\frac{1}{2}$ and add 10.

Solution: $\dfrac{\frac{30}{1}}{\frac{1}{2}} = \dfrac{30 \times \frac{2}{1}}{\frac{1}{2} \times \frac{2}{1}} = 30 \times \frac{2}{1} = 60; \quad 60 + 10 = 70$

Answer: 70

A number of students misinterpret the problem to mean take ½ of 30; that is, they divide 30 into two parts. These students have a reading problem, and they are confused as to what division by a fraction means. They need help in reading problems involving fractions.

RELATING MATHEMATICS TO THE ENGLISH LANGUAGE

When Confucius was asked what he would do if he had the responsibility for administering a country, he said that he would improve language. If language is not correct, he stated, then what is said is not what is meant; if what is said is not what is meant, then what ought to be done remains undone; if this remains undone, morals and arts would deteriorate; if morals and arts deteriorate, justice will go astray; if justice goes astray, the people will stand about in helpless confusion.

CONFUCIUS (C. 551–479 B.C.)

Mathematics teachers can help students recognize that mathematics is a language with a specialized vocabulary that is very precise. Mathematicians can usually communicate (exchange ideas) with other mathematicians all over the world whereas English-speaking people have difficulty many times communicating with one another within the same country because of the ambiguity of language. The English language can be precise, but at times it is used to obfuscate, confuse, and evade issues. When we read, we must separate fact from opinion and fantasy; we must detect propaganda techniques or bias in the writing, and so on. In mathematics, rules are strictly adhered to; mathematics is not used to obfuscate or confuse.

Mathematics teachers can help raise the consciousness level of students by making them more sensitive to the need for more precision in the English language. If the English language problem that the mathematicians must solve is not precisely stated, it would be difficult to solve it. Mathematicians must understand the problem before they can make a precise mathematical translation of the English language problem they wish to solve.

In the English language, as well as in other languages, word meanings depend on syntax, that is, the pattern or word order. For example, in the following sentences, the words *spring* and *well* have different meanings based on the way they are positioned in the sentence.

I like water from a *spring* rather than from a *well*.
We asked the child who was not *well* to stop jumping on the *spring*.

Teachers can help make learning mathematics more dynamic and practical if they show students how to relate the mathematical terms and skills to the English language terms and skills. For example, there is a *syntax* too in mathematics; that is, the way terms are presented in *relation* to other terms influences the meaning of the term. The syntax of mathematics is quite rigid. If you deviate in mathematical syntax, the meaning is usually drastically changed. For example:

$$A > B$$
$$B > A$$

Now, read the following sentences. Note that they too have the same terms, but the order (syntax) is different. The meanings of the sentences are entirely different.

The man bit the dog.
The dog bit the man.

Here are some other examples to show how mathematics and English are similar.

$A + B = C$ is equivalent to $B + A = C$ (These two equations are similar because of the associative property of addition.)
John and Carol are going to the party is equivalent to *Carol and John are going to the party.*

If students are helped to see that small deviations can lead to misunderstandings in mathematics, they may come to recognize that imprecision in language can also lead to lack of communication or misunderstandings. Teachers who help their students to see the relationship between the English language and mathematics are helping their students to succeed in mathematics, as well as to succeed in English. Good readers should be able to succeed in mathematics because it is nothing more than a shorthand form of a language with precise rules.

It is possible that students who have a fear of working with numbers will have less anxiety if they can see the relationship between their language and mathematics. Numbers as letters are symbols that need to be decoded, and all mathematical operations are symbols, too, that represent very specific things to do. As words are organized into patterns that convey unique meanings, so are alphanumeric (consisting of both letters and numbers and often other symbols) symbols arranged into patterns that convey unique meanings. Obviously, lack of common meanings of either mathematical symbols or words would result in faulty communication.

Many textbooks are including a section entitled "Application," which

FIGURE 9-1. Peppermint Patty has difficulty with word problems; they just don't make the right connections for her.

presents mathematical problems of interest to students (see Figure 9-2). Activities such as these help emphasize the relationship between language and mathematics, as well as the practical applications of mathematics.[2]

MATHEMATICAL DEFINITIONS

Numbers are a way of making order out of chaos. Read the following excerpt:

> On a recent trip to New York I got off at Pennsylvania Station. I walked to the taxi platform, but the train had been crowded and soon dozens of people poured out of the station for cabs. Some of them waved and yelled; some stepped in front of the cabs rushing down the incline; some, who had porters in their employ, seemed to be getting preferential treatment. I waited on the curb, convinced that my gentle ways and the merits of my case would ultimately attract a driver. However, when they did, he was snatched out from under me. I gave up, took the subway, cursing the railroad, the cabbies, and people in general and hoping they would get stuck for hours in the crosstown traffic.
>
> Several weeks later, on a trip to Philadelphia, I got off at the 30th St. Station. I walked to the taxi platform. A sign advised me to take a number. A dispatcher loaded the cabs in numerical order, and I was soon on my way to the hotel. It was rapid, it was pleasant, it was civilized. And this is a fine, though exceedingly simple, way in which mathematics may affect social affairs. . . . The numbers have an order, and can be used to simulate a queue [line of people] without the inconvenience and indignity of actually forming a queue. The numbers are a catalyst that can help turn raving madmen into polite humans.[3]

Definitions are also necessary to order, for they make communication clearer and more precise. In mathematics, many undefined terms are introduced and explained by the use of examples, and their meanings are learned from using them in a number of ways.

[2]Jan Fair and Sadie C. Bragg, *Prentice Hall Algebra 1* (Englewood Cliffs, N.J.: Prentice Hall, 1991), p. 218.

[3]"The Criterion Makers: Mathematics and Social Policy," *The American Scientist*, 50 (Sept. 1962):258A.

APPLICATION: Marathon Running

Did you know that the Olympic marathon race was originally run in the 1896 Olympics in Athens, Greece? This race commemorated an unknown messenger who ran 24 miles to annouce a Greek victory. Preparing for a modern day marathon requires careful training and physical conditioning. In order to run a distance of 26 miles and 385 yards, marathon runners need to build up greater distances and faster times. Keeping careful track of their performances enables these long distance runners to structure a proper training schedule.

No official records are kept for marathon races due to varying course conditions and degrees of difficulty. The following table shows the men's and women's marathon gold medalists for the 1988 and 1984 Olympics.

Gelindo Bordin	Italy	1988	2 h 10 min 32 s
Rosa Mota	Portugal	1988	2 h 25 min 40 s
Carlos Lopes	Portugal	1984	2 h 9 min 55 s
Joan Benoit	U.S.A.	1984	2 h 24 min 52 s

EXAMPLE 1 While training for a marathon, Jane plans to run at least 40 mi each week. On Wednesday she is only able to run 4 mi. What is the least number of miles she must average daily by next Wednesday to meet her distance goal?

$$m = \text{number of miles run each day}$$
$$6m = \text{number of miles run for the 6 days}$$
$$6m + 4 \geq 40$$
$$6m \geq 36$$
$$m \geq 6$$

Therefore, Jane must average at least 6 mi each day for the next 6 days.

Figure 9-2. This excerpt from a mathematics textbook illustrates a practical application of mathematics.

A set is a well-defined collection of things. Students can learn this concept from various examples. For example, the set of men or the set of women, the set of fruit, the set of whole numbers, the set of odd numbers, and so on. The set of tall women is not precisely delineated; therefore it cannot be used mathematically. The term *tall* is a relative term, and not until the term *tall* is defined precisely can we refer to a set of tall women.

Teachers can use inductive teaching to help their students to gain mathematical definitions. Inductive teaching requires that a number of examples that aptly illustrate the definition are given and that students can derive the correct definition or generalization from the examples. For example, have students try to determine the definition of *empty set*. On the board put the following examples:

Empty set is the set of all surgeons in the class.

Empty set is the set of all $6 bills.

Empty set is the set of all four-footed animals who talk.

Empty set is the set of all persons who have wings.

Empty set is the set of all 90-year-olds who swim seventy miles every day.

Empty set is the set of all unicorns.

From the examples, the students should be able to define *empty set* as "a set that contains no members."

Set theory is an excellent concept to introduce beginning at the elementary school because it strongly emphasizes the interrelationship between classification and mathematics. Learning to organize information and to communicate in a clear, precise manner is essential not only in mathematics but in everyday life. Think of all the times during the day when you have to organize objects and information.

INTERPRETIVE, CRITICAL, AND CREATIVE COMPREHENSION QUESTIONS FOR MATHEMATICS

In Chapter 3, we discussed how important the art of questioning is and showed that the type of question that is asked will determine the kinds of responses that will be received. More importantly, the questions asked will determine the level of thinking that will be needed to answer the questions. Mathematics, as well as the other content areas, requires that teachers ask questions beyond the literal level. This section will present a discussion of the kinds of questions that teachers can ask at the various comprehension levels.

Emphasis will be given to the interpretive, critical, and creative comprehension skills rather than to literal comprehension skills. In mathematics, literal comprehension would apply to problems in which all information, including the basic operations, is explicitly stated and students merely have to do the basic operations. For example, a teacher asks the students to compute the following equations:

$$9 + 3 = ?$$
$$17 - 8 = ?$$
$$12 \times 9 = ?$$

The word problem in mathematics often presents difficulty to students because it requires that students translate the usually imprecise English language to very precise mathematical language. If the question and the essential nature of the problem are very close, then it is a convergent word problem and should not present much difficulty for students. Usually, this is the first level at which students are introduced to word problems. For example:

> Jack had $15 and spent $5 in one store and $3 in another store. How much money did he have left?
>
> Solution: $5 + $3 = $8
>
> $15 − $8 = $7

Answer: $7

Although the problem is not a difficult one and at an elementary level, it still requires interpretive skills to determine what mathematical operations are required to solve the problem.

Here is another example of an elementary problem at a little higher level of sophistication:

> Jack had $15 and spent $5 in one store and $3 in another store. What part of the original amount did he spend?
>
> Solution: $\dfrac{5}{15} + \dfrac{3}{15} = \dfrac{8}{15}$

Answer: $\dfrac{8}{15}$

The student needs interpretive skills to determine what the mathematical translation of the English language problem is and then what mathematical operations to apply to solve the problem. The preceding problem is a little more difficult because it involves fractions.

Here is another elementary problem that is a convergent word problem because the question and the essential nature of the problem are very close.

> A student has 7 marbles in his pocket. He has 5 green ones and 2 red ones. What is the probability that the boy will reach into his pocket and pick a red marble?

The essence of the problem concerns how to compute probability, which is what the question asks.

Answer: $\dfrac{2}{7}$

There are times, however, when the question does not contain the essence of the problem. This would be the case where the question that is asked is analogous to the topic of the problem and the essence or heart of the problem would be found by determining what is special about the topic. The essence of a problem has to do with gaining insight into the problem—with understanding the problem. It is usually something we must infer. Because of this, we would not be far off by saying that it is analogous to gaining the main idea of a paragraph. The teacher might want to give students direct practice in finding the essence of various word problems using the technique that is analogous to finding the main idea of paragraphs. See the following section for more on the essence of a problem or gaining insight into a problem.

Teachers can challenge students by asking them some of the following interpretive questions:

1. How do you go about making an estimate?
2. Is the given word problem succinctly stated? Explain.
3. Has the writer given us any extraneous information?
4. Do we have all the information we need to solve the problem?
5. What is the essential problem?

Some critical thinking questions follow:

1. Is the answer reasonable?
2. How would you judge or evaluate whether the answer makes sense?

At the divergent level the teacher can ask the following type of questions:

1. Is there a simpler, more direct way to solve the problem?
2. Are there other ways to solve the problem?
3. What other problem is similar to this one?
4. Here is an equation. Can you come up with word problems to which this equation would apply?
5. How can this problem be used in the everyday world?

A GUIDE FOR SOLVING WORD PROBLEMS

This section will present a technique that is helpful to solving mathematical word problems. Here are the steps:

1. Read the word problem *carefully.*
2. Determine whether you understand the question, that is, what is to be found. If you do not understand the question, reread the entire statement of the problem.
3. Write succinct definitions of the variables. This means that you should write down the facts by translating English to precise mathematical forms.
4. Organize all material. This requires categorizing skill.
5. Make a concise mathematical translation of the English language problem; that is, construct a mathematics model for the word problem. Determine the essence of the problem.

6. Evaluate to determine whether there is enough information to solve the problem and whether there is any extraneous information. Discard all extraneous information; that is, put it into the category of information to be ignored.
7. Apply mathematical operations necessary to solve problem. The calculator, computer, or hand operation is used.
8. Evaluate answer (evaluation includes estimation). Compare answer to your estimate. Is the answer reasonable and based on given facts? Is there another way of solving the problem? Is there another way of calculating whether your answer is correct; that is, does the answer agree with all facts?

Special Note:
Finding the essence of the problem sometimes gives you the solution immediately, and you do not have to go through all the presented steps. *Example:* If you have 10 empty coke bottles, how much soda would you find in these bottles? The problem statement is the essence of the problem. Translate English into mathematical statement. (*Empty* translates into 0.) $10 \times 0 = 0$. The answer is 0. To solve this problem, you needed to know the mathematical fact that anything multiplied by 0 equals 0. The fact that there are 10 coke bottles is an extraneous one. $N \times 0 = 0$. The key to solving this problem was in translating *empty* to 0.

To help you to gain a better understanding of the steps involved in solving a word problem, we will do one together in which we will go through all of the steps.
Note that the following type of example allows the student to exercise verbal reasoning and to see how closely related this is to quantitative reasoning or to mathematical logic. Both require high-level thinking. Here is the problem:

A manufacturer makes two kinds of television sets, a console and a portable. He has equipment to manufacture any number of console sets up to 400 per month or any number of portable sets up to 500 per month, but he can only manufacture 600 sets of both kinds per month in all. It takes 50 labor-hours to manufacture either a console or a portable, and the manufacturer has available 30,000 labor-hours per month. The labor force is 25 percent female and 75 percent male. If the manufacturer realizes a profit of $60.00 on each console set and $50.00 on each portable, find the number of each type of set he should manufacture to realize the greatest profit.

STEP 1: Read the word problem *carefully.*
STEP 2: The problem statement paragraph contains facts as well as the question. The question must be separated from the facts. The problem question is as follows: Find the number of each type of set that should be manufactured to realize the greatest profit.

STEPS 3 AND 4: We need to translate English into precise mathematical forms. We need to state all our facts.

Number of console sets made in a month = X
Number of portable sets made in a month = Y
Profit per console = \$60.00
Profit per portable = \$50.00
Maximum number of consoles produced = 400
Maximum number of portables produced = 500
Maximum total number = 600 This translates into equation

$$X + Y = 600$$

$X \le 400$
$Y \le 500$
50 labor-hours to produce a console
50 labor-hours to produce a portable
Manufacturer has available 30,000 labor hours
75 percent males ⎫
25 percent females ⎬ equals work force

STEP 5: We have to make a concise mathematical translation of the English language problem and then see if we can determine the essence of the problem.

Profit realized on consoles = $60X$
Profit realized on portables = $50Y$

Total sets made = $X + Y = 600$ **(equation 1)**
Total profit = $60X + 50Y$ **(equation 2)**

$X \le 400$
$Y \le 500$

The essence or insight into this problem is that there is no labor penalty for making consoles over portables and that the manufacturer makes more profit on manufacturing consoles. Therefore, the problem reduces to making the maximum number of consoles and using the maximum capacity that exists to making consoles. This is the essence of the solution to the problem, succinctly stated. Once we have gained insight into the problem, we can proceed with a solution. *Note:* The essence of the problem is arrived at after the facts are stated and translated into a mathematical model.

STEP 6: The extraneous information is the breakdown of the labor force into percentages for males and females and the number of labor-hours available (30,000). The 30,000 verifies that the 600 set capacity is correct, but it is unnecessary for solving the problem. Also, we must assume that the work and pay for both males and females are equal as no other information was given. We have enough information to solve our problem.

STEP 7: As there is more profit for console sets than for portable sets and there appears to be no penalty, that is, no additional labor-hours to manufacture consoles versus portables, our first priority is to build the maximum number of consoles we can. Therefore, $X = 400$. Plugging this into equation (1), we see that $Y = 200$ because the maximum sets that can be manufactured is 600. Plugging these values for x and y into the profit equation produces

$$(60 \times 400) + (50 \times 200) =$$
$$24,000 + 10,000 = \$34,000$$

If one did not know or had not been able to obtain the essence or insight into the problem, the standard method of solution would be as follows:

$$P = \text{Profit}$$
$$x + y = 600 \tag{1}$$

Solve for y:

$$y = 600 - x \tag{3}$$
$$P = 60x + 50y \tag{2}$$

Substitute for y in P equation:

$$P = 60x + 50(600 - x)$$
$$P = 60x - 50x + 30,000$$
$$P = 10x + 30,000$$

Profit varies linearly with x. Therefore, you maximize profit by maximizing x. The largest x according to our definition is 400.

$$P = 400 \times 10 + 30,000$$
$$= 4,000 + 30,000$$
$$= \$34,000$$

STEP 8: How do we know that \$34,000 is the maximum profit? As this is an open-type problem seeking a maximum or minimum, all other solutions should be wrong. There are a number of ways that we can verify that the manufacturer is making the maximum number of consoles on which he can make a profit. Before we do this, we should try to get an estimate of what the answer should be. In estimating the answer, we might assume that he could make all consoles, which would result in a \$36,000 profit, or all portables, which would result in a \$30,000 profit. The answer lies between these two unallowable extremes.

One way to check the answer is to check other cases to make

sure that they are less. One case would be to have the same number of consoles as portables. For example:

$(300 \times 50) + (300 \times 60) = 33,000$ (The answer is less than \$34,000.)

Another case would be to take the maximum number of portables and the minimum number of consoles. For example:

$(500 \times 50) + (100 \times 60) = 31,000$ (The answer is less than \$34,000.)

You can do this for a number of other cases. Another way to evaluate your answer is to plot the profit equation $P = 10x + 30,000$. Here is a graph of the profit plotted as a function of x, the number of consoles that are produced.

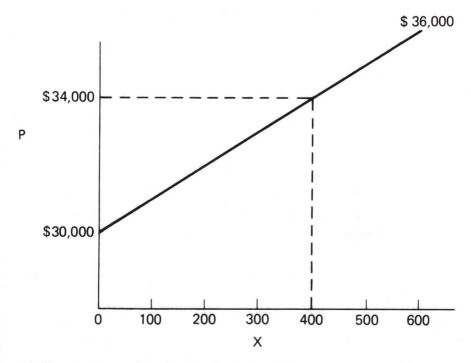

FIGURE 9-3. Graph of Profit Equation $P = 10X + 30,000$

Now impose maximum limit for x, which is 400, and obtain answer. Maximum profit = \$34,000.

VOCABULARY EXPANSION IN MATHEMATICS

A viable technique to help students expand their vocabulary and become more proficient in mathematics is that of learning the meanings of combining forms. In mathematics teachers can help their students see the power of combining forms by showing them how knowledge of a few combining forms can help them unlock the meanings of many words. For example, by knowing a few combining forms, students can define correctly many terms in the metric system, as well as other words. The scenario that follows is instructive.

Scenario:
The teacher, Ms. Johnson, tells her students that they will be studying the metric system. To help them learn many of the terms in the metric system, she will present a lesson on combining forms. Ms. Johnson explains to her students what combining forms are. She then asks them which is more, a centimeter or a millimeter. She tells them that by knowing a few terms they could very easily answer a number of such questions. She presents the following list of combining forms to her students and asks them to memorize the combining forms and their meanings.

deca	ten
deci	tenth
cent, centi	hundred, hundredth
mill, milli	thousand, thousandth
kilo	thousand

Ms. Johnson also tells her students that *centi, milli,* and *deci* are usually used to designate "part of." Ms. Johnson asks the students if they think they have memorized the few combining forms. She gives them a little quiz in which she covers up the meanings and asks the students to write the meaning or meanings for each of the combining forms. She then covers up the combining forms and asks the students to write the combining forms.

Ms. Johnson then presents the combining form *meter,* explaining that the combining form *meter* means "to measure." The term *meter,* however, means a unit of length equal to approximately 39.37 inches in the metric system. Ms. Johnson then presents the following words to her students and asks them to try to write the meaning of each by using their knowledge of combining forms.

decameter	(ten meters)
decimeter	($\frac{1}{10}$ meter)
centimeter	($\frac{1}{100}$ meter)
millimeter	($\frac{1}{1000}$ meter)
kilometer	(1,000 meters)

After going over the meanings with her students, she puts a number of other words on the board and asks her students to try to figure out the meanings of the words by using their knowledge of combining forms.

decade	(ten years)
century	(one hundred years)
centennial	(one-hundredth anniversary; pertaining to a period of one hundred years)
million	(1,000,000)
decimate	(to destroy one tenth of)

Ms. Johnson tells her students that all through the term she will be presenting combining forms to them to help them expand their vocabulary and to help them to read their mathematics book better.

Ms. Johnson was true to her word. Here are examples of some other combining forms and words derived from them that she presented to her students:

poly = many	polygon = many-sided figure
gon = figure having (so many) sides	trigon = three-sided figure
tri = three	tetragon = four-sided figure
tetra = four	pentagon = five-sided figure
penta = five	hexagon = six-sided figure
hexa = six	septagon = seven-sided figure
septa = seven	octagon = eight-sided figure
octa = eight	equivalent = equal
sym = same	symmetrical = same
equi = equal	

SAMPLE READING/MATHEMATICS ACTIVITIES

Mathematical Analogies

Directions: Read each analogy statement carefully to determine whether it is true or false. If the analogy statement is true, write *true*, if the analogy statement is false, write *false*, and then correct the final term in the analogy so that the statement will be true.

1. Decade is to century as century is to <u>year</u>.
2. Centimeter is to millimeter as one is to <u>ten</u>.
3. Centennial is to one as bicentennial is to <u>two</u>.
4. Meter is to kilometer as one is to <u>thousand</u>.
5. Thousand is to hundred as hundred is to <u>ten</u>.
6. Thousand is to million as one is to <u>hundred</u>.
7. Kilogram is to gram as thousand is to <u>one</u>.
8. Milligram is to gram as one is to <u>thousand</u>.

9. Meter is to millimeter as one is to <u>million</u>.
10. Kilometer is to meter as thousand is to <u>one</u>.

Answers: 1. F (millenium) 2. F (one-tenth) 3. T 4. T 5. T 6. F (thousand) 7. T 8. T 9. F (one-thousandth) 10. T

Directions: Find the relationship between a pair of words, and then complete the analogy with a word that would fit.

1. Centimeter is to millimeter as decameter is to ——————.

2. Ten is to decimal as two is to ——————.

3. One is to thousand as meter is to ——————.

4. One is to ten as decade is to ——————.

5. Triangle is to three as hexagon is to ——————.

6. Two is to binary as five is to ——————.

7. Hundred is to C as thousand is to ——————.

8. One is to thousand as thousand is to ——————.

9. Millimeter is to centimeter as centimeter is to ——————.

10. One is to cardinal as first is to ——————.

Answers: 1. meter 2. binary 3. kilometer 4. century 5. six 6. quinary 7. M 8. million 9. decimeter 10. ordinal

Mathematics Categorizing

Directions: Choose the word from each set that does not belong.

1. quart, gallon, inch, bushel
2. centigrade, Fahrenheit, Kelvin, Faraday
3. arc, line, circle, curve
4. bit, byte, word, sentence
5. meter, liter, gram, quart
6. octagon, polygon, triangle, hexagon
7. infinitesimal, minute, mammoth, small
8. round, square, cylindrical, oval

9. mean, medium, average, median
10. binary, quinary, digital, decimal

Answers: 1. inch 2. Faraday 3. line 4. sentence 5. quart 6. polygon 7. mammoth 8. square 9. medium 10. digital

Directions: Put the given words and numerals from the word list into at least ten groups according to a common feature for each group. (Some may fit more than one group.)

Word list

word	kilometer	23
geometry	ounce	tiny
binary	ton	bushel
7	yard	cubic yard
27	1	square foot
mile	byte	11
pound	foot	decimal
36	quinary	cubic foot
18	gram	square rod
algebra	bit	mammoth
huge	trigonometry	
centimeter	45	

Answers: Units: bit, byte, word
Mathematics: geometry, algebra, trigonometry
Number system: binary, quinary, decimal
Metric system: centimeter, kilometer, gram
Prime numbers: 1, 7, 11, 23
Multiples of 9: 18, 27, 36, 45
Volume: cubic yard, cubic foot
Area: square foot, square rod
Length: mile, yard, centimeter, kilometer
Size: huge, tiny, bit, mammoth
Weight: ton, pound, ounce, gram
Measures: (include all from volume, area, and length)

Ideas for Activities

1. Have students read a word problem very carefully. Then have them determine whether enough information has been given to solve the problem. Choose three problems. Delete pertinent information from two of them.

2. Have students read a word problem. Give them five statements on the word problem. Have them determine whether the statements are true or false.

3. Have students brainstorm all the ways that persons use numbers. Set

a time limit; the student who has the greatest number of examples is the winner.

4. Have students skim the newspapers for articles that use some form of mathematics. Discuss these with the class.

5. Have students read the classified section of some newspapers. Have them make a comparison of salaries for similar types of positions. Ask them what variables they have to look at to determine which is the best offer.

6. Have students choose two large food markets. Have them do a comparison of prices for similar food items and similar brands. Have them make a decision as to which market they would choose to shop in.

7. Present certain charts or diagrams to your students. Make up a number of statements about each chart or diagram. Have students state whether the statement is true or false.

COMPUTERS' PLACE IN MATHEMATICS

Computers, together with powerful software, have allowed individuals to manipulate more complex data and from this to obtain new complex results without knowing the intricate details of computer programming. The computer performs the calculations; however, students still need to know how to access the programs and to read and interpret instructions. Also, students must be able to analyze and interpret the results. Part of this entails noticing patterns and inconsistencies.

There are a number of mathematical computer-assisted programs available at all grade levels. These programs, as in other content areas, can be used in a number of different ways based on the teacher's purposes. For example, there are programs that provide drill and practice for students who need help in a specific area. There are other programs that present demonstrations and tutorials. "A program on constructing a robot helps students learn about logic and circuit design as they take notes, test ideas, and learn to program robots. The tutorial would teach about robot anatomy, circuity, logic, and computer chips."[4] Still another use would be simulation. "A simulation on running a business combines knowledge of mathematics and economics. Students learn about market surveys, expert help, bank loans, franchises, and operating decisions."[5] Instructional games are often very enjoyable and effective ways to help students overlearn information and gain important skills.

[4]Carla Mathison and Linda Lungren, "Using Computers Effectively in Content Area Classes," in *Content Area Reading and Learning.* Diane Lapp, James Flood, and Nancy Farman (eds.) (Englewood Cliffs, N.J.: Prentice Hall, 1989), p. 312.
[5]Ibid.

GRAPHIC SUMMARY OF CHAPTER

Here is a graphic summary of Chapter 9. If you have read the chapter, this graphic illustration should help you remember its main points. Under or beside each heading, you might want to jot down some of the information you recall, as well as some of the key concepts in this chapter. This can act as a good review. You can then check your key concepts against those that follow the graphic summary.

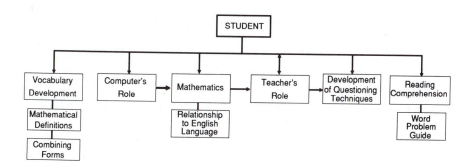

KEY CONCEPTS IN CHAPTER

- Mathematics is the science of numbers.
- In the world of numbers, students must be able to read.
- Mathematics is a language with a specialized vocabulary that is very precise.
- Numerals, as well as letters, are symbolic representations.
- In mathematics, the way terms are presented in relation to other terms influences the meaning of the term.
- The syntax of mathematics is quite rigid.
- Mathematics teachers need to help individuals recognize the need for more precision in the English language.
- Mathematics teachers can help make mathematics more relevant for students by helping them see the relationship between mathematics and language.
- Mathematics requires individuals to work at high levels of comprehension.
- The students must use comprehension skills plus mathematical ability to solve word problems.
- In mathematics, many undefined terms are introduced and explained using examples.

- Word problems in mathematics require individuals to translate the usually imprecise English language to very precise mathematical language.
- Guides for solving word problems help make problem solving easier.
- Combining forms is a viable way to expand an individual's mathematics vocabulary.
- Even with advanced computer technology, students still need to be able to read and interpret results.

SUGGESTIONS FOR THOUGHT QUESTIONS AND ACTIVITIES

1. Prepare a mathematics lesson in a specific area, using a guided reading approach.
2. Construct some questions that would require your students to think beyond the literal comprehension level.
3. Construct some fun mathematics activities.
4. You have been asked to give a talk to your local parent-teacher association concerning the relationship of the English language to mathematics. What will you say?
5. How can you help students to be better problem solvers?
6. What is the place of vocabulary expansion in the mathematics program?
7. Write down all the combining forms that you can think of that will help students expand their mathematics vocabulary.
8. State the characteristics of the kinds of computer software you would like to see made available to mathematics teachers.
9. Review some of the computer software currently on the market for mathematics classes. Note whether they contain the characteristics you stated in number 8.

SELECTED BIBLIOGRAPHY

CURRY, JOAN. "The Role of Reading Instruction in Mathematics." In *Content Area Reading and Learning*. Diane Lapp, James Flood, and Nancy Farnan (eds.) Englewood Cliffs, N.J.: Prentice Hall, 1989, pp. 198–213.
EARLE, R.A. *Teaching Reading and Mathematics*. Newark, Del.: International Reading Association, 1976.
EARP, N.W. "Procedures for Teaching Reading in Mathematics." *Arithmetic Teacher* 17 (November 1970): 575–579.
FREEMAN, GEORGE F. "Reading and Mathematics." *Arithmetic Teacher* 20 (November 1973): 523–529.
LAPOINTE, ARCHIE E., NANCY A. MEAD, and GARY W. PHILLIPS. *A World of Difference:*

An International Assessment of Mathematics and Science. Princeton, N.J.: Educational Testing Service, 1989.

MULLIS, INA V.S., EUGENE H. OWEN, and GARY W. PHILLIPS. *America's Challenge: Accelerating Academic Achievement—A Summary of Findings from 20 Years of NAEP.* Princeton, N.J.: Educational Testing Service, 1990.

O'MARA, DEBORAH A. "The Process of Reading Mathematics," *Journal of Reading* 25 (October 1981): 22–30.

RILEY, JAMES D., and ANDREW PACHTMAN. "Reading Mathematical Word Problems: Telling them What to Do Is Not Telling Them How to Do It." *Journal of Reading* 21 (March 1978): 531–534.

10

Integrating Reading and Writing Across the Curriculum

OVERVIEW

INTRODUCTION

Do any of the following comments sound familiar?

Student Comments:

"In high school I had to write only one theme."
"I find it difficult to write anything."
"I hate to write."

"English is my worst subject."
"Oh, no! We have to really write on the new SATs—on the multiple choice, I had a chance; now I don't."
"I have a lot of difficulty understanding what I read."

Teacher Comments:

"How is it possible for someone to go through school and not be able to write a simple sentence correctly?"
"Students today cannot write."
"Why can't students understand what they are reading?"
"My students think the topic and main idea are similar."
"Teaching English is getting harder and harder."

Reading and writing permeates all the content areas. If students have difficulty in these areas, the problem will manifest itself in all subject matter areas. And, unfortunately, it appears that students do have difficulties in these areas. Industry decries the fact that high school and college graduates lack skills needed in the workplace. In particular, individuals lack problem-solving ability and reading ability that requires higher-order thinking.

The report from *America's Challenge: Accelerating Academic Achievement* shows that "our present education performance is low and not improving."[1] The twenty year summary of findings from the National Assessment of Educational Progress states that "taking the results of both the age- and grade-level (9-, 13-, and 17-year-olds) reading assessments into account, it appears that most students develop the ability to read for surface understanding as they progress through the school years. That is, they can identify specific information and the 'gist' of the material. Yet, when either the material and reading tasks themselves become more challenging, as suggested in our national goal, far fewer students display competency. In particular, they appear to have considerable difficulty analyzing and synthesizing what they have read."[2]

The results of the writing assessment are even more worrisome than that of reading. "Looking across the three grade levels (grades 4, 8, and 12) and the different types of writing tasks given in the assessments, one finds that many students have difficulty communicating effectively in writing. No more than 47 percent of the students at any grade level wrote adequate or better responses to the informative tasks, and no more than 36 percent of the students wrote adequate or better responses to the persuasive tasks. Although performance was somewhat better on the narrative writing tasks, no more than 56 percent of the students wrote adequate or better responses."[3]

---

[1]Ina V.S. Mullis, Eugene H. Owen, and Gary W. Phillips, *America's Challenge: Accelerating Academic Achievement*, National Assessment of Educational Progress (Princeton, N.J.: Educational Testing Service, 1990), p. 3.

[2]Ibid., p. 16.

[3]Ibid., p. 18.

The summary of writing results should not be surprising because if students lack higher-order thinking ability in reading, they would lack this ability in writing also. In addition, in the early 1980s, many decried the fact that writing, which is a fundamental skill that is closely related to reading, is often treated as the stepchild of the English curriculum. At that time it was reported that "for every $3,000 spent on children's ability to receive information, $1.00 was spent on their power to send it in writing,"[4] and "for every two hours spent in teaching reading, only five minutes are spent on teaching writing."[5] There were also reports at that time about how far behind in research writing was in relation to reading. But the most devastating was the report on teachers' preparation in writing. It was reported at that time that elementary teachers had little formal training in writing;[6] it should not be surprising, then, that when students advance to the upper grades, many may lack writing skills.

It is disappointing that after all the clamor for writing across the curriculum and the emphasis on the writing process, the results over the past decade remain the same; that is, "there has been little overall change."[7]

Reading helps reading, and writing helps writing. Everyone agrees. The question is: How do we get students to read and write? Also, how do we help them gain the thinking skills that will help them advance beyond the plateau on which they have remained? One way may be to concentrate more on the integration of reading and writing so that students can gain better insights into both.

The emphasis in the nineties should be on writing as a process that is interrelated with reading and the content areas. ". . . writing is a way to learn history and science, not just a way to report what has been learned."[8] Writing is a valuable mode of learning, and this is aptly shown in the study skills sections (see "Reading and Writing as Modes of Studying" in Chapter 6). In these sections, the emphasis is on using writing to learn; writing about a topic makes us think about it. Content-area teachers are being urged more and more to help their students improve their writing in all subject matter courses, not just in English composition classes. All teachers are called on to give students writing assignments that demand reasoning ability and that require students to relate their new experiences and information to their past experiences and knowledge.

Now that the SATs are incorporating a writing sample in their 1993–94

[4]Donald H. Graves, "A New Look at Writing Research," *Language Arts* 57 (November/December 1980): 914.

[5]Donald H. Graves, "We Won't Let Them Write, *Language Arts* 55 (May 1978): 638.

[6]Sean A. Walmsley, "What Elementary Teachers Know About Writing, *Language Arts* 57 (October 1980): 733.

[7]Arthur N. Applebee, Judith A. Langer, Ina V.S. Mullis, and Lynn B. Jenkins, *The Writing Report Card, 1984–88*, The National Assessment of Educational Progress (Princeton, N.J.: Educational Testing Service, 1990), p. 6.

[8]Arthur N. Applegate, *Writing in the Secondary Schools: English and the Content Area* (Urbana, Ill.: National Council of Teachers of English, 1981): p. xii.

edition "to recognize the importance of writing skills in college,"[9] there will probably be a more concentrated focus on helping students acquire the writing skills they need.

This chapter will present some strategies to help English and other content-area teachers incorporate a reading-writing approach to teaching in their classrooms. It should help raise content-area teachers' consciousness levels to the importance of reading and writing in all content areas. areas.

KEY QUESTIONS

After you finish reading this chapter, you should be able to answer the following questions:

1. What are the findings on students' achievement in reading and writing?
2. How are reading and writing interrelated?
3. What does an integrated reading-writing approach stress?
4. What is the relationship of the topic of a paragraph to the main idea of a paragraph?
5. Why should writers be concerned with the main idea of paragraphs?
6. What is the relationship of the topic sentence to the main idea of a paragraph?
7. What is the function of the main idea in a paragraph?
8. How can teachers help students to be better analyzers of what they read?
9. What are the functions of linking words in a paragraph?
10. How can the supporting details of a paragraph be organized?
11. What type of activities will help show students how closely interrelated reading and writing are?
12. What are some computer programs that can help students read and write better?
13. What are some cautions about students' use of computers in writing?

KEY TERMS IN CHAPTER

You should pay special attention to the following key terms:

> integrated reading-writing approach   story grammar

[9]John Fremer, Senior Development Leader, Educational Testing Service, January, 1991.

THE INTERRELATEDNESS OF READING AND WRITING

This is a book on reading instruction, so readers of this text may wonder about the author's concern over the state of writing in the schools. First, it is important to state that concern over the status of writing in the schools is justified here because of the interrelatedness of the two. Without writing, there would be no reading. Writing reinforces word recognition and discourse structure and increases familiarity with words. Through writing students are able to gain a better understanding of the author's task in getting his or her ideas across. Writing can make students keener analyzers of reading; writing is a thinking process. As writers, we are also readers looking over our own shoulder and trying to determine whether what we have written makes sense and whether it accurately expresses what we wanted to convey. Writing forces us to pay attention to the logical arrangement of our words into sentences and to the arrangement of our sentences into a paragraph. As readers, we use the sequence and organization of ideas to help us comprehend the writer's message as well as to help us remember it. If we read widely, we will have a broad range of topics from which to draw for our own writing. Also, through reading we will come to recognize what skills are necessary to be a good writer. Reading helps us acquire knowledge and often furnishes the stimulus for creative writing. Reading helps us to develop vocabulary and a language sense and helps us to become familiar with a variety of sentence structures used in both speaking and writing. Reading good literature exposes us to the beauty of language written in such a way that it seems to capture a sentiment or thought perfectly.

Both reading and writing need time; that is, students must be given the opportunity and time to spend in reading and writing. Students also need instruction in both as well as a knowledge of results. It seems that one effective way to make the best use of time would be to integrate the teaching of reading and writing in content-area courses. The integration of reading and writing does not mean that the two would always be taught together; it does mean that, whenever feasible, the two would be taught together.

Special Note:
Even though "research on reading-writing relationships has made enormous strides both topically and methodologically, . . . the research on reading-writing relationships should be viewed as still in its infancy."[10]

Scenario: A Ninth-Grade English Class
Mrs. Percy has been teaching English for twenty-five years, and for most of that time, she has been using her version of a holistic approach; she tries to

[10]Robert J. Tierney and Timothy Shanahan, "Research on the Reading-Writing Relationship: Interactions, Transactions, and Outcomes," in *Handbook of Reading Research*, Vol. II. Rebecca Barr, Michael L. Kamil, Peter Mosenthal, and P. David Pearson, eds. (New York: Longman, 1991), p. 274.

FIGURE 10-1. Yes, good writing is hard work. However, it is easier if you are well read.

integrate all the language arts and uses whole pieces of good literature whenever she can. And, most importantly, she has her students do lots and lots of reading and writing. She uses reading as a springboard for writing and students' writing as a vehicle for reading.

Mrs. Percy always begins the school year by presenting an account of a well-known writer's process of writing so that students can better visualize the reading-writing connection. Then, throughout the semester, she engages her students in various activities that reinforce this connection.

Mrs. Percy tells her students that before they begin reading a number of works by a certain author, she would like to imaginatively put them into that author's skin to see what the author does while in the process of writing. She then proceeds to tell her students about a particular author's method of writing. Here is an example of what she tells her students:

> Catherine is a well-known and celebrated writer, who is envied, as well as admired by many because she is so prolific and appears to write with great ease. It's as if words are magically formed in her mind, and she has merely to record them.
>
> Catherine, however, knows differently. She knows how much work and effort she puts into each of her books. Before she writes anything, she spends a great amount of time thinking, even if she already has the central theme in her mind's eye. The book she's working on now is set in the South. To write this book, she'll have to do a great amount of research. Even though Catherine writes fiction, and this book is a mystery, most of her work has been acclaimed because she uses authentic settings and relies heavily on historical facts. In other words, Catherine does her homework before beginning to write. She reads all about the time period she is writing about as well as about the place and the types of characters who inhabited the various place or places. After researching their way of life, customs, habits, and so on, Catherine sits down to write.
>
> Catherine, however, does not just sit and write, write, write. Contrary to what many people believe, Catherine writes, reads what she has written, re-

vises, rereads, revises again, rereads, stops to think about various points, re-reads, and then goes on. This pattern of writing, reading, revising, rereading, and so on continues throughout the writing.

Catherine knows that writing is hard work, and good writing is even harder work!

After the story, Mrs. Percy tells her students that she wants them to keep a log of what they do from the moment they start thinking about what they are going to write until they have completed their project. She feels that this will give them the best insight possible into the reading-writing connection.

TECHNIQUES TO INTEGRATE READING AND WRITING

An integrated reading-writing approach stresses the teaching of the two together in such a way that each acts as a stimulus and aid for the other. By combining the instruction of reading and writing, students can become more sensitive to the kinds of strategies writers use to convey their ideas and readers use to receive the ideas. Writing, as well as reading, will be seen as a problem-solving process that requires specific skills and reasoning ability. In this chapter we will see how we can combine reading and writing

FIGURE 10-2. These students are working together on a report.

FIGURE 10-3. These students are in the library gathering information for their report.

so that they enhance one another. For each presented topic, background information will first be given, and then suggestions and activities will be presented integrating reading and writing. The emphasis in this chapter will be on the paragraph and on main ideas, because students in all content areas must be able to determine the main idea of what they are reading.

Even though the material in the following sections is more suited for an English classroom, all content-area teachers, not just English teachers, can adapt the techniques presented in this chapter to suit their students' needs and their specific subject matter. At the beginning of the term, content-area teachers could apprise their students of the kinds of reading and writing assignments they will have, and, at that time, they could discuss with their students the interrelatedness of reading and writing, as well as present some of the strategies and techniques their students will need to accomplish their assignments. (See sections on summarizing and notetaking in Chapter 6, as well as "The Integration of Study Skills in Content-Area Classes" in Chapter 5.)

The Main Idea of a Paragraph

Throughout this book, the emphasis is on helping students gain higher-order thinking skills so that they can be independent thinkers. Studies show that students can work at literal levels, but many have difficulty working at interpretive, critical, and creative levels. As we have stated a number of times already, if we want to maintain a democracy that is free, we need autonomous thinkers; we need a knowledgeable populace that can think for itself.

Finding the main idea is necessary in order to get the essence of what we are reading. And we need individuals to be able to do this for themselves; individuals who depend on others to interpret information for them because they do not understand it have forfeited their independence. This endangers a democracy.

In Chapter 3, we discussed a technique for finding the main idea of paragraphs and group of paragraphs. In that procedure, we said that a paragraph is always written about someone or something. The someone or something is the *topic* of the paragraph. We also said that the writer is interested in telling his or her readers something about the topic of the paragraph. To find the main idea of a paragraph, we must determine what the topic of the paragraph is and what the author is trying to say about the topic that is special or unique. Once we have found these two things, we should have the main idea. As discussed in Chapter 3, finding the main idea is not easy, but it is essential to gaining an understanding of what has been read and to retaining information. Many people have difficulty in finding the main idea of a paragraph because they confuse the main idea with the topic of the paragraph. Some students are under the impression that the topic sentence and the main idea are always the same. If teachers were to integrate the writing of paragraphs with finding the main idea of paragraphs, these faulty concepts might be dispelled. Also, the exposure to many different types of paragraphs would help students to see that the topic sentence is not always the first sentence in a paragraph and that it is possible for any sentence in the paragraph to be the topic sentence. They would learn, too, that the topic sentence usually anticipates both the main idea and its development, that some paragraphs may not have a topic sentence, that a topic sentence may or may not contain the main idea, and that, even though a topic sentence exists and is explicitly stated (fully and clearly) in the paragraph, the main idea may not be explicitly stated. Students would also learn that the topic sentence is that sentence that names the topic of the paragraph and that every paragraph must have one main idea.

Activities—Reading and Writing

1. Give the students many opportunities to find the main idea of paragraphs, and help them to analyze what they did. (The paragraphs chosen would depend on the content area, and they should be related to material that students are studying at the time.)

Sample Activity
Directions: Read the following paragraph. After you read the paragraph, choose the word or words that *best* answer the two questions that follow the paragraph.

In high school and in college, John's one goal was athletic success so that he could be in the Olympics. John's goal to be in the Olympics became such an obsession for him that he could not do anything that did not directly or indirectly relate to achieving this goal. He practiced for hours every day. He exercised, ate well, and had at least eight hours of sleep every night. Throughout school, John allowed nothing and no one to deter him from his goal.

a. What is the topic of the paragraph?
   1. exercise and practice
   2. work
   3. Olympics
   4. John's goal
   5. athletic success
   6. attempts

Answer: 4

b. What is the author saying about John's goal to be in the Olympics (the topic) that is special and that helps tie the details together?
   1. That it needed time.
   2. That it was a good one.
   3. That it required that John exercise a great deal.
   4. That it was not a reasonable one.
   5. That it was the most important thing in John's life.
   6. That it required good health.
   7. That it was too much for John.

Answer: 5

If you put the two answers together, you have the main idea of the paragraph. Main idea: The goal, being in the Olympics, was the most important thing in John's life.

Discussion

This type of activity will help students recognize that the topic of a paragraph and its main idea are not the same.

2. Have the students find the main idea of different paragraphs. (Again, the various paragraphs should be related to what students are studying at the time.)

Sample Activities

Directions: Find the main idea of each of the following paragraphs.

What makes an airplane fly is not its engine nor its propeller. Nor is it, as many people think, some mysterious knack of the pilot, nor some ingenious gadget inside. What makes an airplane fly is simply its shape. This may sound absurd, but gliders do fly without engines, and model airplanes do fly without pilots. As for the insides of an airplane, they are disappointing, for they are mostly hollow. No, what keeps an airplane up is its shape—the impact of the air on its shape. Whittle that shape out of wood, or cast it out of iron, or fashion it, for that matter, out of chocolate and throw the thing into the air. It will behave like an airplane. It will *be* an airplane.[11]

Main Idea: *What makes an airplane fly is its shape.*

It was nine o'clock the next morning and I was sitting in English class. In other words, my body was sitting there but my mind was far away. Mr. Finley, the teacher, was discussing *To Kill a Mockingbord* and the whole thing was so boring that I had stopped listening. No matter what book we read in English, it is always a story about youth going through experience and improving itself. Southern youth. Northern youth. European youth. To judge from these books you would think that youth did nothing but go through experience and come out great at the end. If Mr. Finley ever gave us a book in which youth went to pieces at the end, I would be more interested.[12]

Main Idea: *A student is sick of books about the improving effect of experience on youth.*

In many parts of Africa, the use of traps, poisons, and dogs has virtually exterminated the leopard. In my youth, we thought that the only good leopard was a hide stretched out for drying. But now we are discovering that the leopard played an important part in maintaining nature's balance. Leopards used to kill thousands of baboons every year, and now that the leopards have been largely wiped out baboons are proving to be a major control problem in many parts of the colony. The perfect way to keep them in check is by allowing their natural enemy, the leopard, to destroy them. So leopards are now widely protected and allowed to increase in numbers. Such is the strange way that man works—first he virtually destroys a species and then does everything in his power to restore it.[13]

---

[11]Wolfgang Langewiesche, "Why an Airplane Flys. (Source unknown.)
[12]Barbara Wersba, *The Dream Watcher* (New York: Atheneum, 1969).
[13]From J. A. Hunter, *African Hunter* (New York: Harper & Brothers, 1952).

Main Idea: _Leopards are now widely protected because they play an important part in maintaining nature's balance._

Discussion
Have the students review the procedure for finding the main idea.

3. Give students opportunities to explain why they gave a particular answer as the main idea.

Sample Activity
Directions: Read the following paragraph, which is an excerpt from *One Day in the Life of Ivan Denisovich* by Alexander Solzhenitsyn (New York: Bantam Books, 1963). Choose the statement after the excerpt that *best* states the main idea. Explain why you chose the statement you did and explain why you did not choose each of the other statements.

> The escort chief went out shouting at them for a while but he saw it was no use—they wouldn't go any faster. But he couldn't tell the guards to shoot at them for this—the prisoners were sticking to the law and marching in their columns by lines of five. The escort chief didn't have the right to make them go any faster. (In the mornings that's what saved their lives. They went out to the job real slow. Anybody who went fast didn't stand a chance to live out his time in the camp. That way you got too hot before you even started on the job and you wouldn't last too long.)

1. The escort chief couldn't tell the guards to shoot at the prisoners for going too slowly.
2. The escort chief didn't have the right to make the prisoners go any faster.
3. Prisoners in all prisons must move slowly in order to survive.
4. The prisoners moved slowly in the morning in order to survive.
5. The prisoners, who moved slowly in the morning, were within their rights to do so.

Answer: _Statement 4 is the main idea. All of the sentences in the paragraph help develop statement 4. The answers in statements 1, 2, and_

.5 are too specific. Each statement is a fact found in the paragraph, but each is too narrow to be the main idea of the paragraph. Statement 3 is a generalization not found in the paragraph.

Discussion
Have the students review the procedure for finding the main idea. Have them recognize that, to find the main idea, they first had to find the topic of the paragraph and then what was special about the topic.

4. Have the students state the topics of a number of paragraphs, and then compare them to the main idea of each paragraph.

Sample Activities
Directions: Find the topic of each of the presented paragraphs in item 2.

Answers: Paragraph 1—What makes an airplane fly
Paragraph 2—A student's taste in books
Paragraph 3—The protection of leopards

Discussion
Again stress to the students that the topic and the main idea are not similar. The main idea of a paragraph is more fully stated than the topic. Review with students the technique for finding the main idea.

5. Have the students read paragraphs that have sentences in them that do not help to develop the main idea of the paragraph. Have students pick out those sentences that do not belong.

Sample Activity
Directions: Find the sentence in the following paragraph that does not belong.

John knew that he needed help. His parents always said that he would out-grow his baby fat. Well, it may have happened to his older brothers, but it hadn't happened to him. Instead of outgrowing his baby fat, he was getting fatter each day. He wanted to try out for the basketball team, but what chance did he have? He knew that he wasn't doing something right. As a result, John asked his parents to take him to a doctor for help.

Answer: He wanted to try out for the basketball team, but what chance did he have?

Discussion
Have the students recognize that all the sentences in a paragraph should develop the main idea of the paragraph. Have the students find the main idea of this paragraph (John needs help to lose weight), and then have them go over every sentence in the paragraph to see if it helps to develop the main idea.

6. Have students write paragraphs related to relevant content-area material. Have students state the main idea of their paragraphs.

Sample Activity
Have students read their textbook assignment in a particular area and write a paragraph on what they think the author's most important point is. Have students analyze their own paragraph to make sure that it says what they want it to, that it has only one idea, and that all the sentences of the paragraph develop the main idea. Have students write their main idea.

Discussion
This type of activity helps integrate the reading-writing connection. It helps students gain an insight into main idea and also to gain a better understanding of both the role of the reader and the writer. It helps students recognize that every paragraph should have one main idea only and that every sentence should help develop the main idea.

The Topic Sentence of a Paragraph

The topic sentence is often the first sentence in a paragraph, but, as has already been stated, it does not have to be. The topic sentence tells what the paragraph will be about by naming the topic. It also usually gives clues to the development of the main idea of the paragraph. From the topic sentence you can anticipate certain events. You can determine that the subsequent sentences will supply supporting details, such as examples, comparison/contrasts, sequence of events, cause-and-effect situations, and so on, to support the main idea.

The main idea can be developed in many different ways. Whichever technique is used to develop the main idea, it must be presented in such a way that it supports and adds understanding to the main idea.

Activities—Reading and Writing

1. Have the students reread the first paragraph under "The Topic Sentence of a Paragraph" and state the main idea of it.

Answer: The topic sentence helps you to anticipate events.

2. Have the students read topic sentences, and have them state what they expect to follow in the paragraph.

Sample Activities
Directions: Read the following topic sentences, and state what you expect to follow in the paragraph

a. The earthquake had terrible effects on all who were in it.

   Sample Answer: *Examples of the terrible effects are expected.*

b. Life in a spaceship makes unusual demands on a person.

   Sample Answer: *A description and examples are expected of the unusual demands of life in a spaceship or an explanation of why this is so.*

c. Fame can bring joys, but it can also bring problems.

   Sample Answer: *An explanatory contrast between the joys and problems of fame is expected.*

d. Scientists must be especially careful in experiments dealing with humans.

   Sample Answer: *Reasons for the need to be especially careful is expected.*

Discussion
Help students to recognize that answers may vary, but all the answers must logically follow from the topic sentence.

3. Have students write topic sentences and state what they expect to follow in the paragraph.

Sample Activities
Directions: Write a topic sentence for the following topics.

a. George Washington's Foreign Policy _____

b. The Boston Tea Party _____

c. The Scientific Method _____

Directions: State what you expect to follow from each of your topic sentences.

a. _____

_____

b. _____

_____

c. _____

_____

Discussion
Again, have students recognize that answers may vary for what will follow from the topic sentences that they have generated, but what follows should be logically related to the topic sentence.

4. Have students read paragraphs and state their topic sentences.

Sample Activities
Directions: Here are two paragraphs from literary works. Read each and state the topic sentence for each of the paragraphs. Remember that the topic sentence helps you to anticipate events and that all the sentences in the paragraph should be related to the topic sentence.

a. Topic Sentence: _____

_____

Some students have such hostility and anger for any authority that they refuse to do anything that they are told to do. They stubbornly resist any direction—especially if it pleases someone in authority. They violate rules and try to beat the system. Their most important need is to prove that an authority (parent, teacher, policeman) is wrong. Success in any other endeavor is secondary to this need.[14]

b. Topic Sentence: _____

_____

With the first noisy gathering of the mountain jays for their flight south, the people began to scatter from the great council at Bear Butte. The Oglalas and Brules of the upper Platte country started first, moving off westward around the Black Hills, to separate later at some fork in the travois trail or to make their winter camps together. Then the Two Kettles and the No Bows left, and the Blackfoot and the Hunkpapas, until only the pole of the great council lodge stood on the sacred place, to fall under some faroff winter storm, back to the earth from which they grew.[15]

Discussion
Help students to recognize that the topic sentences of the paragraphs should state the topic, and all the sentences in the paragraph should be related to the topic sentence. Review also with the students that a good topic sentence either contains, or helps the reader to anticipate, the main idea of the paragraph.

5. Have students state what they expect to follow from some topic sentences and then write the second sentence for each of the topic sentences.

Sample Activity
Directions: Read the following topic sentence, and state what you expect to follow from it. Then write the second sentence for the topic sentence.

If you are tall, well coordinated, and like to play basketball, you have a chance at a career in this sport.

---

[14]From Gary Phillips, "The Turned Off," *Today's Education*, 63:3 (October 1974).
[15]From Mari Sandoz, *Crazy Horse* (Lincoln: University of Nebraska Press, 1961).

Answers:

1. You expect examples to follow of persons who are tall, are well coordinated, and like to play basketball, and who have been successful in basketball.
2. For example, look at Michael Jordan, Patrick Ewing, and Earvin (Magic) Johnson.

Discussion

Again, have students recognize that their second sentences will vary; however, each of the second sentences should be related to the topic sentence, and each should logically follow what went before.

Using Linking Words in Writing Paragraphs

One way to give a paragraph "flow" and order is to use linking words and phrases such as *nevertheless, for example,* and *first.* However, these linking words, which give rhythm and sense to the sentence and the paragraph, do not have to begin every sentence.

Some often-used linking words and phrases are *first, before, then, next, after, now, hence, so, on the other hand, also, finally, perhaps, besides, moreover, however, therefore, nevertheless, for example, for the reason, unfortunately, fortunately, thus, as a result, in addition, in the meantime,* and *furthermore.*

The sample paragraph that follows contains some linking words.

The day my dad came home and announced that he was being transferred was the turning point in my life. You can imagine how I felt. We had lived in the same town, on the same street, and in the same house all my life. As a result, everything was familiar to me. I knew every tree, every crack in the sidewalk, every bump in the road, and everything there was to know in a small town. Also, all my friends lived close by, and we all rode our bikes to school every morning. I liked it here, and I didn't want to move. It wasn't fair that my dad should be transferred. Why couldn't they transfer someone else's dad?

Activities—Reading and Writing

1. Give the students a paragraph that has its sentences out of order. Have them organize the sentences into a logical paragraph.

Sample Activity

Directions: Here are a number of sentences. Arrange them into a paragraph.

1. Now, he could no longer put off his decision.
2. However, he didn't feel like an adult.

3. Everyone said that he was an adult, and as an adult he would have to decide on his life's work.
4. He felt confused and angry at the pressures being placed on him.
5. He had reached a stage in life when he would have to make decisions.
6. Perhaps he could wait until after the summer.
7. In the past, he had put off making any decisions concerning his future.

Answer: Organized in the following manner, the sentences make a logical paragraph: 5, 7, 1, 3, 2, 4, 6.

Discussion
Point out to the students that a paragraph may be ordered in a number of different ways and that the kind of details that are used will depend on the type of paragraph that is being written. Regardless of the ways in which a paragraph may be ordered, all paragraphs should be logically written.

2. Give the students an incomplete topic sentence and a list of linking words. Have them use these to write a paragraph.

Sample Activity
Directions: Use the given incomplete topic sentence and the linking words or phrases to write a paragraph.

Linking Words and Phrases

first	also	therefore
then	finally	nevertheless
next	after	for example
perhaps	then	for the reason
hence	inside	thus
so	moreover	as a result
on the other hand	however	yet

Incomplete Topic Sentence: The funniest thing that happened to me was

_____

_____

_____

_____

_____

Discussion
Have students go over their own paragraphs as readers. Have them analyze their paragraphs to see if they express one main idea and if all the sentences in the paragraph help to develop the main idea.

Supporting Details of a Paragraph

As already stated in Chapter 3, the supporting details of a paragraph are especially useful because readers use the organization of the paragraph to help them to retain information. Also, teachers often use the structure of the reading material to determine the strategies they will suggest to their students.

Review with your students these points: (1) the supporting details of a paragraph can be presented as examples, comparison/contrasts, sequence of events, and cause-and-effect situations; and (2) each paragraph should consist of one main idea and all the sentences of the paragraph should develop the main idea. Help your students to gain a better understanding of these concepts by presenting the following information and examples.

Details support, explain, or illustrate the main idea of a paragraph. They are facts that are essential to the main idea, and they furnish information about, and give meaning to, the main idea.

Important or supporting details may be arranged in a number of different ways, depending on the writer's purposes. Usually, a writer uses a combination of methods in presenting the supporting details. Here are examples of some ways in which details may be arranged.

Sequence of Events *Sequence of events* is used if the writer wishes to give you an arrangement of something in some kind of order. It can be time order, stages, steps, and such. You will usually find sequences of stages and steps in science books. For example:

> The scientific method is a technique that scientists use in research experiments. It consists of a number of steps. A scientist usually must first survey the literature relating to the problem. He or she then identifies and defines the problem. After this, the scientist comes up with a problem hypothesis, which is a possible solution to the problem. From the hypothesis, the scientist deduces certain consequences. He or she then constructs an experimental plan, conducts the experiment, and determines whether the results are significant or not.

Examples Supporting details may be arranged according to *examples*. The writer states an idea and then illustrates and supports it with examples. This technique is used the most often by writers because it is one of the simplest to carry out, and it is very effective. When a writer uses this technique, he or she usually gives you some clue in the topic sentence so that you expect examples to follow. For example, the writer might begin a paragraph with some of the following topic sentences:

1. Several stories have been told about Custer's last stand.
2. In a man's lifetime, he sees a number of different types of organisms.
3. The wives and families of prisoners of war suffered much anguish.
4. The editorial staff have established certain standards for papers being submitted to the school magazine.
5. There are a number of uses for a paper milk carton.
6. People in the United States who do not speak English have a number of problems.

In sentence 1, you expect examples of some stories. In sentence 2, you expect a list of the various organisms a man sees in a lifetime. In sentence 3, you expect examples of the anguish that wives and families of prisoners of war went through. In sentence 4, you expect a list of the standards. In sentence 5, you expect examples of uses for paper milk cartons. In sentence 6, you expect examples of the problems persons who do not speak English face in the United States.

In each of the presented sentences, the words *a number of, several, many, certain,* and *much* signal that examples will follow. However, not all topic sentences contain such obvious signals as *a number of, much,* and so on. For example, read the following group of sentences:

1. The fly is useful to scientists for research purposes.
2. A large tire tube can be lots of fun.
3. The members of a recently discovered primitive tribe appear to be healthier than modern man.

In sentence 1, you expect examples of how the fly is useful for research purposes. In sentence 2, you expect a list of ways in which a large tire tube can be fun. In sentence 3, you expect a list of ways in which the members of the primitive tribe are healthier than modern man. Here is a paragraph illustrating supporting details arranged according to examples:

> If you are the oldest child in the family, you are expected to be all things to all people. Your brothers and sisters look up to you, and your parents expect you to be special. As a matter of fact, they will point to you as an example for the other children. (It's pretty difficult trying to have fun if someone is always looking over your shoulder.) If that isn't bad enough, you also have the most responsibilities. Believe me, being the oldest child in the family is not what it's cracked up to be.

Comparison/Contrast *Comparison/contrast* is used when the author wants to show the similarities or differences in happenings, things, ideas, or situations. The writer may show both similarities and differences rather than one or the other. In explaining complex problems, an author especially may use comparison/contrast, as well as other methods of arranging details.

Today there are a number of social scientists and psychologists who are raising chimpanzees in their homes with their own children. In one case, a psychologist compared the development of the chimpanzee with her own child. She found that at six months the chimpanzee was brighter than the human child of the same age. The chimpanzee seemed more alert and aware of her surroundings than the human child. Even at the age of two the difference between the chimpanzee and the human child was not very great. Although the chimpanzee could not speak and the human child could, she had learned gestures which she used to communicate with others around her.

The writer uses similarities and differences in presenting the supporting details. The similarities are the age of the child and the chimpanzee, the environment in which the chimpanzee and child live, and what is being tested. The differences are the two records of development.

Special Note:
Comparison is usually used to show the similarities of one person, idea, thing, and so on to another. Contrast is usually used to show the differences.

Cause and Effect   A much used method of arranging supporting details is that of *cause and effect*. In this arrangement the author can state the cause and then provide the results or effects. Conversely, the author can state the effect or result and then give the causes or reasons leading up to it.

Homes that are improperly insulated may cause problems for their inhabitants. First of all, it will cost more to heat such a house than one that is well insulated. Second, it will waste energy. Third, it will make the house uncomfortable to live in because drafts or cold air is able to penetrate the poorly insulated walls. Also, the poorly insulated walls could cause the inhabitants to have more colds, a health problem that results in higher expenses for doctors and medicine.

The main idea of the paragraph is that an improperly insulated house may cause problems. The writer arranged the supporting details according to cause and effect. The "cause" is an improperly heated house. The "effects" are the problems such as higher cost of heating, waste of energy, and so on.

Activities—Reading and Writing

1.   Have the students read a number of paragraphs and then try to determine the main idea of each as well as how the writer has arranged the supporting details of each.

Sample Activity
Directions: Here are a number of paragraphs. For each paragraph, state the main idea, and then state how the writer has arranged the supporting details of each paragraph.

a. De Hostos was born in Mayagüez, Puerto Rico, in 1839. Educated on the island and in Spain, he struggled for the autonomy of Cuba and Puerto Rico, and for an end to slavery, in the early 1860s. Later he became convinced that self-determination for Puerto Rico and Cuba was not possible unless the islands were independent, and he left the island to join with more revolutionary elements. In New York he edited the official newspaper of the Cuban revolutionaries, *La Revolution*. When Cuba's ten-year war for independence ended in apparent failure, de Hostos moved to Chile, where he became active in the cause of women's rights.[16]

Answers: The main idea of the paragraph is that the major events in the life of de Hostos are presented. The writer uses sequence to present the supporting details.

b. You could determine pretty accurately the personalities of Maria and Rosa from their manner of walking. When Maria walks, it seems as though the whole building vibrates. Each step she takes is heavy-footed and determined. You know when Maria is around. Rosa, on the other hand, has a light-footed walk that you can hardly hear. You never know she's around until she suddenly appears. Rosa's presence is hardly ever felt and at times you don't even realize that she's there.

Answers: The main idea of the paragraph is that the personalities of Maria and Rosa could be determined pretty accurately from their manner of walking. Here both comparison and contrast are used. Maria's and Rosa's personalities are being compared to their manner of walking. Each girl's personality is similar to her individual walk. The writer also uses contrast to show differences between Rosa and Maria.

c. A boy wants something very special from his father. You hear it said that fathers want their sons to be what they feel they cannot themselves be, but I tell you it also works the other way. I know that as a small boy I wanted my father to be a certain thing he was not. I wanted him to be a proud, silent, dignified father. When I was with other boys and he passed along the street, I wanted to feel a glow of pride: "There he is. That is my father."[17]

Answers: The main idea of the paragraph is that as a boy the author wanted to be proud of his father. The writer uses a combination of methods to present the supporting details. The methods used are comparison/contrast and examples.

Discussion
Help the students to recognize that the supporting details help to develop the main idea and that most writers usually use a number of methods to

16From Byron Williams, *Puerto Rico: Commonwealth, State, or Nation?* (New York: Parent's Magazine Press, 1972).
17From *Sherwood Anderson's Memoirs: A Critical Edition*, ed. Ray Lewis White (Chapel Hill: University of North Carolina Press, 1939).

present their supporting details rather than just one. The examples that were given that used only one method were chosen to emphasize that method.

2. Have students write paragraphs using given supporting details and topics.

Sample Activity
Directions: Here are a topic and some supporting details about the topic. Write a paragraph on this topic, using the given supporting details.

TOPIC: The Uses of Propaganda in Television Commercials.
INFORMATION: Propaganda techniques are used to get persons to buy things.

> There are a number of propaganda techniques.
> The most often used propaganda technique is that of bandwagon.
> People don't like to feel that they are left out.
> Television commercials try to make people feel left out if they don't buy a specific product.

Discussion
Help students to recognize that paragraphs will vary according to the approach that writers take even though the topic sentence and supporting details are similar.

3. Have students write various paragraphs in which the details are arranged in different ways.

Sample Activity
Directions: Write a short paragraph in which the details are arranged in some kind of sequence. A sample paragraph is provided.

> After thirteen years, I at last finished a novel. The first seven years were spent in a kind of apprenticeship—the book that came out of that time was abandoned without much regret. A second one was finished in six weeks and buried. It took six years to write the third novel, and this one was finally published.[18]

Discussion
Again discuss with students how paragraphs will vary. Have students analyze their paragraphs to see if all their sentences develop the main idea. Have the students state the main idea of their paragraphs.

[18]From Cynthia Ozick, "We Are the Crazy Lady," Ms. Magazine (Spring 1973).

The Concluding Sentence of a Paragraph

Help students to recognize that a good paragraph does not end with some minor point or detail. It generally ends with some strong point, a conclusive statement, a restatement, or a question relating to what has gone before. Also, such terms as *in conclusion, in ending, to sum up, in summary,* and so on should generally be avoided. Have the students read a number of paragraphs from literature to see how the authors ended their paragraphs. Here are two examples from *The Adventures of Tom Sawyer* by Mark Twain.

> 1. Tom Sawyer had found a new and weighty problem that was disturbing his mind. Becky Thatcher had stopped coming to school. He had struggled with his pride for a few days and tried to whistle her out of his thoughts, but he failed. He began to notice that he was hanging around her father's house at night and feeling miserable. Becky was ill. What if she should die!
> 2. That thought kept haunting him. He no longer took an interest in war, not even in piracy. The chart of life was gone; there was nothing left but dreariness. He put his hoop away, and his bat; there was no joy left in them anymore.

Sample Activity

Directions: Here is a paragraph that is missing a concluding sentence. Write a concluding sentence for the paragraph.

> Whenever my friend, her brother, and I would have to walk past a certain house in our neighborhood, we would cross the street and walk on the other side. The house, which has two monstrous lion statues in front of it, has been boarded up for as long as we can remember. Adults avoid talking about the "house," but when they do, they do so in hushed tones.

_____

_____

_____

_____

Discussion

Help students to recognize that their concluding sentences will vary; however, each of the sentences should be one that is related to the topic sentence and that helps to develop the main idea of the paragraph.

OTHER WAYS TO INTEGRATE READING AND WRITING

The activities that have been presented in this chapter to integrate the reading and writing of paragraphs can be carried over to the writing of whole compositions and can be expanded to include critical and creative reading skills. Following are a few suggested activities to integrate reading and writing in the critical and creative reading areas.

1. Have students read a number of statements in which the author is trying to sway readers. Have students analyze the statements. Then have them write statements concerning a topic that causes persons to feel negatively. After that, have them write some statements that cause persons to feel positively about a topic.

   Help students to recognize that the way the writer presents information can sway readers unless they are alert. For example, you could have them read a number of newspaper headlines on the same story and have them determine the position of the writer. For example:

   Country X Changes Its Regime

   An Iron Hand Takes Over Country X

   Country X Is in the Grips of Disaster

   Country X Witnesses a Smooth Takeover

2. Present political cartoons without captions to students, and have them write one-sentence captions for the cartoons.

3. Have students read a number of commercials or speeches that use propaganda techniques. Analyze the commercials and speeches with the students. Then have them write a speech and a number of commercials using different propaganda techniques.

4. In English literature or composition classes, have students read some story, and then have them change the ending of the story.

5. In English literature or composition classes have some students read a story, and then have them write another adventure for the main character in the story.

6. In a content-area course such as history, have students read on a topic of special interest to them, and then have them write an article evaluating what they have read about the topic.

7. After studying a topic, have students write what they feel are the most important points they learned about the topic and then have them evaluate its significance to society today.

Here are some other activities that require students to read and write more than a paragraph.

1. Have students read various autobiographies and then have them write their own autobiography.

2. Have students read some biographies and then have them choose another person in their class and write that person's biography. (Discuss with students the kinds of background information they will need.)

3. Have students read two different biographers' versions of a well-known person. Have them write an analysis of the two versions. Dis-

cuss with them how they would go about determining which version is authentic.

4. Have students choose a character from one of Shakespeare's plays that has been discussed in class. Have them write a critical analysis of the character.

5. Encourage students to choose an area of public concern about which they would like to learn more. Have them do investigative reporting in this area and then write the report for the school paper.

6. Your class has been reading many plays. Have your students imagine they are television producers. Ask them to determine which play that they have read would be suited for television. Have them write their rationale.

COMPUTER PROGRAMS THAT EMPHASIZE THE READING-WRITING CONNECTION

Knowledge of text structure or story grammar, which in narrative includes "the setting of a story (including characters, location, and time), the basic theme, key episodes of plot, and a resolution of the problem that motivated the characters to action,"[19] often helps students better understand what they are reading. It can also help students write better.

There are a number of computer programs that help students learn about text structure. One type of program models for students a particular text structure or pattern, which students read, and then students "plan and write according to the style modeled."[20] Some available programs that "help students to accomplish this goal include those in the series Thinking Networks for Reading and Writing and Playwriter and the program *Story Tree.*"[21]

Interactive/prompt tutorials also help students learn text structure. Programs, such as *Organize* and *Writing Process Workshop*, "provide interactive tutorials on the components of a particular discourse structure."[22] Students interact with the computer and input their ideas based on important aspects of a particular type of discourse.

There are a number of programs available with various kinds of capabilities. Some have limited word processing capabilities, whereas others can help students write an original draft, revise versions of it, as well as help edit it.

Some software uses modeling techniques and semantic maps to help students gain insights into how text is organized. For example, a student

[19]Cornelia A. Dowd and Richard Sinatra, "Computer Programs and the Learning of Text Structure," *Journal of Reading* 34 (October 1990): 105.
[20]Ibid.
[21]Ibid.
[22]Ibid.

reads a selection and then "processes the ideas in an active and meaningful way by constructing a semantic network with the help of the computer."[23] This technique helps the student understand the "story's major episodes and supporting events and is taught that the configuration of the narrative map corresponds to the structure of this type of discourse."[24]

Computer programs with their built-in motivational attraction are a viable way to help students learn about text structure and to stimulate them to write.[25] However, no program should be used as an end in itself. Teachers must help students recognize that many of the advances made in word processing software and the special programs that are available that check spelling, word usage and even writing style will not make the need to write and gain writing skills obsolete. Word processor spell checks and computer thesauri are useful tools for word processor users, but individuals have to be able to write something before these can be applied. The people using these programs are generally writers who have acquired writing skills and usually use these programs as a check, not as ends in themselves to compensate for a lack of skills.

If we make students computer dependent for everything they do, we will be raising a generation of illiterates. Ironically, computer literacy could lead to illiteracy. Even if spell checks, thesauri, and other programs are available in the schools, and students use these tools as aids in the editing process, it does not negate the need for helping students attain writing skills.

Teachers should be especially wary of the computer programs that attempt to analyze writing style and word usage because they are limited at best. There should be warning labels for them saying, "Beware, these tools can be detrimental to your writing style." They tend to level everyone's style to a sameness and "may do more harm than good."[26] As William Safire says, "The beginner, despite the disclaimers in the manuals, is likely to be intimidated and forced into a short-sentence, simple-word mold fit for ten-year-olds or Ernest Hemingway, while many a pro will be rattled by the mechanistic carping at any expression of personal style."[27] He says further that the "robots are years away from matching what the average teacher can offer."[28] Even if computers can eventually offer programs that are more sophisticated and can distinguish correctly among certain types of sentences, we all need to gain skill in writing and try to acquire our own style.

Knowledge of the availability of these programs is good, but students who lack writing skills and are overdependent on program checkers cannot do independent thinking. Ironically, they become the robots.

[23]Ibid.
[24]Ibid.
[25]See Dowd and Sinatra for a discussion of a number of such programs.
[26]William Safire, "Writer vs. Robot," *The New York Times Magazine*, Section 6, January 8, 1989, p. 13.
[27]Ibid.
[28]Ibid.

A FINAL WORD: READING AND WRITING ACROSS THE CURRICULUM

Throughout this book, the emphasis has been on broadening the role of content-area teachers. From the studies in the various subject-matter areas in the past few decades, it appears that students are not attaining the concepts that they should be getting. This is probably not because of the dummying down of books as some would like us to believe; it is probably because students have not gained the kinds of reading and writing skills they need to get the most from their content-area courses and textbooks. Rather than lambasting these lacks, content-area teachers at all levels must themselves have these reading and writing skills at their fingertips so that reading and writing skills can be used to help students gain relevant content concepts. A major goal of the 1990s should be to implement reading and writing across the curriculum.

GRAPHIC SUMMARY OF CHAPTER

Here is a graphic summary of Chapter 10. If you have read the chapter, this graphic illustration should help you remember its main points. Under or beside each heading, you might want to jot down some of the information you recall, as well as some of the key concepts in this chapter. This can act as a good review. You can then check your key concepts against those that follow the graphic summary.

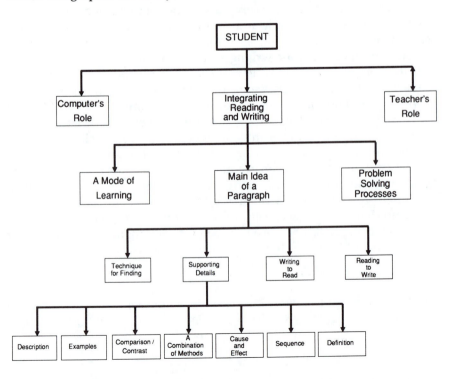

KEY CONCEPTS IN CHAPTER

- Writing is a fundamental skill that is closely related to reading.
- All content-area teachers, not just English teachers, should be concerned with writing and reading.
- Writing is a mode of learning and not just a means to convey information.
- Reading and writing enhance one another.
- Reading and writing both require time.
- Students need many opportunities to read and write in all content areas.
- The integration of reading and writing stresses the teaching of both so that each acts as a stimulus and aid for the other.
- Both reading and writing are problem-solving processes that require higher-level thinking.
- Finding the main idea independently is necessary to get the essence of what we are reading.
- A paragraph has only one main idea.
- Stating the main idea of their own paragraphs helps students' gain an insight into main idea.
- Reading and writing their own paragraphs gives students insight into how a paragraph is organized.
- The topic sentence usually anticipates both the main idea and its development.
- The main idea can be developed in a number of ways.
- The supporting details in a paragraph must develop the main idea.
- Some computer programs can be good motivational techniques to stimulate students to write.
- Computer programs should not be used as ends in themselves.

SUGGESTIONS FOR THOUGHT QUESTIONS AND ACTIVITIES

1. You have been placed on a special committee to help to evaluate the reading and writing program in your school. You are interested in combining the teaching of reading and writing. How would you go about convincing your colleagues to do this? What arguments would you use?
2. Develop two activities in which reading and writing are combined.
3. Discuss how an analysis of reading helps writing and how an analysis of writing helps reading.
4. Select some passages from literature that you could use to help your

students to recognize that the topic sentence of a paragraph is not always the first sentence of a paragraph.

5. Select some passages from literature to analyze, and then have your students write a paragraph.

6. Have your students choose one of their compositions to analyze. Have them read each of the paragraphs. Have them check to see if each paragraph expresses one main idea and if each sentence of the paragraph helps to develop the main idea.

7. Analyze some computer software that integrates reading and writing. Write a critique of the programs.

SELECTED BIBLIOGRAPHY

APPLEBEE, ARTHUR N., JUDITH A. LANGER, LYNN B. JENKINS, INA V.S. MULLIS, and MARY A. FOERTSCH. *Learning to Write in Our Nation's Schools: Instruction and Achievement in 1988 at Grades 4, 8, and 12.* National Assessment of Educational Progress. Princeton, N.J.: Education Testing Service, 1990.

ATWELL, MARGARET A. "The Evolution of Text: The Interrelationship of Reading and Writing in the Composing Process." Doctoral Dissertation, Indiana University, 1980.

EMIG, JANET. "Writing as a Mode of Learning." *College Composition and Communication* 28 (February 1977): 122–128.

GLATTHORN, ALLEN. "Thinking, Writing and Reading." In *Content Area Reading and Learning.* Diane Lapp, James Flood, and Nancy Farnon (eds.) Englewood Cliffs, N.J.: Prentice Hall, 1989, pp. 283–296.

RUBIN, DOROTHY. *Teaching Elementary Language Arts,* 4th ed. Englewood Cliffs, N.J.: Prentice Hall, 1990.

SAGER, MOLLEE B. "Exploiting the Reading-Writing Connection to Engage Students in Text." *Journal of Reading* 33 (October 1990): 40–43.

TIERNEY, ROBERT J., ANNA SOTER, JOHN F. O'FLAHAVAN, and WILLIAM McGINLEY. "The Effects of Reading and Writing upon Thinking Critically." *Reading Research Quarterly* 24 (spring 1989): 134–173.

TIERNEY, ROBERT J., and TIMOTHY SHANAHAN. "Research on the Reading-Writing Relationship: Interactions, Transactions and Outcomes." In *Handbook of Reading Research,* Vol. II. Rebecca Barr, Michael L. Kamil, Peter Mosenthal, and P. David Pearson (eds.) New York: Longman, 1991, pp. 246–280.

11

Reading for Appreciation: Gaining a Lifelong Habit

When you read something that seems to "get under your skin," that excites you, that stirs you, and that makes you "experience," you have probably felt the *joy* of reading.

INTRODUCTION

Reading helps reading; the problem is that many students are not reading. It is easy to understand why students who have reading problems are not reading, but we have a large population of students who have no discernible reading problems who are also not reading. Why?

Read the following typical and atypical statements made by young people:

Typical Statements

"I have baseball practice."
"I have band practice."
"I'm trying out to be a cheerleader."
"I'm meeting the gang at George's house."
"I have to watch a special TV program."
"Let's go see that great movie."
"Let's listen to the new tape."
"I have piano lessons."
And so on . . .

Atypical Statements

"I can't wait to get home to finish that terrific book I'm reading."
"Let's get together to discuss that great book."
And so on . . .

Young people must contend with enculturated attitudes, as well as with competing activities, which vie for their time and attention. Pressure from peers, parents, teachers, and society abound. Be well-rounded! So-

FIGURE 11-1. Reading helps reading!

cialize! Join clubs! Try out for athletic teams! Attend meetings! Show class spirit! And so on. Studies show that the most popular students are those who are brilliant, athletic, and *nonstudious*. And what student doesn't want to be popular?

It used to be that the typical statements given earlier were generally made by males and the atypical statements, by females. However, this is not true anymore. Pressures weigh heavily on females too. It is possible that the statement "I have baseball practice" is being voiced by a female rather than a male. The result is that the reluctant readers' population is probably increasing.

Also, the fact that students are reading less may be contributing to the reported lower SAT (Scholastic Aptitude Test) scores. The less students read, the less their vocabulary is expanded. As there is a high correlation between vocabulary and aptitude tests, this may account for the lower SAT scores. In order to try to offset the lower SAT scores, many people often jump on the bandwagon with *the cure-all*, saying "Let's go back to 'the basics.' " The need for skills in the basics is fine, but it is not the whole answer. Many of the young people who are not reading have no reading problems; they are just not choosing to read in their leisure time. Also, if students' specific reading disabilities are removed, it does not necessarily follow that these students will become readers. In order to become readers, students must have the time and the desire to read; they must have acquired an appreciation for reading; and they must have a need to read.

What better place is there for students to develop a love for reading than in their English literature classes? The relationship of reading to English literature is obvious; in English literature classes students must engage in reading, and reading comprehension is essential to understanding what is read. Also, usually, one of the major goals of all literature courses is to inspire students with the joy that can be found in books. Interestingly, even though a number of students do attain some concepts about plot development, setting, symbolism, and so forth in their English literature courses, many may not acquire that concomitant essential ingredient that is necessary for them to continue reading—that of appreciation. It seems to me that this may be because English teachers need the help and commitment of all teachers to promote wide reading in their classes. The goal of all teachers should be to inspire the student with the joy that can be found in books because this inspiration, once acquired, is one that should remain with students for the rest of their lives. This chapter is concerned primarily with helping all content-area teachers, not just English literature teachers, to help their students become lifelong readers.

KEY QUESTIONS

After reading this chapter, you should be able to answer the following questions:

1. What is reading for appreciation?
2. What is Sustained Silent Reading?
3. What is the relationship of role modeling to reading?
4. How should content-area teachers prepare their rooms so that students will be stimulated to read?
5. What kinds of books should content-area teachers provide for their students?
6. How can teachers use television as a positive force for reading?
7. What is bibliotherapy?
8. How can teachers use bibliotherapy to stimulate students to read?
9. What are some bibliotherapy themes that would lend themselves to being introduced in school?
10. What must a teacher know in order to work with bibliotherapy in his or her class?

KEY TERMS IN CHAPTER

You should pay special attention to the following key terms:

appreciative reading
attitude
bibliotherapy
creative problem solving

Drop Everything and Read (DEAR)
role modeling
starter shelves
Sustained Silent Reading (SSR)

WHAT IS READING FOR APPRECIATION?

Go to three different dictionaries and you'll probably find a different mix of definitions for the term appreciation. *Webster's New Collegiate Dictionary* defines *appreciation* as "**1 a:** sensitive awareness; especially the recognition of aesthetic values; **b:** judgment, evaluation: especially a favorable critical estimate; **c:** an expression of admiration, approval, or gratitude; **2:** increase in value."[1]

The *Random House College Dictionary* defines appreciation as "**1.** gratitude . . . **2.** act of estimating the quality of things according to their true worth. **3.** clear perception or recognition, especially of aesthetic quality. . . ."[2]

Webster's New World Dictionary of American English defines appreciation

[1]Merriam-Webster, *Webster's New Collegiate Dictionary* (Springfield, Mass.: G.C. Merriam Co., 1977), p. 56.
[2]*Random House College Dictionary,* Revised Edition (New York: Random House, 1988), p. 66.

as "**1.** the act or fact of appreciating; specif., **a)** proper estimation or enjoyment **b)** grateful recognition, as of a favor **c)** sensitive awareness or enjoyment, as of art **2.** a judgment of evaluation. . . ."[3]

When we talk about reading for appreciation, we are usually talking about sensitive awareness, especially the recognition of aesthetic values. The recognition of aesthetic values includes both enjoyment and the making of a value judgment. Probably because of the evaluation component, some people place appreciation at the highest level in a taxonomy of reading. These individuals believe that a person cannot attain appreciation unless he or she has a complete understanding at the highest level of what is being read.

In this book, appreciative reading is regarded as a separate domain with a hierarchy of its own. It is, therefore, possible for an individual to gain an appreciation for a piece of literature, even though he or she does not have a complete understanding of it. For example, a poem can be enjoyed because of its delightful sounds, rhythm, or language, even though it is not understood. Of course, the greater the understanding, the higher the appreciation, but appreciation is still possible without complete understanding at various lower levels.

Appreciative reading in this book is defined as reading for pleasure and enjoyment that fits some mood, feeling, or interest. Reading for enjoyment allows readers to vicariously experience many adventures and to engage in "something interesting and exciting."[4] It gives individuals things to discuss with other people, and very importantly, "reading for enjoyment is associated with reading achievement."[5]

FOSTERING APPRECIATIVE READING

In the introduction, it is stated that one of the major problems with fostering appreciative reading is competing with other enjoyable activities that vie for students' time and attention. Some principals, however, are trying to do just that by "going out on a limb to encourage reading."[6] They have found that such programs as the "I-dare-you approach wherein the principal offers the students a wacky reward for meeting reading goals—gets students reading in record numbers."[7] "Principals have jumped into pools of

---

[3]*Webster's New World Dictionary of American English*, Cleveland: Webster's New World Dictionaries, 1988), p. 67.

[4]John T. Guthrie, and Vincent Greaney, "Literacy Acts," in *Handbook of Reading Research*, Vol. II, Rebecca Barr, Michael L. Kamil, Peter Mosenthal, and P. David Pearson eds. (New York: Longman, 1991), p. 88.

[5]Ibid.

[6]*Reading Today* (Newark, Del.: International Reading Association, April/May 1990), p. 13.

[7]Ibid.

Jello, sat on a roof for a day, and even worn a monkey suit and sat in a cage in the library all day."[8]

The "wacky dare" program may work for the short term, but will students continue to read on their own and recognize that reading is its own reward? Long-term results need lots and lots of nurturing, and educators know that the key is to instill a love of reading in children at very young ages before they come to school. This is the ideal; unfortunately, it does not happen for many of our children. Therefore, one of the responsibilities teachers of young children have, besides promoting awareness of print in their students, is to help instill in them a love of books. This responsibility does not end, however, with teachers of young children; it must continue all through the grades.

Attitudes and Reading

Attitudes exert a directive and dynamic influence on all our lives, and once set, are difficult to change. It is often the concomitant learnings, such as attitudes, which will remain with us more than the subject matter we learned in class. Therefore, in content-area classes, teachers must be ever vigilant that what they do in teaching content does not stifle their students' love of reading. They must show through example and what they do that they value reading for enjoyment.

THE IMPORTANCE OF PROVIDING TIME FOR A READING FOR APPRECIATION PROGRAM

Every good reading program must have a component in it dedicated to appreciative reading. Learning to read and reading to learn are important parts of any reading program, but appreciative reading is what determines whether persons will read and continue to read throughout their lives. If children develop an appreciation of books at an early age, it will be more difficult for other activities and media to compete. One important factor is to make the decision to have a reading for appreciation program. Many educators give lip service to the appreciation component of the reading program, but they do not implement it. The only way that educators can show that they value a reading for appreciation program is to set aside time for the program. If time is set aside, there is a chance for success. As stated earlier, young people have to contend with many enjoyable activities that compete for their time and attention; reading for pleasure is often given a low priority in the competitive battle. By setting time aside during the school day for reading for enjoyment, educators would be giving students a chance to whet their appetites for books. What is especially encouraging is

[8]Ibid.

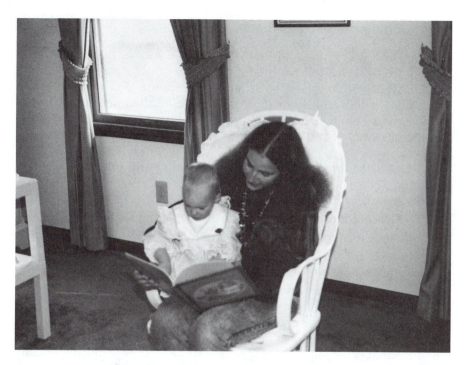

FIGURE 11-2. Melissa's mother and father have lots of books in their home, and they read to Melissa every day. Melissa is on her way to becoming a good reader.

that the Drop Everything and Read Program (DEAR)[9] or Sustained Silent Reading (SSR) seems to have caught on. Many school systems have initiated DEAR or SSR in their schools, and the response to it has been excellent. DEAR or SSR is a very simple program to institute, but it needs the backing and commitment of *all* school personnel for it to work, and some adjustments need to be made for it to work effectively in the secondary school.

DEAR or SSR requires that teachers follow certain rules:[10]

1. Each student must read.
2. The teacher must read at the same time that the students read.
3. Students read for a specified time period.
4. Students are not responsible for any reports on what they have read, and no records are kept of what students have read.
5. Students choose any reading material that they like.

SSR is obviously easier to initiate in the elementary grades than in the upper grades; however, it can be practiced in the upper grades if teachers are committed to the importance of having students engage in independent silent reading and if proper provisions are made so that it fits smoothly into the content program. The idea of having a bell ring and everyone from the superintendent to the custodian drop everything and read (DEAR) is intriguing and may work in some school systems; however, common sense dictates that this can cause some difficulties. For example, what if a student in a science class is in the middle of dissecting a frog or involved in a very intricate experiment? What if a student in an art class is in the middle of a project that demands immediate attention? What if a student is in the midst of solving a very complicated math problem that requires extensive concentration? What should these students do? The bell to drop everything and read may prove very frustrating for these individuals. Also, what if these students are in a special classroom or laboratory? They may be able and willing to drop everything and read, but the facilities may not be very conducive to reading.[11] DEAR or SSR is an excellent idea, but the program can work only if, as stated earlier, *all* teachers are committed to making it work. Content-area teachers should be involved in planning when the period for SSR should take place in their classes, and they should provide many types of reading matter for their students. Of course, even if a school system or

---

9Sustained Silent Reading (SSR) rather than DEAR is the more familiar phrase used for practice in independent silent reading. The original phrase was Uninterrupted Sustained Silent Reading (USSR).

10Adapted from Robert A. McCracken, "Initiating Sustained Silent Reading," *Journal of Reading* (May 1971): 521–524, 582.

11Marilyn Joy Minton, "The Effect of Sustained Silent Reading upon Comprehension and Attitudes among Ninth Graders," *Journal of Reading* (March 1980): 502.

FIGURE 11-3. These students are meeting in a group to discuss the books they are reading.

individual school is not committed to having an SSR program, any individual teacher can initiate and implement one in his or her own class.

Also, teachers can adapt SSR to fit their classes in a number of different ways as long as it does not violate the major purposes of SSR—to get students to read voluntarily and to enjoy what they read. One suggestion is to incorporate discussion as part of SSR.[12] Teachers can set aside some time after reading and have students state in one or two sentences what they liked about what they read. Another variation is to have students meet in groups of four or five and discuss what they are reading, and still another is to have students pair off with a partner and discuss the books between them.

ROLE-MODELING AND READING

When the character Fonze in the former television situation comedy "Happy Days" took out a library card in a particular episode, librarians across the country were swamped with requests for library cards by persons who had never had one before. An analysis of the results of young

[12]See Richard B. Speaker, Jr., "Another Twist on Sustained Silent Reading: SSR + D," *Journal of Reading* 34 (October 1990): 143–144.

FIGURE 11-4. This teacher is a good role model for her students.

children's watching "Sesame Street" found that a significant number of children who watched "Sesame Street" entered school with prolearning and proreading attitudes even though the attainment of these attitudes was not the objectives of the program.[13] It has been hypothesized that because children like to watch other children on television, "peer role-modeling of reading behaviors could motivate and reinforce positive attitudes toward reading."[14]

A number of television shows in the eighties and nineties have gotten the message as to the power of role modeling because some are making a concerted effort to show characters reading a book. Some even suggest books that people might like to read that are related to the show they have just seen. These encouragements to read from a major media source are good, but the irony is that television is often the culprit that competes for the individual's attention. (See "Television and Reading" in this chapter.)

Teachers at all grade levels who are enthusiastic about books and portray this enthusiasm to their students will infect their students with this enthusiasm. Some researchers reported in the literature how one junior high school teacher's habit of silently reading a newspaper for the first five minutes or so of his class stimulated other students in his class to model his behavior.[15] A teacher who is seen to be deeply immersed in a book during the lunch hour will also have a marked influence on students.

13Pamela M. Almeida, "Children's Television and the Modeling of Proreading Behaviors," in Chester M. Pierce, ed., *Television and Education* (Beverly Hills: Sage Press, 1978), pp. 56–61.
14Ibid., p. 59.
15Robert A. McCracken and Marlene J. McCracken, "Modeling Is the Key to Sustained Silent Reading," *The Reading Teacher* (January 1978): 407.

SETTING THE ENVIRONMENT FOR READING IN CONTENT-AREA CLASSROOMS

Most people expect the English literature classroom to be pleasant, inviting, conducive to reading and filled with books. A good English classroom should be replete with books; lots and lot of books at various interest and readability levels. The bulletin boards should have recommended book lists, award-winning books, book jackets from a number of popular books, students' recommendations and evaluations of various books, as well as some art work depicting a scene or characters from books. Good English literature classrooms should be dead giveaways because of their emphasis on books and other printed materials. However, this emphasis on books should not be restricted only to English classrooms—all content-area classes should have some sections devoted to books and other printed materials. For example, the classroom could have a shelf that contains various journals, magazines, newspapers, and so on, and another shelf or shelves filled with books. The books and other printed materials should be germane to the particular subject and students should be encouraged to browse through them. Teachers should also use these as part of their instructional program, as well as for their Sustained Silent Reading program. All teachers could whet their students' appetites for the books on display by putting tantalizing captions in front of them. This could arouse students' curiosity and stimulate them to go beyond the covers of the book. Teachers could challenge students who have read some of the books to create the captions for the books that would motivate other students to want to read the books. The same techniques could be used for articles in magazines and journals.

How to Stock the Shelves

Once content-area teachers have made the decision to have a special corner in their classrooms devoted to books and other printed material, they have to decide on what specific books and materials to include. One writer suggests the term *starter shelf*[16] for these books and materials because that is most descriptive of the shelf or shelves. The books that are chosen are merely to start the students reading voluntarily. The teacher starts the collection, but the students can contribute to it; and the books are changed periodically based on students' interests, needs, and reading ability levels.

The use of the starter shelf will depend on the intent of the teacher, as well as the needs of the students. Some teachers may want to stock the shelves with books relevant to each specific unit that is being studied at the time; others may want to have a core of general books. Some teachers may want to have a supply of fiction books related to the topics under discus-

[16]Adapted from David M. Bishop, "Motivating Adolescent Readers via Starter Shelves in Content-Area Classes," Alfred J. Ciani, ed. *Motivating Reluctant Readers* (Newark, Del.: International Reading Association, 1981): 49.

sion; others may want to have only nonfiction books. Some may want to have reading materials on topics of general interest and concern in the particular subject area. For example, in science courses, there might be reading matter on human engineering, drugs, space probes, cloning, biofeedback, nuclear and solar energy, and so on; in mathematics courses, there might be books and materials on artificial intelligence that probe the possibility of computers' ability to reason as humans, computer simulation; and so on. (See "Selected Bibliography" at the end of this chapter for some resource materials to help teachers stock starter shelves.)

Teachers must remember that the main purpose of the starter shelves is to get students to read on their own. Teachers should, therefore, not demand that students write a book report for every book that they choose to read from the starter shelf, nor should teachers require students to read a certain number of books from the starter shelf during the term. The starter shelf should act as a stimulus for students; it should be a place, as already stated, that students go to voluntarily; it should be a place that will "hook students on books."

The number of books chosen for the starter shelf would be determined by the amount of space available for the books and other reading material, the ability to attain the necessary materials, as well as the intent of the teacher and needs of the students. If the content-area teacher is teaching a number of classes with students at varying reading ability levels,[17] he or she will probably need different materials for each of the classes. This can cause a problem, especially if the content-area teacher does not have a permanent classroom. Also, some schools have such a high incidence of vandalism that they cannot afford to leave any material on display unsupervised. One school system has overcome these difficulties in a few ways. One way is to have built-in open shelves that can be locked with a roll down top when the classroom is not in use or unsupervised. Another way is to have the starter shelf on wheels. Teachers have their materials on a rolling cart which they take with them if they have no permanent classroom. Yet another way is to have teachers use colorfully decorated file boxes that they take with them to each class. The file boxes contain approximately 50 paperback books and 2 or 3 magazines that are at the reading ability levels of the students in the particular class. The file boxes and rolling carts are treated in the same way as stationary starter shelves; that is, the teachers change the books based on the topic being studied, and students can add to the collection at any time.

STUDENTS' INTERESTS AND CHOICE OF BOOKS

The *Journal of Reading* since 1987 has published yearly lists of books preferred by middle, junior high, and senior high school students. Trade

17See "Selected Bibliography" for resource references.

books (books not designated as textbooks) are requested from publishers. The submitted books undergo a rigorous process of selection in which students have the final say. The school sites chosen for field testing the books are usually a mix of different types of schools and represent different parts of the country.

It is not surprising then that the books chosen reflect this mix. The 1990 Young Adult Choices include novels dealing with "alcoholism, drunk drivers, and equal access to activities and sports for girls. Vietnam appears as a topic again."[18] In addition, "there are growing-up stories set in the inner city, the suburbs, and rural areas."[19] Fantasy stories dealing with the unknown, as well as nonfiction books dealing with the Holocaust, the sinking of the Titanic, and whales were also chosen.

In the latter part of the 1980s, children's and young adults' books began to deal with more and more realism. This realism is continuing into the 1990s. (See Bibliotherapy Themes for a discussion of some topics that were heretofore considered taboo.)

Criteria for Choosing Books to Help Foster Better Understanding in a Multicultural Society: A Special Note

Teachers have an excellent opportunity to help foster better relations among different peoples of the world by the kinds of books they choose for their classroom libraries, because books can act as a bridge to promote better understanding among all cultures.

When teachers choose books for their classroom libraries, they should put themselves in the position of their students and ask themselves how they would feel if they were to read the book. For example, would the book make them come back for more? Does the book interest them? Are the characters presented in a manner that does not demean any cultural group? Are the characters from various cultures portrayed with traits and personalities that are positive? A "no" answer should disqualify the book.

The importance of providing students with books that convey hope and with which students can identify because they mirror their lives cannot be overemphasized. Another factor, which is as important, concerns the image that individuals obtain when they read a book about people with different racial or ethnic backgrounds. Young people are greatly influenced by what they read; the way individuals are portrayed in books will have a profound effect on young people's perceptions of them.

Good books can open doors through which can pass better understanding, mutual respect, trust, and the hope of people living together in harmony and peace.

---

[18]"Young Adults' Choices 1990," *Journal of Reading* 34 (November 1990): 204.
[19]Ibid.

TELEVISION AND READING

Since television first began there has been an ongoing debate on the influence of television viewing on students' reading. The researches have not been definitive. Some suggest that "television viewing has a considerable negative impact on reading achievement only for children who watch for relatively many hours—more than 4 to 6 hours a day."[20] Television also seems to affect different groups of children in different ways. The reading achievement of children who come from high socioeconomic status homes decreased when they watched greater amounts of television, whereas the converse appeared to be true for those who come from low socioeconomic status homes; that is, heavier viewing for these children increased their reading achievement.[21]

In a recent Gallup Poll the public ranks the educational value of television lower than family, school, or peers.[22] However, if used properly, television can have some positive effects on students' learning and reading.

As stated earlier, students watch television. That is a fact. On the average, young adults generally do not watch television as much as young children, but they do spend time watching some shows. Teachers should capitalize on this knowledge and try to make television a stimulus for reading. There are a number of programs available that are concerned with reading suitable for young adults. These could act as a catalyst for reading. For example, some networks have a number of shows presented after school that adapt well-known novels with themes that would be of interest to students. Prime Time School Television prepares an instructional guide for the shows. It gives teachers advance notice of air dates, provides a synopsis of the program or series, and suggests points to look for while students watch the program; it offers follow-up activities and subjects for school use; and it includes a helpful print and nonprint bibliography of related materials.

Teachers could use these shows as a springboard for critical and creative thinking comprehension lessons. They could also use them as a means of encouraging reading if books with similar themes are readily available for students. Teachers could have students read the book beforehand, and then they could discuss how the television production presents the book or whether the television production has aptly presented the book. For example, when the filmed dramatization of Albert Speer's memoirs, "Inside the Third Reich" was shown on television, history teachers could have introduced their students to the book and then asked the students to view the

---

[20]Johannes W.J. Beentjes and Tom H.A. Van Der Voort, "Television's Impact on Children's Reading Skills: A Review of Research," *Reading Research Quarterly* 23 (fall 1988): 401.
[21]Ibid.
[22]George Gallup, Jr., "Parents Disturbed by TV Content; Most See Growth in Problem," *The Gallup Poll*, April 9, 1989.

production. After the production, the teacher could have had different students read Speer's memoirs as well as other books that portray the same time period. Then students could have discussed the television production, Albert Speer's memoirs, and other books written about the same period.

Another example would be when Public Television presented a series on the Civil War. History teachers could have assigned students to watch the series and then to compare what they saw with what they were reading as to authenticity. The teachers could also have challenged their students to give their ideas on what they would have done differently in the presentation of the series.

Scripting or script reading is another technique that teachers might investigate for stimulating students to read. Script reading consists of having students read a script before it is broadcast. In class, students discuss the subject matter, main ideas, vocabulary, and issues.

BIBLIOTHERAPY

Bibliotherapy is another technique that can be used to interest students in books. If students see that books can help them, this may encourage them to read more. Also, bibliotherapy encourages students to try to seek answers in a positive, intellectual, and logical manner.

Have you ever felt that you were different from others, that some things bothered only you, that you were peculiar because you liked certain things? Have you ever resented being the smallest or the tallest in class? Have you ever felt guilty because you had bad thoughts about some member of your family? Have you ever been embarrassed because you were frightened about things nobody else seemed to be frightened about? Have you ever felt that your parents got their divorce because of you? Have you ever worried about death or dying? Have you . . . ?

We could go on and on with the emotions that fill us and the problems that we all may have faced or still may face. Have you ever read a book in which the main character had a problem exactly like yours? Didn't it make you feel good to know that you were not the only one with such a problem? Weren't you relieved?

If you have ever read a book in which the main character had a problem exactly like yours and if the book helped you to deal better with your problem, you were involved in bibliotherapy.

Defining Bibliotherapy

Reading guidance given by teachers and librarians to help students with their personal problems is regarded as bibliotherapy. Bibliotherapy is the use of books to help individuals to cope better with their problems. The use of books (or bibliotherapy) to help persons is not a new phenomenon. As far back as 300 B.C., Greek libraries bore inscriptions such as "The Nourishment of the Soul" and "Medicine for the Mind." Alice Bryan, a noted librarian, in the late 1930s advocated the use of books as a technique of guidance to help readers "to face their life problems more effectively and to gain greater freedom and happiness in their personal adjustment."[23] However, it probably was not until Russell and Shrodes published their articles on the "Contributions of Research in Bibliotherapy to the Language Arts Program" in 1950 that teachers attempted to bring bibliotherapy into the classroom. Russell and Shrodes discussed their belief that books could be used not simply to practice reading skills, but also to influence total development. They defined bibliotherapy as "a process of dynamic interaction between the personality of the reader and literature—interaction which may be utilized for personality assessment, adjustment, and growth." They also say that this definition:

> . . . is not a strange, esoteric activity but one that lies within the province of every teacher of literature in working with every child in a group. It does not assume that the teacher must be a skilled therapist, nor the child a seriously maladjusted individual needing clinical treatment. Rather, it conveys the idea that all teachers must be aware of the effects of reading upon children and must realize that, through literature, most children can be helped to solve the developmental problems of adjustment which they face.[24]

In a definition of bibliotherapy, the term *cope* is important to note. When individuals use coping mechanisms, they are solving their problems by dealing with reality. They are behaving in a positive manner. The coping mechanism used in bibliotherapy is *empathy*.[25] Empathy refers to an individual's being able to project himself or herself into the personality of another and know how that person feels. Unless persons have experienced what someone else feels, either firsthand or vicariously through books, they cannot empathize with the other individual.

Identifying with a character in a story is the important first step in bibliotherapy. *Empathy* is the next step. In this step the reader projects himself or herself imaginatively into the character's "skin." How the storybook character deals with problems and handles his or her emotions can help the reader gain *insights* (the third step) into how to adjust or deal with his or her own real-life problems.

Matching Books to Individuals

Bibliotherapy will not take place by just reading a book, and not all books are suited for bibliotherapy purposes. For bibliotherapy to be effective,

---

[23]Alice I. Bryan, "The Psychology of the Reader," *Library Journal* 64 (January 1939): 110.

[24]David Russell and Caroline Shrodes, "Contributions of Research in Bibliotherapy to the Language Arts Program, I," *The School Review* 58 (September 1950): 335.

[25]*Catharsis* is the term usually used by psychoanalysts or psychiatrists to explain the second step in the process of bibliotherapy. The term *empathy* is used in place of *catharsis* because it is less burdened by clinical connotations.

there must be a proper match between the individual and a book. Although there are times when some books by pure serendipity do help an individual to cope better with his or her problems, it is best not to leave the selection of the book to chance or accident. Some books are better suited to specific individuals than others. For example, to give a child who is "frightened out of his wits" a book such as *Call It Courage* or *Julia of the Wolves* would be ludicrous. A child who is "frightened of his own skin" will not identify with a courageous protagonist. A book depicting a brave character will upset and disturb the frightened child more. This individual needs a book in which the protagonist is frightened by everyone and everything, but learns to deal with his or her problem.

The Uses of Bibliotherapy

Bibliotherapy helps individuals to cope with their problems in a number of ways. It helps persons realize that they are not the only ones to have a particular problem. It allows the readers to see that there is more than one solution to a problem and that they have some choices. It helps the readers to see basic motivations of others in situations similar to their own and to see values involved in human, rather than in material, terms. It provides facts needed in solving a problem, and it encourages the reader to plan and carry out a constructive course of action.[26]

Bibliotherapy can also be used in both preventive and ameliorative ways. That is, some individuals, through reading specific books, may learn how to handle certain situations before they have taken place. Other persons may be helped through books to overcome some common developmental problem they are experiencing at the time. For whatever purpose bibliotherapy is used, it will only be of value if teachers are knowledgeable about *how* to use bibliotherapy in their classrooms.

In order to use bibliotherapy effectively in the classroom, teachers should know about students' needs, interests, readiness levels, and developmental stages.

Bibliotherapy Themes

The kinds of problems that lend themselves to bibliotherapy are varied, and many have already been stated in an earlier section. Bibliotherapy themes depend on the age of the students as well as on their developmental needs. In Chapter 2, the developmental tasks of adolescents according to Havighurst are presented. These tasks could be used as a guide by teachers in choosing books for their students. There are times when teachers may find that a student has a special problem with which he or she must cope. For example, a student may have difficulty coping with his or her parents' divorce, the death of a loved one, or an illness. It may be that the student is new to the school, or the student may be too fat or too thin. It could be that the student finds growing up confusing; drugs, alcohol, and dating can also cause great anxieties for many students.

It was stated earlier in this chapter that in the latter part of the eighties, children's and young adults' books began to deal with more and more realism. In the past few years, a number of books have surfaced that address such delicate topics as incest and child abuse, topics that were once taboo and certainly not in the domain of the teacher. Today, however, teachers are being asked to be on the lookout for signs of possible physical and sexual abuse among their students and to identify them to their school principal and nurse.

If teachers suspect they have such victims in their classes, they might want to read aloud to the class a book that deals with these topics. However, because of the sensitivity of these areas, teachers should use bibliotherapy only in consultation with the school psychologist. The reading aloud of the book is not enough to help the victims. The book, however, may help these young people recognize that they are not alone and that they are not "bad" or "evil"; it may also encourage them to tell someone about their problem.

An even more controversial issue that society is grappling with that has entered the classroom deals with the treatment of AIDS victims. In the 1990s, we will certainly see more and more books emerge that may help young people cope better with this issue. Another difficult issue that probably more books will address, which is almost paradoxical in the age of AIDS, is that of teenagers' earlier sex experiences and the proliferation of teenage pregnancies.

The Teacher and Bibliotherapy

By reading books that deal with themes such as those stated in the previous section, students can be helped to cope better with their emotions and problems. Perceptive teachers sensitive to their students' needs can help their students by providing the books that deal with the same problems that their students have. However, because teachers are not clinicians, students who are having serious adjustment problems should be referred for help to the guidance counselor or school psychologist. Also, teachers must be careful not to give students who are anxious about a situation a book that would increase their anxiety. A teacher should also not single out a student in front of the class and give him or her a book that very obviously points out that student's defects. It would probably embarrass and upset the student more.

The school librarian and the special reading teacher may be excellent resource persons to help the teacher to choose books for bibliotherapy purposes. For best results, teachers should work very closely with them.

After teachers use reference sources or the aid of librarians to identify some possible books for bibliotherapy, they should peruse the books to determine whether the books meet certain important criteria. Books for bibliotherapy should deal with problems that are significant and relevant to the students. The characters in these books should be "lifelike" and presented in a believable and interesting manner. The characters' relationship to others in the book should be equally believable, and they should have motives for their actions. The author should present a logical and believable plot using vivid descriptive language, humor, adequate dialogue, and emotional tone. The situations presented by the author should be such that minor problems can be separated from main problems. The episodes in the book should lend themselves to being extracted and discussed so that students can formulate alternate solutions. Also, the author should present enough data so that students can discern generalizations that relate to life situations. The book should also be written in such a manner that the readers' imaginations are so stirred that they can "enter the skin of another."

A good teacher, one who is perceptive to the needs of students and who recognizes the importance of individual differences, will be in a better position to determine when a problem lends itself to being presented to the whole class or when it should be handled on an individual basis. As was stated earlier, when a teacher wishes to give individual students books for bibliotherapy purposes, the students should not be singled out lest they feel ostracized or humiliated.

As in most things, there is not any one sure way of introducing an individual to a book. However, if the book is at the readability and interest level of the person, if the book fulfills a need, and if the person is given time to become absorbed in the book, chances are that the person will read the book. Although there are a number of "ifs" in the preceding sentence, all of them can be overcome by an interested and concerned teacher.

Bibliotherapy Techniques

Many times a teacher may find that a number of students in the class share a similar problem. Therefore, the teacher might want to introduce the problem in some way to the class and use a bibliotherapy technique to help the students to cope with their problem.

One way to interest individual students in books for bibliotherapy purposes would be to choose an episode from a book to read aloud to the class. The chosen episode should present the main character in a problem situation. Also, the protagonist should be one with whom the teacher feels a number of students can identify. After the episode is read, a discussion should take place on how the character resolves his or her problems. The author's solution should not be given. The book may then be offered to those individuals who would like to read it. The teacher using this technique should have several copies of the book available because many of the students will probably want to read it.

Bibliotherapy and Creative Problem Solving

Another technique the teacher could have used is bibliotherapy and creative problem solving. In this method, almost the whole book is read aloud to the class. Before the ending, the students, using clues from the book try to determine how the main character's problem is resolved. They are encouraged, also, to generate their own solutions. After the ending is read, the students are asked to compare their solutions with the author's. Then they can discuss which they liked better and why.

Following is an example of how to use bibliotherapy in a high school English class. The book chosen for the whole class is Barbara Wersba's *Run Softly, Go Fast.*

This book is chosen because it can be used with a large group. It has passages that can be excerpted from the book, it lends itself to being read aloud, it can be used with less mature as well as with more mature persons, and the protagonist is one with whom many students can relate.

The instructor initiates a discussion on the "pains of growing up." Students are encouraged to discuss some of the problems that they or their friends may have encountered. Then the instructor reads an excerpt from *Run Softly, Go Fast*. The excerpt consists of the first few pages of the book. In these pages, David, a young man, is reminiscing about his father's recent death and funeral. We learn about David's feelings about his father, his life, and what he thinks his father thought. A discussion should follow about the book character and the vehemence he feels toward his father. Students should be encouraged to give their feelings and views about the protagonist. Ask the students whether they think David actually hated his father. A discussion concerning children's perceptions of their parents and how these perceptions change with increasing age should also take place.

The next excerpt read aloud is about David's feelings about his childhood and his relationship to his father at that time. First, the following is read; ". . . My whole childhood is wrapped up in the sound of his voice talking about the future. I would be handsome when I grew up, a ladykiller. I would go to college and major in business and be a success. He was so ignorant of who I really was . . ."[27] After a discussion of this passage, David's reminiscing about a dream he had after a drowning incident is read. In this excerpt David finds security and love in his father's presence. He says, "And I knew . . . I knew that for the rest of my life he would come when there was danger. A million miles could separate us, but he would come and find me. . . . And then I fell asleep, with him holding my hand, this man who was my father. . . ."[28]

How brittle is a child's love. What happens that causes David to have such animosity toward his father that he refuses to see him for two years and then only visits his father on his deathbed?

[27]Barbara Wersba, *Run Softly, Go Fast* (New York: Atheneum, 1971), p. 14.
[28]Ibid., p. 15.

Students are asked to read the rest of the book on their own. After about a week's time, a discussion concerning David and his relationship to his father should take place. In the discussion, students should be encouraged to give their feelings and to tell about the effect, if any, that the book had on helping them to gain some insight into their own feelings.

If students begin reading books that relate to themselves and that help them to gain a better understanding of themselves, it is possible that more students will choose to read. (See "Selected Bibliography" for a list of references that should help teachers choose books for their students.)

GRAPHIC SUMMARY OF CHAPTER

Here is a graphic summary of Chapter 11. If you have read the chapter, this graphic illustration should help you remember its main points. Under or beside each heading, you might want to jot down some of the information you recall, as well as some of the key concepts in this chapter. This can act as a good review. You can then check your key concepts against those that follow the graphic summary.

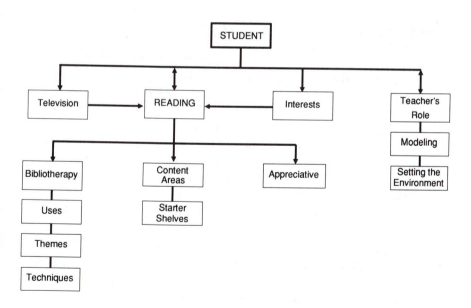

KEY CONCEPTS IN CHAPTER

- Reading helps reading.
- Students have many competing activities that vie for their time and attention.
- Teachers must provide time in their classrooms for reading.

- Appreciative reading is reading for pleasure and enjoyment that fits some mood, feeling, or interest.
- Attitudes exert a directive and dynamic influence on individuals' behavior.
- SSR or DEAR refers to students spending time in independent silent reading purely for the sake of reading.
- Teachers should be good reading role models for their students.
- Content-area classrooms should have both fiction and nonfiction books related to the topics being studied.
- Books can help foster better relations among all groups of people.
- Television viewing affects different groups of students in different ways.
- Bibliotherapy is the use of books to help individuals cope better with their emotional and adjustment problems.
- Teachers must be very careful about how they use bibliotherapy in their classrooms.

SUGGESTIONS FOR THOUGHT QUESTIONS AND ACTIVITIES

1. Check the television schedule for upcoming programs that you can use as a stimulus for interesting students in books for your content-area course.
2. Brainstorm some activities that could be used as a catalyst to stimulate students to read.
3. Choose a theme that you feel would lend itself for bibliotherapy use in the classroom. Choose some books from which you can excerpt some material that relates to the theme. Read the excerpt to the class, and have them discuss it. Have them try to come up with a solution.
4. You have been chosen to give a talk to your colleagues on how bibliotherapy can be used effectively in the classroom. What will you say?
5. Compile a list of books that could be used for bibliotherapy purposes.
6. Compile a list of books for your subject area that you would use to initiate a "starter shelf" in your classroom.
7. Discuss the effects of television on reading.
8. Brainstorm some ways that teachers can use to stimulate students to read voluntarily.
9. Have a debate on whether certain controversial topics should or should not be presented in the school.

SELECTED BIBLIOGRAPHY

BEACH, RICHARD W., and JAMES D. MARSHALL. *Teaching Literature in the Secondary School.* Orlando, Fla.: Harcourt Brace Jovanovich, 1991.

BISHOP, DAVID M. "Motivating Adolescent Readers via Starter Shelves in Content-area Classes." in *Motivating Reluctant Readers.* Alfred J. Ciani (ed.) Newark, Del.: International Reading Association, 1981.

BOHNING, GERRY, and MARGUERITE RADENCICH. "Informational Action Books: A Curriculum Resource for Science and Social Studies." *Journal of Reading* 32 (February 1989): 434–437.

BROWN, ELEANOR F. *Bibliotherapy and Its Widening Applications.* Metuchen, N.J.: Scarecrow Press, 1975.

CIANI, ALFRED, (ed.) *Motivating Reluctant Readers.* Newark, Del.: International Reading Association, 1981.

CLARY, LINDA MIXON. "Getting Adolescents to Read." *Journal of Reading* 34 (February 1991): 340–345.

DONELSON, KENNETH L., and ALLEEN PACE NILSEN. *Literature for Today's Young Adults.* Glenview, Illinois: Scott, Foresman, and Company, 1989.

DUKE, CHARLES R. "Tapping the Power of Personal Response to Poetry." *Journal of Reading* (March 1990): 442–447.

GUTHRIE, JOHN T., and VINCENT GREANEY. "Literacy Acts." In *Handbook of Reading Research,* Vol. II. Rebecca Barr, Michael L. Kamil, Peter Mosenthal, and P. David Pearson (eds.) New York: Longman, 1991, pp. 68–96.

JALONGO, MARY RENCK. "Bibliotherapy: Literature to Promote Socioemotional Growth." *Reading Teacher* 36 (April 1983): 796–803.

LOUIE, BELINDA Y. "Literacy in Young Adult Literature." *Journal of Reading* 33 (January 1990): 282–284.

MATHISON, CARLA. "Stimulating and Sustaining Student Interest in Content Area Reading." *Reading Research and Instruction* 28 (1989): 76–83.

"Young Adults' Choices for 1990: Teenagers' Best Liked Books." *Journal of Reading* 34 (November 1990): 203–209.

12

Diagnostic Techniques for Reading in Content Areas

INTRODUCTION

Not too long ago, this author was a luncheon speaker for educators in a large inner-city school district. During lunch, a principal at her table said that he was in charge of three schools. The speaker was incredulous. "How is that possible?" she asked. "Oh, it's really easy. You see, I never go to two of the schools because it's too dangerous to go there. No teaching takes place there. We have all the incorrigibles in those two schools. The kids there can't read nor write. Many are just marking time until they leave. I spend all my time at the third school. That's the only place it pays to be."

What do you say to statements such as that? There really is no easy reply. The truth is that many of the students in the two schools he is in charge of have been arrested and found guilty of innumerable violent crimes; many are drug users and pushers. Many have assaulted and maimed teachers. Many are back on the streets and in the schools because of their age; as youthful offenders, many are released—only to start their pattern over and over again.

These young people who, at a very early age, have given up on society and themselves for different reasons usually have one thing in common—they can't read. Perhaps their lives would not be different if they had learned to read; but somehow, it might have. If intervention had taken place earlier, it might have made a difference. For these young people who have chosen deviant paths it may be a moot point. However, we can't afford to give up. We must attempt to provide alternatives for these young disenchanted people and at the same time provide intervention at an early enough age so that those with reading problems will not become the new disenchanted. Teachers are a powerful group of people; they can make the difference!

Content-area teachers have enough to contend with; they certainly do not need the added burden of having to diagnose their students' reading difficulties. However, good content-area teachers need to know something about diagnosis so that proper intervention can take place. This chapter will not attempt to make reading diagnosticians out of content-area teachers; it will attempt to provide content-area teachers with some insights into why their students may be having difficulties in the content areas and provide teachers with some procedures that they can use in their content classes to help identify those students who may have difficulty reading their textbooks. This chapter will also present a portrait of a secondary school reading specialist.

KEY QUESTIONS

After reading this chapter, you should be able to answer the following questions:

1. Why is it important to know whether a textbook is at the reading ability level of a student?
2. How can you determine a student's various reading levels?
3. What is the role of the student in diagnosis?

4. What is a group informal reading inventory?
5. What is an informal "on-the-spot" approach to diagnose students' ability to read their textbooks?
6. What is cloze procedure?
7. What are the functions of readability formulas?
8. What is the role of the reading specialist in the secondary school?

KEY TERMS IN CHAPTER

You should pay special attention to the following key terms:

cloze procedure	independent reading level
cloze test	instructional reading level
content domain	listening capacity level
content-referenced tests	listening capacity test
diagnosis	norm-referenced tests
frustration reading level	norms
group informal reading inven- tory	objective
group informal vocabulary test	readability formulas
group listening capacity test	reading specialist
group tests	standardized tests
	textbook readability

DIAGNOSING A STUDENT'S READING DIFFICULTIES IN THE CONTENT AREAS

In content-area classes, teachers cannot ignore important diagnostic principles when they are teaching because diagnosis and instruction are interrelated. Teachers who are sensitive to the needs of their students must be able to recognize certain cues that act as warning signals to alert them to some problem. These teachers recognize that early diagnosis is important and the handmaiden of prevention.

Content-area teachers do not have to be reading specialists to be able to recognize that a student has a reading problem. Content-area teachers can also take certain measures at the beginning of the year to avert problems from developing. The adage "An ounce of prevention is worth a pound of cure" is an apt one.

In diagnosis the teacher is interested in defining the nature of the student's difficulty as soon as possible so that the difficulty can be nipped in the bud.[1] If the content-area teacher suspects that a student's problem in

[1]See Dorothy Rubin, *Diagnosis and Correction in Reading Instruction*, 2nd ed. (Boston: Allyn & Bacon, 1991).

the content area may be caused by a reading problem, the teacher can do a number of things. The first option the teacher has is to refer the student for testing by a reading specialist. On the surface, this may appear to be the easiest thing to do, but for practical purposes, it may not be. In many schools the ratio of students to the reading specialist is very high; that is, there may be one reading specialist for every 100 students or for a whole secondary school. By the time the reading specialist tests the student, the term may be half over. Probably the best method would be for the teacher to consult with the reading specialist and, together with the student, try to learn as much as possible about the student's reading behavior.

DIAGNOSIS AND STUDENT INVOLVEMENT

The main purpose for diagnosis is to determine what is causing a student's problem so that a program can be developed to help a student overcome the difficulty. Student involvement is crucial. Unless the student recognizes that he or she has a problem, unless the student understands what that problem is, and unless the student is interested in overcoming the problem, nothing much will probably be accomplished.

The teacher can help the student to become involved in the following ways:

1. The teacher should help the student recognize his or her strengths as well as weaknesses.
2. The teacher should not overwhelm the student with a listing of all his or her difficulties at once.
3. The teacher should try to elicit from the student what the student thinks his or her problems are, why the student feels that he or she has these problems, and what the student feels are the causes of his or her problems.
4. The teacher and the student together set attainable goals for a specific problem area.
5. Together, the next step is determined.

CONTENT COURSES AND TEXTBOOK READABILITY

In content-area classes, it is essential that teachers match their students with textbooks at their appropriate reading ability levels. The achievement of this goal is a major step that requires some knowledge of readability levels and the techniques for determining these.

Teachers at the junior and senior high schools have many students in their content classes who are not reading at grade level. This can cause many difficulties for such students, and it may be that a student's dislike of a course is because he or she cannot read the textbook. A student who is not reading at grade level would probably have difficulty reading a social studies, science, or mathematics textbook whose readability is at the same grade level. Teachers will have to provide these students with special guidance and direction if they cannot get subject matter books that contain the same content concepts at the students' reading ability levels. Some of these students may need guidance and help beyond that which the content-area teacher can provide; these students would need to be referred for special help. (See Chapter 14.)

Special Note:
It would be very difficult to get a subject matter book for a student who is reading below grade level at the student's reading ability level and have the textbook cover the same material. If a student is in ninth grade, the subject matter book for eighth grade mathematics covers different material. Also, the student may be good in mathematics but have a reading problem. If a book from the lower grade level is used, the student would be penalized in mathematics.

What follows are practical techniques and procedures that content-area teachers can use to learn about their students' reading and learning behavior and their textbooks. Emphasis is given to group informal techniques rather than to individual techniques because individual reading inventories such as the informal reading inventory are usually given in the secondary schools by the reading specialist. Also, it is highly unlikely that secondary school content-area teachers will have the time or the inclination to administer individual diagnostic reading tests to students. Before we discuss these techniques, it is important that something be said about reading levels.

Special Note:
Teachers in elementary schools who are responsible for teaching reading, as well as content-area subjects, to their students in a self-contained classroom would probably be more likely to use individual diagnostic techniques to determine their students' problem in reading content material. It is, however, beyond the scope of this book to supply the specific information that teachers would need to be able to administer an individual informal reading inventory to their students. The selected bibliography section at the end of this chapter presents books that supply this type of information for those who desire it.

As already stated, the emphasis in this chapter is on those techniques that content-area teachers would be able to use easily and that apply directly to their area or that can readily be adapted to their specific content-area.

Determining Reading Levels

When content-area teachers give their students a group informal reading inventory, they are interested in determining at what level their students are able to read their textbooks. This point has been made a number of times already because it is such a vital one for content-area teachers. The teacher's method of instruction will vary based on whether the students' textbooks are at their independent, instructional, or frustration reading levels. The group informal reading inventories that teachers give to their students are used to determine this information. Before we move on to discuss these various techniques, we should discuss what is meant by the terms *independent*, *instructional*, and *frustration* levels.

The informal reading inventory (IRI), which originated from the work of Emmett A. Betts and his doctoral student, Patsy A. Killgallon, is used to determine three reading levels and a capacity or listening capacity level. The criteria for reading levels on the individually administered IRI were determined by Betts, and many individual and group informal reading inventories still use the same levels or modifications of them. The levels as determined by Betts and his percentages that designate the levels follow. Note that criteria are given for silent comprehension reading only because when content-area teachers give group informal inventories they are only determining a student's silent comprehension reading ability.

Betts Reading Levels

Independent Level*	Students read on their own without any difficulty.	Comprehension—90% or above
Instructional Level	Teaching level.	Comprehension—75% or above
Frustration Level	This level is to be avoided. It is the lowest level of readability.	Comprehension—50% or less
Listening Capacity Level*	Highest level at which a pupil can comprehend when someone reads to him or her.	Comprehension—75% or above

*Betts also called the *independent level* the *basal level*, and the *listening capacity level* was called the *capacity level*.

In designating these levels Betts not only gave percentage determinants, he also gave other criteria that the teacher should look for at each level.[2] And according to Betts, "it is wiser to look at the verbal and nonverbal clues in performance."[3]

[2]Adapted from Emmett A. Betts, *Foundations of Reading Instruction* (New York: American Book Co., 1946), pp. 445–454.
[3]Jerry L. Johns, "Emmett A. Betts on Informal Reading Inventories." *Journal of Reading* 34 (March 1991): 493.

Independent Level This level "is the highest level at which an individual can read and satisfy all the criteria for desirable reading behavior in silent- and oral-reading situations."[4] At the independent level the student can read successfully on his or her own without any assistance. When the student is reading silently at this level, he or she should be able to achieve a minimum comprehension score on literal and interpretive questions of at least 90 percent. The pupil should also be free from such observable evidence of tension as frowning, movements of feet and hands, finger pointing, and holding the book too close or too far.

The independent level is an important one for the student, teacher, and librarian. It is at this level that the student will read library or trade books in school and at home. The reference books that students choose to read for a special project or assignment should also be at their independent level because they will be reading these on their own. If they choose books to read independently that are too hard for them, that will deter them from reading.

Instructional Level The instructional level is the one at which teaching is done. It is at this level that content-area teachers can use such procedures as a directed reading approach to prepare their students to read their textbooks. (See "A Guide for Using a Directed Reading Approach in Reading Content Material" in Chapter 1.) This level must not be so challenging that it frustrates the student. At this level there should be a minimum comprehension score of at least 75 percent for silent reading on literal and interpretive questions. As on the independent level, there should be no observable tensions or undue movements of feet and hands. There should be freedom from finger pointing, lip movements, and head movements; and there should be acceptable posture.

Frustration Level This is the level to be avoided; however, for diagnostic purposes, it is helpful for teachers to know what this level is so that they can avoid giving students reading material at this level. Also, even though this is the level to be avoided, some students' textbooks are at the students' frustration level, and, as stated in an earlier section, it may not be possible to provide these students with a different textbook. If this is the case, teachers must make very special provisions for these students. (See Chapter 14 for examples of very special provisions for special students that teachers can use or adapt for students whose textbooks are at their frustration level.) The fact that a student has reached his or her frustration level is evidenced by the student's attaining a comprehension score of 50 percent or less on literal and interpretive questions for silent reading.

At the frustration level, the student has difficulty anticipating meanings and is not familiar with the facts presented in the selection. The student shows his or her frustration by frowning, constantly moving in a

4Betts, p. 445.

nervous fashion, finger pointing, blinking, or faulty breathing. The student may also be unwilling to read.

At this level, when the student reads silently, he or she reads at a slow rate, uses lip movements, and makes low vocal utterances.

Listening Capacity Level The listening capacity level, as first determined by Betts, is the "highest level of readability of material that the learner can comprehend when the material is read to him."[5] Betts also established the minimum comprehension score of at least 75 percent, based on both factual and inferential questions for listening capacity.

Content-area teachers can use Betts reading levels as a guide; they should not use them as absolutes. Teacher judgment is essential in determining what standards to use for specific classes. Also, even though minimum criteria are usually given for estimating the various reading levels of IRIs, these are actually general standards because of teacher judgment. Another point that should be made is that Betts reading levels were determined based on basal readers. When these levels are applied to content textbooks, such factors as interest, specialized or technical vocabulary, concept load, and so on, should be considered.

GROUP INFORMAL READING INVENTORIES

The first technique for content-area teachers that will be described to determine whether students can read their textbook can be called an "on-the-spot" approach because it does not require any special materials. It uses students' textbooks to determine whether these books are at the reading ability level of the students. This technique should be applied at the beginning of the term after the teacher has acquainted students with the textbook. (See "Knowing the Textbook" in Chapter 5.) In this group approach the content teacher chooses a passage of about 1,000 to 1,500 words from the middle of the book that is representative of the book. The students read the passage silently and then write the answers to given questions on the passage, or they write a summary of the passage, or they write the main or central idea of the passage, and so on. (The types of questions that teachers construct for their group informal reading inventory will depend on teachers' purposes. Usually teachers use a combination of literal and interpretive questions, but critical comprehension questions may be asked also.) Teachers must recognize that this group "on-the-spot" approach has many limitations. If students have writing problems, teachers will be testing these students' writing problems rather than their reading problems. Also, if a student has word recognition problems, these could be interfering with the student's ability to comprehend the passage.

The "on-the-spot" approach is helpful in spite of all the caveats that

[5]Ibid., p. 439.

were given in the previous paragraph. If students have difficulty answering a number of questions on the passage, it will alert the teacher to the fact that the students have a problem. The teacher can try some other diagnostic techniques as well as enlist the help of the reading specialist to try to determine what the problem is.

Special Note:
Teachers should make sure that the questions they construct for their group informal reading inventory are all text dependent; that is, the answer for each question directly depends on the students' reading the excerpted text material.

GROUP LISTENING CAPACITY TEST

A group listening capacity test would help the teacher determine whether students have the comprehension ability to read their textbooks. It would also help the teacher gauge his or her students' ability to listen to oral reports and lectures. A listening capacity test is given to determine a student's comprehension ability through listening, and it is helpful in assessing a student's reading ability, especially if a student has some word recognition problems.

The procedure for preparing an informal "on-the-spot" group listening capacity test is similar to the other "on-the-spot" technique, but the method for giving it differs. The teacher chooses a passage from the middle of the textbook that is about 250 words and prepares questions on the passage that include interpretive and literal comprehension questions and perhaps some critical comprehension ones. (Note that the passage chosen for the listening capacity test is shorter than the one chosen for the group informal reading inventory.) The teacher reads aloud the passage and then asks the questions and the students write the answers to the questions. (Again, the teacher must make sure that he or she is testing reading ability rather than writing ability.) The teacher is interested in determining the students' listening capacity level, which is the highest level at which a learner can understand material when it is read to him or her. The minimum comprehension score of at least 75 percent is usually used. (See "Determining Reading Levels" in this Chapter.)

Special Note:
A listening comprehension test helps estimate a student's reading potential; however, if the student has some hearing problem, the test would not be an accurate estimate of that student's reading potential. Obviously, any hearing impairment would invalidate any type of listening test given to assess comprehension.

GROUP INFORMAL VOCABULARY TEST

Another approach teachers can use to determine whether their students will have problems reading their textbooks, as well as to determine the amount of guidance they should give to their students, involves textbook word lists. The word list should contain twenty to twenty-five words. The teacher selects these from the textbook by opening the book randomly to different pages and by selecting one or two words from each page until a total of twenty to twenty-five words is reached. (The teacher should avoid including technical words because the students would probably not have met these words before.) The words that the teacher chooses should be those that he or she thinks might cause difficulty for students or words that the teacher feels students need to know in order to comprehend the concepts being explained.

The students are given the words in the context of a sentence and asked to define the word. If twenty words are used and if a student misses five or more of the words, the student will probably need special help.

Special Note:
Teachers should be cautious about choosing a word list from a book's glossary because many times the glossary is composed primarily of scientific or technical terms. These terms are usually defined within the textbook, and many authors also provide a key for the pronunciation of these words.

CRITERION-REFERENCED TESTS

A special section is being presented on criterion-referenced tests in this chapter because these tests can effectively assess individual students' specific needs. At the beginning of the term and throughout the term, teachers can use these tests to determine whether students have the specific skills needed to either read required content material or to obtain the desired objectives of their lessons.

Teachers can easily construct test items to correspond to their objectives, and if students do not have a needed skill, corrective techniques would be applied.

What Are Criterion-Referenced Tests?

Criterion-referenced tests are based on an extensive inventory of instructional objectives in a specific curriculum. The objectives are presented in behavioral terms.

Criterion-referenced tests are designed to diagnose specific behaviors of individual students. They are used to gain more information about the students' various skill levels, and the information is used either to reinforce, supplement, or remediate the skill development being tested. The test results help the instructor plan specific learning sequences to help the students master the objective they missed.

Criterion-referenced tests can be administered to an individual or to a group, and they may be teacher-made or standardized. Criterion-referenced tests are considered standardized if they are published tests that have been prepared by experts in the field and have precise instructions for administration and scoring. They are not norm-based; however, some may provide a means for comparing students to a norm group even though this is not the purpose of criterion-referenced tests but rather that of norm-referenced tests.

Criterion-referenced tests are concerned primarily with mastery of objectives, which are based on classroom curriculum. On criterion-referenced tests an individual competes only with him- or herself. There is very little difference in appearance between a norm-referenced test and a criterion-referenced test; however, differences do exist, as already noted, in the purposes for the tests.

For a criterion-referenced test to be valid, a content domain must be specified, and the test items must be representative of the content domain. Test makers identify various content-area domains and write measurable objectives within each domain; then detailed item specifications are developed. These item specifications are supposed to "ensure detailed coverage for the skills stated in the objectives."[6] Usually, there are a number of items written for each objective to ensure reliable measurement.

Here is an example of a teacher-made criterion-referenced test. Note that the general and specific areas are provided and that the test item is correlated to the objective for the specific area. The important factor is not the terminology used but whether we can infer that the test item does indeed measure what it is supposed to; in this case, the ability of the student to state the central idea of the group of paragraphs.

GENERAL AREA: history
SPECIFIC SKILLS NEEDED
FOR LESSON: central idea
OBJECTIVE: The student will state the central idea of the group of paragraphs selected from their reading assignment.

The students are asked to read a group of consecutive paragraphs carefully and then to state the central idea of the passage. The teacher can construct the question so that the students have to choose the *best* answer from those supplied, or they have to come up with their own answer.

If many students have difficulty finding the central idea of the passage, the teacher should directly teach the skill to the whole class by using

[6]*California Diagnostic Reading Tests Technical Report*, (Monterey, Calif.: CTB/McGraw-Hill, 1989), p. 5.

related content material. If only one or a few students have difficulty in the specific skill being tested, the teacher could provide a special guide for directly teaching the skill using related material to just those students who need it.

Many teachers in their everyday lessons utilize instructional objectives and then prepare tests to determine whether students have achieved them. The test that is correlated to the specific objective would be considered a criterion-referenced test.

Special Notes:
"Criterion-referenced tests and norm-referenced tests are no longer seen as a strict dichotomy."[7] Some tests are more useful for norm-referenced use than for criterion-referenced use, depending on the purpose for the test. Some tests have been prepared for use as both criterion-referenced and norm-referenced; that is, test users can compare a student's test results to a national norm or to a set of predetermined specific objectives. When a criterion-referenced test has equated norms, it means that "the scores on one test have been statistically matched to the scores on a normed test."[8]

Content domain may refer to the content of an entire book, or, for a particular test, a set of objectives would define its content domain.

CLOZE PROCEDURE

Can you supply the _____ that fits this sentence? When you came to the missing word in this sentence, did you try to gain closure by supplying a term such as *word* to complete the incomplete sentence? If you did, you were involved in the process of *closure,* which has to do with the ability of the reader to use context clues to determine the needed word. To gain *closure,* we must finish whatever is unfinished.

The cloze procedure was primarily developed by Wilson Taylor in 1953 as a measure of readability, that is, to test the difficulty of instructional materials and to evaluate their suitability for students. It has since been used for a number of other purposes, especially as a measure of a student's comprehension ability.

Cloze procedure is not a comprehension skill; it is a technique that helps teachers gain information about a variety of language facility and comprehension ability skills. A cloze test or exercise is one in which the reader must supply words that have been systematically deleted from a text at a particular grade level.

There is no set procedure for determining the length of the passage or

[7]Michael Zieky, Director of Technical Assistance and Training, Educational Testing Service, 1991.
[8]Ibid.

the number of deletions that a passage should have. However, if teachers wish to apply the reading levels criteria that have been used in research with the traditional cloze procedure, they must follow certain rules. First, only words must be deleted, and the replacements for these words must be the *exact* word—not a synonym. Second, the words must be deleted in a systematic manner. The researchers who have developed the criteria for scoring cloze tests state that "any departure from these rules leaves the teacher with uninterpretable results."[9]

The traditional cloze procedure consists of choosing a passage that is representative of the material being tested and deleting every fifth word of the passage. The passage that is chosen should be able to stand alone; that is, it should not begin with a pronoun which has its antecedent in a former paragraph. The first sentence of the passage should remain intact. Then beginning with either the first, second, third, fourth, or fifth word of the second sentence, every fifth word of a 250-word passage should be deleted.

At the intermediate-grade level and higher, the passage length is usually 250 words, and every fifth word is generally deleted. For maximum reliability, it is suggested that a passage should have at least fifty deletions. If we were to use this as our criterion, we could see that we need the length of a passage to be at least 250 words, with every fifth word deleted. Obviously, a cloze technique would not yield as reliable a score for a short passage as for a longer one.

Scoring the Cloze Test

If we have deleted fifty words, the procedure for scoring the cloze test is very easy. All we have to do is multiply the number of correct insertions by two and add a percentage symbol. For example twenty-five correct insertions would be equal to 50 percent. If we have not deleted exactly fifty words, we can use this formula in which the number of correct insertions is divided by the number of blanks and multiplied by 100 percent.

$$\text{Formula:} \quad \frac{\text{Number of Correct Insertions}}{\text{Number of Blanks}} \times 100\%$$

$$\text{Example:} \quad \frac{40 \text{ Correct Insertions}}{60 \text{ Blanks}}$$

$$\text{Example:} \quad \frac{40}{60} \times 100\% = (40 \div 60) \times 100\% = 67\% \quad \text{(Rounded to nearest digit)}$$

For a traditional cloze test in which only exact words are counted as correct and every fifth word has been deleted, a score below 44 percent

[9]John R. Bormuth, "The Cloze Procedure: Literacy in the Classroom," in William D. Page, ed. *Help for the Reading Teacher: New Directions in Research* (Urbana, Ill.: National Conference on Research in English, 1975), p. 67.

would indicate a frustration level which is the level to be avoided. At the frustration level, the student has difficulty anticipating meanings and is not familiar with the facts presented in the selection. The student may show his or her frustration by frowning, constantly moving in a nervous manner, and so on. A score between 44 and 57 percent would indicate the instructional level, which is considered the one at which teaching is done. At this level the material must not be so challenging that it frustrates the student nor so easy that the student becomes bored. Scores above 57 percent would indicate the independent level, the level at which the student can read well without any assistance.

It is important to note that these criteria should be used only if the exact words are used and if every fifth word has been deleted from the passage.

Reading Levels Scale for Cloze Procedure

Independent Level	58% and above	(the level at which the student can read with no assistance)
Instructional Level	44%–57%	(the teaching level)
Frustration Level	43% and below	(the level to be avoided)

Variations of the Traditional Cloze Procedure: An Emphasis on Diagnosis

Variations of the cloze technique are usually used. For example, instead of deleting every fifth word, every noun or verb is deleted or every function or structure word (definite and indefinite articles, conjunctions, prepositions, and so on) is deleted. This technique is used when the teacher wishes to gain information about a student's sentence sense. Example:

Where _____ the energy go?

Another variation of the cloze technique would be to delete key words in the passage. This technique is useful for determining whether students have retained certain information. Example:

A procedure in which the reader must supply words is called the _____ procedure.

Cloze technique can also be adapted for use in a number of other ways. Students can be presented with a passage in which parts of words are given, and they must complete the incomplete word. Example:

The m_____ enlarges minute objects.

Another adaptation is to present the students with a passage in which every *n*th (the number chosen) word is deleted. They must then choose words from a given word list that *best* fits the blanks.

Teachers can use the cloze technique for diagnostic, review, instructive, and testing purposes. In the construction of the exercise, the key thing to remember is the *purpose* of the exercise. If the purpose is to test a student's retention of some concepts in a specific area, then the exact term is usually necessary; however, if the purpose is to gain information of a student's language facility, ability to use context clues, vocabulary development, or comprehension ability, the exact term is not as important because often many words will make sense in a passage.

Cloze Technique in Science

Here is a sample of the type of cloze technique that teachers can use with their students to determine their ability to use context clues to figure out the missing words.

Structures in living things range from simple to complex. There are "levels of

organization" among (1)_____ things. In your earlier studies in (2)_____, you

probably learned about electrons, protons, and (3)_____ and how they are

organized into (4)_____. Perhaps you are familiar with the idea of (5)_____

being organized into molecules, and you may know that (6)_____, in turn,

may be (7)_____ into cell parts such as the nucleus, (8)_____, and cell mem-

brane.

Answers: 1. living 2. science 3. neutrons 4. atoms 5. atoms 6. these 7. organized 8. cytoplasm.

READABILITY FORMULAS

As already discussed, the cloze procedure can be used as a measure of a book's readability, but it usually is not; it is usually used for instructional purposes. Also, the cloze procedure is not a formula. There are, moreover, techniques for determining the readability of written material that are easier and quicker to apply; that is, readability formulas exist that are applied directly to the written material to determine the reading difficulty of the written material.

Most readability formulas are based on both sentence length and syllabication; however, some may also use word lists. Readability formulas do not take other variables—such as experiential background of students, maturation, purpose of reading, and so on—into account. They also do not measure the abstractness of ideas nor the literary style nor quality of the written material. Readability formulas are not absolutely reliable, for different formulas on similar material may not produce the same scores. When a readability formula produces a score of grade eight, it does not mean that all eighth graders will be able to read the book. It merely means that a number of eighth graders—approximately five to seven out of ten such readers— will probably have little trouble with the book. Although readability formulas are imperfect tools, they do have value, for they give some idea of the difficulty of a book for specific groups of readers.

Regardless of which formula teachers use, they should be familiar with the methods for estimating readability. Teachers do not have to work out the exact estimates for each book, but by observing the sentence length and syllables, or sentence length and kinds of words, that is, the difficulty of the words used in a paragraph, they can estimate whether a book is at the proper level for their students to read independently. (See Appendix B for an example of a readability formula.)

THE READING SPECIALIST: AN IMPORTANT RESOURCE FOR CONTENT-AREA TEACHERS

Most middle schools, junior high schools, and high schools have special reading teachers who work with students who have reading difficulties. One of the biggest problems special reading teachers have is getting content-area teachers to use their services. Many view the reading specialists as separate from the content-area programs. This is unfortunate. What follows is a portrait of a secondary school reading specialist. This scenario should help content-area teachers gain a better insight into the role of special reading teachers in their schools.

Scenario: Portrait of a Secondary School Reading Specialist
Mrs. Hill is a former English teacher. Ten years ago her principal suggested that she take some reading courses because the school needed a reading specialist, and he thought she would be a good choice. At first Mrs. Hill wasn't too excited about the idea. She was, after all, an English teacher, and she enjoyed teaching English literature. Mrs. Hill realized, however, that for a few years she had not really been doing what she loved because so many of her students had reading problems. Because of this, she told her principal that she would take a few reading courses and let him know how she felt in a few months. The reading courses helped Mrs. Hill gain many insights into the problems her students had, and she decided to go on for a master's degree in reading. When she told her principal that she would like the reading specialist's job once she finished her degree, he told her that he had to hire someone from within the system, and it had to be a secondary

school person. Therefore, she was the most logical candidate. The principal also said that because Mrs. Hill was a secondary teacher herself, she would be more readily accepted than a reading teacher from the elementary grades.

After much thought, Mrs. Hill decided to take the position for the next school year. She knew she had her work cut out for her but was excited about the challenge. She had taken three reading courses the preceding semester and was taking three more this semester, and she intended to take another three courses in the summer. She was visiting reading labs in various schools and talking to other reading specialists. Interestingly, many of the people she spoke to were also former English teachers.

Ten years later: Mrs. Hill is a reading specialist today, and in the past ten years she has learned a lot about herself and her colleagues. It's amazing how many people acted differently toward her when she returned to school as a reading specialist. Mrs. Hill saw herself as having a number of roles, an important one being a consultant to the content teachers and helping them recognize how reading comprehension could be used to enhance content areas. Her colleagues, however, would have none of that. They listened to what she had to say at the faculty meetings, but then they went into their rooms, closed their doors, and did what they had always done before.

Mrs. Hill has had an uphill struggle, but she feels it was worth it. Of course, not all her colleagues today embrace her suggestions about incorporating reading comprehension into the content areas, using guide sheets, and instructing students in study-skills techniques for the particular content area, but most of them do. Today, she is a consultant as well as a reading teacher; she is not just locked away all day in a room with different groups of students. Mrs. Hill's colleagues now recognize that one of her major roles is to help them to help their students within their regular classes. This was her biggest battle, but she was determined to win it. She felt that she had to if she were to become an effective reading specialist within the school. Her colleagues liked research data, so she got the data for them. She showed them that studies indicate a consistent negative relationship between the time students spend in "pull-out" classes and reading.[10] This is probably so because the "pull-out" program usually becomes the complete reading program rather than a supplemental one; it is gener-

---

[10]G.V. Glass and M.L. Smith, *Pull-out in Compensatory Education*, paper prepared for Office of the Commissioner, U.S. Office of Education, 1977.

ally not integrated with the students' other courses, and the students miss what is going on in the class from which they were pulled.[11]

Mrs. Hill also advertised her services by distributing attractive fliers to her teachers describing her services. The fliers gave teachers an overview of the many areas that reading encompasses. One flier contained a comprehensive questionnaire, which Mrs. Hill invited the teachers to fill out; it would give Mrs. Hill information about the needs of the teachers in her school. Most of the teachers did fill out the questionnaire and Mrs. Hill set up appointments with each of these teachers. It was a lot of work, but it was worth it.

Mrs. Hill is proud of the reading lab at the secondary school and of the special program that she and a number of other special personnel and content-area teachers from within the district helped to develop for students with severe reading problems. This program is integrated with the content-area courses. Students are given reading instruction as part of their English class, and all other content-area teachers emphasize reading comprehension skills in their classes.

Mrs. Hill also works with those students who need to acquire functional or survival reading skills to help them cope with the outside world. She helps them learn how to read and fill out employment forms and how to read maps, menus, traffic manuals, and other information involving driving. She also helps them with advertisements, in particular, classified advertisements.

Mrs. Hill, who is respected by her colleagues and much sought after by them, now has a multifaceted role at the secondary school. She acts as a consultant, teacher, diagnostician, helper, and manager. She works with teachers, with administrators, with other special personnel, and directly with students. She also directs the reading lab in the school. Her only problem is that she does not have enough time during the day.

Today Mrs. Hill is happy that she took her principal's advice because she feels that she is making a significant contribution. If you are a teacher, there is nothing more exciting than having a student at the secondary school level awaken to the world of books and knowing that you have helped to bring this about. *It's not too late.*

---

[11]The term *pull-out program* may be used in a number of different ways in the literature. The term *pull-out* in this textbook refers to those programs in which students are taken from another class to have reading instruction.

GRAPHIC SUMMARY OF CHAPTER

Here is a graphic summary of Chapter 12. If you have read the chapter, this graphic illustration should help you remember its main points. Under or beside each heading, you might want to jot down some of the information you recall, as well as some of the key concepts in this chapter. This can act as a good review. You can then check your key concepts against those that follow the graphic summary.

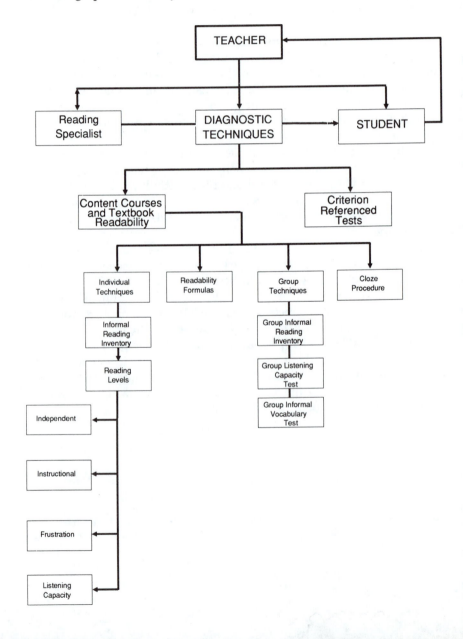

KEY CONCEPTS IN CHAPTER

- Early diagnosis of reading problems is important and is the handmaiden of prevention.
- Student involvement is essential for effective diagnosis and correction.
- In content courses teachers must match students and books.
- In content courses teachers usually employ group informal diagnostic techniques rather than individual ones.
- The Betts Reading Levels include the independent, instructional, frustration, and listening capacity levels.
- The independent reading level is the one at which the individual can read on his or her own.
- The instructional reading level is the teaching level.
- The frustration level is the one to be avoided.
- The listening capacity level is the highest level of comprehension the learner can attain when material is read aloud.
- Group informal reading inventories have a number of limitations.
- Vocabulary word lists from students' texts should be used with caution.
- Criterion-referenced tests are primarily concerned with the mastery of objectives.
- On criterion-referenced tests, an individual competes only with him- or herself.
- Cloze procedure is a technique that helps teachers gain information about a variety of language facility and comprehension skills.
- Readability formulas should be used with caution.
- Readability formulas exist that are applied directly to written material.
- Reading specialists and content-area teachers should work together for the common good of the students.
- Content-area teachers should consult the reading specialist if they suspect that a student has a reading problem.

SUGGESTIONS FOR THOUGHT QUESTIONS AND ACTIVITIES

1. Choose a specific content area, and then prepare a criterion-referenced test for a number of instructional objectives in the content area to determine students' specific needs. (Prepare a separate criterion-referenced test item for each instructional objective.)

2. Choose a selection from a content-area textbook. Apply the Fry readability formula to the selection to determine its readability level.

3. Choose one of the "on-the-spot" techniques presented in this chapter, and administer it to a student to determine whether the student's textbook is at the student's reading ability level.

4. You have been chosen to give a talk to your colleagues on the content-area teacher's role in diagnosing reading difficulties. What will you say?

5. Prepare a cloze test to use with a group of students in a content area of your choice.

SELECTED BIBLIOGRAPHY

BADER, LOIS A., and KATHERINE D. WIESENDANGER. "Realizing the Potential of Informal Reading Inventories." *Journal of Reading* 32 (February 1989): 402–408.

BLANTON, WILLIAM, ROGER FARR, and J. JAAP TUINMAN. (eds.) *Reading Tests for the Secondary Grades.* Newark, Del.: International Reading Association, 1971.

CONOLEY, JANE CLOSE, and JACK J. KRAMER (eds.) *The Tenth Mental Measurements Yearbook.* Lincoln, Neb.: Buros Institute of Mental Measurements, Univ. of Nebraska, 1989.

DESANTI, ROGER J. "Concurrent and Predictive Validity of a Semantically and Syntactically Sensitive Cloze Scoring System." *Reading Research and Instruction* 28 (winter 1989): 29–40.

FRY, EDWARD. "Reading Formulas—Maligned But Valid." *Journal of Reading* 33 (January 1989): 292–297.

FRY, EDWARD. "A Readability Formula for Short Passages." *Journal of Reading* 33 (May 1990): 594–597.

HANSELL, T. STEVENSON. "Four Methods of Diagnosis for Content Area Teaching." *Journal of Reading* 24 (May 1981): 696–700.

JOHNS, JERRY L. *Basic Reading Inventory.* Dubuque, Iowa: Kendall/Hunt, 1988.

JOHNSON, MARJORIE S., ROY A. KRESS, and JOHN J. PIKULSKI. *Informal Reading Inventories,* 2nd ed. Newark, Del.: International Reading Association, 1987.

MEHRENS, WILLIAM A., and IRVIN J. LEHMANN. *Measurement and Evaluation in Education and Psychology,* 4th ed. Fort Worth, Tex.: Holt, Rinehart and Winston, 1991.

RUBIN, DOROTHY. *Diagnosis and Correction in Reading Instruction,* 2nd ed. Boston: Allyn & Bacon, 1991.

SWEETLAND, RICHARD C., and DANIEL J. KEYSER. *Tests,* 3rd ed. Austin Tex.: PRO-ED, 1990.

13

Observation as a Diagnostic Technique in the Content-Area Classroom

OVERVIEW

Introduction: A Scenario
Key Questions
Key Terms in Chapter
Making Observations Objective
    Poor Readers Can Be Good
    "Con Artists" in Content
    Classes
Anecdotal Records
    Determining the Information to
    Be Recorded
Checklists
    Group and Individual
    Checklists

Checklists and Rating Scales
Other Helpful Student Behavior
    Study Techniques
    Informal Interviews
    Interest Inventories
    Projective Techniques
Graphic Summary of Chapter
Key Concepts in Chapter
Suggestions for Thought Questions
    and Activities
Selected Bibliography

INTRODUCTION: A SCENARIO

Mr. Johnson teaches poetry to ninth and tenth graders. No one has to tell him that this is not the students' favorite kind of literature. This may not have always been so, but, unfortunately, as students go through the grades, they seem to like poetry less and less. From the looks of his students on the first day of class, he knows that he has his work cut out for him.

Fortunately for his students, Mr. Johnson is a very patient and creative teacher, who loves what he does and who feels that everyone has within him- or herself a creative spark that is waiting to be ignited. His greatest joy is to nurture this spark. He wants to make poetry come alive for his students. He wants to help them feel, taste, and breathe poetry. And he wants them to come away with the idea that it is not "sissy" stuff.

In order to accomplish his goals, he needs to know as much as possible about his students. The adage "Actions Speak Louder Than Words" is an apt one for him. It's one thing for an individual to say he or she is doing something; it's another to actually observe the person doing what he or she says he's doing. Mr. Johnson knows this and, as a result, tries to use as many techniques as possible to learn the most he can about his students. One technique on which he relies very heavily is observation.

Mr. Johnson knows that direct observation is helpful to the teacher who wants to become aware of the attitudes, interests, and appreciations of students.

Mr. Johnson is correct. For example, teachers can observe whether students are volunteering to read aloud or to answer various types of questions. They can observe whether students are volunteering to participate in discussions and to work on group projects and whether they voluntarily choose to read during their free time. They can see which students consistently do their homework and extra work. The best method to determine whether students have learned something is to observe whether they are doing or using what they have learned.

This chapter will help you gain information about the kinds of techniques teachers in content-area classes or, for that matter any other classes, can use to learn more about their students' interests, attitudes, and appreciations.

KEY QUESTIONS

After reading this chapter, you should be able to answer the following questions:

1. What are the purposes of observation?
2. How can observation be made as objective as possible?
3. What is an anecdotal record?
4. What is an informal interview?
5. Why do teachers use interest inventories?
6. What are projective techniques?
7. When are projective techniques used?

KEY TERMS IN CHAPTER

You should pay special attention to the following key terms:

anecdotal record

checklist

informal interviews

interest inventory

observation

projective technique

rating scale

MAKING OBSERVATIONS OBJECTIVE

Observation is a technique; it is a means for collecting data. So that observations are of value, teachers must be as objective as possible and avoid making generalizations about a student's behavior too early. For example, by observing that a student on one or two occasions puts his or her head on the desk, the teacher makes the statement that the student is tired. This may be so, but it may not be. There are a great many reasons why a student might put his or her head on the desk.

Here are some helpful suggestions on how to make observations as objective and useful as possible.

1. Use checklists and anecdotal records (observed behavior without interpretation) to record observations. (See next section.)
2. Observe a student over an extended period of time before making any inferences about the student's behavior.
3. Avoid the projection of one's own feelings or attitudes onto the student's behavior.
4. Observations should be used in conjunction with other measurement techniques.
5. Make sure that only observed behavior is recorded.
6. Look for a pattern of behavior before making any inferences about behavior.
7. Record observed behavior immediately or as soon as possible.
8. Recognize that checklists and anecdotal records do not reveal the cause or causes of the observed behavior or behaviors; they only help to identify patterns of behavior from which one can try to deduce the existence of possible problems.
9. Do not oversimplify a student's observed behavior.
10. Date observations.

364 | Special Areas

Poor Readers Can Be Good "Con Artists" in Content Classes

It's difficult to be a good observer unless you know what signs to look for. A good experience would be to observe a class over a period of time and then to observe one student only. You would probably find that there are certain students who seem to act up almost all the time for no reason at all. At times, you might feel that these students' only mission in life appears to be to disrupt class and do anything to get a "rise" out of the teacher. Everyone knows who these students are, and they do need help. Their behavior is a symptom of some problem, and every time they act up, they are showing us this.

However, there is another group of students who also needs our help, but, because of their actions in class, they are not as easy to spot and, as a result, are often deprived of the help they need.

These students rather than making a scene, do just the opposite; they "hide out."[1] Their nonverbal behavior may actually belie what they are really feeling and thinking. In other words, these students have learned how to "con" teachers into thinking they are attending and doing the work when in essence they are not because they have reading problems. They are good "con artists."

Good teachers need to know what to look for to pinpoint these students so that they can be helped. One big clue should be that these students do not do well on their tests, yet they come to class each day; they sit up front, they appear to be paying attention; and they nod and smile at you. Because of this behavior, teachers usually assume that these students are paying attention and doing their work and, as a result, do not call on them to answer questions in class. On the other hand, certain kinds of deviant behavior also seems to pay off for those students who want to avoid being called on in class. Teachers tend not to call on students who avoid eye contact with them and who are disruptive.[2] As a result, "teachers who focus on effective instruction from only their perspectives fail to appreciate the needs of unsuccessful readers and may inadvertently reinforce students' reading failure."[3]

ANECDOTAL RECORDS

Teachers are often confused about what to record as worthy of observation. Because of this, checklists (see next section) are very helpful; however, checklists do not usually have an inclusive list of student behavior. Teachers

[1]See William G. Brozo, "Hiding Out in Secondary Content Classrooms: Coping Strategies of Unsuccessful Readers," *Journal of Reading* 33 (February 1990): 324–328.
[2]Ibid., p. 326.
[3]Ibid., p. 324.

usually supplement checklists with anecdotal information, which is the recording of *observed behavior* as objectively as possible. In recording observed behavior, teachers should attempt to put down exactly what has taken place *as soon as possible*. The date and time of the incident should be recorded, and the teacher's interpretation of the observed behavior may be given; however, the teacher's interpretation or possible explanation for the student's behavior should be put in brackets or set off in some way to avoid confusion with the actual observed behavior. It is best for the teacher to record merely the observed behavior and to observe the student over an extended period of time before making any hypotheses as to the cause or causes of the behavior. If the teacher observes the student over an extended period of time, the teacher is more likely to see a pattern of behavior.

Determining the Information to Be Recorded

What information should be recorded? This is a difficult question to answer and, as already stated, is often confusing for the teacher. As a result, anecdotal information usually consists of unusual observed behavior. Teachers may, however, be losing important information that could help them to gain insights into a student's problem if they record only unusual behavior.

From the preceding discussion, it is obvious that exact guidelines cannot be given as to what should or should not be recorded. Alert teachers, however, who are aware of the individual differences of the students in their classes will recognize those situations that warrant recording. Here are some examples:

1. Susan always seems to want to go to the lavatory. Record when she goes and the frequency. It may be a physiological or emotional problem, or it may be that she wants to "escape" from a certain classroom situation.

2. Frank is always "acting up" and causing disruptions in class. Record when Frank "acts up" to see whether there is a pattern. It may be that this is Frank's way of avoiding doing something. What is he avoiding? Is he bored, or is he frustrated? Is something bothering him?

3. Sara hardly ever raises her hand to ask or answer any questions. She rarely talks to anyone. Record when Sara does ask or answer some question. Then try to come up with some hypotheses that give possible reasons for this behavior.

It's important to note that observations do not explain the causes of behavior. As stated earlier, observation is a technique for gathering information; it helps teachers to learn more about the behavior of students. If used carefully in conjunction with other techniques and test data, it can help teachers to generate possible causes for behavior. The possible causes must then be verified by more extensive and scientifically collected data, such as standardized tests.

Special Note:
Teachers should be extremely careful about what anecdotal information becomes part of a student's permanent records because federal legislation has been passed that allows parents access to their children's school records.

CHECKLISTS

Checklists usually consist of lists of behaviors that the observer checks as present or absent. Checklists are a means for systematically and quickly recording a student's behavior. They are not tests. Although checklists are not tests, it is possible to present or devise a test to enable the rapid filling out of a checklist of behaviors; in other words, the test is administered to get the result, which is the student's profile.

Checklist formats may vary. Some checklists use rating scales, some are used for a whole class or group, and some are used for an individual student. The purpose of the checklist should determine the kind of checklist that is used.

Group and Individual Checklists

Checklists that are used to display the behavior of a whole class or of a group of students in a specific area are sometimes preferred by teachers because they do not have to go to individual folders to record a student's behavior, and teachers can, at a glance, determine who needs help in a specific area and who does not. A group checklist is helpful in planning instruction for the group as well as for the individual, whereas the individual checklist is useful in assessing the strengths and weaknesses of an individual student only. Both types of formats are helpful. A teacher who, at a glance, wishes to see a complete profile of a child may prefer the individual approach, whereas the teacher who wishes to see a profile of students' strengths and weaknesses in specific skills for instructional planning purposes will probably prefer a group checklist.

Whether a group or individual checklist is used, the checklist should contain an itemized list of behaviors in a particular area, there should be space for dates, and there should be space for special notes. On p. 367 is an example of an individual checklist that content-area teachers can use to determine a student's reading behavior in a content class.

Special Note:
Group checklists usually do not have the space for notes that individual checklists have. This may be one disadvantage of a group checklist.

Student's Name: _____

Class: _____

Teacher: _____

Diagnostic Checklist for a Student's Reading Behavior in a Content Class

	Yes	No	Sometimes
1. The student can state the meaning of a word in context from the textbook.			
2. The student can give the meaning of specialized terms used in the textbook.			
3. The student can recall information from the textbook that is explicitly stated.			
4. The student can state the main idea of a paragraph from the textbook.			
5. The student can state the central idea of a group of paragraphs from the textbook.			
6. The student can summarize a chapter from the textbook.			
7. The student can state the details that support the main idea of a paragraph.			
8. The student can state the details that support the central idea of a group of paragraphs from the textbook.			
9. The student can answer questions concerning content material that require inferential reasoning.			
10. The student can hypothesize why the writer presented the material.			
11. The student can draw analogies about what he or she is reading.			
12. The student can apply what he or she has read to solve problems.			
13. The student can critically examine what the writer has presented.			
14. The student can go beyond the textbook to come up with alternate solutions.			
15. The student voluntarily chooses to read.			
16. The student raises his or her hand to answer questions.			
17. The student contributes to classroom discussions on the readings.			
18. The student brings in books for the starter shelf.			
19. The student chooses to read more on a specific topic.			

Checklists and Rating Scales

A checklist that uses a rating scale is actually an assessment instrument. This type of checklist serves different purposes from one that records observed behavior. An assessment checklist can be used by the teacher at the end of a unit to help to determine a student's progress. It can be used with the student so that the student is aware of his or her progress in a specific area. When the assessment checklists are used, the checklists of observed behavior and the anecdotal records should be used as supplementary information or as aids in verifying the student's rating. If rating scales are used, it is important that criteria be set up beforehand that help teachers to determine what rating to give to a particular student. For example if a student consistently answers questions incorrectly that are based on his or her textbook assignments, that student would receive a rating of 3 on a scale of 1 to 3 in which 1 is the highest and 3 is the lowest. If the student almost never makes an error in answering questions, that student should receive a rating of 1 on a scale of 1 to 3. If a student sometimes answers questions incorrectly, the student would receive a rating of 2 on a scale of 1 to 3. Here is an example of a group checklist with a rating scale.

Textbook Questions Rating Scale (Group)

	Carol	John	Sharon	Seth
	1 2 3	1 2 3	1 2 3	1 2 3
Chapter 1				
Chapter 2				
Chapter 3				
Chapter 4				
and so on				

OTHER HELPFUL STUDENT BEHAVIOR STUDY TECHNIQUES

Direct observation is helpful in gaining information about students, but there are some important student characteristics that cannot be gained through direct observation. Student attitudes or feelings and student interests are examples of essential student characteristics that cannot be directly observed. Projective techniques, informal interviews, and inventory-type measures exist that can help teachers learn about those aspects of students that cannot be directly observed. Achievement tests can help teachers learn about the amount of knowledge students have, and intelligence tests can help teachers learn about the student's rate of learning or his or her approximate potential for doing work in school; projective techniques, informal interviews, and interest inventories can help teachers understand their students better.

In all programs it is important for teachers to look at both the cognitive and noncognitive characteristics of their students because students' attitudes and interests will affect what they learn and whether they learn. Teachers must be cautioned against assuming the role of a psychologist or therapist and should avoid any suggestion that they are searching for underlying causes for a student's psychological behavior. Teachers should avoid administering any psychiatrically oriented type of instrument to their students.

Informal Interviews

The easiest way to learn about a student's likes or dislikes is to ask him or her. Content-area teachers, however, do not have as many opportunities to do this as the teachers in the lower grades who have students for the whole day. They could, however, set up special times during the day or week to meet with students for a consultation in the form of an informal conference. This is a good technique because it helps teachers build rapport with their students as well as gain information about them. This technique is, however, very time-consuming, especially for those content-area teachers who have from about 100 to 150 students, so other techniques are needed also.

Special Note:
Teachers should avoid setting up special interviews to discuss students' interests after school. Students may look upon this as a punishment of some sort. Of course, if teachers, by chance, meet some of their students after school and converse with them, this is an excellent opportunity to learn about their interests.

Interest Inventories

Interest inventories can be standardized or teacher-made. The purpose of an interest inventory is to help teachers learn about the likes and dislikes of their students regarding something. In an English class, teachers are particularly interested in a student's likes or dislikes regarding certain activities so that they can use this information to help stimulate students to read. For example, if teachers learn from an interest inventory that a student who is a reluctant reader likes mechanics and cars, they could choose books in this area at the student's reading ability level to help to stimulate him or her to read. (See Chapter 11, entitled "Reading for Appreciation: Gaining a Lifelong Habit.")

Interest inventories usually employ statements or questions or both to obtain information. The statement or questionnaire method enables the teacher to gain a great amount of information in a relatively short period of time, but there is a major difficulty with this method. When people fill out an inventory-type instrument, they are not always truthful. Many times individuals give "expected responses"; that is, they answer with responses that they feel the tester expects or wants rather than with responses based on what they actually do or based on how they really feel. Students who wish to create a favorable impression on their teacher especially may answer in an "expected direction." Teachers cannot completely do away with the faking that is done on inventory-type instruments, but they can help to control it. Teachers who have a good rapport with their students and who have a good affective environment in their classrooms will be able to gain the trust of their students. Before administering the inventory, these teachers can discuss with their students the purpose for the inventory and try to impress upon the students how important it is for them to try to put down exactly the way they feel rather than what they think they should put down.

Interest inventories can be individually administered, administered to a small group, or administered to the whole class. The interest inventory is usually used in a group situation, but it is individually administered if the student's reading problem prevents him or her from filling it out.

The interest inventory that follows is one that can be used by content-area teachers in the lower grades, as well as at the upper grades.

Name _____ Grade _____ or Subject _____

1. What topic do you like the best in this course?
2. What has been your favorite assignment so far this term?
3. What topic would you like to learn more about?
4. Have you done any extra reading this term?
5. If you answered yes to question 4, state in what area you did the extra reading.

Some teachers may want to learn about their students' attitudes toward receiving help in study skills. These teachers could present their students with a questionnaire that elicits information about their students' study and learning skills needs. Here are some items that could be used:

1. Do you have difficulty doing homework in this course?
2. Do you feel you need help in reading your textbook?
3. Do you feel more time should be spent on explaining homework assignments?
4. Would you like to have a tutor assigned to help you?
5. Do you need help in notetaking?
6. Do you need help in listening to lectures or talks?

Projective Techniques

Projective techniques are subtle procedures whereby individuals put themselves into a situation and reveal how they feel. Projective techniques are more revealing than the inventory-type methods that were discussed in the preceding section because in a projective technique the student is less likely to fake an answer. This is so because the student does not know what the *correct* or *best* answer is, for there is no correct or best answer. On a projective test students are more likely to give the answer that is natural for them and, as a result, reveal how they really feel.

There are, however, a number of problems with using projective techniques. The major problem has to do with the interpretation of the student's responses. Because of difficulty with interpretation, projective tests are not very trustworthy; however, projective techniques do have some definite benefits for teachers with students who have problems in a content-area course. Projective methods can help teachers gain some insights into the way students who have problems feel about themselves without the students' realizing this. Teachers may also gain information as to why the students think they have a problem. The teacher could then use this information to try to help the students.

Special Note:
Teachers should use projective tests with caution and not try to read too much into the students' responses. Also, teachers should not administer those tests that require clinical analysis by a psychologist.

The examples of projective tests that follow are simple ones that classroom teachers can administer to their students. These tests can be administered to a group or individually.

Sentence Completion Test The sentence completion test is one that is easy to administer in a relatively short period of time. Students are given some unfinished sentences that they are asked to complete as rapidly as possible. This kind of test can be given orally to those students who have difficulty reading or writing, or it can be given to a whole group at once. Here is an example of some typical sentences:

> Reading is . . .
> History is . . .
> Science is . . .
> Mathematics is . . .
> Homework is . . .
> Group work is . . .
> I believe I can . . .
> I prefer . . .
> My favorite . . .

Here is a sample of a short inventory that elementary school teachers teaching content areas in self-contained classrooms could give to their students:

Name _____

Grade _____

Directions: Read each incomplete sentence, and then complete only those that you feel apply to you.

1. I like _____ the best.

2. I like _____ the least.

3. I have difficulty doing _____ homework.

4. I never have difficulty doing _____ homework.

5. I like to read books about _____.

6. I have difficulty understanding material in _____.

7. I never have difficulty understanding material in _____.

Wish Test   The wish test is similar to the sentence completion test except that the phrase *I wish* precedes the incomplete sentence. Here are some typical examples:

> I wish I were . . .
> I wish I could . . .
> I wish reading were . . .
> I wish history were . . .
> I wish science were . . .
> I wish mathematics was . . .
> I wish assignments were . . .
> I wish textbooks were . . .
> I wish school were . . .
> I wish I were . . .
> I wish my teacher . . .

GRAPHIC SUMMARY OF CHAPTER

Here is a graphic summary of Chapter 13. If you have read the chapter, this graphic illustration should help you remember its main points. Under or beside each heading, you might want to jot down some of the information you recall, as well as some of the key concepts in this chapter. This can act as a good review. You can then check your key concepts against those that follow the graphic summary.

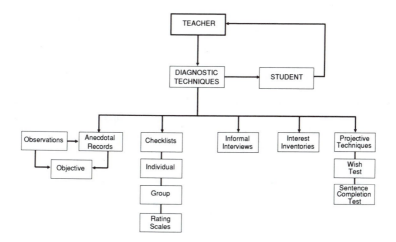

KEY CONCEPTS IN CHAPTER

- Observation is a technique for collecting data.
- Patterns of behavior must be observed before inferences can be made.
- Anecdotal records and checklists are means for recording behavior.
- Teachers should be on the lookout for certain patterns of usual behavior as well as unusual behavior.
- Anecdotal information is the recording of observed behavior as objectively as possible.
- Checklists are usually lists of behaviors that the observer checks as either present or absent.
- A checklist that uses a rating scale is actually an assessment instrument.
- Informal interviews are a viable means to learn about students' likes and dislikes.
- Interest inventories usually employ statements or questions to gain information about students.
- Projective techniques are subtle procedures whereby students put themselves into a situation that reveals how they feel.

SUGGESTIONS FOR THOUGHT QUESTIONS AND ACTIVITIES

1. Prepare a checklist that would give you information about a student's ability to answer questions and read in a content-area class.
2. You have been asked to give a talk to your colleagues concerning the use of observation techniques in content classes. What will you say?

3. Choose a content area, and then prepare a checklist to help you learn about students' attitudes toward the subject.

4. Choose a student from a content-area class. Observe the student over a period of time. Keep an anecdotal record of the student's behavior in the particular class.

5. Prepare an interest inventory that you could use in a particular content class to learn about the students' feelings toward the reading assignments they have to do in class.

SELECTED BIBLIOGRAPHY

BROZO, WILLIAM G. "Hiding Out in Secondary Content Classrooms: Coping Strategies of Unsuccessful Readers." *Journal of Reading* 33 (February 1990): 324–328.

CONOLEY, JANE CLOSE, and JACK J. KRAMER (eds.) *The Tenth Mental Measurements Yearbook*. Lincoln, Neb.: Buros Institute of Mental Measurement, University of Nebraska, 1989.

POPHAM, W. JAMES. *Modern Educational Measurement*, 2nd ed. Chapter 13: "Observations and Ratings," pp. 288–304. Englewood Cliffs, N.J.: Prentice Hall, 1990.

RUBIN, DOROTHY. *Diagnosis and Correction in Reading Instruction*, 2nd ed. Boston: Allyn & Bacon, 1991.

SWEETLAND, RICHARD C., and DANIEL J. KEYSER. *Tests*, 3rd ed. Austin, Tex.: PRO-ED, 1990.

14

Special Students in Content-Area Classrooms: Providing for Their Needs

All the children of all the people have a right to an education.

—PUBLIC LAW 94-142

INTRODUCTION: A SCENARIO

While in college, Frances J. Jackson majored in history with a minor in secondary education, and when she graduated she got a position as a social studies teacher in a large inner-city high school. When her friends heard where she was going to be teaching, they tried to talk her out of it. Even some of her professors were concerned for her.

Frances, or rather Fran as most of her friends call her, comes from the inner-city herself. She is a very intelligent and articulate young woman who has always wanted to teach. Also, she chose teaching as her profession because she knows firsthand how a good teacher can help turn a student's life around. She knows that a teacher can make a difference in one's life, especially for a student who does not have many advantages.

When school started in the fall, Fran was excited about teaching. She felt well-prepared because she had gone through what many consider a very good program, had many field experiences, and had a good grasp of her subject matter. She came filled with energy, excitement, idealism, and hope. What else could she need? How could anything go wrong? However, "the best laid plans of mice and men oft go awry."

Fran was prepared for almost everything. However, she was not prepared for the wide range of students she would have in her classes nor for the multicultural mix of students who had limited English proficiency. She also did not feel adequately equipped to deal with the mainstreamed students who were in some of her classes.

The first week of school was a learning experience for Fran. She became oriented to the school; she learned where it was safe to go and where it wasn't. She also got to know her students. Many of her students had trouble reading their history and geography textbooks, and many who could decode the words didn't understand what they were reading. Very few read a newspaper and knew elementary facts about their state or country.

Fran was aware of the studies on at-risk students. Her professors had discussed the dismal results of the National Assessment of Educational Progress reports, especially among minority students. However, she somehow had not expected it to be as bad as she found it. She felt unprepared to cope with so many students who had reading problems at the secondary level.

She had come from a poor home, but she had always loved school and worked hard to learn and get the most she could from her classes. She hadn't expected so many students to be cynical, uncaring, and filled with despair. It reminded her of the lines from Robert Frost's poem "Death of the

Hired Man." "Nothing to look backward to with pride, and nothing to look forward to with hope. Not now or never any different."

After the first month of school, Fran was exhausted and disappointed, but she was not ready to give up. She would bang on doors and get the help she needed. It's now the middle of the term, and she is still being promised special help and smaller classes next term.

Fran is a realist. She knows she needs help now, so she went back to her college and talked to her former professors. She asked them to recommend books and possible techniques she could use in her social studies classes. Fran also met with the reading specialist in her school to discuss with him some of the things she could do to help her students who had reading problems.

Fran has learned that no teacher—whether he or she is teaching in an elementary school or in secondary school—is immune from having students mainstreamed into his or her classroom or from having students who have reading problems. The more teachers know about these students, the better able they will be to adapt the content material to their needs. (Students who have physical impairments, such as orthopedic problems, usually do not require any special curricular changes.)

This chapter will present information on borderline children (slow learners) and gifted students because these two groups are usually found in regular classrooms, as well as those who may be mainstreamed into regular classrooms. Information will also be presented on individualizing instruction for students with reading problems to help them read their content books.

It is hoped that this kind of information will help Fran and others like her.

KEY QUESTIONS

After reading this chapter, you should be able to answer the following questions:

1. What is Public Law 94-142?
2. What is mainstreaming?
3. Who is the "average" child?
4. What are some of the characteristics of borderline students?
5. What types of provisions should teachers make for borderline students?
6. What are some of the characteristics of gifted students?
7. What types of provisions should teachers make for their gifted students?
8. Who are the exceptional students?

9. What does "learning disability" mean?
10. How can teachers individualize instruction in content areas?
11. Who are the at-risk students?
12. How can teachers use computers to help at-risk students?
13. How can teachers incorporate learning centers in content classes?
14. How can teachers use peer tutoring in content classes?

KEY TERMS IN CHAPTER

You should pay special attention to the following key terms:

at-risk students
average children
borderline children (slow learners)
exceptional children
IQ gifted children

learning center
learning disability
mainstreaming
mental age
peer tutoring
Public Law 94-142

WHAT IS PUBLIC LAW 94-142?

Public Law 94-142 advocates a free appropriate education for all children in the least restrictive environment. This has brought to the fore the importance of the uniqueness of each child. In the regular classroom there is usually a wide range of ability levels, which generally includes the borderline (slow-learning) and the gifted child.[1] As a result of Public Law 94-142, exceptional children may be mainstreamed into the regular classroom. In order to be able to work with such children, all teachers, not just special education teachers, must become more knowledgeable of exceptional children. The more teachers know about the children with whom they work, the better able they will be to provide for their individual differences and needs.

THE MENTAL AGE SPAN IN CONTENT-AREA CLASSES

The mental age span in content-area classes varies according to the class and the grade level. The teacher in a regular self-contained classroom in an elementary school usually has students with similar chronological ages but with a mental age span of about five years. It could be more. Mental age

---

[1]Although gifted children are classified as exceptional children, they are generally found in the regular classroom. Borderline (slow-learning) children are not classified as exceptional children in the revised AAMD (American Association on Mental Deficiency) definition.

(MA) refers to a child's present level of development; it helps to indicate the child's present readiness. As children progress through the grades, the span between the borderline (slow-learning), average, and gifted child becomes wider.

However, in junior high and particularly in high school, self-selection takes place whereby a number of classes become more homogeneous and have a narrower ability level. This would be particularly true for the sciences and mathematics. Students who choose to major in science and mathematics usually have similar interests and must have a certain ability level. Obviously, you would not find slow learners in advanced science and mathematics classes, unless, of course, they've been misplaced.

The wide range of ability levels would usually be found in foundation courses and in the social sciences. However, as stated earlier, no one is immune from mainstreaming because it is possible for some exceptional students to be mainstreamed in advanced courses as well as in others. For example, even though mentally retarded students would not be mainstreamed into advanced courses, students with physical handicaps could be.

Special Note:
It is important to note that students with similar mental ages and different chronological ages will not have similar mental abilities. For example, a child with a chronological age of ten and a mental age of six has an IQ of 60. A child with an IQ of 60 will not progress in reading like a child of five with a mental age of six and a half, who has an IQ of 130.

WHO IS THE AVERAGE CHILD?

The first question that comes to mind whenever anyone labels someone an average child is: Is there really an "average" child? Actually there probably is not. Every child is an individual and as such is unique and special. However, for research purposes we tend to look upon the average child as that individual who scores in the IQ range from 90 to 110. Studies are based on averages. Averages are necessary as criteria or points of reference. Only after we have determined the criteria for "average" can we talk about "above or below average."

WHO ARE THE EXCEPTIONAL CHILDREN?

The phrase exceptional children is usually applied to those children who deviate so much from "average" children that they require special attention. "These children require special education because they are markedly different from most children in one or more of the following ways: they may have mental retardation, learning disabilities, emotional disturbance, physical disabilities, disordered speech or language, impaired hearing, impaired sight, or special gifts or talents."[2]

Even though the emphasis on exceptional children has been on differences, there is a concerted effort today to try also to focus on their similarities. "Exceptional children are not different from 'average' children in every way."[3] It is important that teachers be aware of these differences and similarities so that they can provide for these students' needs if they are mainstreamed into a regular classroom. A discussion of some of the things content-area teachers can do to provide for mainstreamed students is given in this book; however, for an in-depth discussion of exceptional children, students should refer to special education textbooks (see "Selected Bibliography").

Learning Disabilities

The definition of learning disabilities is one that needs special attention because there is so much confusion concerning this term. Researchers have found that the characteristics of children labeled "learning disabled" vary so much that it is impossible to list common characteristics. The way the term is used seems to vary not only from state to state but from school district to school district within a state.

Although there is a great amount of confusion and controversy concerning the term *learning disability* and although studies have shown that there is in existence a multitude of definitions and synonyms for this term, there is one definition that is most widely accepted and acted on. The definition that is usually given for learning disability is that endorsed by the federal government in 1977:

> "Special learning disability" means a disorder in one or more of the basic psychological processes involved in understanding or in using language spoken or written which may manifest itself in an imperfect ability to listen, think, speak, read, write, spell, or do mathematical calculations. The term includes such conditions as perceptual handicaps, brain injury, minimal brain dysfunction, dyslexia, and developmental aphasia. The term does not include children who have learning problems which are primarily the result of visual, hearing, or motor handicaps, of mental retardation, emotional disturbance, or environmental, cultural or economic disadvantage.[4]

From this definition there does not appear to be any logical explanation for an individual's learning disability. Also, the learning disability may

---

[2]Daniel P. Hallahan and James M. Kauffman, *Exceptional Children: Introduction to Special Education*, 4th ed. (Englewood Cliffs, N.J.: Prentice Hall, 1988), p. 6.

[3]Ibid., p. 2.

[4]Federal Register, "Procedures for Evaluating Specific Learning Disabilities," Washington, D.C.: Department of Health, Education, and Welfare, December 29, 1977, p. 65083.

go undiagnosed because the student is of average or above-average intelligence, so the teacher thinks the student is either lazy or lacks discipline.

Teachers should be especially vigilant in content-area classes for those students who are of average or above-average ability who are having some kind of learning problems because these students may have a special learning disability. Teachers should refer these students for special testing. Teachers must, however, be leery of labeling youngsters as learning disabled without adequate and substantive documentation. For example, the Black English trial in Ann Arbor showed that the school district had labeled the Green Road children as "learning disabled" and "emotionally impaired" without due consideration to their racial and linguistic backgrounds. Unfortunately, "the staff was handicapped by their inadequate knowledge of the children's characteristics and the biased nature of the tests they were using."[5] An example is given whereby the "speech therapists weren't aware that the Wepman test included a number of oppositions that are mergers in the Black English vernacular; pin vs. pen, sheaf vs. sheath, clothe vs. clove, and so forth."[6] (See "Dialect and Language Differences" in Chapter 2.)

MAINSTREAMING

The impetus of mainstreaming was triggered by Public Law 94-142. Public Law 94-142 is a federal law that is designed to give handicapped children a "free appropriate public education." It requires state and local governments to provide identification programs, a special education, and related services such as transportation, testing, diagnosis, and treatment for children with speech handicaps, hearing impairments, visual handicaps, physical disabilities, emotional disturbances, learning disabilities, and mental retardation handicaps. Public Law 94-142 also requires that whenever possible, handicapped students must be placed in regular classrooms. *Mainstreaming* is the placement of handicapped children in the least restrictive educational environment that will meet their needs.

Handicapped children who are moved to a regular classroom are supposed to be very carefully screened. Only those who seem able to benefit from being in a least restrictive environment are supposed to be put into one. The amount of time that a handicapped child spends in a regular classroom and the area in which the child participates in the regular classroom depend on the individual child.

For mainstreaming to be successful, regular classroom teachers must be properly prepared for this role, and teachers must enlist the aid and cooperation of every student in their class. Classroom teachers must pre-

[5]William Labov, "Objectivity and Commitment in Linguistic Science: The Case of the Black English Trial in Ann Arbor," *Language in Society* 11 (August 1982): 168.
[6]Ibid., pp. 168–169.

pare their students for the mainstreamed child by giving them some background and knowledge about the child. The amount and type of information given will, of course, vary with the grade level. Regular classroom teachers should also have the students involved in some of the planning and implementation of the program for the mainstreamed child.

For example, if English teachers are expecting physically handicapped children to be admitted to their classes, they can help to prepare their students by having them read some books that portray a physically handicapped child in a sensitive and perceptive manner. Teachers might read some excerpts from Helen Keller's *The Story of My Life* or Marie Killilea's book *Karen*. After reading the excerpts, teachers can engage the students in a discussion of the handicapped child's struggles, fears, hopes, concerns, goals, and dreams. Teachers can then attempt to help the children in their class recognize that they have feelings, hopes, and fears similar to many handicapped children's. Teachers should also help their students to understand that a child with a physical handicap does not necessarily have a mental handicap. As a matter of fact, many handicapped persons are very intelligent and able to make many contributions to society. The teacher can then discuss with the children how they think they can make the new child who is coming to their class feel at home. The teacher might also use special films and television programs to initiate interest in the handicapped and to help gain better insights about them.

Instructional Provisions for Mainstreamed Students

Besides preparing the children in the regular classroom for the mainstreamed child, an individualized program must be developed for each mainstreamed child in cooperation with the child's parents, the special education teacher, or consultants. The program should be one that provides a favorable learning experience for both the handicapped child and the regular classroom students. That is, the integration of a handicapped child should not take away from the program of the regular classroom children.

Children who have orthopedic and other health impairments do not need any special provisions as far as basic reading skills, textbook assignments, or additional instructional materials are concerned. Some students will need special furniture, and their achievement may have to be monitored by using tape recorders; that is, the tests would have to be given orally, and the student would record answers on a tape. Students with speech impairments and students who have emotional disturbances also need no special adjustments except that children with emotional disturbances need an environment that is calm, low in tension, and high in motivation, whereas students with speech impairments need help in making oral reports, so committee assignments should be used for this.

Students who have visual impairment and hearing impairment or deafness will need a number of special adjustments. Students with visual problems should be given front row seating, and a "buddy" system should be established for them. The "buddy" would be responsible for making carbon copies of notes and of chalkboard assignments. Students with visual impairments do not need any special help in basic skills for mastering the content concepts, but they do need help in visually reading the textbook and other instructional materials. The textbook must be either read orally to the students, or the students themselves can read it with a magnifier. Some instructional material can be reproduced in large print or put on tape. (This is done with the permission of the publisher.) Students with visual impairments should have their examinations orally given, recorded on tape, enlarged on a closed-circuit TV, or translated into Braille. Students with hearing impairment, like students with visual impairment, need a number of special provisions. These students need front row seating so that they can lip-read, and those who are deaf may need a special sign language translator. Students with hearing impairment usually need very well-outlined lesson presentations and the rephrasing of complex sentences, as well as special guides to help them interpret what they are reading. Captioned films for the deaf should be used whenever possible, and students with hearing impairment should be assigned to a committee for any type of oral reporting.

Another group of exceptional students who are being mainstreamed into regular classrooms and who need a number of special provisions are students with learning disabilities. Such students require a structured daily schedule and, like students with hearing disabilities, they need well-outlined lessons, rephrasing of complex sentences, and special guides to help them interpret what they are reading. These students also need their written test questions to be rephrased and to be assigned to a committee for oral reports.

THE BORDERLINE CHILD OR THE "SLOW LEARNER"

The borderline child is usually described as a dull average child who is borderline in his or her intellectual functioning. These children's IQ scores range from approximately 70 to 85. As a result, they generally have difficulty doing schoolwork. Borderline children are not, however, equally slow in all their activities or abnormal in all their characteristics. It is difficult at times to differentiate borderline children and children with specific learning disabilities from underachievers produced by disadvantaged environments.[7]

Borderline children, who have many times been referred to as *slow learners*, are between the "average" child and the mentally retarded child.

[7]Samuel A. Kirk, Sister Joanne Marie Kliebhan, and Janet W. Lerner, *Teaching Reading to Slow and Disabled Learners* (Boston: Houghton Mifflin, 1978), p. 3.

Special emphasis is being given to this group of children because most classroom teachers have children in this IQ range in their regular classrooms, but many teachers may not know how to provide for them.

Providing Instruction for the Borderline Child

Teachers in regular classrooms have many times been frustrated because they have had children who do not seem to be able to learn material that is considered "average" for the specific grade level. Not only is the teacher frustrated, but so is the child. A child who according to an individual IQ test scores in the 70 to 85 range would have difficulty working at grade level. Because of social promotion (children are promoted according to chronological age rather than achievement) children are moved along each year into a higher grade. As slow learners go through the grades, their problems generally become more pronounced and compounded unless they are given special attention.

The term slow learner is probably a misnomer, because the term implies that a child needs more time to get a concept, but eventually will acquire it. Actually, there are some concepts that slow learners cannot acquire no matter how long they work on them because slow learners usually cannot work in the abstract. Obviously, the teacher should not use inductive or deductive teaching techniques in working with slow learners. Slow learners generally can learn material if it is presented at a concrete level. Slow learners usually must be given many opportunities to go over the same concept; slow learners must continue practice in an area beyond the point where they think that they know it, in order to *overlearn* it. The practice should be varied and interesting to stimulate the students. Many games and gamelike activities could be used for this purpose. Slow learners have a short attention span, so learning tasks should be broken down into small discrete steps. Slow learners generally need close supervision, and they may have difficulty working independently. Distractions must be kept at a minimum, and each task should be very exactly defined and explained. It is necessary to define short-range goals, which slow learners can accomplish, to give them a sense of achievement. Slow learners are usually set in their ways, and once they learn something in one way, they will be very rigid about changing.

The teacher should recognize that individual differences exist within groups as well as between groups. Obviously, there will be individual differences among slow learners.

The Borderline Child in Content-Area Classes

Many students who are slow learners are found in the secondary schools, and, as already stated, these students are in regular classes. These students, however, are not able to work or read at grade level, and many attend remedial reading classes because they have many reading problems.

Content-area teachers must work very closely with the reading specialist to help these students gain many of the skills that they need to survive in the world of school and in the outside world. (See "The Reading Specialist: An Important Resource for Content-Area Teachers" in Chapter 12 for a scenario describing a reading specialist at the secondary school.) Teachers must provide extremely structured guides for these students, and the students need to follow a structured daily procedure. They need expanded interpretation of whatever concepts are being taught, and the material must be written in simple sentences without any abstract words. The lessons for these students must also be very easy to follow. All skills that are needed to attain certain concepts must be directly taught in very simple clear language, and students must be helped to see exactly where the skills apply to the content material. Teachers should use as many concrete examples as they can, and they should not present vocabulary words in isolation. Whenever possible, pictorial representations, real objects, or actions should be used to help student attain vocabulary words.

Special Note:
Students with an IQ of about 70, at the beginning of the ninth grade, according to the Bond and Tinker formula for reading expectancy, should be reading at approximately a 6.6 grade level.

Bond and Tinker formula:

$$(\frac{IQ}{100} \times \text{Years of Reading Instruction}) + 1 = \text{Reading Expectancy at End of Year}[8]$$

The Bond and Tinker formula is an idealized one for students with low IQs. The chances are high that the students are not reading according to their ability level and that they have a number of other problems. It's obvious that these students cannot do ninth grade work and that they need special help.

GIFTED CHILDREN

Gifted children fall into the category of exceptional children because this group of children deviates greatly from "average" children.

When one talks about the gifted, immediately visions of small children wearing horn-rimmed glasses and carrying encyclopedias come to mind. This is a myth. There are many definitions of the gifted. In recent years the definition of the "gifted" has been broadened to include not only the verbally gifted with an IQ above 132 on an individual IQ test such as the Stanford-Binet Intelligence Scale but also those individuals whose performance in any line of socially useful endeavor is consistently superior.

[8]The Bond and Tinker formula begins at grade one; that is, at the end of grade one the child is considered to have been in school one year.

Marland's national definition in a congressional report alerts educators to the multifaceted aspects of giftedness:

> Gifted and talented children are those identified by professionally qualified persons who by virtue of outstanding abilities are capable of high performance. These are children who require differentiated educational programs and services beyond those normally provided by the regular school program in order to realize their contribution to self and society.
>
> Children capable of high performance include those with demonstrated achievement and/or potential ability in any of the following areas:
>
> 1. General intellectual ability.
> 2. Specific academic aptitude.
> 3. Creative or productive thinking.
> 4. Leadership ability.
> 5. Visual and performing arts.
> 6. Psychomotor ability.[9]

Characteristics of Gifted Children

Gifted children, on the average, are socially, emotionally, physically, and intellectually superior to "average" children in the population. Gifted children have, on the average, superior general intelligence, a desire to know, originality, common-sense, willpower and perseverance, a desire to excel, self-confidence, prudence and forethought, and a good sense of humor, among a host of other admirable traits.

Gifted children's language development is usually very advanced. They generally have a large stock of vocabulary and delight in learning new words. Many have learned to read before they came to school; they usually have wide-ranging interests that they pursue in extensive depth, and they are usually voracious readers. However, without guidance, many gifted students will often not read very challenging books.

Although many gifted students enjoy writing and engage in writing frequently and for their own pleasure, some may lack basic writing skills. This happens because it is often taken for granted that highly able students have all the basic skills that they need at their fingertips. This is not so. Gifted children, like all other children, must attain these skills.

Instructional Provisions for Gifted Students

Gifted students need special attention because of their precocious learning abilities. However, when gifted children are not given special attention, they still usually manage to work on grade level. As a result, gifted children are often ignored. Regrettably, gifted children are actually the most ne-

[9]S.P. Marland, *Education of the Gifted and the Talented* (Washington, D.C.: U.S. Office of Education, 1972), p. 10.

glected of all exceptional children. Attention is given to those who have "more need." Margaret Mead, the renowned anthropologist, has written about this attitude toward the gifted, which is still applicable today:

> Whenever the rise to success cannot be equated with preliminary effort, abstinence and suffering, it tends to be attributed to "luck," which relieves the spectator from according the specially successful person any merit. . . . In American education, we have tended to reduce the gift to a higher I.Q.—thus making it a matter of merely a little more on the continuity scale, to insist on putting more money and effort in bringing the handicapped child "up to par" as an expression of fair play and "giving everyone a break" and to disallow special gifts. By this refusal to recognize special gifts, we have wasted and dissipated, driven into apathy or schizophrenia, uncounted numbers of gifted children. If they learn easily, they are penalized for having nothing to do; if they excel in some outstanding way, they are penalized as being conspicuously better than the peer group, and teachers warn the gifted child, "Yes, you can do that, it's much more interesting than what the others are doing. But, remember, the rest of the class will dislike you for it.[10]

Gifted children, like all other children, need guidance and instruction based on their interests, needs, and ability levels. Although gifted children are intellectually capable of working at high levels of abstraction, unless they receive appropriate instruction to gain needed skills, they may not be able to realize their potential. Gifted children should not be subjected to unnecessary drill and repetition. Gifted children gain abstract concepts quickly. They usually enjoy challenge and have long attention spans.

It is interesting to note, however, that the kinds of activities that stimulate gifted students are not significantly different from those that are used in teaching other students. For example, two doctoral dissertations, which focused on the literature and composition objectives of the Pittsburgh Scholars Program in English, for Grades ten and eleven, present thirty different "Strategies for Teaching Scholars English." The strategies that they present are those that most teachers use. They include such techniques as teacher lecture, class discussion, independent project by a group or individual, vocabulary enrichment activities, and so on.[11]

Although the strategies may not be significantly different from those used by teachers for other students, the manner in which the material is presented should be guided by knowledge of the characteristics of gifted students. The atmosphere in the classroom should be one in which gifted students are respected as persons who are capable of independent work and leadership, and the subject matter that is presented should allow for

[10]Margaret Mead, "The Gifted Child in the American Culture of Today," *The Journal of Teacher Education* 5 (September 1954): 211–212.

[11]Natalie Apple, "A Study of the Literature Objectives of the Pittsburgh Scholars Program in English, Grades 10 and 11," Doctoral dissertation, University of Pittsburgh, 1979; Patricia Tierney, "A Study of the Composition Objectives of the Pittsburgh Scholars Program in English, Grades 10 and 11," Doctoral dissertation, University of Pittsburgh, 1979.

student involvement, choice, and interaction. Also, the instruction for gifted students should focus on those activities that involve the higher levels of the cognitive domain; that is, gifted students should spend the most time in activities that require analysis, synthesis, and evaluation. Gifted students should also be encouraged by their teachers to be intelligent risk-takers, to defend their ideas, to delve deeply into problems, to seek alternate solutions to problems, to follow through on hunches, and to dream the impossible dream.

AT-RISK STUDENTS

At-risk students are those students who are in danger of failing in school because they lack basic literacy skills. These children often come from low socioeconomic status homes, and when they enter school, they are usually already behind those children who come from middle-class homes.

In a number of chapters in this book we have discussed the importance of learning to read in the early grades. We have also stated that the longer a student remains a nonreader, the more difficult it is to help that child get back to grade level, let alone his or her ability level. These students are a challenge to all educators!

The term "at risk" or "high risk" is heard quite often today: however, the surfacing of another label will not make these students' problems go away. Labels cannot do that! Efforts in the right direction can. Children who come from educationally disadvantaged homes need early identification and special programs that emphasize the language arts beginning in preschool or kindergarten. They need intervention as early as possible And this intervention must continue throughout the grades.

Teachers at all grade levels must recognize those students who lack learning to read as well as reading to learn skills. "Students are at risk in reading when they have developed limited cognitive skill in handling the demands inherent in the task of learning from texts. However, another factor, metacognitive in nature, is just as likely to create an at-risk situation for students—a lack of knowledge of their own reading processes."[12] In other words, not only must students who have reading problems want to get help, they must also recognize "when and why they are not comprehending."[13] This is not easy because years of failure have severely damaged these young people's self-images. They do everything and anything to avoid print material, which further compounds their problem.

Teachers can try to enhance these students' self-concept by providing them with a tailored program that will ensure success. A directed approach

---

[12]Richard T. Vacca and Nancy D. Padak, "Who's at Risk in Reading?" *Journal of Reading* 33 (April 1990): 487.

[13]Ibid., p. 488.

to teaching reading using relevant content material would be especially effective for these students. (See Chapter 1.) In addition, computer programs can be very helpful if the students are properly oriented to the program and special provisions are provided for them (see "Individualizing Instruction with Computer Programs, Reading, and At-Risk Students" later in this chapter).

Content-area teachers must be patient with their high-risk students and seek all the help they can get, especially from the reading specialist. Also, if these students are involved in special reading programs, and many are, the program must be suited to the individual student so that the student can relate what he is learning in the special reading program to the subjects he or she is taking. Obviously, the reading specialist and the content-area teacher must work together.

It's good that the term at risk is focusing attention on the problems of these students; however, the term at risk has risks of its own. Teachers "must take special care that the term 'at risk' is not used as a prediction of failure, that it does not become a negative label that perpetuates a self-fulfilling prophecy."[14]

INDIVIDUALIZING INSTRUCTION IN CONTENT AREAS

Teachers in content areas can use individualized instruction to help slow learners and at-risk students acquire certain skills they may need and to provide special enrichment for gifted students. (Individualized instruction can, of course, be used for other students also.) There are many different types of individualized programs, which range from informal ones developed by teachers to those that are commercially produced. It is beyond the scope of this book to give a description of the various organizational patterns or the individualized programs that exist; books have been written on these. However, a brief description of some of the characteristics of both teacher-made and commercially produced individualized programs would be useful.

Teacher-Made Programs

Informal programs can vary from teacher to teacher. However, most of the programs usually use instructional objectives, which are taken from curriculum guides, study guides, and instructors' manuals. To accomplish the objectives, the teachers usually select activities and materials from a number of sources, the teacher and student confer periodically, and the teacher keeps a check on the student's progress by keeping adequate records.

[14]Linda Gambrell, guest ed., "Journal of Reading: A Themed Issue on Reading Instruction for At-Risk Students," *Journal of Reading* 33 (April 1990): 485.

Commercially Produced (Published) Programs

A variety of different commercial programs exist, and they have a number of things in common. Most of the programs use instructional objectives for each curriculum area. Usually each curriculum area is divided into small discrete learning steps based on graduated levels of difficulty. A variety of activities and materials generally combined in a multimedia approach is used, and usually built into the commercial programs is a system of record-keeping, progress tests, and checklists.

Some Common Characteristics of Individualized, Teacher-Made, and Commercially Produced Programs

In almost all individualized programs, students work at their own pace. Learning outcomes in individualized programs are based on the needs, interests, and ability levels of the students. Activities are interesting and challenging, and they usually employ a multimedia approach. The activities are based on desired outcomes, students work independently, and there is some system of record-keeping.

For Whom Does Individualized Instruction Work? Students who have short attention spans, who have difficulty following directions, and who have reading problems will obviously have difficulty working independently.

FIGURE 14-1. This teacher meets individually with students to provide for their specific needs.

Teachers will have to help these students set limited, short-range objectives that can be reached in a short period of time. For those students with severe reading problems, the teacher will have to rely very heavily on audio tapes to convey directions. Students who are slow learners (see sections on slow learners) will also need special help; special programs will have to be devised for them. Students who have no discernible achievement problems but who have never worked in an individualized program before will also have difficulty unless they are properly oriented to the program. (*Note:* Do not confuse the need to work independently in an individualized program with the need to provide for the individual differences of students in the class. For example, a student who is a slow learner will usually have difficulty working independently, but the teacher still needs to provide an individual program for this student based on his or her special needs.)

Some Common Sense About Individual Programs Preparing individual outcomes and a specially tailored program for each student in each content area can be a monumental task. Therefore, what is generally done is to use outcomes and programs already prepared, either teacher-made or commercially made, and then match these to the needs of individual students. For such an individualized program to work effectively, teachers must have a variety of individualized programs available for their students, and they must know the individual needs of their students. (See section on learning centers.)

It is also important to state that the individualized program should not be the student's whole program. Students need to work in groups and need teacher contact and interaction, as well as peer contact and interaction; they need a variety of methods and materials to sustain their interest; they need continuous diagnosis and evaluation; and they, as well as their content-area teachers, must be considered as partners in the quest for knowledge.

Learning Centers in Content Classes

Many content classes use learning centers as an integral part of their instructional program. It is one way to individualize a student's instruction. Usually, a special area in the content classroom is set aside for the learning center. The materials to stock a learning center may be either teacher-made or commercially produced. Some of the requirements for a good learning center are as follows:

1. Is in an easily accessible area.
2. Is attractive.
3. Provides for students on different maturational levels.
4. Has clearly stated behavioral objectives so that students know what they are supposed to accomplish (outcomes).

5. Provides for group and team activities as well as individual activities.
6. Allows for student input.
7. Asks probing questions.
8. Has some humorous materials.
9. Provides activities that call for divergent thinking.
10. Uses a multimedia approach. (Includes such instructional materials as textbooks, library books, programmed materials, sets of pictures, realia [real things], commercial and teacher-prepared audio tapes, filmstrips, film, TV, radio, tape recorders, maps, globes, manipulative materials, and games.)
11. Has carefully worked out learning sequences to accomplish objectives.
12. Has provisions for evaluation and record-keeping.

Designing a Learning Center   Students in a political science class are discussing propaganda techniques. The teacher would like students to be able to recognize these techniques in reading the political speeches that they are studying. Here is the learning center that this teacher designed for the students.

In the following plan for developing a learning center, notice the similarity to the development of a lesson plan.

1. Motivating technique: necessary to attract attention. This could be realia (real objects), pictures, humorous sayings, and so on.
   Example: Familiar commercials with pictures are listed on learning center bulletin board (propaganda learning center).
2. Instructional objectives: necessary so that students know what they are supposed to accomplish (outcomes).
   Examples: (propaganda learning center)
   a. Define *propaganda.*
   b. Define *bias.*
   c. Explain what is meant by a propaganda technique.
   d. List five propaganda techniques.
   e. Describe each of the five propaganda techniques you chose and give an example of each.
   f. Read a given political speech, and state what propaganda techniques the politician uses.
   g. Explain the politician's position on three major issues.
   h. Team up with another student and, using a propaganda technique, write a political speech to influence your peers to vote for a particular candidate.
3. Directions to accomplish objectives: necessary so that students know what to do to accomplish objectives. Step-by-step instructions are

given for the students to accomplish the objectives. Students are told to

a. read instructional objectives so that you know what you are supposed to accomplish.

b. go to file drawer one, which contains the learning activities to accomplish objective one.

c. complete each learning activity and record your progress on each before you go on to the next objective. (This depends on the learning center. In some learning centers, the students must accomplish the objectives in sequence; in others this is not necessary. For the propaganda learning center, some of the learning objectives must be accomplished in order. Obviously, before students can write a political speech using propaganda and bias, they must be able to define *propaganda* and *bias*, they must be able to explain propaganda techniques, they must be able to recognize them, and they must be able to give examples of them.)

Summary of Steps in Preparing a Learning Center

1. Select a topic.
2. State objectives.
3. Identify experiences.
4. Collect materials.
5. Prepare activities.
6. Make schedules (which students use center and when).
7. Prepare record forms (each student using center must have one).

Peer Tutoring

Many times teachers in content classes resort to peer tutoring to help those students who are having special problems. Peer tutoring can be especially useful in working with slow learners. Peer tutoring benefits both the tutor and the tutee. Peer tutoring usually helps the student who has been encountering difficulty in an area to gain skill in the area and also to gain confidence in working with the skill. It also helps the tutee feel more at ease about participating in a large group. The tutor also gains because it helps him or her to overlearn the skill that is being taught, and it helps to enhance his or her self-concept. The tutor is looked upon with prestige and respect by the teacher and his or her peers.

Individualizing Instruction with Computer Programs, Reading, and At-Risk Students

In a number of chapters in this book, we have discussed the place of computer software in the content areas. This topic is being presented here again because microcomputers are an especially effective way to individualize instruction in all classrooms. Computers are good motivating techniques; students like the privacy the computer affords and, in particular, its non-judgmental component.

There are a few problems, however. One, which has already been noted in an earlier chapter, is that computers are more likely to be used to teach about computers rather than to help students in content areas (see "Computer Software and Social Studies," in Chapter 7). Another is that "there are clear racial/ethnic differences in computer competence, favoring White students over Black and Hispanic students. These differences are present even between students who have comparable levels of experience. But the differences are accentuated by greater experience with computers among White students."[15] In addition, at-risk students, those who come from low socioeconomic homes, are at a decided disadvantage over other students when it comes to computer competence and experience.[16] This is unfortunate because it is these students who can especially benefit from this excellent resource if properly used.

One educator, who used a number of reading and test-preparation software with selected at-risk students, reported some very encouraging results.[17] "These students saw the computer as an opportunity to explore without fear of failure, thereby developing a sense of self-control, inner power, and autonomy with their learning."[18]

However, it is still the software that is supreme, and this is the major problem. There is not enough reading and content-area software available for at-risk students. Many of the programs are at too high a level for them. A good idea would be to use some of the steps from the Guide for Using a Directed Reading Approach in Reading Content Material, which was presented in Chapter 1, to prepare students for the program.

The following steps describe what one teacher does when orienting high-risk students to a particular program.

STEP 1: Mrs. Miller previews every program so she is familiar with its format and content. In doing this, she notes any technical and nontechnical terms that might cause problems for her students. In addition, she notes whether the concept level is at the experiential level of her students.

STEP 2: She presents the terms to her students and helps them gain an understanding of them.

STEP 3: She discusses with the students the key concepts which they will be using. She then builds topic information.

---

[15]Michael E. Martinez and Nancy A. Mead, *Computer Competence: The First National Assessment*, National Assessment of Educational Progress, (Princeton, N.J.: Educational Testing Service, 1988): 6.

[16]Ibid.

[17]Shelley B. Wepner, "Computers, Reading Software, and At-Risk Eighth Graders," *Journal of Reading* 34 (December/January 1990/1991): 264–266.

[18]Ibid., p. 265.

STEP 4: Mrs. Miller orients the students to the program by setting purposes for them and by making sure they understand the instructions.

STEP 5: Mrs. Miller checks on her students when they are working on the computer to make sure they understand what they are doing, and she keeps records on exactly what programs the students are working on. Each student is also responsible for keeping records on the programs he or she is using.

The students in Mrs. Miller's class are doing very well because this teacher takes nothing for granted. She has spent the necessary time to make sure the students know how to access the computer and follow instructions. She has also helped prepare them for the program. Mrs. Miller is using the computer as part of her teaching-learning program rather than as an appendage to it.

GRAPHIC SUMMARY OF CHAPTER

Here is a graphic summary of Chapter 14. If you have read the chapter, this graphic illustration should help you remember its main points. Under or beside each heading, you might want to jot down some of the information you recall, as well as some of the key concepts in this chapter. This can act as a good review. You can then check your key concepts against those that follow the graphic summary.

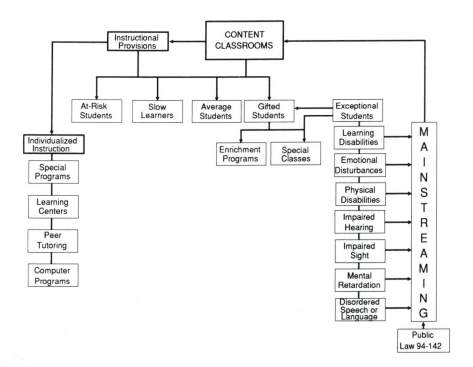

KEY CONCEPTS IN CHAPTER

- Public Law 94-142 advocates a free appropriate education for all children in the least restrictive environment.
- As students progress in school, the mental age span among borderline, average, and gifted students increases.
- Exceptional students are those who deviate so much from the average that they require special attention.
- Borderline students are not considered exceptional children.
- Borderline children are those whose IQs range approximately from 70 to 85.
- Gifted students are classified as exceptional children.
- Gifted children are those whose IQs are above 132 on an IQ test such as the Stanford Binet, or whose performance in any line of socially useful endeavor is consistently superior.
- "Average children" are those whose IQs range approximately from 90 to 110.
- The definition of *learning disability* varies greatly.
- Teachers must be very cautious about labeling students.
- Mainstreaming was triggered by Public Law 94-142.
- For mainstreaming to be successful, content-area teachers and their students must be properly prepared.
- At-risk students are those who are in danger of failing in school.
- Individualized instruction can accommodate the needs of special students.
- Microcomputers are an effective way to individualize instruction in the classroom.
- Learning centers are used in individualized programs.
- Peer tutoring helps both the tutor and the tutee.

SUGGESTIONS FOR THOUGHT QUESTIONS AND ACTIVITIES

1. You have been told that a student with a hearing impairment will be mainstreamed into your content area class. What will you do to prepare for this student?
2. Observe a class in which there is a learning disabled student. Prepare a special guide for this student that will help him or her master the concepts being taught in class.
3. Do the same as in item 2 for a student who is a slow learner.
4. Observe a class in which a student has been mainstreamed. Discuss

with the teacher what special provisions have been made for this student.

5. Discuss with the principal of a school how many and which exceptional children have been mainstreamed into the high school.

6. You have been asked to present a talk to your local parent-teacher association concerning mainstreaming at the secondary school level. What will you say?

7. You have been told that a physically handicapped child will be mainstreamed into your content-area class. How will you prepare your students for this student? What will you do to prepare for this student?

8. What strategies would you use to help students in your content classes who are at risk of failing?

9. Prepare a learning sequence from your content area for gifted students that could be incorporated in a learning center.

10. Discuss how computer programs can help individualize instruction.

SELECTED BIBLIOGRAPHY

KIRK, SAMUEL A. *Teaching Reading to Slow and Disabled Learners.* Prospect Heights, Ill.: Waveland Press, 1988.

KLETZIEN, SHARON B., and MARYANNE R. BEDNAR. "Dynamic Assessment for At-Risk Readers." *Journal of Reading* 33 (April 1990): 528–533.

LARRIVEE, BARBARA. *Effective Teaching for Successful Mainstreaming.* New York: Longman, 1985.

LOUV, RICHARD. "Hope in Hell's Classroom." *The New York Times Magazine* Section 6 (November 25, 1990): 30–32, 63, 66–67, 74.

TERMAN, LEWIS M., and MELITA H. ODEN. *The Gifted Child Grows Up. Genetic Studies of Genius,* vol. 4. Stanford, Calif.: Stanford University Press, 1947.

THISTLETHWAITE, LINDA L. "Critical Reading for At-Risk Students." *Journal of Reading* 33 (May 1990): 586–593.

VAN TASSEL-BASKA, JOYCE L., and PAULA OLSZEWSKI-KUBILIUS (eds.) *Patterns of Influence on Gifted Learners.* New York: Teachers College Press, 1990.

WEPNER, SHELLEY. "Computers, Reading Software, and At-Risk Eighth Graders. *Journal of Reading* 34 (December/January 1990/1991): 264–268.

YSSELDYKE, J.E. "Similarities and Differences between Underachievers and Students Classified Learning Disabled." *The Journal of Special Education* 16 (1982): 73–85.

Appendix A

General Checklist for Textbook Readability

	Excellent	Good	Fair	Poor
1. Physical Characteristics				
a. Print				
(1) Clear				
(2) Readable				
(3) Proper size				
(4) Proper spacing between lines				
b. Paper				
(1) Good weight				
(2) Durable				
(3) Nonglossy				
c. Binding				
(1) Reinforced				
(2) Book firmly in its cover				
2. Content (General Characteristics)				
a. Valid information; that is, information is related to topic being studied.				
b. Content is covered in proper depth for particular grade level.				
c. Concepts are presented in clear and understandable language.				
d. Key concepts and/or topics are presented at the beginning of each section or in the margins.				

General Checklist for Textbook Readability *(Continued)*

	Excellent	Good	Fair	Poor
e. Topic sentences are generally presented at the beginning of paragraphs.				
f. Topic sentences help readers anticipate the main ideas of the paragraphs.				
3. Readability				
a. Vocabulary is suitable to particular grade level.				
b. Sentence length is suitable to particular grade level.				
4. Features				
a. Material is presented creatively.				
b. Objectives are presented at the beginning of each chapter.				
c. Special notes are given to explain certain terms or concepts.				
d. Index is complete.				
e. Glossary—special terms used in text are defined.				
f. Bibliographies—include up-to-date materials.				
g. Summaries are given at the end of each chapter.				
h. Purposes are set forth for each chapter in the form of questions.				
5. Visual Content or Illustration				
a. Charts and graphs are sprinkled throughout the text.				
b. Pictures and cartoons are sprinkled throughout the text.				
6. Treatment of Minorities				
a. Every group of people is treated with dignity and respect.				
b. No group is stereotyped.				
c. Each group is accurately portrayed.				
7. Treatment of Gender				
a. Males and females are treated as equals.				
b. Stereotypes are avoided.				

Appendix B

FRY READABILITY FORMULA

Graph for Estimating Readability – Extended

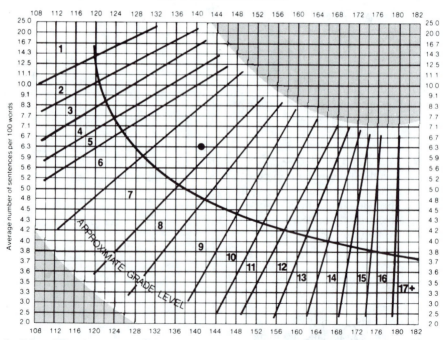

Average number of syllables per 100 words

by Edward Fry, Rutgers University Reading Center, New Brunswick, N.J. 08904

Note: This "extended graph" does not outmode or render the earlier (1986) version inoperative or inaccurate, it is an extension. (REPRODUCTION PERMITTED—NO COPYRIGHT)

Expanded Directions for Working Readability Graph

1. Randomly select three (3) sample passages and count out exactly 100 words each, beginning with the beginning of a sentence. Do count proper nouns, initializations, and numerals.
2. Count the number of sentences in the hundred words, estimating length of the fraction of the last sentence to the nearest one-tenth.
3. Count the total number of syllables in the 100-word passage. If you don't have a hand counter available, an easy way is to simply put a mark above every syllable over one in each word, then when you get to the end of the passage, count the number of marks and add 100. Small calculators can also be used as counters by pushing numeral 1, then push the + sign for each word or syllable when counting.
4. Enter graph with *average* sentence length and *average* number of syllables; plot dot where the two lines intersect. Area where dot is plotted will give you the approximate grade level.
5. If a great deal of variability is found in syllable count or sentence count, putting more samples into the average is desirable.
6. A word is defined as a group of symbols with a space on either side; thus, *Joe, IRA, 1945,* and *&* are each one word.
7. A syllable is defined as a phonetic syllable. Generally, there are as many syllables as vowel sounds. For example, *stopped* is one syllable and *wanted* is two syllables. When counting syllables for numerals and initializations, count one syllable for each symbol. For example, *1945* is four syllables, *IRA* is three syllables, and *&* is one syllable.

EXAMPLE:	SYLLABLES	SENTENCES
1st Hundred Words	124	6.6
2nd Hundred Words	141	5.5
3rd Hundred Words	158	6.8
AVERAGE	141	6.3

READABILITY 7th GRADE (see dot plotted on graph)

Glossary

Accommodation. Individual develops new categories rather than integrating them into existing ones—Piaget's cognitive development.

Adolescence. The period of life from puberty to maturity terminating legally at the age of majority.

Affective domain. Concerned with the feelings and emotional learnings that individuals acquire.

Affixes. Prefixes that are added to the beginning of a root word and suffixes that are added to the end of a root word.

Analogies. Relationships between words or ideas.

Analysis. Breaking down something into its component parts.

Anecdotal record. Recording observed behavior over a period of time.

Antonyms. Words opposite in meaning.

Appeal to inappropriate authority. A fallacy; people attempt to prove or disprove their argument by referring to well-known individuals, who are not authorities on the matters in question.

Appeal to pity. A fallacy; consists of asking that a proposal be accepted on the grounds of feeling sorry for someone rather than establishing the truth or falsity of something.

Appendix. A section of a book containing extra information that does not quite fit into the book but that the author feels is important enough to be presented separately.

Appreciative reading. Reading for pleasure and enjoyment from books that fit some mood, feeling, or interest.

Argument from ignorance. A fallacy; people attempt to prove their argument by stating that no one has ever disproved it; the opposite is also true.

Assimilation. A continuous process that helps the individual to integrate new incoming stimuli to existing concepts—Piaget's cognitive development.

At-risk students. Those students who are in danger of failing in school because of their backgrounds or other factors.

Attacking the person. A fallacy; directing attention to the person by attacking his or her character rather than trying to disprove the truth of what is said.

Auding. Highest level of listening, which involves listening with comprehension.

Attitude. Exerts a directive and dynamic influence on an individual's behavior.

Average children. Often referred to as those who score in the IQ range approximately from 90-110.

Bias. A mental leaning, prejudice, partiality, or a slanting of something.

Bibliotherapy. The use of books to help individuals cope better with their emotional and adjustment problems.

Bilingual. Using or capable of using two languages.

Black English. A variation of standard English; in the class of nonstandard English (*which see*).[1]

Borderline children (slow learners). Students whose IQs usually range approximately from 70 to 85.

Bottom-up reading models. Models which consider the reading process as one of grapheme-phoneme correspondences; code emphasis or subskill models.

Brainstorming. Generating many different ideas without inhibition.

Buzz words. Words that take on particular importance in the discussion of a topic and are reminders of a wide range of information; information reminders in very small packages.

Central idea. See **Main idea.**

Checklist. A means for systematically and quickly recording a student's behavior; it usually consists of a list of behaviors that the observer records as present or absent.

Cloze procedure. A technique that helps teachers gain information about a variety of language facility and comprehension ability skills.

Cloze test. Reader must supply words that have been systematically deleted from a passage.

Cognitive development. Refers to development of thinking (*which see*).

Cognitive domain. Hierarchy of objectives ranging from simplistic thinking skills to the more complex ones.

Combining forms. Usually defined as roots borrowed from another language that join together or that join with a prefix, a suffix, or both to form a word; for example *aqua/naut.*

Comparison. A demonstration of the similarities between persons, ideas, things, and so on.

Complex question. A fallacy; refers to questions that cannot be answered with a simple yes or no.

Comprehension. Understanding; the ability to get the meaning of something; the act or action of grasping (as an act or process) with the intellect.

Computer-assisted instruction. Instruction using computers.

Concentration. Sustained attention. It is essential for both studying and listening to lectures.

Concepts. A group of stimuli with common characteristics.

Connotative meaning. Includes all emotional associations of a word; based on an individual's background of experiences.

Construct. Something that cannot be directly observed or measured—such as intelligence, attitudes, and motivation.

Content-area teacher. Primarily concerned with the teaching of content concepts.

Content domain. Term that refers to subject matter covered.

Context. The words surrounding a word that can shed light on its meaning.

Context clue. An item of information from the surrounding words of a particular word in the form of a synonym (*which see*), antonym (*which see*), definition (*which see*), description, example (*which see*), and so on, that helps shed light on the particular word.

Contrast. A demonstration of the differences between persons, ideas, things, and so on.

Creative problem solving. A technique used with bibliotherapy (*which see*) to help students determine how the main character's problem is solved.

Creative process. There appears to be four stages to the creative act for most people: preparation, incubation, illumination, and verification.

Creative reading. Uses divergent thinking skills to go beyond the literal comprehension (*which see*), interpretation (*which see*), and critical reading levels (*which see*).

Criterion-referenced tests. Based on an extensive inventory of objectives in a specific curricu-

---

[1]*Which see* refers to the immediately preceding word that is defined elsewhere in the glossary.

lum area; they are used to assess an individual's performance in respect to his or her mastery of specified objectives in a given curriculum area.

Critical reading. A high-level reading skill that involves evaluation; making a personal judgment on the accuracy, value, and truthfulness of what is read; requires critical thinking.

Cultural diversity. A mix of people from different cultural and ethnic backgrounds.

Database management systems. Ways to manage or classify data on the computer.

Deductive teaching. Students are given a generalization and must determine which examples fit the rule, going from general to specific.

Denotative meaning. The direct, specific meaning of a word.

Developmental tasks. Those tasks that must be met and successfully accomplished if a person is to achieve an effective adult role.

Diagnosis. Act of identifying difficulties and strengths from their signs and symptoms.

Dialect. A variation of language sufficiently different to be considered separate, but not different enough to be classified as a separate language.

Digit span. Refers to amount of words or numbers an individual can retain in his or her short-term memory.

Directed reading approach to teaching content. The direct teaching of any needed reading or study skill using relevant content material so that students can attain the content concepts being studied.

Divergent thinking. The many different ways of looking at things.

Drop Everything and Read (DEAR). Same as Sustained Silent Reading (*which see*).

Equilibrium. According to Piaget, a balance between assimilation (*which see*) and accommodation (*which see*) in cognitive development (*which see*).

Example. Something representative of a whole or a group.

Exceptional children. Those children who deviate so much from the "average" that they require special attention.

Fact. Something that exists and can be proved true.

Fallacies. False beliefs or mistaken ideas about something.

Fallacious arguments. Incorrect reasoning but may be psychologically or structurally persuasive.

False cause. A fallacy; people try to convince others that a preceding event causes an event that follows.

Finding inconsistencies. Finding statements that do not make sense.

Frustration reading level. The student has difficulty anticipating meanings and is not familiar with the facts presented in the selection. It is the level to be avoided.

Gifted children. The academically gifted are usually those with an IQ above 132 on the Stanford Binet Intelligence scale; however, gifted also refers to those whose performance in any line of socially useful endeavor is consistently superior.

Glossary. A list of the meanings of specialized words or phrases.

Graphic summary. A visual representation of material presented in a chapter, section, or so on.

Group informal vocabulary test. Given to determine whether students will have trouble reading their textbooks, as well as to determine the amount of guidance to give students.

Group informal reading inventory. An "on-the-spot" approach that uses students' textbooks to determine whether these books are at the reading ability level of the students.

Group listening capacity test. Helps teacher determine whether students have the comprehension ability to read their textbooks.

Group tests. Administered to a group of persons at the same time.

Halo effect. A response bias that contaminates an individual's perception in rating or evaluation.

Homographs. Words that are spelled the same but have different meanings.

Homonyms. Words with the same pronunciation but with different meanings (and, usually, different spelling).

Homophones. Same as homonyms (*which see*).

Hypothesis. A possible solution to a problem; a tentative assumption made to be tested.

Independent reading level. Student reads on his or her own without any difficulty.

Index. A list of topics discussed in a book and page numbers where discussed.

Individualized instruction. Student works at own pace on material based on his or her needs, interests, and ability.

Inductive teaching. Students discover generalizations by being given numerous examples that portray patterns, going from specific to general.

Inference. Understanding that is not derived from a direct statement but from an indirect suggestion in what is stated.

Informal tests. Teacher-made tests (*which see*).

Informal interviews. Teachers converse with students to learn about their interests and feelings.

Instructional reading level. At this level the material must not be so challenging that it frustrates the student nor so easy that the student becomes bored. It is the level at which teaching is done.

Integrated reading-writing approach. The use of reading to stimulate writing and the converse, that is, the use of writing as a stimulus for reading.

Intelligence. Ability to reason abstractly.

Interactive instruction. The teacher intervenes at optimal times to enhance instruction.

Interactive reading models. The top-down processing of information is dependent on the bottom-up processing and vice versa.

Interest inventory. A statement or questionnaire method that helps teachers learn about likes and dislikes of students.

Interpretation. A reading level that demands a higher level of thinking ability because the material involved is not directly stated in the text but only suggested or implied.

IQ. Intelligence Quotient; mental age divided by chronological age multiplied by 100.

Irrelevant conclusion. A fallacy; directing attention to something else, something not applicable to the matter in question.

Learning center. An integral part of the instructional program and vital to a good individualized program. An area is usually set aside in the classroom for instruction in a specific curriculum area.

Learning disability. Difficult to define; definition given most often is: a disorder in one or more of the basic psychological processes involved in understanding or in using language spoken or written, which may manifest itself in an imperfect ability to listen, think, speak, read, write, spell, or do mathematical calculations.

Listening capacity level. The highest level at which a learner can understand material when it is read aloud.

Listening capacity test. Given to determine a student's comprehension through listening; examiner reads aloud to students and then asks questions about the selection.

Listening vocabulary. The number of different words one knows the meaning of when they are said aloud.

Literal comprehension. The ability to obtain a low-level type of understanding by using only explicitly-stated information.

Main idea. The central thought of a paragraph. The term *central idea* is usually used when referring to a group of paragraphs, an article, or a story. The procedure, however, for finding the main idea and the central idea is the same for both.

Mainstreaming. The placement of handicapped children in the least restrictive educational environment that will meet their needs.

Mathematics. The science of numbers.

Mental age. In intelligence testing, a score based on average abilities for that age group.

$$MA = \frac{IQ \times CA}{100}$$

Metacognition. Thinking critically about thinking; refers to individuals' knowledge about their thinking processes and ability to control them.

Modeling strategy. Thinking out loud; verbalizing one's thoughts to help students gain understanding.

Motivating technique. Aid teacher uses to gain students' attention and direct their energies toward a particular goal.

Motivation. Internal impetus behind behavior and the direction behavior takes; drive.

Nonstandard English. A variation of standard English owing to socioeconomic and cultural differences in the United States.

Norm-referenced tests. Standardized tests with norms (*which see*) so that comparisons can be made to a sample population.

Norms. Average scores for a given group of students or groups of students.

Notetaking. A useful study and paper-writing tool.

Objective. Desired educational outcome.

Objective tests. Those that usually have only one correct answer for a given question.

Observation. A technique that helps teachers collect data about students' behavior.

Opinions. Based on attitudes or feelings; they can vary from person to person, but cannot be conclusively proved right or wrong.

Outlining. Helps students organize long written compositions; it helps also for studying because it serves as a guide for the logical arrangement of material.

Overlearning. Helps persons retain information over a long period of time; occurs when individuals continue to practice even after they think they have learned the material.

Peer tutoring. A student helps another student gain needed skills.

Perception. A cumulative process based on an individual's background of experiences. It is defined as giving meaning to a sensation or the ability to organize stimuli on a field.

Perceptual domain. Part of the reading process that depends on an individual's background of experiences and sensory receptors. (See *Perception*.)

Phonics. The study of the relationships between letter symbols of a written language and the sounds they represent.

Political cartoons. Political cartoonists' vehicle for using satire to ridicule and hold up to contempt what they feel are vices, follies, stupidities, abuses, and so on.

Projective technique. A method in which the individual tends to put himself or herself into a situation, revealing how he or she feels.

Propaganda. Any systematic, widespread, and deliberate indoctrination or plan for indoctrination.

Public Law 94-142. Advocates a free appropriate education for all children in the least restrictive environment.

Question Answer Relationships (QARs). Helps students distinguish between "what they have in their heads" and information that is in the textbook.

Questions. A good way for students to gain a better insight into a subject; questioning also gives the instructor feedback and slows the instructor down if he or she is going too fast; also part of SQ3R (*which see*).

Rating scale. An evaluative instrument used to record estimates of particular aspects of a student's behavior.

Readability formulas. Applied directly to the written material to determine the reading difficulty of the written material.

Reading. Bringing meaning to, and getting meaning from, the printed page.

Reading comprehension. A complex intellectual process involving a number of abilities. The two major abilities involve word meanings and reasoning with verbal concepts.

Reading in a scientific manner. Reading critically; not blindly accepting everything that is presented.

Reading process. Concerned with the affective (*which see*), perceptual (*which see*), and cognitive (*which see*) domains.

Reading specialist. Person very knowledgeable in reading who acts as a consultant to teachers and also works with students who have reading problems.

Reading strategy. An action or a series of actions that helps construct meaning.

Reading taxonomy. A hierarchy of reading comprehension skills ranging from the more simplistic to the more complex ones; a classification of these skills.

Reading teacher. Primarily concerned with helping students gain skill in reading.

Recite or recall. The process of finding the answer to a question in one's memory without rereading the text or notes; part of SQ3R (*which see*).

Role modeling. An observer imitates the behavior of a model.

Role playing. A form of creative drama in which dialogue for a specific role is spontaneously developed.

Schema theory. Deals with relations between prior knowledge and comprehension.

Scientific method. A technique scientists use in research experiments that consists of a number of steps.

Self-fulfilling prophecy. Teachers' assumptions about children become true, at least in part, because of the attitude of the teachers, which in turn becomes part of the children's self-concept.

Semantic clue. Meaning clue.

Semantic mapping (graphic organizer). A graphic representation used to illustrate concepts and relationships among concepts such as classes, properties, and examples.

Set. A well-defined collection of things.

Skimming. Reading rapidly to find or locate information.

Slow learners. Same as borderline children (*which see*).

Special circumstance of person. A fallacy; an acceptance of something is urged because of the person.

SQ3R. A widely used study technique that involves five steps: survey, question, read, recite or recall, and review.

Standard English. English in respect to spelling, grammar, vocabulary, and pronunciation that is substantially uniform, though not devoid of regional differences. It is well established by usage and the formal and informal speech and writing of the educated and is widely recognized as acceptable wherever English is spoken or understood.

Standardized tests. Tests that have been published by experts in the field and have precise instructions for administration and scoring.

Starter shelves. Books chosen are merely to start the students to read voluntarily; books are changed periodically based on students' interests, needs, and reading ability levels.

Story grammar. In narrative includes the setting of a story (including characters, location, and time), the basic theme, key episodes of plot, and a resolution of the problem that motivated the characters to action.

Strategy. A systematic plan for achieving a specific objective or result.

Study procedures. (1) Build good habits, (2) devise a system that works for you, (3) keep at it, (4) maintain a certain degree of tension, and (5) concentrate.

Subjective tests. Usually essay tests; answers are not merely right or wrong; tests are a demonstration of reasoning, thought, and perception.

Summary. A brief statement of the essential information in a longer piece. The central idea of an article and the important events should be stated in a summary, although not necessarily in the sequence presented in the article. The sequence should be followed if it is essential to understanding. A summary does not include the summarizer's opinions.

Supporting details. Additional information that supports, explains, or illustrates the main idea. Some of the ways that supporting details may be arranged are as cause and effect, examples, sequence of events, descriptions, definitions, comparisons, or contrasts.

Survey. To gain an overview of the text material; part of SQ3R (*which see*).

Sustained Silent Reading (SSR). Practice in independent silent reading.

Synonyms. Words similar in meaning.

Synthesis. Building up the parts of something, usually into a whole.

Teacher-made tests. Tests prepared by the classroom teacher for a particular class and given by the classroom teacher under conditions of his or her own choosing.

Telegraphic writing. The use of one or two words to recall a complete message.

Textbook readability. Matching students with textbooks at their appropriate reading ability levels.

Thinking. Covert manipulation of symbolic representations.

Top-down reading models. These models depend on the readers' background of experiences and language ability in constructing meaning from the text.

Topic sentence. States what the paragraph will be about by naming the topic.

Vocabulary consciousness. An awareness that words may have different meanings based on their context and a desire to increase one's vocabulary.

Word problem in mathematics. Requires individuals to translate the usually imprecise English language to very precise mathematical language.

Word recognition. A twofold process that includes both the identification of printed symbols by some method so that the word can be pronounced and the association of meaning to the word after it has been properly pronounced.

Index

DATE DUE